CHRISTOPHER MARLOWE

Volume I

The Tragicall History of
CHRISTOPHER MARLOWE

VOLUME ONE

By *John Bakeless*

GREENWOOD PRESS, PUBLISHERS
WESTPORT, CONNECTICUT

Copyright 1942 by the President and Fellows of Harvard College

Reprinted with the permission
of Harvard University Press

First Greenwood Reprinting 1970

Library of Congress Catalogue Card Number 70-106681

SBN 8371-3352-1 (SET)
SBN 8371-5157-0 (VOL. 1)

Printed in the United States of America

PREFACE

To ITS author, at least, it is a somewhat startling reflection that this study of Christopher Marlowe has occupied most of the interval between two World Wars, almost as many years as the entire life of its subject. Begun in 1920, it has expanded — almost of its volition rather than of mine — from the original effort merely to discover the sources of *Tamburlaine* into an effort to bring together everything that can now be known about Christopher Marlowe. No such attempt can ever be completely successful; but I trust that twenty-two years' endeavor after thoroughness, completeness, and accuracy have at least reduced the inevitable blunders and omissions to a minimum.

The book was already in essentially its present form when, in 1936, a grant from the John Simon Guggenheim Memorial Foundation enabled me to spend some months in research in British archives. The results of this and subsequent study had been digested and the manuscript was almost entirely in the hands of the publisher in November, 1940, when I was ordered to active duty. It was entirely in print in 1941, but the reading of the proofs has necessarily been much delayed by the duties of a General Staff officer in time of war. Under these circumstances, it has been impossible to make use of several studies published in 1941 and 1942. Even the bibliography cannot claim to be complete after 1940, although it has been possible to include some later material.

It would be an endless task to list all who have aided me, but a few debts are too great to pass without remark. From the beginning of the study almost to its end, I benefited by the advice and criticism of the late George Lyman Kittredge. Mr. C. F. Tucker Brooke, long known as the most distinguished of Marlowe students, has been prolific in suggestions, keen in criticism, and constantly helpful in lending material from his personal collection. Mr. John Livingston Lowes has, from my student days, been a constant source of help, encouragement, and new ideas. My wife has labored patiently and long, first with my notes and later with my proofs; without her help during the war period, it would have been nearly impossible to go to press at all.

Publication has been generously assisted by a grant from the American Council of Learned Societies, through the Modern Language Association, and by a second grant from the Guggenheim Foundation.

It is pleasant to record three unexampled bits of generosity. Mr. Frank W. Tyler, of Canterbury, placed at my disposal his discovery of the Benchkyn Will and several documents relating to John Marlowe; Mr. Charles Graves, of Edinburgh, turned over to me his collection of Milton-Marlowe parallels, previously unknown; and Mr. John Robert Moore, of Indiana University, aided by his student, Mr. Merrill V. Eaton, searched long and hard to track down for me in Defoe's voluminous writings an obscure allusion to *Faustus* which had eluded everyone else. It is correspondingly melancholy in these tragic days to contemplate the aid I have received from German, Japanese, and Bulgarian scholars. Whether as scholar or as soldier, an American may permit himself the hope that these kindly and courteous gentlemen represent the best in their respective nations as truly as their present rulers represent the worst.

The book has had the benefit of critical readings by various authorities. The late B. Sprague Allen read and criticized most of the manuscript some years ago. Various portions have been read by Mr. J. Q. Adams and Mr. Giles E. Dawson, of the Folger Shakespeare Library; by Mr. Samuel Claggett Chew, of Bryn Mawr; and by Mr. Mark Eccles, of the University of Wisconsin. In acknowledging their aid, I must, of course, pronounce the customary absolution: They have saved me from many errors. For such as remain, responsibility is properly my own.

I have naturally incurred innumerable obligations to libraries. The greatest is to the Harvard College Library, in which I have received every conceivable aid for nearly a quarter of a century. Chief among my many benefactors on its staff have been Mr. W. B. Briggs, Mr. William A. Jackson, Mr. Robert H. Haynes, and Miss Alice Reynolds. Mr. A. P.

DeWeese and Mr. Gerald McDonald, of the New York Public Library, together with Miss Reynolds, have verified practically all of the references not accessible to me in Washington during the last two arduous years. Mr. W. N. C. Carlton, Librarian Emeritus of Williams College, has solved numerous baffling bibliographical puzzles; and Mr. David J. H. Cole and Mr. John E. Alden, of the Library of Congress, have far exceeded any merely professional obligations in the help they have given me.

A group of New York University librarians have long assisted me in this and other books — especially Mr. Robert B. Downs, Director of the Libraries; Mr. Theodore F. Jones, Director of the University Heights Library; Mr. Mulford Martin, Librarian of the Commerce Library; Mr. Nelson W. McCombs, Librarian, Mr. Alfred B. Lindsay, Assistant Librarian, and Mr. H. Gambier-Bousfield, Chief of the Readers' Department, of the Washington Square College Library. Both the Yale and the Columbia University libraries have been kind enough to give me visitors' privileges whenever required.

In British archives and libraries I have received much friendly assistance — notably from Mr. H. R. Creswick, Mr. H. L. Pink, Mr. D. G. Harrison, and Mr. H. R. Mallett, of the University Library, Cambridge; Sir Will Spens, Master of Corpus Christi College, and Mr. T. R. B. Sanders, Estates Bursar; Mr. William J. Baker, Registrary's Clerk, Cambridge University; Mr. E. Lobel, Mr. J. R. Liddell, and Mr. Ian G. Philip, of the Bodleian; Dr. J. A. Venn, President of Queens' College, Cambridge; the officials of the Public Record Office, especially Mr. Noel Blakiston and Mr. J. R. Crompton; Mr. W. P. Blore, of the Cathedral Library, Canterbury; Mr. H. T. Mead, formerly Librarian of the Royal Museum and Public Library, Canterbury; and the Rev. Geoffrey Keable, Rector of the Church of St. George the Martyr. Canon F. J. Shirley, Headmaster of the King's School, lent every possible assistance in my study of Marlowe's schooldays there. In Australia, Mr. H. M. Green, of the Fisher Library, University of Sydney, located for me some of the less known writings of the late J. LeGay Brereton, whose personal bibliography is sometimes as obscure as his Elizabethan studies have been brilliant.

A few mechanical details should be noted. Quotations from Marlowe follow Brooke's 1910 edition. Quotations from Shakespeare follow Neilson's 1906 Cambridge edition. Except in occasional passages where it seemed to lend a special flavor, or where the mingling of two forms in the original seemed interesting, the long ∫ has been altered to modern *s*. A few glaring misprints in original texts have been silently corrected. Italics have been introduced into some quotations to draw attention to special passages — otherwise italics appear in the sources.

I have given the name of Marlowe's murderer as "Friser" in view of Miss de Kalb's discovery that the man himself spelled it so. To be strictly logical, I might on the same grounds have called my poet "Marley," following his own and his family's spelling; but it would be the purest pedantry to alter now the universally accepted form.

J. B.

Washington, D. C.
3 September, 1942

CONTENTS

VOLUME I

VOLUME II

ILLUSTRATIONS

VOLUME I

VOLUME II

ABBREVIATIONS

Archiv .... [Herrig's] *Archiv f. d. Studium d. neueren Sprachen und Literaturen*
BM .... British Museum
BN .... Bibliothèque Nationale
CHEL .... *Cambridge History of English Literature*
CUL .... Columbia University Library
DF .... *Doctor Faustus*
EFB .... English Faust Book
ES .... *Englische Studien*
F .... Goethe's *Faust*
Fgt. .... *Faust* Fragment
Folger .... Folger Shakespeare Library
GFB .... German *Faust* Book
HCL .... Harvard College Library
HEDL .... [A. W. Ward's] *History of English Dramatic Literature* (1899)
HEDP .... [J. P. Collier's] *History of English Dramatic Poetry* (1831)
H&L .... *Hero and Leander*
Jahrb. .... *Jahrbuch der Deutschen Shakespeare-Gesellschaft*
JB .... Author's collection
JEGP .... *Journal of [English and] Germanic Philology*
JM .... *Jew of Malta*
LC .... Library of Congress
MLN .... *Modern Language Notes*
MLR .... *Modern Language Review*
Morgan ...... Pierpont Morgan Library
n.d. .... No date of publication
n.p. .... No place of publication
NS .... New series of a periodical
NYPL .... New York Public Library
NYU .... New York University Library
N&Q .... *Notes and Queries*
OS .... Old series of a periodical
PMLA .... *Publications of the Modern Language Association*
PRO .... Public Record Office, London
PRO, Cant. ... Public Record Office, Canterbury
PQ .... *Philological Quarterly*
RES .... *Review of English Studies*
SAT .... Samuel A. Tannenbaum's collection
SP .... *Studies in Philology*
STC .... *Short Title Catalogue*
Tamb. .... *Tamburlaine*
TLS .... London *Times Literary Supplement*
ULC .... University Library, Cambridge
Urf. .... *Urfaust*

CHRISTOPHER MARLOWE

CHAPTER I

MARLOWE AND HIS FAMILY

Sunrise and thunder fired and shook the skies
That saw the sun-god Marlowe's opening eyes.
SWINBURNE: Prologue to *The Broken Heart*

BOTH THE WORK and the life of Christopher Marlowe are closely linked with the early work and the early life of William Shakespeare. So far as their work is concerned, the lesser poet is the forerunner of the greater. He is chief among those who prepared the way, both as an experimenter in dramatic form and as the creator of the "mighty line," in which the talented young rustic, coming up from Stratford a few years before the death of his brilliant predecessor, was to find an instrument lying ready to his hand.

As early as 1587 — when Shakespeare was perhaps a schoolmaster near Stratford, perhaps a horse-boy outside Burbage's "Theatre," in Finsbury Fields, or its rival, the "Curtain" — the first production of *Tamburlaine* had startled London and made the young scholar from Cambridge the most famous and successful playwright of his day. Without Marlowe, Shakespeare would doubtless have been Shakespeare still; but he would have been a different Shakespeare.

So far as their early lives are concerned, the two men were almost exactly contemporaries. Marlowe, the university man, blazes suddenly into an early glory, soon extinguished. Shakespeare, the countryman, develops slowly after a long period of obscurity. Their paths cross only in the last few years of Marlowe's life.

Yet, though Marlowe had achieved a permanent place in English literature and was dead of his murderer's dagger-thrust when Shakespeare had scarcely begun to write, the two men were nearly of an age. On February 26, 1563, says the register kept in the Church of St. George the Martyr, Canterbury, "was

Chriſtened Chriſtofer the ſonne of John Marlow."[1] This means, of course, the year 1564 by modern reckoning. Exactly two months later, to the day, in the Church of the Holy Trinity, in Stratford, a hundred and fifty miles away, John Shakespeare and his wife, Mary Arden, brought their first son to be christened. The greatest dramatist of English literature had been born in the home of a provincial alderman in Warwickshire; and in Kent the dramatist who was to form Shakespeare's early style and guide his first efforts on the London stage was a baby in the cradle of a cobbler's house. Both fathers were commoners, engaged, among other things, in some form of leather working. Both mothers seem to have been of slightly higher social station.

The date of Shakespeare's birth is a matter of inference. As he was christened on April 26, and as children are said[2] to have been customarily christened on the third day after birth, it is inferred that Shakespeare was born on April 23. Similar reasoning would place the day of Marlowe's birth on February 23; but the date is sometimes given, on no very satisfactory evidence, as February 6.[3]

The cobbler's son in Canterbury came of an even less distinguished family than the small-town businessman's son in Warwickshire. Mary Arden was of gentle blood, though her marriage with the prosperous Stratford alderman brought her down to his social level. Master John Shakespeare, though he later fell on evil days, was long a leading citizen of the little country town by the Avon, who toward the end of his life, through the efforts of his famous son, made good his own claim to a coat of arms, "non sanz droict." The Marlowe family had no such claims to distinction and no pretensions to gentility; nor, it is easy to surmise, did the pious folk of the cathedral town of Canterbury — after Christopher Marlowe's prospects of holy orders to follow a university career had faded — regard the reports that must have trickled back from London of their neighbor's son's successes among the godless play-folk as adding much luster to the name of Marlowe.

---

[1] MS. Register of St. George the Martyr. Cf. J. M. Cowper: Register Booke . . . of St. George the Martyr . . . 1538–1800, p. 10. Cowper abbreviates his entries, which, though accurate as to fact, do not exactly reproduce the original.

[2] Sidney Lee: Life of Shakespeare, p. 8; J. Q. Adams: Life of William Shakespeare, p. 21n.   [3] See I. 12 and n.

Illustrious or not, however, Marlowe is a good old Kentish name. The name of Shakespeare can be traced back to the twelfth century and beyond the Channel. Though neither so old nor so distinguished, the Marlowes are of right English — usually the purest Kentish — stock.

The word "Marlowe," itself, is probably either a geographical name, derived from the village of Marlowe, in Buckinghamshire, or else an occupational name derived from the trade of the "marler," one who digs marl — a clay mixed with carbonate of lime and used as a fertilizer — or one who spreads it on the land. The word does not appear in the Oxford Dictionary earlier than 1810; but it had probably been in popular use for generations, since this method of fertilization is referred to in the forest charter of Edward III.[4] The name sometimes appears as Le Marler.

The form Marley — which both John Marley and his son, the dramatist, actually used — is presumably derived either from OE *mere* and *leáh* (ME *ley*), meaning a dweller at the "lake lea," or else from *mære-leáh*, a "boundary lea." The hopeless confusion of sixteenth-century spelling makes certainty impossible. If the name is derived from the village of Marlowe, it has the respectability of the Domesday Book, where the little town appears as Merlowe. This is supposed to be derived from OE *mere* and *hlæw*, a hill or tumulus.[5] Robert Ferguson relates the form Marley to ON *margligr, kind or affable.[6] Obviously, in such a matter certainty is impossible and, fortunately, not very important.

As early as the fifteenth century, Marlowes begin to appear in the Canterbury records — usually tradesmen, often prosperous, sometimes wealthy. Occasionally the name crops up outside of Kent, the owners being, in all probability, offshoots of the Kentish family — a surmise for which there is no direct evidence, but one which is rendered plausible by the frequency with which the name appears in Kentish records and by the recurrence of the four Christian names, John, Thomas, Richard, and Christopher, wherever Marlowes are found.[7]

[4] Charles Wareing Bardsley: *Our English Surnames*, pp. 221–222n.
[5] Henry Harrison: *Surnames of the United Kingdom*, II. 14.
[6] Robert Ferguson: *English Surnames*, p. 321. Cf. Bardsley, *loc. cit.*
[7] For records of the non-Kentish Marlowes, see author's MS. dissertation, HCL.

The first recognizable member of the clan in Canterbury records is one William Morle, fuller, who in 1414 becomes a freeman "by redemption," or "emption," that is, by purchase. His son Thomas Morle, also a fuller, becomes a freeman without payment, since he is a freeman's son, in 1459. Both entries are still preserved in the city accounts, where the admission of freemen is recorded.[8] There is also Simon Morle, a vintner, who was admitted as a freeman of the city in 1438.[9] He seems to have been a man of substance. In 1443/4 the corporation

Paid Simon Morle Vintner for red wine given to the Lord John Stafford Archbishop of Canterbury by the Bailiffs and Citizens of Canterbury against the time of his Inthronization in the Church of Christ Canty [10]   } 3-6-8

In 1445/6 the corporation paid Simon four marks, compensation for a pipe of wine which he had presented to Cardinal Beaufort on his visit to Canterbury the preceding Christmas.[11] Later he joined with one John Sheldwich to advance four pounds to be presented to Margaret of Anjou, "at the time of her pilgrimage to Canterbury to St. Thomas the Martyr." There is also a John Marle, lockyer, who appears among the "Intrantes" of Northgate, 1425-26.[12]

Not until 1467, however, do we find a Marlowe who can, with any degree of probability, be put forward as an ancestor of the dramatist. This honor belongs to John Marley, or Marle, who appears as a freeman in 1467. The entry of his admission runs:

John Marle de parochia ste crucis extra portam occidentalem tanner xvj die Junij Anno regni/ Regis Edwardi quarti vij admiffus & juratus eft ad libertatem Ciuitatis predicte Et soluet x ˢ/ Ande soluet in manibus iijˢ iiijᵈ Et in festo exaltationis ste crucis. . . . vjˢ viijᵈ

Since he pays for his freedom, this John Marle can hardly be the son of Thomas Marle; the sons of freemen became freemen without payment. He may, however, have been the son of

<hr/>

[8] These documents are now in the Royal Museum and Public Library (Beaney Institute), Canterbury.

[9] J. M. Cowper, *Roll of the Freemen of Canterbury*, col. 288; *MS. Accounts, 1393–1445*, vol. I, fol. Exxxix.

[10] Bunce MSS., II. 256.

[11] Royal Hist. MSS. Commission: Appendix to 9th *Report*, I. 140. Cf. Bunce MSS., II. 256.

[12] Cowper, *Roll of the Freemen*, col. 288; *MS. Accounts, 1445–1506*, vol. II, fol. Ciiij.

John Marle, lockyer, who was merely one of the "intrantes" dwelling outside the city but permitted to trade in it on payment of a yearly "fine." He may also have been the son of Simon Morle.

Richard Marley, tanner, the son of John Marley, tanner, appears in the records in 1514. The entry of his freedom runs:

Md the feid day and yere Rychard Marley of Westgatftrete next Canterbury tanner was admytted and sworne to the libertyes [flourish] of the feid Citie for the which he paied nothynge [flourish] for that he was the sonne of John Marley tanner freman of the feid Citie byfore the feid Rychard Marley tanner was borne [flourish] [13]   *nihil*

Accompanying entries fix the year as 1514.

John Marley, the tanner, is probably the great-great-grandfather, and Richard Marley probably the great-grandfather, of the author of *Tamburlaine* and *Doctor Faustus*. The dates, the names John and Christopher, which reappear in the poet's known father and supposed grandfather, the comparatively small population of sixteenth-century Canterbury, the similarity of trade — tanners and shoemakers were one guild and have at least leather in common — taken together with the tendency of crafts to pass from father to son, all strengthen the suggestion that there is a blood relationship of some kind, and that probably this relationship is direct ancestry.

It is more difficult to place John Marlen, a mattressmaker, who appears in 1523/4 among the "Intrantes" in the parish of Westgate.[14]

The tanner's trade had been so prosperous for Richard Marley that one can only conclude that the citizens of Canterbury must have been particularly hard on the leather in their shoes and aprons and buff jerkins, and that tanning must have been a singularly profitable trade. In his will, which is dated 1521, Richard Marley[15] is able not only to provide for his

---

[13] *MS. Accounts, 1512–1520*; Cowper, *op. cit.*, col. 57. See *Consistory Court Register*, XIII, fol. 51, for transcript of his will.

[14] J. M. Cowper: *Intrantes of Canterbury*, col. 184. The original entry is at the very bottom of the list of Intrantes for 1523/4. *MS. Accounts, 1523–1527*.

[15] The reader need feel no qualms over the variety of spellings. The surname is variously given as Marlowe and Marlow as late as 1900; and in the sixteenth and seventeenth centuries as Morley, Marley, Marly, Marlye, Marlen, Marlin, Marlinge,

family but to direct his executors to "Cause to be gylt well And workemanly the Crucyfyx of our lord with the Mary and John Stondyng vppon the porch of the seyd North dore" of the parish of Westgate Holy Cross, Canterbury.[16]

Near this crucifix the old tanner — let us hope none of his descendants ever saw the grave-digging scene in *Hamlet* or heard the grave-digger's comments on the durability of tanners' bodies — wished to be buried. "A fore the Crusyfyx of our lorde as nygh the commyng Jn of the North dore there as conuenyently can be" runs his last request. This crucifix did not long remain, however, for in 1640 William Somner, who had seen the old will, records that "the Crucifix is gone, and the King's Arms set up in place of it." [17]

This very wealthy man's will, dated June 12, 1521, specifically alludes to "Crystofer my son." The will of a Christopher Marley, presumably the same, appears in the records March 5, 1540. In it the testator describes himself as "christofer marley tanner of the parrissh of westgaytt dwellynge within the walles of the cetye of canterburye." [18] The father-and-son relationship is further established by the directions for burial contained in both wills. Richard Marley, the father, had directed that he should be buried in the churchyard of the parish of Holy Cross. The son, Christopher Marley, directs that he be buried in the parish of Westgate. The full name of this parish is "Westgate Holy Cross" or "Holy Cross of Westgate." Both belonged to the same parish. Their bones probably rest today under the roadway south of the Westgate, which has cut across the old churchyard by the North Door.

Genealogical evidence, however, is less satisfactory in the

Marlyne, Marline, Merlin, and Marlyn. Even the weekly entries in the Buttery Book show a wide variation in Marlowe's name and most others.

This sort of thing was common enough among Elizabethans. Everyone knows the variety of Shakespearean spelling. Sir Walter Raleigh spelled his own name in two ways, and others spelled it in fifty or sixty ways. (Cf. Henry Stebbing: *Sir Walter Raleigh*, pp. 30–31.) Marlowe's own father and mother spell Mistress Marlowe's Christian name differently in their wills.

[16] The will is in the *Consistory Register* in the Canterbury Branch of the Public Record Office, 32/13, formerly XIII. 6. All the Marlowe wills are accurately transcribed by Professor C. F. Tucker Brooke, in the appendices to his *Life*.

[17] William Somner: *Antiquities of Canterbury* (2nd ed. revised by Nicolas Battely, 1703), pt. I, p. 168.

[18] The will is in the *Archdeaconry Register* in the Canterbury Branch of the Public Record Office, 17/21, formerly XXI. 258 ff.

next generation. Christopher Marley's wife, Joan,[19] was with child at the time of the will. The husband, apparently anticipating immediate death, willed "to the child that she goyth with all if hitt be a man child mye dwellynge howse & the hangynge of the howse the meate table the beste chayer & a house Joynynge to mye dwellynge howse callyd the old hall with the lande longeth therto in fee symple."

Five hitherto unknown legal documents discovered by Frank W. Tyler, Esq., of Canterbury, strongly suggest that John Marlowe, shoemaker and father of the poet, was actually born at about this time.[20] These consist of a will which both John Marlowe and his son Christopher witnessed, a deposition by John Marlowe relating to the will, and three other depositions by the same witness on various other matters. There is no possible question that these papers refer to the poet's father. He is identified by his trade and himself refers in one deposition to his son, Christopher, and to John Moore, one of his sons-in-law. Unfortunately, however, legal papers of the period give approximate instead of exact ages, a fact which makes it impossible to fix John Marlowe's date of birth definitely. In the first deposition, in 1565, he says that he is "Etatis circiter xxxta annorum"; in the second, in 1586, he says that he was "etatis circiter l ta annorum"; in the third, in 1593, he is "etatis l annorum et amplius"; and in the fourth, in 1602, he says that he is "etatis Circiter lxiiij annorum." In other words, he implies in the first deposition that he was born about 1535; in the second, about 1536; in the third, some time before 1543; and in the fourth, about 1538. This is quite as vague as the document recording the Scrope trial, in which Geoffrey Chaucer is said to be "del age de xl. ans et plus," almost in the exact words of the 1593 deposition of John Marlowe.[21]

The old shoemaker is no more specific as to the date at which he came to Canterbury. In the 1565 deposition, he said that he had lived in the city "circiter decem annos," that is, since 1555; in 1586 this becomes "per xlta annos," that is, since 1546; in 1593, he changes this to "per xxxij annos vel eo circiter," ap-

---

[19] Not identical with Joan Marley, widow, of Chilham, whose will is dated 1534.

[20] For further references to these documents, see I. 24–27.

[21] Chancery Misc. Rolls. Bundle 10, no. 2. See Caroline A. Spurgeon: *Chaucer Criticism and Allusion*, I. 8.

parently since about 1561; and in 1602, he changes again to "per xlta annos aut circiter," or since about 1562. He is equally indefinite about the length of time during which he had been a parishioner of St. George's.

Although it is quite impossible to prove the date of John Marlowe's birth, it is probable enough that he was born in the summer or autumn of 1540, when Mistress Joan Marley, widow of Christopher Marley, tanner, of Westgate, would have been expecting her child. It is noteworthy that John Marlowe names one of his children Christopher and another Joan, as if in honor of his parents, and that all his signatures spell the name "Marley."

John Marlowe invariably gives the village of Ospringe, ten miles west of Canterbury, as his birthplace, but as the parish records have been destroyed it is useless to seek a baptismal record, which would give the parents' names, as well as the date. It would, however, have been natural enough for the widow to withdraw to a neighboring town, ten miles west of Canterbury, if she had friends or relatives living there, and equally natural for her child to return to Canterbury as he grew older. If he really was the son of Christopher Marley, the tanner of Westgate, he fell heir to a fair amount of property there.

Of the subsequent history of John Marlowe and his family we know a good deal. Innumerable documents testify that he was a shoemaker. As a young man he is apprenticed to Gerard Richardson, according to an entry in the city accounts of Canterbury:

Item Received of garrard Rychardffon ffor the inrollment of John Marley his aprentys [22] } ij^s j^d

We know that this is the right John Marley because his master was a shoemaker, who had been admitted by marriage in 1550.[23] The municipal records are not quite clear about the date but are clear enough to show that the new apprentice was enrolled just after Elizabeth came to the throne. This must have been either in 1559 or 1560.[24] The latter date is the more probable,

[22] MS. Accounts, 1558–1568, vol. XII.
[23] J. M. Cowper: Roll of the Freemen, col. 296.
[24] The accounts run from Michaelmas to the Feast of St. Margaret (the day before

for on July 3, 1593, it is officially stated that he had lived in Canterbury for thirty-two years.[25] This indicates that he left Ospringe in 1560. Since the Elizabethan year began March 25, the months of April, May, and June, 1593, are probably not to be counted in.

While he was still an apprentice and three years before he became a freeman, John Marlowe was married to Catherine Arthur in the Church of St. George the Martyr on May 22, 1561, by the rector, the Reverend Arthur Swetinge. We still find the entry:

The 22nd day of May were married John Marlow and Catherine Arthur.[26]

His bride was probably the daughter of the Reverend Christopher Arthur, who had once been rector of St. Peter's, Canterbury, and seems to have come of an old Kentish family who, like the Ardens of Warwickshire, were entitled to bear arms. But the Arthur family had fallen on evil days. Catholic Queen Mary's hand had borne heavily upon the married clergy, and the Reverend Christopher had very likely been ejected from his living as a "reforming priest."

Though Catherine Arthur may have come from the minor gentry, prosperity, then as now, was at least as good a recommendation in a suitor as the blood of a gentle family. It is not by any means certain that the Reverend Christopher Arthur lived to see his daughter married; but, if he did, he can hardly have objected, in view of the eminent respectability of Master John Marlowe.

If at the time of his marriage John Marlowe was already a member of the Guild of Shoemakers and Tanners, to which it is quite certain that he later belonged, he must have complied with the old decree of Burghmote which provided that "if any of the seide fraternitie, dwelling in the liberties of the seide citie, intende to be married, then he shall give knowledge of

---

Michaelmas) of the following year. The year is given in one entry as the first year of Elizabeth (1558–59), which would give 1559 as the probable date.

25 Deposition of John Marlowe, July 3, 1593. *Depositions of Witnesses, 1591–4.* Cathedral Library, Canterbury, X, 11, 6, p. 147b.

26 J. M. Cowper: *Register Booke . . . of St. George the Martyr*, p. 100. All of these family entries have been checked by the original, in the possession of the rector, the Rev. Geoffrey Keable.

hit to the wardeyns of the seide fraternyte three daies before
the marriage, and then the seide wardens to give a command-
ment to the bedill of the same fraternite to name the brethren
in due time to go with him from his dwelling-place unto the
parisshe church where the matrimony shall be solemnised, and
to offer with him."[27]

Mary and Christopher Marlowe. — The next year the first
child of the union, Mary Marlowe, was born. The entry appears May 21, 1562:

The xxi[th] of May was Christened Mary the daughter of John Marlowe.[28]

Nothing more is heard of her, and it is probable that she is the
unnamed child referred to in a burial entry of 1568:

The 28th day of August was buried the daughter of John Marlow

Nearly three years after the marriage, the first son, who was
to become poet, dramatist, and Shakespeare's predecessor, was
born.[29] The approximate date can be established with tolerable
accuracy, though not definitely, from the registers of the King's
School, Canterbury — where scholars had to furnish proof of
age prior to admission — as February, 1563/4. The baby was
christened February 26, 1563/4, at the Church of St. George
the Martyr, at an ancient baptismal font still in use.[30] He had

---

[27] John Brent: *Canterbury in the Olden Time* (2nd ed., 1879), p. 152. Ingram, p. 14,
refers to the first ed., pp. 43-44.
[28] J. M. Cowper: *Register Booke . . . of St. George the Martyr*, p. 9, and the original.
[29] *Ibid.*, p. 9.
[30] J. M. Cowper: *Register Booke . . . of St. George the Martyr*, p. 10. Sixteenth-
century birth dates are rarely so definitely established as the nineteenth- and twentieth-
century scholars who write about them assume. Even the year of Marlowe's birth was
unknown until Dyce published his 1850 edition (I. i.). The biographer immediately
preceding Dyce (Lardner's *Cyclopedia,* "Lives of the English Dramatists," I. 49)
asserted that "the time of this writer's birth cannot be ascertained." Sir Egerton
Brydges (*Restituta,* II. 128) gives the date as 1566. Even a scholar like Malone says
only that Marlowe "was born about the former part of Edward VI." (MS. note in his
copy of Langbaine, now at the Bodleian, numbered Malone 131.) Collier, in his
Shakespeare (1853 ed., I. xxxiv n.), surmises that Marlowe was born in 1563, and adds
that "Oldys placed the event earlier." Ingram and the later encyclopedias agree on
February 6, a date for which there is no evidence. J. G. Lewis, the first English writer
to publish a separate brochure on Marlowe, ignores the day and gives the year as 1563,
confusing old and new style reckoning. Few of the more recent authorities presume to
fix the date of birth. Sidney Lee in the DNB, Ashley H. Thorndike in the *Encyclopedia
Americana,* and an anonymous writer in the *New International* content themselves with
the year, as does Professor C. F. Tucker Brooke. The date is given as February 6,
without citation of authority, in Philip Henderson: *And Morning in His Eyes,* p. 19.

been born, according to ancient Canterbury tradition — which is unsupported by documents, but which has never been disputed [31] — in the house now known as No. 57 St. George's Street, almost immediately opposite the church, in whose upper story the old woodwork that the child Marlowe must have seen still remains.

The same reasoning that is ordinarily used to establish the day of Shakespeare's birth would — as has been said — make Marlowe's February 23, 1563/4. The entry reads:

The 26th day of ffebruary was Chriftened Chriftofer the fonne of John Marlow [32]

They are as relentless as Time itself, these ancient records. One by one, the children of the Canterbury shoemaker appear on the register of christenings. One or two die almost at once. In a few years some appear on the marriage register. Then, after another lapse of years, they begin to appear on the register of burials — all but one, who sleeps in an unknown grave somewhere in the church or churchyard of St. Nicholas, Deptford.

These church records were normally kept in triplicate. Each rector kept a register of marriages, christenings, and burials in his own church, and sent the cathedral authorities two duplicates. One of these went to the archbishop; one to the archdeacon.

The three sets of records should agree; but, with embarrassing frequency, certain entries will appear in one source and not in the other. Ordinarily the church register, being kept from day to day, should be regarded as the more accurate; but this was not always the case. Details appear to have been forgotten in the haste attending some ceremonies, and these details seem to have been filled in or corrected when the rector or the parish clerk made up the transcript.

The register of St. George the Martyr, during these years, is not the original but a copy. In 1599 the minister and churchwardens had the records of christenings, marriages, and burials copied, beginning with the entries of 1538. Unfortunately "finding the saide records (some of them) vnperfectly wrotten,

---

[31] Letter of T. H. Mead, Esq., formerly director of the Royal Museum and Public Library, Canterbury.
[32] Cowper, *Register Booke*, p. 10.

and confuzedlye bounde toghether, they could not so orderly proceade, as they desired." [33]

The annual transcripts are therefore much earlier in date and, though copies, quite as likely to be accurate as the register itself. The archbishop's transcripts of St. George's at this period have not survived, but the archdeacon's are still safely stored in Christ Church Gate.

Second Son. — A second son was born in 1568, and the register for that year contains the entry:

The last day of October was Christened the sonne of John Marlow [34]

In the burials appears the entry:

The 5th day of November was buried the sonne of John Marlow.

The Two Thomas Marlowes. — Another son was christened July 26, 1570. The register reads:

The 26th day of July was christened Thomas the sonne of John Marle

This is confirmed by the transcript. His burial is recorded a few days later:

The 7th day of August was buried Thomas ẙ sonne of John Marlow.

This is also confirmed by the transcript.

At some time between 1573 and 1576, John Marlowe and his family moved from the parish of St. George's, in the eastern part of the city, to St. Andrew's parish, in its very center. In St. Andrew's Church, therefore, the last of John Marlowe's children was christened in 1576. Like the little boy who had died in 1570, he also was named Thomas. Again one gets the impression that the Marlowes clung stubbornly to family names. The entry runs:

Thomas Marley the sonne of John — 8 of Aprill [35]

---

[33] *Register,* fol. 2r.

[34] The archdeacon's transcript says: "the last day off october was crystenyd the sonne off John Marle [1568/9]."

[35] Tucker Brooke (*Life,* p. 8n) discovered this and other entries in St. Andrew's. The records of this parish are now in the custody of the rector of St. Margaret's, Canterbury.

and is confirmed by the transcript. This child must also have died early, for there is no mention of him in his parents' wills.

Besides Mary Marlowe, the first daughter, there were four others, whose lives can be traced through the church registers. The Reverend Alexander Dyce was the first to discover these entries.[36] He erred grievously, however, by confusing a certain "Marget the daughter of John Marlow," [37] born in 1548, with the dramatist's sister; and he also missed much that was lying in the records.

Margaret Marlowe. — Christopher Marlowe did, however, have a sister named Margaret, born some time in 1565 or 1566. The date is illegible, according to Dyce, though Brooke and Cowper agree in making it December 11, 1565. As it appears in the register it runs:

The iith day of December was Christened Margarit the daughter of John Marloe

In the archdeacon's transcript for 1566 it is perfectly clear:

the xviij day off desember was crystenyd Marget the daghter off John Marlo.

The record of this christening is a good example of disagreement between the register and the transcript. The carelessness of the entry is remarkable. The father's name as first written in the transcript looks like "Marley." This has been corrected in pale ink by changing the last syllable to "lo." The first name was originally written "Will'm," but this has been erased and changed to "John."

When at length it does appear in the archdeacon's transcript, the date is given as December 18, 1566. Such discrepancies are not uncommon, and we shall find another case in the record of the marriage of Joan Marlowe. Margaret Marlowe married John Jorden, Jurden, or Jordane, who is presumably the same "John Jurden," described as a "taylor," who became a freeman August 7, 1590, less than two months after his marriage. Apparently he was allowed to become a freeman by redemption at a specially low fee because of his marriage to a

---

[36] Dyce's ed. of 1850, I. i.
[37] J. M. Cowper: *Register Booke . . . of St. George the Martyr*, p. 6, and the original.

freeman's daughter, but this is not specifically stated. The record of his admission runs:

Memorandum that the viij day of Auguſt Anno xxxij^{do} John Jurden of the cytie of cant*er*bury taylor was Admytted & ſworne to the liberties of this cytie for the which he payd but x^s Agreed by bourmouth ^{38} } x $^•$

There is a record of the marriage in the register of St. Mary Bredman for 1590:

The xvth day of June were maryed John Jorden & Margaret Marlowe.^{39}

This was the only marriage of the year 1590. It is presumably their child, "Margarett, daughter of John Jordane," who is buried at St. George's March 13, 1638/9.^{40} Jorden seems to have been a fairly successful businessman. By 1594/5, a few years after his marriage, he is taking one Henry ffontayne as an apprentice, and in 1601/2 he is taking a certain William Parcey.^{41}

Joan Marlowe. — Joan Marlowe, also referred to as Jane, was apparently christened in St. George's, August 20, 1569. The register reads:

The 20th day of August was Christened John the sonne of John Marlow ^{42}

but there is no further notice of such a son, and no record of Joan's christening unless this is it. As her name was frequently spelled "Johan" in the sixteenth century, the mistake when the carelessly kept register was copied some years later is not surprising.

The marriage itself is recorded in the register of St. Andrew's:

Iohn More & Jayne Marley — 22· of Aprill [1582] ^{43}

^{38} J. M. Cowper: *Roll of the Freemen of Canterbury*, col. 280. *MS. Accounts, 1587–9*^{2}, vol. XV, fol. 92.

^{39} Brooke: *Life*, p. 10. The transcript says: "John Jorden and Margret Marlo wer maried ye 15 of June 1590."

^{40} J. M. Cowper: *Register Booke . . . of St. George the Martyr*, p. 167, and the original. On the admission of freemen, see Bunce: *Minutes*, no. XXXVII, but cf. erratum noted in XXXVIII. The transcript gives the date as March 1.

^{41} Both entries in the "Enrolling of Apprentices" for these fiscal years. (*MS. Accounts, 1592–1602*, vol. XVI.)

^{42} The entry thus appears in the register itself. Cowper's reprint somewhat shortens it.

^{43} Recorded in the archdeacon's transcript as: "John More & Jayne Marley — xxijth

This is followed by two entries in the city accounts, one in 1583 and one in 1585, recording the admission of John Moore to the freedom of the city because he has married "Jane the daughter of John Marley of the feid cytie." [44]

The triple record of the marriage has led to much speculation which is really quite needless. A prospective freeman frequently did not make the payments necessary to his freedom until some time after he was entitled to it. John Moore did not appear before the city fathers until eight months after his marriage, a circumstance in which there is nothing at all remarkable. His second admission as freeman probably means that he had failed to make his payments or that some other irregularity required correction. There is no need to suppose that there was any need of a second marriage ceremony. Being nearly thirteen, Joan Marlowe was by Elizabethan standards quite old enough for marriage.

The entries whereby Moore became a freeman are as follows:

Moore   Memorandum that the xviijth day of January [1583]
         Anno xxv^{to} Regine Elizabeth/ John Moore of the cytie
         of Caunterbury shoemaker was/ admytted & allowed
         to the liberties of this cytie for the/ which he payd but
         xj^d ob becaufe he maryed with Jane/ the daughter of   } xi^d ob
         John Marley of the feid cytie shoemaker/ who was a
         freeman of the seid cytie before the/ byrth of the
         feid Jane

The second entry runs:

Moore   Memorandum that the fame day & yere [1585] John
         Moore of the cytie of/ Caunterbury shoemaker was
         admitted & alloyed to the liberties/ of this cytie for the
         which he payd but xi^d ob Agreed by the/ wyle(?) of   } xl'
         burgmoote becaufe he maryed [illegible; elided] Jane/
         daughter of John Marloe of this cytie shoemaker who /
         was a freeman of this cytie before the byrth of/ the
         feide Jane

Other entries show that "the fame day & yere" means September 13, 1585. Presumably the Joan Moore buried at

Apriell." The register is now in charge of the rector of St. Margaret's, Canterbury. The entry was first discovered by Professor Brooke.

44 J. M. Cowper: Roll of the Freemen of Canterbury, col. 139; MS. Accounts, 1577–1587, vol. XIV (both entries); Brooke: Life, p. 9.

St. Mary Magdalen, August 19, 1598, was Mistress John Moore.

Anne Marlowe. — "An daughter of John Marlow," was christened at St. George's July 14, 1571,[45] and is not heard of further until her marriage to John Crawford, shoemaker, who a few months later became a freeman. The church register of St. Mary Bredman for 1593 contains the entry:

The xth day of June were maried John Crauforde & An Marlowe [46]

only a few days after the murder of the dramatist, who had flashed through the whole of his meteoric career at Cambridge and in London while the little girl was quietly growing up in Canterbury. News transmission, except for a few newsbooks and the government intelligence service, was extremely slow, however, and it is probable that no tidings of the tragedy in London reached Canterbury for weeks. There is no allusion to the murder in any Canterbury record so far discovered.

The entry of John Crawford's admission reads:

Crauforde   M*emorandum* that the xxix[th] day of January A*nn*o xxxvj° Regin*e* n*ost*re Elizabeth John Crauforde of the Citye of Caunterbury Shoemaker was admitted and ſworne to the liberties of this Citye for w*hi*ch he paid but xj[d] oƀ [flourish] becauſe he maryed with Ann Marlowe the daughter of John Marlowe of this Citye Shoemaker who was a freeman of this Citye before the birth of the ſaid Ann and was firſt ſene and lyked of by Bourmoth [47]   xj[d] oƀ

Dorothy Marlowe. — On October 18, 1573, the last of John Marlowe's daughters was christened. She does not appear in the register of St. George's,[48] but the archdeacon's transcript has on this date the entry:

the same daye was crissened daretye the daughter of John Marlye.

---

[45] The archdeacon's transcript reads: "the xiiij day off July was crystend An the daghter off John Marle."

[46] The archdeacon's transcript reads: "The 10 of June were maried John Crauford & An Marlowe [1593]."

[47] Cowper, *Roll of the Freemen of Canterbury*, col. 112; *MS. Accounts, 1592–1602,* vol. XVI, fol. 9. (Various sections of this book have independent numbering of folios.) Brooke: *Life*, p. 10.

[48] J. M. Cowper: *Register Booke . . . of St. George the Martyr*, p. 12, and the original.

Though younger than her sister Ann, she was only a year later in marrying. The register of St. Mary Bredman records in 1594 that

The xxx^{tith} day of June were maried Thomas Graddell & Dorithie Marle.

Thomas Cradwell received his freedom in the year of his marriage. The entry in the municipal accounts runs:

Graddell. Memorandum that the xxviijth daye of September ⎫
        Anno xxxvj° Regine nostre Elizabeth [flourishes] ⎪
        Thomas Graddell of the Citye of Caunterbury ⎪
        vintener was admitted and ſworne to the liberties ⎪
        of this Citye for which he paid but xj^d oƀ becauſe ⎬ xj^d oƀ̃
        he maried with Dorathe the daughter of John ⎪
        Marlowe of this Citye Shoemaker who was a free- ⎪
        man of this ſaid Citye before the byrthe of the ⎪
        ſaid Dorathe and that the ſaid Thomas was firſt ⎪
        ſene and lyked of by Bourmoth [49] ⎭

It was probably their son, John Gradwell, of All Saints, Canterbury, yeoman and bachelor, who married April 25, 1622. He is described as the son of Thomas Gradwell.[50]

It will be noted that all of John Marlowe's sons-in-law, except John Jurdane, appear in the list of freemen by marriage. That is, they became freemen by marrying the daughters of a freeman and paying elevenpence halfpenny. Hence the careful records of their marriages in the city records.[51]

It is fairly easy to recreate imaginatively the conditions under which the shoemaker's lad grew up in Canterbury. Facts do not bear out the accepted tradition as to the extreme poverty of John Marlowe's household. The shoemakers were a rather prosperous guild in sixteenth-century Canterbury. The Burghmote decreed in 1518 "that every brother shoemaker, cobbeler, or

[49] J. M. Cowper: *Roll of the Freemen of Canterbury*, col. 327; *MS. Accounts, 1592–1602*, vol. XVI, fol. 10v. These folios run for the year only.

[50] J. M. Cowper: *Canterbury Marriage Licenses*, 1st ser., 1568–1618. None of the Marlowe marriages appear in this. The entries in the registers of St. Andrew's and St. Mary Bredman were not published until Professor C. F. Tucker Brooke printed his *Life* (p. 8 and n). They were supplied to him by the Rector of St. Margaret's, Canterbury, who is in charge of the MS. records of the other two churches. The married names of surviving daughters are given in the probate note affixed to John Marlowe's will. See Brooke: *op. cit.*, pp. 93–94.

[51] J. M. Cowper: *Roll of the Freemen of Canterbury*, p. xi.

corner, that will sett up and occupy as a maister within the said citie and libertye of the same, shall pay to the wardens of the seide crafte, or ever he sett up and occupy, 3s. 4d. to the maintenance of the aforeseide brotherende, upon payne of forfeiture of 6 lbs. of wax." This was a fairly large fee for the period.

An ordinance further demands "That the bedill shall see that the dedde body of every brother have four torches to bring him to the grave, and four tapers to be lighted or borne about his corpse or herse if his body be in the church in the time of dirige or mass, except there be two corpses in one day, when the seide torches and tapers are to be equally divided between them." [52] Shoemakers must have been relatively prosperous to keep up such ceremonial.

It is true that John Marlowe's only surviving son went to Cambridge on a scholarship, but this does not necessarily imply dire financial straits at home. Acceptance of a scholarship for a promising lad no more indicated poverty then than it does now. University education in the sixteenth century was a thing for the nobility and for promising sons of the people who might become priests. Indeed, it is quite possible that, then as now, a businessman successful in a small way was not inclined to help along the crazy modern notions of a queer and disappointing son, with a mad way of making verses and no inclination for the shoe and leather trade. It is doubtful whether the man who raised devils to visit the study of Faustus, or saw with his mind's eye the face that launched a thousand ships, ever looked upon the cobbling career or the hide and leather business with any very notable degree of sympathy.

There may have been scenes of heavy parental wrath in the Marlowe household before young Christopher went off to the university, and it is perhaps significant that after maturity Christopher Marlowe seems to have had little to do with his family, though he had other Kentish associations. But however John Marlowe may have looked upon his son's aspirations, there is no reason to suppose that he was an especially unsympathetic parent; he was certainly on friendly terms with his son when they jointly witnessed Mistress Benchkyn's will in 1585; and it is sheer libel upon an ornament of the Canterbury Guild

[52] John Brent: *Canterbury in the Olden Time* (1879), pp. 151–152.

of Shoemakers and Tanners to suggest that he could not provide — and provide fairly well — for his family. We can probably regard Dekker's *Shoemaker's Holiday* or, better yet, Thomas
Deloney's novel of shoemakers' lives, *The Gentle Craft*, in which
Dekker found his source, as fair, though idealized, pictures of
what life was like in the Marlowe household.

John Marlowe must have been in decent circumstances most
of his life. His father had bequeathed him two houses, furniture, and land, and he was able to marry while still an apprentice, almost three years before he became a freeman.

Not until April 20, 1564, in the sixth year of Queen Elizabeth's reign, do the municipal records of Canterbury record
that:

ỹ xxth day of aprill in ỹ yere a fforeseid John Marlyn of Can-
terᵇᵘʳʸ shomaker was admitted & sworne to the liberties of
ỹ citte ffor ỹ whitche he paid but iiij^s j^d becaws he was in-
rowlyd withyn ỹ Citte accordyng to ỹ customes off ỹ saeme [53]   } iiij^s j^d

The fee which he pays is about average for a man becoming
a freeman of Canterbury by "emption" or "redemption."
The records show similar fees of from 6s. 8d. to 13s. 4d. Presumably his birth at Ospringe prevented his claiming the rank
of freeman, at a special fee, to which sons of Canterbury freemen were entitled, or perhaps there was some irregularity about
his father's status.

There was every reason why a young shoemaker should wish
to be a freeman. The guild of "the Brethren of the Assumption
of Our Lady, of the Crafts and Mysteries of Shoe-Makers,
Coriours and Cobbelers" was an important organization. Only
freemen of the city could "holde craft and opyn windowes,
withoute leve ther; other may nott, withowte agrement of the
chamber." In other words, the freemen controlled the trade of
Canterbury. The following special privileges are among those
set forth in 1529:

Oñ. ys, that fremen may come to the counsell of the same cyte,
and thēr speke and be herd; wher other shalbe voyde, and be put
away.

*   *   *   *

[53] *MS. Accounts, 1558–1568*, vol. XII. J. M. Cowper: *Roll of the Freemen of Canterbury*, col. 212, lists him among the freemen by apprenticeship.

Fremen bethe quyte of toll of costumus of lastage and of shewyng, over all Yngeland, and be all the costis of the see

* * * *

Thēr schall be no freman of Caunt'bery be condempnyd, ne convyct be foryn men, for eny trespass, but only be 'her concitezens

* * * *

Yeff eny freman of Caunt'bery shuld be takē be his body, or arreynyd, wherfore he schuld suffre emprisonment, he schall no where be imprisonyd, but only in the pr'son of Caunt'bery, ne no where be demyd [i.e., judged], but be concitezens of the same cite, be her charter.

* * * *

Yeff a freman of Caunt'bery be condēpnyd in eny dett, at sewte of eny man, he may have xv dayes of payement, under suerte.

Yeff a freman emplete eny other man of dett, the plaintiff may pursue his dett, wyth iij hands, and have his axyng.

* * * *

A Freman of Caunt'bery may ax and have part of vyteyll and corn, and other that comyth to be sold yn the markett.

Yeff a freman of Caunt'bery take aprēntys to terme of yers, in the fyrst yere, he may inroll him and pay 2 s., and so to be of record

* * * *

Eny freman's chyld, fre-bore, may pay his fees in the chamber, and then to be a freman, as his fadyr was.

Yeff eny wedde a freman's dawghter, fre bore, he may paye his right to the chamber and be a freman, yeff sche have made none before

* * * *

Fremen of Cauntbery schall have 'her huntyng and ther dysport, wythe-yn boundys of 'her prevelege.[54]

The freemen were "truely sworne uppon a boke" to bear loyal allegiance to the Crown; to maintain the franchises, customs, and usages of the city; not to bring suit against a fellow-freeman outside the city if they could get their rights before the city's own bailiffs; and to take only freemen born as apprentices.[55]

---

[54] Bunce *Minutes*, no. XXIV; Bunce MSS., I. 108.

[55] Bunce MSS., II. 328. Original said to be "at the end of the large book of H6."

There is silence in the Canterbury records with regard to John Marlowe's business activities for the next few years — a silence that strongly suggests the struggle of a young tradesman to achieve that humble measure of success which we find him enjoying toward the close of his life. His deposition in the "libel" case of Hunte vs. Aplegate, in 1565, mentions two apprentices, Lore Atkynson and Harman Verson. Neither of these young men becomes a freeman.

By 1567/8, John Marlowe is sufficiently prosperous to require another apprentice, and we find the entry:

Item *Received* off John Marle fhomaker for th ynrollment off⎫ ijˢ jᵈ
Ric Umbarffeld hys aprentys [56]   ⎭

Richard Umbarffeld disappears from the record, never appearing on the roll of freemen as a good apprentice should, possibly because of death. He may have been the son of John Umberfyld,[57] a smith, who was admitted freeman by marriage in 1562. He would have been old enough to become an apprentice if his father's marriage had antedated his admission as freeman by some years. This was not impossible. John Marlowe himself was married and had children before becoming a freeman.

Four years later we find a payment by John Marlowe listed in the "Receate of maifter wildis Monny" — apparently repayment of a loan due the city. The entry reads:

Rc of John Marlowe for fo muche by him due to the⎫ ijˢ
citie [58]   ⎭

There are many other payments by other men at the same time, the payments running from two to ten shillings.

By July 3, 1583, another of John Marlowe's apprentices, Elias Martyn, is receiving his freedom:

---

[56] *MS. Accounts, 1558–1568*, vol. XII. Discovered by author. Ingram (p. 130) and Brooke: *Life* (p. 15n) mention a loan of five pounds repaid by Henry Carre "out of Streeter's legacy, which Marley the shoemaker had and delivered in at Candlemas. No. XXX. R. Eliz." Ingram also alludes to John Marlowe as a bowman on a manuscript muster roll of the Armada period.

[57] Cowper: *Roll of the Freemen of Canterbury*, col. 150. Harman Umberfyld, tailor, admitted in 1597, was certainly his son. (*Ibid.*, col. 86.)

[58] *MS. Accounts, 1568–1577*, vol. XIII. Discovered by author.

Memorandum that the same day & yere Elias Martyn of the seid Cyte Shoemaker was admytted & alloyed to the liber-ties of this Cytie for the which he payd but iiij[s] i[d] because he was the aprentyce of John Marloe of the seid Cytie Shoe-maker and was enrolled in the chamber of the seid Cytie according to the customs there used.[59] } iiij[s]. jd

The shoemaker seems to have taken another apprentice imme-diately, for by April of 1594 we find:

Memorandum that the xxvj[th] daye of Aprill Anno xxxv° Regine Elizabeth William Hewes late apprentice with John Marlowe of the Citye of Caunterbury Shoemaker was ad-mitted and sworne to the liberties of this Citye for which he paid but iiij[s] j[d] for that he was enrolled in the chamber of y̆ said Citye accordyng the customes there used.[60] } iiij[s] j[d]

Almost at once we find a new apprentice, for in 1594/5 appears the record:

Item received of John Marlowe of the Citie of Caunterbury Shoemaker for the enrollment of Thomas Mychell his appren-tice ij[s] j[d] who was bounde to hym by Indenture dated the xxiij[ti] daye of December Anno xxxvjo Regine Elizabeth for vij yeres from the feaste of the byrthe of our saviour Christ from thence next ensuing.[61] } ij[s] j[d]

Like Umbarffeld, Mychell seems never to have become a free-man and cannot be traced further.

The shoemaker is occasionally summoned to make a deposi-tion for or against one of his neighbors. The first of these is dated February 19, 1565. It avers that about a year earlier, almost at the exact time of Christopher Marlowe's birth, John Marlowe and one Lawrence Aplegate, a tailor of about his own age, had gone to Barham, near Canterbury.[62]

"By the waie as they twoo togither went," they fell into idle and somewhat lewd conversation.

---

[59] MS. Accounts, 1577–1587, vol. XIV. Cowper (Roll of the Freemen of Canterbury, col. 213) thinks the first name may be Elnas. Brooke (Life, p. 15) reads Elias, probably correctly.

[60] MS. Accounts, 1592–1602, vol. XVI, fol. 10; Cowper: op. cit., col. 200.

[61] MS. Accounts, 1592–1602, vol. XVI, fol. 11. These folios are for the year only. Discovered by author.

[62] P.R.C. 39 — 5, Cathedral Library, Canterbury. Aplegate, who became a freeman in 1562, two years before John Marlowe, appears in J. M. Cowper: Roll of the Freemen of Canterbury, col. 3.

The said lawrence Aplegate said theis word*es* or the verie like in
effect good fayth cossin I wolde open a thinge vnto you yf you will
kepe it secret wherupon this deponent pr*o*mising hym that so he wold
the said lawrence proceded saying I haue hadd my pleasure of godlyve
Chappmans Daughter and further syth that diuers tymes syns and
in sondrie places the said Lawrence Aplegate hath most sclanderouslie
affirmed the foresaid word*es* and in repeting and acknoledging the
same wold say that godwiff Chapman didd owe vnto hym the same
Lawrence twoo shilling*es* and quoth he she wold nott pay me the said
twoo shilling*es* but retayned & kepte back the same for that I oc-
cupyed godliff hir Daughter fower times w*hi*ch was for everie tyme
vj d or the verie like word*es*.

Aplegate repeated these scandalous remarks in his own
house; in the Marlowe household in the presence of Mistress
Marlowe, of John Marlowe's two apprentices, Lore Atkynson
and Harman Verson, and in the house of another Harman
Verson, probably the apprentice's father.[63]

One of the two aggrieved ladies brought suit on a charge which
would today be slander, but which in the sixteenth-century
manuscript record is plainly marked "super li*bel*lo." The
plaintiff's name is here given as "Hunte." This suggests that
the daughter brought suit because she had since married and
was therefore eager to clear her reputation.

In the testimony preliminary to the deposition, John Marlowe stated that he was "Etatis circiter xxxta annor*um*"; that
he had lived in Canterbury "circiter decem annor*um*"; and that
he had been a parishioner of St. George's "circiter quatuor vel
quinque annos." In other words, he had been born about 1535,
had lived in Canterbury since about 1555, and had become a
parishioner of St. George's since 1560 or 1561. He also states
that he was "oriundus infra p*arochi*a de Hosprindge." Allowing for a "cockney H," this is the parish of Ospringe, near Canterbury, the birthplace given in three subsequent documents.

On April 19, 1585, an old woman of Canterbury named
Katherine Benchkyn decided to make her will. In itself, this
document is of no importance, but the witnesses happened to
be the poet Christopher Marlowe himself, who was in Canterbury on a short visit from Cambridge; his brother-in-law, John

[63] Harman Verson, glazier, admitted freeman 1552, appears in J. M. Cowper: *Roll of the Freemen of Canterbury*, col. 306.

Moore; his father; and a certain Thomas Arthur, who was probably his uncle. Something over a year later, after Mistress Benchkyn's death, John Marley made a deposition with regard to her will. The official note which precedes the deposition identifies him fully as "Joh*ann*es Marly parrochi*ae* Divi Georgij," as "or*i*und*us* in parrochia de Ospringe," and as "etatis circiter l ta annoru*m* liber*ae* Condic*i*o*n*is."

There is no possible question of identity. The Marlowe family did live in St. George's parish, as the church register abundantly shows. Furthermore, John Marley swears that "this deponentes Soonne Chr*ist*ofer Marley" and "John Moore, this deponentes Soonne in Lawe" were fellow-witnesses. His signature corresponds exactly with his other known signatures.[64] This, then, is the poet's father — he swears to it himself.

On July 3, 1593, John Marlowe made another deposition.[65] In the autumn of 1591, probably in October, he had gone to the house of Leonard Doggerell, in St. Peter's parish, "about som busines that he had w*i*th the said Doggerell for his lether." [66] Doggerell was a currier, that is, a workman who dressed and colored leather after tanning.

In his house at the time were some goods belonging to one John Parfect, who had died. Wishing to distrain upon them for damage, Doggerell asked Marlowe and a certain John Smyth to be witnesses. They all went upstairs while Doggerell went through the legal formula of pointing at two featherbeds and two bolsters and saying: "I distreyn these beds & bolsters for damage fesant." When they came down, Doggerell went through the same formula of distraint upon two playing tables. In the summer of 1593 there was trouble with members of the Parfect family over these chattels, and Marlowe went into court on behalf of his friend Doggerell. There, so far as the Marlowe family was concerned, the little comedy ended.

Some years before this, John Marlowe had added to his

[64] Deposition of John Marly, October 5, 1586. Public Record Office, Canterbury, 39/11, fol. 237.

[65] Deposition of John Marlowe, July 3, 1593. *Depositions of Witnesses, 1591–4.* Cathedral Library, Canterbury, X, 11, 6, p. 147b.

[66] Deposition of John Marlowe, July 3, 1593. *Depositions of Witnesses, 1591–4,* Cathedral Library, Canterbury, X, 11, 6, p. 147b.

cobbling the business of a professional bondsman. He had gone on one bond as early as 1579. By 1588 he had evidently become a responsible tradesman whose bond was always acceptable, for it is recorded repeatedly in the books of various dioceses from the year of the Armada until his death in 1604.

It always appears [67] at the marriages of couples whose social status is relatively humble — twice for innkeepers and frequently for yeomen and husbandmen. His name is variously spelled in these records — Marley, Marlowe, Marloe, Marlow, and Marlyn, but as his trade is always referred to, there is little doubt of his identity. Moreover, all such entries cease after his death, so that there can hardly be a chance of confusion with any other John Marlowe who may have existed.

John Marlowe was presumably one of those "vintners, victuallers, . . . holders and men of lower standing" described by Mr. J. M. Cowper,[68] who "were always on hand and ready to give a bond for £ 40, £ 100, or £ 200, according to the period." Let us hope he was not among those who had "degraded what was intended to be a security into a trade." Being rich enough to provide surety for a hundred pounds as early as 1579,[69] he was probably able to provide decently for his family much earlier and throughout his married life.

About 1588, he became a parishioner of St. Mary's and on October 2, 1602, testified in behalf of the rector, the Rev. James Byssell, in a dispute over tithes.[70] In this deposition he stated that he had been a parishioner "by the space of theis xiiij yeeres last past aut circiter" — a statement to be taken with reservation, in view of the lax chronology of his other depositions.

[67] J. M. Cowper: *Canterbury Marriage Licenses*, 1st ser., 1568–1618. It may have appeared oftener, for Cowper does not always name the sureties. The dates at which he was bondsman are: April 28, 1579 (p. 365), February 8, 1588 (p. 87), July 29, 1589 (p. 88), March 22, 1590 (p. 366), August 10, 1593 (p. 25), September 28, 1593 (p. 72), October 13, 1596 (p. 181), February 24, 1597 (p. 59), June 17, 1597 (p. 267), August 27, 1597 (p. 107), December 7, 1597 (p. 183), July 20, 1599 (p. 169), November 22, 1599 (p. 88), March 31, 1601 (p. 139), October 7, 1602 (p. 287), November 22, 1603 (p. 206), August 11, 1604 (p. 214). The original marriage licenses have long since disappeared, but official records of them are still stored at Christ Church Gate, Canterbury. Cowper lists one more appearance for John Marlowe as bondsman.

[68] J. M. Cowper: *Canterbury Marriage Licenses*, 1st ser., 1568–1618, pp. iii–iv.

[69] See the original entry of license for the marriage of William Corkyne and Joan Corsyne, August 27, 1597, now in Christ Church Gate, Canterbury.

[70] PRO Cant. 39–26–17.

John Marlowe's will, signed January 23, 1604, a day or two before his death, gives no great amount of information as to his pecuniary situation, though there is eloquent evidence of a happy marriage — with all that that implies for his son's childhood — in this simple provision: "As touching my temporall goods my debts & funeralls dischardged & paid J give and bequeath solely to my wife Katherine whome J make my sole executrix." [71]

The will is signed only with a mark; and from this fact some scholars have inferred that John Marlowe was illiterate. But many persons whom one would expect to be literate sign wills of this period only with a mark; and some of the most learned men of the kingdom, ranging from archbishops down and including even St. Thomas à Becket, sign ecclesiastical documents only with a cross. These last, however, are earlier than John Marlowe's time. [72]

John Marlowe is recorded in the list of "burialls" at the Church of St. George the Martyr:

Jan. 26 John Marloe, clarke of St. Maries. [73]

The transcript has the entry:

John Marloe buried the, 26. of Januarie. 1604[/5] [74]

The family had apparently moved to the parish of St. Mary Bredman some time before Margaret Marlowe's marriage in 1590, as John Marlowe's testimony in the tithes case indicates. Being a parish clerk, he must certainly have been literate. His signature on several depositions and on the Archdeacon's transcript of the register of St. Mary Bredman for 1591/2 are in perfectly clear and easy script. [75]

When his widow, Mistress Katherine Marlowe, comes to make her will, [76] March 17, 1605/6, she has such an abun-

[71] *Archdeaconry Register*, Canterbury Branch of the Public Record Office, 17/52, formerly LII. 373.

[72] Data from W. P. Blore, Esq., Librarian, and Frank W. Tyler, Esq., Sub-Librarian, of the Cathedral Library. See also Oscar James Campbell: "Shakespeare Himself," *Harper's*, 181: 172–185 Jy 1940.

[73] J. M. Cowper: *Register Booke . . . of St. George the Martyr*, p. 179, and the original.

[74] Now at Christ Church Gate, Canterbury.

[75] Now at Christ Church Gate, Canterbury.

[76] *Archdeaconry Register*, Canterbury Branch of the Public Record Office, 17/54, formerly LIV. 267.

dance of worldly goods to dispose of—presumably inherited from her husband — that her testamentary arrangements give an almost classic glimpse of the interior of a moderately prosperous Elizabethan home. Mistress Marlowe has a maid, musically named Mary May, who is affectionately remembered with "my red petticoate, and a smocke." Goodwife Morrice — twice mentioned, first to become the richer by "one pillowecoate" and again to receive "my petticoate that I doe weare daylye and a smocke and a wastcoate" — is, to judge by the nature of the bequests, another servant. Katherine Reve, who receives only "one payre of pillowecoates," may be still another.

There are gold and silver rings, numerous silver spoons, six pairs of sheets for each daughter, besides "a dosen of napkins to be divided equallye because some are better then other." There are also articles of furniture and clothing, five pounds in cash — no mean sum for the early seventeenth century — bequests of furniture, and other property not enumerated, all to be bestowed upon her son-in-law and executor, John Crawford. The widow's will, written by Thomas Hudson, is signed, like her husband's, with a mark and is witnessed by Goodwife Sarai Morrice and Mary Maye, who like their mistress found signatures a little too much effort.

The wills of Marlowe's parents, made more than ten years after their son had been stabbed to death, may not be the best of evidence as to the conditions under which he grew up, but there is none better available. They certainly demonstrate comfort and prosperity in the old couple's declining years, and, since self-won comfort and prosperity are rarely attained at a bound, they suggest at least a fair degree even during their son's lifetime. Shoemakers in provincial cities of the sixteenth century did not attain to such luxuries as gold rings and silver spoons easily, unless — as may have been the case with the Marlowes — their immediate ancestors had also enjoyed moderate prosperity. "That is a poor peasant," wrote a German visitor to England, "who has no silver-gilt salt-cellars, silver cups, and spoons." [77]

Although John Marlowe appears, then, to have been a fairly

[77] L. von Wedel's Journal, *Trans. Royal Hist. Soc.* (NS) 9: 268 (1895).

substantial citizen of Canterbury, he was obviously not so blessed with worldly goods as some of the earlier Marlowes. The Richard Marley who made his will June 12, 1521, was so wealthy that it required six pages of legal foolscap to dispose of all he had. This includes brass household utensils, appar- ently valuable, clothing and furniture, a store of bark and leather, real estate in Canterbury and outside the city (includ- ing three messuages in Northlane, Kent), and a good deal of money. There are various bequests for religious purposes. The money derived from sale of his stock of bark and leather was to provide ten pounds for his son Christopher, supposed grand- father of the poet; twenty shillings to a friend, "Maister Man for hys good counsell"; four pounds to his brother-in-law, Thomas Colpholl; and three pounds to "Thomas ffowle ouersear of the same my testament"; and a payment of six- pence weekly for life to his mother, Kateryn Marley. His wife Alice was to have the real estate until his son Christopher came of age.[78]

The son, Christopher Marley, whose will was made on March 5, 1539/40, seems to have been a thrifty soul, and the estate prospered in his care. He left twenty-one nobles to his mother, Alice Marley; twenty pounds to his wife, together with twenty acres of land; and ten pounds as a dowry for his daughter Elys (Alice). To the unborn child who may have been John Mar- lowe, father of the dramatist, he leaves two houses, furniture, and land.

From the series of wills and from the record of John Mar- lowe's business, one gets a picture, not of wealth, but of modest comfort on an humble scale.

[78] *Archdeaconry Register*, vol. XXI, fol. 258 f., in Public Record Office, Canterbury Branch.

CHAPTER II

EDUCATION: THE KING'S SCHOOL

The fruitfull plot of Scholerisme grac't.
Doctor Faustus, 16
—

ONCE CHRISTENED in St. George's, Christopher Marlowe disappears from written records until he enters the King's School, Canterbury, when payments on his behalf begin to require occasional mention of his name. Until 1578, then, we may picture the future dramatist living much the same life that another clever and imaginative lad was living in Stratford — with the difference that the cobbler's son dwelt in the seat of the Primate of England, with a more bustling life to catch the eye and stir the mind than the hills and quiet fields along the Avon could offer.

Both boys must have seen the mystery, miracle, and morality plays which had not yet begun to yield their popularity completely to the newer and more worldly drama that was rapidly springing up in the capital. At least once during Shakespeare's boyhood strolling players visited Stratford, and the references to Herod, the old Vice, and his lathe dagger which are scattered through his plays suggest many a visit to the Corpus Christi Cycle in neighboring Coventry.

In Canterbury, little Kit Marlowe was probably having even better opportunity to see the drama of his day. Canterbury was interested in drama and had been long before Marlowe was born. As early as 1473/4, the accounts record payment of five shillings to the players of the Duke of Clarence.[1] In 1504/5, the old pageant of St. Thomas, a procession through the streets which halted from time to time to act out the martyrdom of Thomas à Becket, had been revived with what was, for that day, great realism. The city officials held that the play was "as well to the hono*ur* of the same cite as to the pr*o*fite of all Vitelers &

---

[1] Bunce MSS., II. 27, in the Royal Museum and Public Library.

other occupations," and that failure to perform it was "to the grete hurte & decay of the seide Cite."[2]

The revivers paid eighteen pence for two bags of feathers, which seem to have been colored red and scattered to represent the spurting blood of the martyr. The parts of the murderous knights were acted by children, and probably the other parts as well.[3] There are entries for "four men to help to carry the pageant," "Linen Cloth for St. Thomas's Garment," a sword, a horse, and other properties.[4]

These pageants were suppressed in 1536/7 and then revived for a time under Queen Mary. Marlowe, therefore, never saw them. Nor can he have been influenced directly by the premature attempt at a theatrical company undertaken by some impresario of 1557 — attempts which were promptly and rudely put down, because the city fathers and Bloody Mary's Privy Council regarded them as "very sedicious."[5] This was probably a Protestant dramatic outburst against the Catholic government. Two letters from the Privy Council are still extant, directing that "the parties are to be punyshed as persons that sewe further sedicons." A copy of the offending drama had been forwarded to London for examination and the actors themselves imprisoned, for all of which the Privy Council returned "our hartie comendacons," signing themselves "your loving frendes."

There were other theatrical productions in Canterbury, however, both religious and secular. The religious drama may have lasted as late as Marlowe's childhood and so have influenced his developing tastes. The secular drama of the city certainly continued throughout his lifetime.[6] A decree of the Burghmote had early set up a special guild of Corpus Christi to act the sacred drama, and a special cycle was regularly presented each Lent and on other special festivals of the Church. In 1504 the Burghmote had ordered that "alle manner of crafts and mis-

[2] *Ibid.*, II. 359.

[3] J. Charles Cox: *Canterbury*, p. 103.

[4] Bunce MSS., I, 47.

[5] Canterbury Archives, Bundle LII, nos. 27 and 29 (Royal Museum and Public Library). The episode is alluded to by John Brent: *Canterbury in the Olden Time* (2nd ed., 1879), pp. 158–159.

[6] John Brent: *Canterbury in the Olden Time* (2nd ed., 1879), pp. 158–159.

triers, within the same cite, be so incorporated, for the sus-
tentacion and contynuance of the seide play, by the fest of
Seint Michel next comyng. And, yf eny suche crafte or crafts
be obstynatt or wilfulle, and will nott make sute to the Burge-
mote, for the performacion of these premissis by the seide faste,
to forfett to the seide chamber xxˢ. and theire bodies to be
punysshed, futhermore." [7]

It was presumably for these productions that we find [8] the
accounts in 1543 recording payment of 15s. "for stuff, bought
at London, for the play," also £1 3s. 3d. "for stuff, and making
of Cloaths for the Tormentors in the play," 10d. for "drink
given to the players, at divers times," 3s. 4d. "to my Lord
Warden's players, who played in the Guildhall." There are
other payments to "my Lord Protector's players."

Christopher Marlowe, as a lad of six, may have seen the performances of the Lord Warden's Players, who visited Canterbury in 1569/70. As a lad of ten, he could hardly have failed
to see the performances recorded in the city accounts for December, 1574: "Item payd to the Lord of Leycester his players
for playing." [9] Other companies of players visited the city after
young Christopher had gone to the university — Lord Morley's
men in 1581/2, the Earl of Hertford's in 1582, Lord Leicester's
between 1585 and 1588. Lord Strange's men, who probably
had already produced some of Marlowe's plays in London,
appeared in Canterbury in 1592. It is conceivable that John
and Catherine Marlowe actually saw their son's plays on the
stage. [10]

However these, or similar, performances may have interested
the youthful Marlowe in dramatic writing, stimulus may also
have come from school plays, produced on the raised dais of
the Almonry Chapel at the King's School. [11] About the time of
Marlowe's birth it was the custom for the schoolboys to act
plays, and this was probably still the custom while he was a

---

[7] Bunce *Minutes*, no. XXII. Bunce MSS., II. 359.

[8] Bunce *Minutes*, no. V; Bunce MSS., I. 49.

[9] The payment to Leicester's men is in *MS. Accounts, 1568–1577*, vol. XIII. Recorded
under "Expenses," 1574/5. See also Bunce *Minutes*, no. V; Bunce MSS., I. 49.

[10] John Tucker Murray: *English Dramatic Companies*. See Index under "Canterbury."

[11] *The King's School* (pamphlet, 1910), p. 10.

King's Scholar. There are no documents to prove it, but various documents show dramatic performances at the school just before and just after his time. The treasurer's accounts for 1562/3 record a payment of £14 6s. 8d. to the headmaster, "Mr. Ruesshe forrewards given him at settynge out of his plays at Christmas, per capitulum." [12] The *Acta Capituli* for the period between 1560 and 1563 likewise contain a payment of 56s. 8d. "to the scholemaster and scholars towards such expensys as they shall be at in settynge furthe of Tragedies, Comedyes, and interludes this next Christmas." Documents of the early seventeenth century continue to record frequent performances. [13]

It is possible to trace other broad general influences which must have affected the mind of a child who was certainly unusually sensitive and impressionable, amid a life of extraordinary richness, roughness, splendor, crudity, and brutality — in short, the usual life of early Elizabethan days. Canterbury stood on the highway leading to the Channel ports and thence to the hurly-burly of the Low Countries. Travelers, soldiers, sailors, merchants, priests, officials, spies, messengers, were perpetually passing back and forth. It is like enough that some of those stories of *Tamburlaine* and *The Massacre at Paris* — whose general origin is clear enough but whose exact provenance it is today so tantalizingly difficult to trace — go back to no printed sources whatever, but to an echo of old travelers' tales which once rang in the eager ears of a wide-eyed and wondering little boy, the son of a Canterbury cobbler.

The fascination which regal pomp and pageantry exercised over the mature Marlowe — a fascination most clearly to be seen in *Tamburlaine*, but evident enough in all the plays and even in the dubious glimpse of his personality given by the Baines libel — must also go back to childhood impressions.

There was ritual splendor enough in the cathedral, even under Protestant Elizabeth, and there was also the liveried ceremonial of the municipality. But there was nothing during Marlowe's childhood to equal Elizabeth's own royal progress through the city and her state visit to the great Archbishop Parker in

[12] *Acta Capituli*, vol. I, fol. 20, Cathedral Library. Cf. CHEL, V. 115; Dorothy Gardiner: *Canterbury*, pp. 69–76; Woodruff and Cape: *Schola Regia*, p. 89.

[13] *Publica Exercita Loveioii Scholarium*, Cathedral Library, MS. E 41, now at the King's School.

August, 1573, when every child in the city, and first among them nine-year-old Christopher Marlowe, must have stood cap in hand, huzzaing in the streets.

To do honor to the Virgin Queen it was ordered that "Mr. Mayor, the Aldermen, and every one of them, ride in their scarlet gowns to meet the Queen; and the Common Council be on foot with their best apparel, and likewise as many of the chief Commoners as have gowns." [14] The city gave Her Majesty two presents, of thirty pounds and twenty pounds each, and smaller sums to the heralds, sergeants-at-arms, trumpeters, footmen, messengers, porters, the Black Guards, the "Captains and Knights marshalmen," musicians, and "Walter the Iester" — all of whom seem to have been entirely receptive. In all, the royal visit cost the city treasury £77 11s. 4d. in gifts, not to mention one pound "paid to Mr. Wyck for making the oration to the Queen." [15]

The ecclesiastical authorities were equally hospitable. As Her Majesty rode up to the west door of the great cathedral, she found Archbishop Parker with three other bishops waiting to meet the royal procession; and as the Queen rode up her "grammarian" — a schoolboy, probably sorely awed and frightened, from the King's School, adjoining the cathedral, where four years later the cobbler's lad was to become a scholar — welcomed her with an oration. Oratory ended, the Queen dismounted and entered the cathedral for evensong. [16] On September 7 the Archbishop entertained the Queen in the great hall of the episcopal palace.

For a fortnight Elizabeth dwelt among her Kentish subjects, setting up her court in the monastery of St. Augustine, which Henry VIII had seized to make a palace. The Queen attended service in the cathedral on Sunday and kept her birthday in the episcopal palace as guest of the wealthy Archbishop. Archbishop Parker describes the Queen's visit in a letter to Archbishop Grindal, of York, in a letter which is still extant:

I met her Highness as she was coming to Dover upon Folkestone Down, the which I rather did, with all my men, to shew my duty to

[14] John Brent: *Canterbury in the Olden Time* (2nd ed., 1879), p. 184.
[15] Bunce MSS., I. 138; II. 194–195.
[16] J. M. Cowper: *Lives of the Deans of Canterbury*, p. 46.

her, and mine affection to the shire, who likewise there met her. And I left her at Dover, and came home to Bekesbourne that night: and after that went to Canterbury to receive her Majesty there: which I did, with the bishops of Lincoln and Rochester, and my suffragan, at the west door. Where, after the grammarian had made his oration to her upon her horseback, she alighted. We then kneeled down, and said the Psalm *Deus misereatur*, in English, with certain other collects briefly; and that in our chimmers and rochets. The quire, with the dean and prebendaries, &c. stood on either side of the church, and brought her Majesty up with a square song, she going under a canopy, borne by four of her temporal knights, to her traverse placed by the communion board: where she heard even-song, and after departed to her lodging at St Augustine's, whither I waited upon her. From thence I brought certain of the council, and divers of the court, to my house to supper, and gave them fourteen or fifteen dishes furnished with two mess at my longer table, whereat sat about twenty; and in the same chamber a third mess at a square table, whereat sat ten or twelve: my less hall having three long tables well furnished with my officers, and with the guard, and other of the court. And so her Majesty came every Sunday to church to hear the sermon; and upon one Monday it pleased her Highness to dine in my great hall throughly [*sic*] furnished with the council, Frenchmen, ladies, gentlemen, and the mayor of the town with his brethren, &c.; her Highness sitting in the midst, having two French ambassadors at one end of the table, and four ladies of honour at the other end. And so three mess were served by her nobility; at washing her gentlemen and guard bringing her dishes, &c.[17] Because your grace desireth to know some part of mine order, I write the more largely unto you.[18]

According to Canterbury tradition, Elizabeth held court not far from the Marlowe house, in a building where the "Queen Elizabeth room" is still pointed out. She lodged in St. Augustine's Abbey, east of the city, and celebrated her birthday in the Archbishop's palace. There was, in consequence, a perpetual stream of lords, gallants, and royal pageantry up and down St. George's Street, past John Marlowe's house, where the boy Kit could see it all. Hence, probably, the famous lines in *Tamburlaine*:

> Is it not passing braue to be a King,
> And ride in triumph through *Persepolis*? [758–759]

[17] It was customary for the Queen to wash her hands publicly before dining. The dishes brought to her were, of course, filled with water.

[18] Dated March 17, 1574/5. Petyt MS. Inner Temple, no. 47, fol. 22. Original draft in Parker's hand. Reprinted as no. CCCLXVIII in *Correspondence of Matthew Parker* (Parker Society, 1853), pp. 475–476.

Perhaps also there is a reminiscence of municipal pageantry in the verses which tell how "the townes-men maske in silke and cloath of gold." [19]

When Elizabeth left Canterbury, both the city and the Archbishop showered her and her court with gifts. The city gave the Queen money and plate; the Archbishop money and a diamond-and-agate salt-cellar.[20]

The magnificence of the royal visit, the stately ceremony of the cathedral, were among the impressions that presumably fixed themselves early upon the mind of a child who must have been curiously receptive to the vivid life of state and municipal pageantry. But these were not all.

There were innumerable other spectacles by no means salutary, at least according to the notions of our more squeamish modern days. Plays, pageants, and royal progresses were all very well in the estimation of the full-blooded Elizabethan burgesses, their lusty 'prentices, their wives and children; but their hearts were stirred to real enthusiasm by such bloodier pastimes as cockfighting, dogfighting, bullbaiting, and — most edifying of spectacles for the godly to behold and most diverting for the ungodly — the execution of criminals. A special decree of the Burghmote provided that no beef might be marketed unless the animal had been baited for the delectation of the populace before being slaughtered [21] — a practical means of providing the rabble, if not with *panem et circenses*, at least with beef and a very passable imitation of the Roman shows, all at a minimum cost to the thrifty fathers of the city. This, however, is asserted by an old Canterbury writer to have been "an ancient order and custom of the city used by the city butchers before their killing; not so much (if at all) for pleasure, as to make them man's meat and fit to be eaten." [22]

Criminals doomed to execution were almost as plentiful as bulls to be baited, and were perhaps little more pitied. Many a heretic was burned at Canterbury during the persecution under

[19] I. *Tamb.* 1552.
[20] Dorothy Gardiner: *Canterbury*, pp. 90–93; "Felix Summerly" [Sir Henry Cole]: *Handbook for Canterbury, passim.*
[21] Ingram, p. 24 and n. 24; John Brent: *Canterbury in the Olden Time* (1st ed.), p. 40.
[22] Charles Cox: *Canterbury*, p. 285. There is no clue to the identity of the "old Canterbury writer."

Bloody Mary, and the burghers were hardened to the sight of suffering. Even earlier, in 1535, the city accounts record charges "for the expences of John A Wood and Robert Eylmyn rydyng to London to the Erytyk — xiiij *s* viiij d." Another entry grimly adds 2*s*. "for a lode and a halfe of wode to burne the seide Erytyk," as well as a sixpenny stake, a pennyworth of gunpowder, and a twopenny staple.[23] Fox's *Book of Martyrs* explains that, when victims of religious persecution were burned, the gunpowder "was not laid under the faggots, but only about their bodies to rid them out of their pains."

Equally dreadful was the fate of Friar Stone, whose sufferings are writ large upon the matter-of-fact account books of the city for 1539/40:[24]

Item paid for half a tonne of tymber to make a paire of gallowes for to hang ffryer Stone	ii⁸ vjᵈ
Item paid to a Carpenter for makyng of the same Gallowes & the Dray	xvjᵈ
Item to a laborer that dygged the holes	iijᵈ
Item paid to iiij men to help Sett vp the gallowes	vijᵈ
Item paid for drynk for them	jᵈ
Item paid for cariage of the same tymber from Stablegate to the Dongeon	iiijᵈ
Item paid for a hardell	vjᵈ
Item paid for a lode of wood & for a hors to drawe hym to the dongeon	ij⁸ iiijᵈ
Item paid to ij men that fet the ketill & parboyled hym	xijᵈ
Item paid to iij men that caryed his quarters to the gates & sett them vp	xijᵈ
Item paid for a Halter to hang hym	jᵈ
Item paid for ij oᵬ Halters	jᵈ
Item paid for Sandwich cord	ixᵈ
Item paid for screwe	jᵈ
Item paid to a woman that scowred the Ketyll	ijᵈ
Item paid to hym that did execucyon	iiij⁸ viijᵈ

Most of these items are only too alarmingly clear. A "hardell" or hurdle is a flat wood framework used to pen cattle. It is very much like the hurdle used by modern athletes and still common enough under its old name in modern Kent. Traitors were usually drawn to execution upon a hurdle instead of a cart. The

[23] *MS. Accounts, 1530–1538*, vol. VIII; Bunce *Minutes*, no. V. For similar stories, see John Brent: *Canterbury in the Olden Time* (2nd ed., 1879), pp. 218–219.
[24] *MS. Accounts, 1539–1545*; Bunce MSS., I. 49.

"Dongeon" was not a prison, but the open field still known as the Dane John in modern Canterbury. Friar Stone's sufferings, obviously a part of the persecution under Henry VIII, leave their trace in Marlowe's *Jew of Malta*. The villain-hero, Barabas, perishes in a boiling cauldron, like the luckless Friar Stone; and a friar is hanged earlier in the same play.[25]

There were few burnings at the stake in Elizabeth's reign and none at Canterbury. Marlowe himself probably never saw an execution by fire, though Francis Kett, who was still in residence at Corpus Christi, Cambridge, during the poet's first year there, was burned at the stake at Norwich a few years later. The memory of horror lingers, however. Such episodes as the torture of Friar Stone must have been remembered and discussed in Canterbury while the boy Kit was growing up; and there were, in any case, plenty of other brutalizing spectacles in Elizabethan England.

Private life was very nearly as savage as official. The dagger that every freeman wore was no mere ornament, though the city ordained "that no man drawe knyfe, nor no other wepyn upon payne of imprisonment of xl days, or to make fyne at xiij^s.iiij^d," and further "that no man, by nighte tyme, goz armyd, ne bere ne sword, ne none other wepyn, aftyr curfue tyme wit*h*oute light." [26]

Nevertheless, the dagger ensured the frequency of bloody broils — Marlowe's was not the only Kentish life that ebbed out through a stab wound. And the law, though it held life cheap enough in awarding its own penalties, was swift enough to avenge private killing. One could escape execution by proving self-defense, as Marlowe himself almost had to do.[27] Or one could escape by pleading "benefit of clergy," reading the "neck verse," and submitting to be branded in the brawn of the thumb with the letter "T." In Marlowe's childhood, Canterbury probably still owned and used the grisly implement mentioned in the city accounts for 1502: "Paid for the ingraving of one Iron to mark Murderers with — 8 d." [28] William Mar-

[25] *Jew of Malta*, 1733–1734.
[26] Bunce *Minutes*, no. XXIII.
[27] See I. 100.
[28] Bunce MSS., I. 47.

lowe, who in 1588 pleaded guilty to stealing a heifer somewhere near London,[29] and Ben Jonson, who killed the actor Gabriel Spencer, owed their lives to this loophole in the law.

For many a poor wretch, there was no escape. At least six men were hanged in Canterbury during Marlowe's childhood.[30] A gibbet was set up in 1529, another in 1540, and another in 1576. In addition, there was a condemned cell in an upper room of Westgate, still a city landmark. Here the convicted criminal could be hurried a few feet to the window and hanged on the city wall. This is what Marlowe is thinking of in *Tamburlaine*, when the governor of Babylon is hanged "vp in chaines vpon the citie walles." The same scene contains a reference to the "Westerne gate." The real Westgate, Canterbury, was almost within sight of John Marlowe's house.[31]

Other reminiscences of his native city in Marlowe's plays are less gruesome. In *The Jew of Malta*, Abigail is shut up in a monastery, like the Maid of Kent, who had been confined in St. Sepulchre's nunnery at Canterbury. Marlowe's friars live in a

> monastery
> Which standeth as an out-house to the Towne

as St. Augustine's Abbey still stands. The nuns' cloister in the play has a "darke entry" because the cathedral's real "Dark Entry" stood just across the green from the King's School, where the schoolboy Marlowe saw it every day. "*Ierusalem*, where the pilgrims kneel'd" on "Marble stones" is a recollection of the stone floors of the cathedral, where pilgrims knelt for centuries. Pilgrimages had ceased in Marlowe's day but the legend lived on.

> The running streames
> And common channels of the City

are typical of Canterbury, where the River Stour divides into two branches, one flowing through the city, the other around it.[32]

29 J. C. Jeaffreson: *Middlesex County Records*, I. 249.
30 Bunce MSS., I. 126, 128; II. 196–197; Bunce *Minutes*, nos. V, VI, and VII.
31 II. *Tamb.* 4220, 4234.
32 *Jew of Malta*, 571 ff., 2261–2262, 1382, 973–974, 2091–2092.

When in two other plays Marlowe refers to making

The papall towers to kisse the lowlie ground,

or when in *Doctor Faustus* he refers to burning "toplesse Towres," [33] or in *The Jew of Malta* to battering towers down, he is probably thinking of the monastery towers razed at Canterbury under Henry VIII.

In the rough school of the Canterbury streets, the shoemaker's son learned to admire the ruffling bravos, who in his plays later paced the Curtain stage as Scythian warriors, Turkish pashas, English nobles, German lords, and magicians. Perhaps the life of the city was too full of color and excitement for him to observe the quieter humors of those less obtrusive but more human souls whom the country lad at Stratford was then observing and noting down upon the tablets of his mind — Dogberry, Justice Shallow, Bully Bottom, and those real Warwickshire men "William Visor of Woncot" and "Clement Perkes o' the hill," who once really existed and left documents behind to prove it, and whose names fall so readily into Davy's speech in the Second Part of *Henry IV*.[34] It may be that here, rather than in any natural limitation of the man, we have the secret of Marlowe's failure in later life to create those human, humorous souls who are the flesh and blood of Shakespeare's plays, and who might have softened and made credible the rant and bombast that conceal half of the real beauty of Marlowe's mighty line.

This was the education for the drama that life in Canterbury gave the cobbler's child.

Records of Christopher Marlowe's formal education begin when in 1579, at fourteen years of age, he enters the King's School, which for centuries had been attached to the cathedral. Here he received a scholarship of one pound, quarterly, from the foundation established for the benefit of promising lads who had already mastered the rudiments of education and who were between the ages of nine and fifteen.

The King's School — founded, says an ancient tradition, by

[33] *Edward the Second*, 397; *Massacre at Paris*, 1215, with slight change in phrasing; *Doctor Faustus*, 1329; *Jew of Malta*, 1444. Cf. Dorothy Gardiner: *Literary Tradition of Canterbury*, pp. 17–20.
[34] V. i. 42–43.

the Archbishop Theodore in the year 600 and passing thereafter through much ill fortune and good — had at length been re-established and given its royal title by Henry VIII, who in 1541,[35] after driving the monks from Canterbury, set up a new collegiate body to administer Canterbury Cathedral and its enormous wealth. The new charter provides for "two public teachers of the boys in grammar" and "fifty boys to be instructed in grammar."

The Twenty-Seventh Cathedral Statute further provides that these shall be

fifty poor boys, both destitute of the help of friends, and endowed with minds apt for learning, who shall be called scholars of the grammar school, and shall be sustained out of the funds of our Church conformably with the limitations of our statutes: whom nevertheless we will not have to be admitted as students before they have learned to read and write and are moderately versed in the first rudiments of grammar, and this in the judgment of the Dean and Head Master, or in the Dean's absence, of the Vice Dean and Head Master. And we will that these boys be maintained at the expense of our Church, until they have obtained a moderate acquaintance with the Latin grammar, and have learned to speak in Latin and write in Latin; for which object they shall be allowed the space of four years, or (if to the Dean and Head Master, or, in the Dean's absence, to the Vice Dean and Head Master it shall seem good) at most to five years and no more. Also we will that no one be elected as a poor scholar of our grammar school who has not completed the ninth year of his age, or who hath exceeded the fifteenth year of his age.[36]

At first thought this seems another argument for the poverty of John Marlowe's household. But in fact the term poor boys "destitute of the help of friends" was very liberally interpreted — so liberally that Archbishop Cranmer, who in 1541 became the first visitor of the King's School, had to resist a tendency to admit only the sons of gentry. Cranmer sturdily demanded: "If the gentleman's son be apt to learning, let him be admitted; if not apt, let the poor man's child [that is] apt enter his room." [37] The boy Kit Marlowe was such a "poor man's child." John Marlowe was certainly not a very poor man, but his son could

---

[35] Bunce MSS. (II. 172) say 1546. Cf. William Gostling: *Walks in and about Canterbury* (2nd ed., 1777), pp. 163–164.

[36] C. E. Woodruff and H. J. Cape: *Schola Regia Cantuariensis*, p. 48.

[37] Woodruff and Cape: *op. cit.*, p. 51; John Strype: *Memorials of . . . Cranmer*, I. 128 (ed. 1812).

hardly have gone to the King's School, and certainly could not have gone to the university, without scholarships.

Scholars were to be admitted to the King's School only as vacancies occurred, and Marlowe obtained his scholarship just in time — on January 14, 1578/9, when he was within the age limit by a few weeks only. Since he had been christened February 26, 1563/4, he would soon have been fifteen and too old. There would have been in that case no more schooling, no career at the university — and the academic influence that shaped and refined the crude popular vigor of the Elizabethan drama would have been exerted by feebler, clumsier hands. The schoolmasters who probably stretched a point in young Marlowe's favor did better than they knew, though it is doubtful whether their pupil's subsequent career filled them with quite the pride they should have felt.

The boy's earlier training is a mystery. Some schooling he must certainly have had, else he could never have entered the King's School at all, much less have won a Cambridge scholarship two years later. In a noble family or an extremely wealthy commoner's household, he might have had a private tutor, but never in the humble home of a cobbler. Since John Marlowe was literate, he may have given young Christopher his earliest instruction, or the lad may, like Richard Boyle, later his associate, have been "instructed in grammar learning by a clergyman of Kent." [38]

There was, however, provision for the public education of citizens' children, by which young Marlowe may have profited. In 1544, the corporation's common clerk had been established in the "Fyle," a shop adjoining the Court Hall, where he — "or one for him" — was directed to "do the duty of his office and instruct children." [39] As a result, Canterbury tradesmen not infrequently were at least well enough educated to write clear and legible hands. Under this municipal pedagogue, whose "Fyle" was but a few minutes' walk from the parish of St. George's, the youthful Marlowe may have learned to read and write and perhaps to construe simple Latin.

[38] Alexander Chalmers: *General Biographical Dictionary* (ed. 1812), VI. 312.
[39] Bunce MSS., I. 171; Bunce *Minutes*, no. V. There is a reference to the Fyle and the Court Hall in *MS. Accounts, 1530–1538*, fol. 15 (1534/5). See also John Brent: *Canterbury in the Olden Time* (2nd ed., 1879), p. 111.

When Marlowe entered the King's School, the head master was John Gresshop, M.A., of Christ Church, Oxford, who was succeeded in 1580 by Nicholas Goldsborough, M.A., of Queen's College, Cambridge. The head master's stipend at this time was but forty pounds a year, while the lower master, Robert Rose, received but ten pounds.[40]

With his entry to the King's School, recorded knowledge of Christopher Marlowe's life — no longer mere plausible conjecture — begins again. We can now follow him, sometimes by the most cursory mention but always by trustworthy documents, almost year by year and sometimes week by week, through the rest of his life.

The surviving accounts show that Marlowe received his stipend as a King's Scholar until Christmas of 1579; and there is little doubt that the payments continued regularly until he went to the university as the year 1580 closed. Unfortunately, the records for his last year at the King's School are missing. The others, carefully kept by John King, treasurer of the cathedral at this period, have been preserved. Marlowe enters in the second term and is in regular standing for the rest of the year. He remained through the Michaelmas (autumn) term of 1580, and was then, at seventeen, ready for the university.

Elementary education in the sixteenth century was strenuous to a degree unknown in our weaker age. School began at six in the morning with responsive repetition of a psalm, and ended with another psalm at five in the afternoon. All non-capitular members of the cathedral dined together at three tables, the third being occupied by the fifty King's Scholars and ten choir boys.[41] Each member of the foundation was given cloth for a new gown at Christmas — a King's Scholar being entitled to two and a half yards, worth 3s. 4d. a yard. In practice, however, the allowances for "commons" and gowns were added to the cash stipends. As the King's Scholars drew a stipend of £1 8s. 4d., the treasurer allowed enough for commons and gown to bring the total payment up to four pounds a year for each scholar, or one pound a quarter.

The King's School enjoyed a brilliant reputation. Richard

[40] Woodruff and Cape: *op. cit.*, pp. 84, 91.
[41] Statute 30. See Woodruff and Cape: *op. cit.*, pp. 52–53.

Boyle, later first Earl of Cork, who was at the school and at Corpus Christi College at the same time as Marlowe, was "exceptionally accurate in his syntax and orthography, and, when mindful, wrote a 'fair hand.' " [42] Other King's Scholars seem to have been equally well trained, and the signatures of several scholars who signed personally for their stipends show that they were skilled in calligraphy. Marlowe's signature is not, alas, among those preserved here; but the solitary signature that survives elsewhere shows that he wrote a clear and easy hand.[43]

The school has always stood near the cathedral. When Elizabeth ascended the throne, masters and scholars met in the "Mint Yard." In 1573, a few years before Marlowe entered, the school moved from the "North Hall" to the Almonry, now called the Grange, on the South Side of the Mint Yard.[44] It was here, therefore, that the future dramatist received the education that prepared him for Cambridge. No record of his ability as a student remains, but his work was presumably satisfactory, or he would hardly have been given the scholarship on which he went to Corpus Christi. This was habitually filled by a boy from the King's School, as it still is.

As schoolmates, the cobbler's son met, on equal terms, the scions of families famous, then or later, in English history. On the books at about this period are such names as Shelley, Dobson, Coldwell, Lewes, Lyly, Sydney, Munday, Russell, Playfair, and Bentham. Benjamin Carrier, or Carier, who became a famous religious polemist, John Boyle, Bishop of Cork in after years, and his brother Richard, already mentioned, were all Marlowe's contemporaries both at the King's School and at Corpus Christi.

Stephen Gosson, author of the *School of Abuse*, had left the King's School in 1572. Like Marlowe, he later became a playwright, but unlike Marlowe he repented of his evil ways, "finding playes of the*m*selues, as filthy as the stables of Augia, impossible to bee cleansed before they be carried out of Englande,

[42] A. B. Grosart: *Life of Richard, the first Earl of Cork*, in *Linsmore Papers*, 2nd ser., V. 197 [CUL].
[43] See I. 25–26, 74–75.
[44] Now largely rebuilt.

wyth a stiffe streame." [45] A boy named William Harvey, who was later to discover the circulation of the blood, became a King's Scholar just after Marlowe had abandoned the university for Bohemian life in London.

[45] *Plays Confuted in Five Actions.* Reprinted by W. C. Hazlitt in *English Drama and Stage*, p. 161.

CHAPTER III

EDUCATION: CAMBRIDGE

Glutted now with learnings golden gifts.
Doctor Faustus, 24

THE BOUNTY of Matthew Parker, Archbishop of Canterbury, who had died in 1575, afforded means to send many a poor man's son to Corpus Christi, Cambridge. To this great priest the literature of England owes the greatest of its early dramatists. Without the scholarship which Parker's will provided, Marlowe could not have gone to Cambridge. Without the bequest of Parker's magnificent collection of books and manuscripts to Corpus Christi, Marlowe might never have written either *Tamburlaine* or *Edward the Second*, both of which almost certainly owe part at least of their inspiration to books still preserved in the collection. Without the success of *Tamburlaine*, Marlowe might never have become a successful dramatist at all — certainly the course of Elizabethan drama would have been different.

The scholarship which Marlowe held was the last of a long series established either under Parker's influence or with funds which he himself provided. The first six scholarships at Corpus Christi, though founded while Parker was master, were not his. They were established in 1548 "ex benevolentia magistri et sociorum," that is, by the college itself. Each of these early scholars was to have "after the rate of 8 *d* per Week for Commons, a small allowance *per ann.* for Landress and Barber, together with a Chamber and his Reading in the Hall free." Later the sum allowed for commons was increased to ten pence and still later to twelve pence. The scholars were to be "such as were likely to proceed in Arts and afterwards to make Divinity their study," a proviso repeated in some at least of the later scholarships.[1] Several years after this, probably about

[1] Robert Masters: *History of Corpus Christi, Cambridge* (1753), p. 200, quoting the Statutes of Corpus; G. C. Moore Smith, MLR, 4: 169 (1909).

1565, Archbishop Parker, who had been Master of Corpus from 1544 to 1553, founded another scholarship, partly with money left by a certain John Mere, of whose will he had been named "supervisor," partly with gifts by himself and by others.[2] This new scholarship first appears in the college accounts for the year ending with Michaelmas, 1565.[3]

In 1567 Parker, who was now archbishop, founded three new scholarships "with certain books and bedding given to the said three Scholars, to their use forever."[4] The holders were to be known as "Norwich scholars," since they were nominated by the mayor and aldermen of Norwich. Accounts for the year 1567–68 show an increase in the amount expended for scholarships from "xi^{li} ii^s" to "xxiij^{li} xi^d," which is presumably due chiefly to the new scholarships, though probably in part to an increase in the allowance made for commons.

On May 31, 1569, Archbishop Parker established three more scholarships. The holders of these, who were to be known as "Canterbury Scholars," were to be nominated by the Dean and Chapter from the students of the King's School, Canterbury, the money for their support being derived from tenements in Westminster.[5]

On May 22 the munificent priest founded two more scholarships with money derived from the Hospital of Eastbridge, Canterbury. Besides these, he founded on August 6 two more Norwich scholarships in addition to those already established in 1567. Nomination of the two new scholars from the schools of Norwich, Wymondham, and Aylsham was entrusted to the Dean and Chapter. No wonder the money spent for scholarships rises in the Corpus Christi accounts to xl^{li} xj^s vj^d! Not only have the scholars increased in number, but their weekly stipend has meantime risen to twelve pence.

In 1575 the college accounts testify to the founding of three more scholarships, and it is almost certain that one of these was

---

[2] Masters, *op. cit.*, pp. 85, 200; John Josselin: *Historiola* (ed. J. W. Clark, 1880), pp. 42–43. On Mere, see Masters, *op. cit.*, p. 200; Parker MSS., nos. 106, 346, 353, 355; and the catalogue of Corpus MSS. by M. R. James.

[3] Moore Smith, *loc. cit.*

[4] "An Instrument Testimonial of Archbishop Parker's gift to the three Colleges in Cambridge." Printed in John Strype: *Life and Acts of Matthew Parker*, III. 351. See also MS. *Statuta &c. &c.*, fol. 36.

[5] Masters, *op. cit.*, pp. 201–202; Strype, *op. cit.*, III. 352.

RECORD OF MARLOWE'S BAPTISM. REGISTER OF THE CHURCH OF
ST. GEORGE THE MARTYR, CANTERBURY
(Fourth line from bottom)

held by Marlowe. Archbishop Parker died May 17, 1575, after having made his will on the fifth of the preceding April. A paragraph in this provides:

Item, Volo quod executores mei paratum reddant cubiculum in eo collegio [sc. Corporis Christi], jam vocatum *a storehouse*, pro tribus aliis meis scholasticis inhabitandis, pro quibus singulis volo tres libras et sex solidos octoque denarios per annum dari, juxta formam quam executores mei scripto suo præscribent. Quorum Scholasticorum primum electum volo per successores meos in scholâ Cantuar. et in eâ urbe oriundum: secundum electum volo è scholâ de Aylesham: et tertium è scholâ de Wymondham: in hiis duabus villis oriundos.[6]

The terms of the will seem to have been carried out at once. Three new scholarships appear at Michaelmas, 1575, but this may have been a hasty and tentative arrangement.[7]

The bursar's records group the newcomers with the five Norwich scholars, instead of with the other Canterbury scholars. One name, Christopher Pashley, appears among them until the first quarter of 1580-81, when Marlowe's name is first substituted for his, then crossed out and replaced by "Pashlye," written above. In the second quarter Pashley disappears altogether and Marlowe takes his place. This suggests that Marlowe had come up to Cambridge with the nomination for the scholarship assured, and had merely been waiting for Pashley to vacate it.

Marlowe was a "Canterbury scholar," but not on the earlier foundation of 1569. It is quite clear that he follows Pashley, and Pashley's scholarship was a new one, beginning in 1575, soon after the Archbishop's death. Marlowe met all the requirements of the Archbishop's will, for he had been born in Canterbury and had been educated at the King's School.

The scholarships were tenable for three years, but if the candidates were disposed to enter into holy orders, they might be held for six.[8] In either case, scholars who desired degrees were

---

[6] Printed by John Strype: *Life and Acts of Matthew Parker*, vol. III, bk. IV, Appendix, pp. 336–337. The significant sections are quoted by Moore Smith, with some minor differences in transcription. There is a copy of the will at Corpus.

[7] Strype, however, suggests (*loc. cit.*) that the will was not in force until 1578, and Masters at least implies that nothing was done until 1580, when John Parker founded the scholarships but reserved the nominations to himself. See John Parker's note on the will printed in Strype, *op. cit.*, III. 336.

[8] Masters, *op. cit.*, p. 98.

thrown on their own resources for one year unless they could
finish in less than the normal period, for the B.A. then required
four years, and the M.A. usually three more. As Marlowe held
his scholarship for six years, he must have been at least ostensibly preparing for the Church; and academic displeasure over
his subsequent plunge into secret government service and into
the theatre may well account for some of the puzzling events of
his last year at Cambridge.

The future dramatist was entering a rather large academic
community. England's two flourishing universities numbered
jointly about three thousand students, almost equally divided.
In 1586 "the number of Schollers and necessary Maesters of
Colleges of the Universitie of Cambridge" is given as 1,500,
and the number of townspeople as 4,990.[9] A list of names in
1581, however, gives the total as 1,862. The religious note was
very marked. Cambridge University included, according to a
statement by the bishops to Parliament, "an hundred preachers
at the least, very worthy men, and not many less in the university of Oxford." [10]

In spite of this the process of secularization had begun, and
the universities were gradually denying theological studies
their original predominance. The nobility and gentry were
beginning to enter the universities in increasing numbers and
producing changes, not all of which were for the better. Fel-
lowships and preferments were frequently obtained through
court influence. Both school and college elections sometimes
favored the rich against the poor.

The increased secularization led to a lessening of interest in
religion, which in turn often led to riotous living. Excessive
drinking was common. Robert Greene declared that he had
"consumed the flower of my youth" while a student at Cambridge "amongst wags as lewd as my selfe." [11] The far from
edifying figure of Credulous Oldcraft in John Fletcher's *Wit at
seuerall Weapons* may well be a reminiscence of Fletcher's own
student days at Corpus Christi, just after Marlowe's departure.

[9] Charles Henry Cooper: *Annals*, II. 435 (1586), quoting Lansdowne MS. 51, fol.
144. See also Lansdowne MS. 33, fol. 85, and CHEL, V. 404.
[10] Cooper: *Annals*, II. 403 (1584). See also John Strype: *Annals of the Reformation*,
III, pt. 2, 305, Appendix XL to bk. I.
[11] *Repentance of Robert Greene*. In Grosart's Greene, XII. 172.

Rigid regulation of dress and other details of university life was a relic of the ecclesiasticism natural in universities which had originally been monastic institutions. The dress prescribed for undergraduates was the long academic gown, reaching to the heels, and a round skull cap essentially like that now worn under the academic "mortar board." [12] William Soone, Professor of Civil Law, wrote in 1575: "Vestitus communis omnibus ratio, pileus sacer. Sacrum dico, qui sacerdotum caput ornat: toga ad talos vsque producta, eadem forma, qua sacerdotum." [13] Graduates were permitted "the superior scholastic and squared cap," but were compelled to avoid such vanities as linen shirts and ruffles.

The University Statutes of 1570, which were in force at the time of Marlowe's entrance, provided that "no one who has been advanced to any degree in the university, shall go forth from his college, except he be clad in a gown reaching down to his ankles and a hood befitting his degree, or at least having a sacerdotal distinction about his neck, — a fine of six shillings and eightpence shall be imposed on any one who disobeys in this respect." [14] The archives of Corpus Christi refer to the "liveries" (*liberatura*) worn by the master, fellows, and scholars. [15]

Elizabethan love of finery had long made itself felt in the university, however, and as early as 1560 minute regulations were drawn up to enforce this semi-monastic garb by providing "that no scholler doe weare any long lockes of Hayre uppon his heade, but that he be polled, notted, or rounded after the aocustomed manner of the gravest Schollers of the Universitie under payne of 6 *s.* 8 *d.*" It was further provided that "no scholler shall weare any Barilled Hosen, any great Ruffs, any clocks with wings." [16] The nether limbs of these devotees of learning were not to be enclosed in "silke or any other stuffe of the like chardge, nor secondly of Galligaskan or Venetian or such like unseemly fashion, and no Slopp [Breeches] but the

[12] J. B. Mullinger: *University of Cambridge*, II. 392.
[13] George Braun, or Bruin: *Civitates Orbis Terrarum*, lib. II of vol. II, fol. 1. The book is also referred to as *De Praecipuis, Totius Vniversi Vrbibus*. The passage is quoted in Cooper: *Annals*, II. 329 (1575). See also *Gentleman's Magazine*, 46: 201 My 1776.
[14] Mullinger, *op. cit.*, II. 389, and *Documents*, I. 482-483.
[15] H. P. Stokes: *Ceremonies of the University of Cambridge*, p. 44.
[16] *Historical Register*, p. 190; Cooper: *Annals*, II. 161-162, quoting MS. Cole, XLII. 290; Hartshorne: *Book Rarities in the University of Cambridge*, p. 446n.

playne small Slopp without any cut, welt, pincke, or such like, nor thirdly of any colour but blacke or sad-colour neere unto blacke, excepte white Hose for boys." The use of silk, even in academic gowns, was restricted to the higher degrees.

Marlowe, the man of the Renaissance, is thinking rebelliously of these medieval restrictions when he makes Doctor Faustus, dreaming of the power that unlawful magic shall make his, exclaim:

> Ile haue them fill the publike schooles with silk,
> Wherewith the students shalbe brauely clad. [118–119]

He is again thinking of English academic dress when he makes Tamburlaine order his generals to don "scarlet roabes" — the traditional dress of Cambridge doctors on great occasions — for the solemnities which celebrate his triumph.[17]

The strictness with which the regulations on dress were enforced must have galled Marlowe's eager spirit. One can see how seriously the authorities took such matters from the sad case of one Stephen Lakes, an erring scholar of Trinity, whom the provost rebuked "for his habit unbecoming a scholar. For he wore under his gown, a cut taffeta doublet of the fashion with his sleeves out, and a great pair of galligastion hose. For this disguised apparel, so unmeet for a scholar, the provost punished him a week's commons." [18]

Just after Marlowe took his B.A., on November 5, 1585, dress was again minutely regulated for graduates (of whom he was now one), for masters, and for higher degree holders. It was provided "that no Graduate remayninge within any Colledge, Hostell, or Hall, or clayminge to enjoye the priviledge of a Scholler, doe weare any stuffe in the outward part of his gowne, but woollen cloth of blacke, puke, London Browne, or other sad color: And the gowne to be made with a standing coller, as the use hath bene, and not falling: And the hood that is worne with the same gowne, to be of the same or like cloth and color that the gowne is of." Graduates were also required to "weare withall in the day tyme a square cap and none other: no hatt to be worne except for infirmities sake." Each was

---

[17] I. *Tamb.* 2306.
[18] Cooper: *Annals*, II. 346 (1576).

forbidden "any stuffe in upon or about his doubtlett, coates, Jerkyn, jackett, cassock or hose, of velvett or silke."

Nor was he to wear any cloth "that shal be embrodred, powdred, pynked, or welted, savinge at the handes, verge, showlder, or coller: or gathered, playted, garded, hacked, raced, laced or cutt, saving the cutt of the welt and button holes, nor of any other redde, grene, and suche other like colour." Offenders were to be "ordered, reformed and punished, from tyme to tyme, both for stuffe, fasshion and colour." [19] One begins to understand the enthusiasm for elaborate costumes revealed in Marlowe's plays, or the wild talk about color, pomp, and splendor in religion with which the Baines libel charges him.

The minute detail of the prohibitions and the frequency with which regulations of academic dress are reiterated suggests that Marlowe's fellows in the university were in pretty constant rebellion against them. In 1587 Burghley complains that college tutors are dressing in "Satten Dublettes, silke and velvett overstockes, and facynge of gownes with velvett and satten to the grownde; and in great fine ruffs, contrarye to lawe and order." [20]

In the following May, Burghley returned once more to dress reform. Many, he complained, had "left the ancient, grave, and comely apparell generally used of all scholars in both Universities." He was especially eager "that no hatt be worne of any Graduate or Schollar," and that "all Scholers being Graduats upon the charges of any Howse, do wear a square cap of clothe, and lykewise scholers of Howses that be no Graduats, and all other Scholers that have taken no degree of Scholers, and do lyve upon their own charges, do weare in the said University a round clothe cap. Saving that it may be lawful for the sons of Noblemen, or the sons and heirs of Knights, to wear round caps of velvet, but no hats." [21] A strange letter from the chief minister of state in the Armada year!

Student life was restricted in other respects with equal severity. Just as Marlowe was entering, a decree of 1580 permitted scholars to "play at the foot-ball, but only within the

---

[19] Cooper: *Annals*, II. 411–412 (1585).
[20] Cooper: *Annals*, II. 448 (1587); Strype: *Annals of the Reformation*, III, bk. II, chap. XII.
[21] Cooper: *Annals*, II. 455 (1588).

precincts of their several colleges." [22] Since James I early found it necessary to enjoin the university against "bear-baiting, bull-bating, common plaies, public shewes, enterludes, comoedies or tragedies in the English language, games at loggats [bowling], and nine-holes," we may assume that most of these iniquitous pastimes were popular in Marlowe's day. It is certain that in 1581 a bear was "bayted in the sermon time betwene one and two of the clock in the afternoone." [23] In 1571 the heads of the colleges prohibited swimming or bathing in any water (*rivi stagnum aut aquam aliam*) in the County of Cambridge. The punishment for the first offense was a public flogging, for the second expulsion, but this applied only to undergraduates. Bachelors of Arts were put in the stocks, and Masters of Arts were punished at the discretion of the master or dean.

Many of the Cambridge students were pitifully poor. "Sure they be not able some of theym to contynue for lacke of necessarye exibicion & relefe," wrote Thomas Lever, of St. John's, adding: "Loke whether that there was not a greate number of both lerned & pore that myght haue ben kepte, mayntayned, and relyeued in the vniuersities: whych lackyng all healpe or comforte, were compelled to forsake the vniuersitye, leue their bokes, & seke theyr lyuynge abrode in the country?" [24]

A list of a student's possessions dating from 1541 shows that he had only "a great thinne Chest, with a hanging Locke & Key," "a long Gowne, with a Whood faced with Russells," two jackets, two doublets, one pair of hose, a cloak, an old shirt, a hat, a chair, a meatknife, eight books, a lute, three sheets, a coverlet, and "a very old Blankett." [25] On the other hand, the Earl of Essex, while a student, spent seven pounds on the furnishing of his rooms, including extra glass for the windows, new hangings of "painted cloth" for the study, and "a place makinge for the trindle bed to drawe through the waule." [26]

---

[22] Cooper: *Annals*, II. 382 (1580); *Stat. Acad. Cantab.*, p. 461; J. J. Smith: *Cambridge Portfolio*, I. 102.

[23] Cooper: *Annals*, II. 383 (1581).

[24] Thomas Lever: *A Sermon preached at Pauls Crosse* (c. 1550), fol. Eiii of the Folger copy. Also in Edward Arber: *English Reprints*, XII. 122, with some errors.

[25] Cooper: *Annals*, I. 398–399 (1540–41).

[26] Cooper: *Annals*, II. 352–353 (1577); Thomas Dinham Atkinson: *Cambridge Described and Illustrated*, p. 260.

Fellows and bachelors usually shared rooms with one, two, or even three students. The seniors took the bedsteads and the younger men slept in trundle beds. *The Returne from Pernassus*,[27] a Cambridge play, makes a former student allude to the time "when I was in *Cambridge*, and lay in a Trundlebed."

Marlowe, as a "pensioner," was probably not so poor as the first student, certainly not so wealthy as the Earl of Essex. Wealthy or noble young men entered the university as "fellow-commoners." Most of the students were "pensioners," like Marlowe, on the "convictus secundus," or second list. A third group of "sizars" performed menial service, and there was even a fourth group of "quadrantarii," or college servants who were allowed to study. Since tradesmen's sons were likely to be sizars, Marlowe was fortunate in having the rank of pensioner, which he doubtless owed to the scholarship he had won. He was probably no poorer than most students, and the Buttery Book shows that he frequently spent a great deal more than his scholarship. But his proud and impetuous spirit resented even a second place. One can guess at some such feeling in the lines in *Hero and Leander*:

> And to this day is euerie scholler poore,
> Grosse gold from them runs headlong to the boore

and the bitter reference to the

> loftie seruile clowne,
> Who with incroching guile keepes learning downe.[28]

Yet, however poverty might pinch, there were compensations. Cambridge seems to have been as beautiful then as it is today. Paul Hentzner, the German traveler who visited the university in 1598, eleven years after Marlowe had taken his M.A., wrote: "All is splendid; the streets fine, the churches numerous, and those seats of the Muses, the Colleges, most beautiful; in these a great number of learned men are supported, and the studies of all polite sciences and languages flourish." [29]

---

[27] *Returne from Pernassus*, II. i. On production of this play see E. K. Chambers: *Elizabethan Stage*, IV. 38–39, and n. in British Museum's copy of the first ed.

[28] *Hero and Leander*, I. 471–472, 481–482. On the three upper ranks of the students, see Venn: *Alumni Cantabrigienses*, I. xxvii.

[29] Paul Henztner: *Journey into England* (ed. 1807), pp. 29–30.

In 1575, just before Marlowe's time, William Soone had written: "The way of life in these colleges is the most pleasant and liberal: and if I might have my choice, and my [Catholic] principles would permit, I should prefer it to a kingdom." [30] "Behind the colleges," says the Diary of the Duke of Stettin-Pomerania, "flows a lovely river, with many bridges leading to a meadow pleasantly laid out with trees as a promenade for the students, who make pretty good use of the cheerful place, and perhaps keep more dogs and greyhounds, that are so often seen in the streets, than they do books." [31]

Corpus Christi, the college which the shoemaker's lad entered, was already an ancient seat of learning. It had been founded by the Gild of Corpus Christi together with the Gild of St. Mary under royal sanction granted in 1352. Its full title was the College of Corpus Christi and of the Blessed Virgin Mary; but it was familiarly known, from the adjoining Church of St. Benet [Benedict], as Benet Hall.[32]

The college was governed by the master and fellows, selecting as fellows "honestos castos humiles, pacificos & modestos, graduatos" — or men about to graduate. They were required to proceed to the S.T.B. and the doctorate. Half or a third had to be in priest's orders. Fellows who were priests received eight marks a year, those in deacon's orders, six marks. They conversed only in Latin, except by permission of the master. The master himself was required to be in residence three months of the year, though this might be reduced to a minimum of thirty days.

Students entering the college took the following oath:

Jurabis quod observabis statuta et laudabiles consuetudines Collegij nostri quamdiu in eo versatus fueris; et quod Magistro vel Custodi Collegij siue Praesidenti ab eo substituto obediens eris in omnibus licitis et honestis; et quòd Collegij honorem et utilitatem quantum in te fuerit tuo consilio et auxilio juvabis, neque quicquam sciens et volens facies quod in damnum, infamiam, aut prejudicium ejusdem Collegij redere posse putaveris, sed potius velis esse benefactor pro tuo posse, sicut te Deus adjuvet in Christo Jesu.

Jurabis etiam quòd agnoscis in conscientia tua Regiam Majestatem

[30] Cooper: *Annals*, II. 330 (1575). Georg Braun, *loc. cit.*
[31] *Trans. Royal Hist. Soc.* (NS) 6: 34–35 (1892).
[32] Josselin: *Historiola*, par. 2.

esse, et juxta verbum Dei esse debere Supremum Gubernatorem Ecclesiarum Angliæ, Scotiæ, Franciæ et Hiberniæ; nec vllum alium externum Principem, Pontificem, aut Prælatum, vllam habere, vel habere debere authoritatem infra hæc regna prædicta, sicut te Deus &c.[33]

Originally established on the site of tenements owned by the brethren of the Gild, Corpus Christi had grown through lease and purchase until, by the middle of the sixteenth century, it occupied most of its present site, except the New Quadrangle, which was not erected until 1823–27.

In 1569, a few years before Marlowe entered, John Josselin, Latin Secretary to Archbishop Parker and Fellow of Queen's College, Cambridge, wrote for Parker's use an *Historiola Collegii Corporis Christi*, which describes the college "as it appears at the present day with walls of enclosure, chambers arranged about a quadrangle, Hall, Kitchen, and Master's Habitation."[34] The college had no chapel in Marlowe's day but used the Church of St. Benet.[35] "Such was the frugality of our ancestors," adds Josselin, that the college dispensed with glass until the time of Henry VIII, when the master and fellows had their windows glazed. Gradually, however, rooms were not only glazed but even paneled and plastered, until the buildings had, in Josselin's words, attained "that elegance and beauty for which they are now [1569] conspicuous."[36]

"Pleasant and liberal" the life in Cambridge no doubt seemed to the shoemaker's son, but for modern tastes it was somewhat strenuous. A contemporary sermon describes the life in St. John's College about 1550:

There be dyuers ther whych ryse dayly betwixte foure and fyue of the clocke in the mornynge, and from fyue vntyll syxe of the clocke, vse common prayer wyth an exhortacion of gods worde in a common chappell, and from sixe vnto ten of the clocke vse euer eyther pryuate study or commune lectures. At ten of the clocke they go to dynner, whereas they be contente wyth a penye pyece of byefe amongest .iiii. hauying a fewe porage made of the brothe of the same byefe, wyth salte and otemell, and nothynge els.

[33] MS. *Statuta &c. &c.*, fol. 28. See also Parker MS. 488, 489, 489.2 and 489.3. [Parker Lib., Corpus Christi.]

[34] Josselin: *Historiola*, par. 2.

[35] H. P. Stokes: *Cambridge Scene*, p. 41.

[36] Josselin: *Historiola*, par. 24.

After thys slender dinner they be either teachynge or learnynge vntyll v. of the clocke in the euenyng, when as they haue a supper not much better then theyr dyner. Immedyatelye after the whyche, they go eyther to reasonyng in problemes or vnto some other studye, vntyll it be nyne or tenne of the clocke, and there beyng wythout fyre are fayne to walk or runne vp and downe halfe an houre, to gette a heate on their feete whan they go to bed.

These be menne not werye of theyr paynes, but very sorye to leue theyr studye.[37]

The Cambridge curriculum in Marlowe's day had just emerged from a series of important changes. The purely medieval curriculum of the Schoolmen had disappeared in 1535, when royal injunctions ended the "frivolous questions and obscure glosses" of scholastic education and substituted classical and Biblical literature, together with such science as was then known. The Code of Edward VI had in 1549 provided for instruction in mathematics, dialectics, and the elements of philosophy for the bachelor's degree; and perspective, astronomy, Greek, and further instruction in philosophy for the master's. The first professorship — the Lady Margaret Professorship in Divinity — established in 1502, was followed in 1540 by the five Regius professorships in law, physics, divinity, Greek, and Hebrew, founded by Henry VIII.

By the time Marlowe entered, the curriculum had been further modified by the Elizabethan Statutes of 1570, which eliminated mathematics from the undergraduate course, but made no further important changes.[38] The undergraduate curriculum, as Marlowe knew it, is specifically outlined:

Primus annus rhetoricam docebito: secundus et tertius dialecticam. Quartus adjungat philosophiam; et artium istarum domi forisque pro ratione temporis quisque sit auditor.[39]

"Merling," of Corpus Christi, thus duly appears among the students of "Mr. Johnes," Professor lecturæ Dialecticæ, in the

---

[37] Thomas Lever: *A Sermon preached at Pauls Crosse* (c. 1550), fol. Eii of the Folger copy. Also in Edward Arber: *English Reprints*, XII. 121–122, with some errors. Also in modern spelling, with several errors, by John H. Ingram in *Universal Review*, 4: 385 Jy 1889.

[38] *Historical Register*, pp. 348–349.

[39] Cap. VI. "De ratione studiorum." *Stat. Univ. Cantab. Documents Relating to the University and Colleges*, I. 459.

list of students dated October 29, 1581.[40] The requirements for
the master's degree remained unchanged:

Hi auditores assidui philosophicae lectionis, astronomiae, per-
spectivae et Graecae linguae sint, idque quod inchoatum antea erat
sua industria perficiant. Intererunt cunctis magistrorum artium
disputationibus aperto capite nec abibunt inde nisi a procuratoribus
petita venia.

There were in Cambridge in Marlowe's time two of the finest
libraries in the kingdom, of which, to judge from the varied
learning of his plays, Marlowe had made ardent use. These
were the libraries of Corpus Christi College and of the university itself. Archbishop Parker's generosity had enriched the
library of Corpus with his personal collections, which it still
preserves. In June of 1581, just after Marlowe entered, a grace
had been passed requiring payments to the Keeper of the Public [i.e., university] Library on admission to degrees.[41] These
varied from 4d. for Bachelors of Arts, and 8d. for Masters of
Arts, to 16d. for doctors.[42]

The regulations safeguarding the books show how they were
treasured. There was a triple inventory, one kept by the vice-
chancellor himself. "All written books and all other bookes of
Imagery with colours, all Globes, Astroglobes, and all other
Instruments mathematicall, with all other books mathematicall, or Historicall (such as shall be thought meet by the
Vice Chauncellor)" were to be "safly locked up in some convenient place within the Library with 2 severall locks and keys,
whereof the one key to remaine with the Vice Chancellor, and
the other to remain with the keeper of the Library." Not
content with this, the library authorities chained some of the
other books. Bills for the renewing of chains in Marlowe's
day are still extant.[43]

The librarian gave two hundred pounds security "to pre-
serve safly all and every one of the Books not locked up." The
library was open "from eighte of the clock untill tenn in the

[40] British Museum, Lansdowne MS. 43, fol. 85, col. 3.
[41] Cooper: *Annals*, II. 387 (1581–1582); *Stat. Acad. Cantab.*, p. 357.
[42] MS. *Grace Book* Δ, fol. 134r; Venn's printed transcript, p. 345; Charles Sayle:
Annals of Cambridge University Library, p. 52.
[43] Sayle: *Annals of the Cambridge University Library*, pp. 51, 53; Cooper: *Annals*,
II. 389.

forenone, and from one to three in the afternone: so that all masters of arte, batchelours of law or physick, or any other of the university above that degree, may have free accesse to the bookes of the saide librairie: so that at one time there be not more than tenne in the said librairie together (excepte the straungers that come only to see and not to tarry); and that none of them tarry above one houre at one booke at one tyme, if any other shall desire to use the sayd booke."

Undergraduates did not have free access to the books, but, since they paid a fee, they must have been allowed to read under some kind of restriction.[44] John Parker had strictly provided that only college officials could take books out of his father's library; but that very restriction suggests that undergraduates were probably allowed access to them within the library itself. There was a special oath with regard to the use of the college libraries.[45]

All books sold in Cambridge were under the control of the vice-chancellor and heads of colleges. Bookbinders, booksellers, and stationers gave forty pounds bond to the university that they would "provide sufficient store of all manner of books fit and requisite for the furnishing of all students continuing or abiding within this university, and the same books to be well bound, and to be sold at all and every time and times upon reasonable prices." In return, the university protected the dealers against the London publishers, who in the absence of adequate copyright, pirated Oxford and Cambridge editions. It was forbidden to expose such pirated editions for sale in Cambridge, and students were forbidden to buy them. The prices of all books printed in Cambridge were fixed by the vice-chancellor.[46] In London, a few years later, Marlowe was to be on friendly terms with some of these very London stationers (a term including both publishers and booksellers, who were often identical), whose shops clustered about the old St. Paul's Cathedral. Thomas Kyd in his letter to Sir John Puckering [47]

<hr />

[44] Cooper: *Annals*, II. 389-390 (1582). A minor typographical blunder has been silently corrected.

[45] MS. *Statuta &c. &c.*, fols. 59, 27, 29.

[46] Cooper: *Annals*, II. 396 (1593); *Stat. Acad. Cantab.*, p. 462; MS. *Grace Book* Δ, fol. 150v; Venn's printed transcript, p. 404.

[47] British Museum, Harleian MS. 6849, fol. 218. See also Brooke: *Life*, p. 105.

alludes to "some stationers in Paules churchyard" as being among "such as he conversd withall," and Gabriel Harvey makes a similar allusion.[48]

Several of the books which the dramatist was later to use as sources were awaiting him in the Cambridge libraries. Both the university and Corpus Christi owned copies of the *Theatrum Orbis Terrarum*, an atlas by the German geographer Wortels, or Ortelius. Both also owned the works of the learned Paulus Jovius, Bishop of Nocera, and of Aeneas Sylvius Piccolomini (Pope Pius II). Corpus owned Baptista Egnatius' *De Origine Turcarum Libellus*. All of these contain material that later appears in *Tamburlaine*. A queer name among the Parker manuscripts at Corpus turns up in *The Jew of Malta*, and the college's copy of Holinshed, from which Marlowe took most of *Edward the Second*, still bears on its title page the donor's name and the year 1587, when the future dramatist was still a student. The university owned a copy of the *Lexicon* of Suidas — which treats of Musaeus, legendary author of the Greek poem that is the source of *Hero and Leander* — and the works of Lucan, whom Marlowe later translated.

All of these volumes are early accessions of the libraries which can be shown [49] to have been received either before his matriculation or else during his period of residence. No one, of course, can prove that he read these particular copies. All one can say is that the books were there and that the poet had more time to read them in his university days than in his later life. It is interesting to note that the *Lamb of God*, by Richard Harvey, who left Cambridge just after Marlowe entered, indicates that Harvey had been reading many of the same books.

Marlowe's interest in the stage was probably further stimulated by the university drama. Plays were more frequent in Cambridge than they had been in Canterbury.[50] The *Mundum*

[48] See I. 113–114, 143.

[49] See the old MS. *Catal: Librorum*, also called the "Donors' Book," in the university library (Anderson Room); the MS. *Rough List of Parker Books*, in the Parker Library at Corpus Christi, especially nos. 47 and 298; and C. Sayle: *Annals of the Cambridge University Library*, pp. 49, 52, 53. Marlowe's use of this source material is discussed in the chapters dealing with individual plays.

[50] G. C. Moore Smith: *College Plays Performed in the University of Cambridge*, pp. 50 ff. For still earlier references, see his "Cambridge Plays before 1585," in *Fasciculus Ioanni Willis Clark dicatus*, p. 266; Robert Masters: *History of CCC* (1753), p. 5;

Book of King's College records "ludos" as early as Christmas Day, 1482, and "le disgysynges" a few years later. Other colleges were not far behind. Their accounts show a succession of payments for "ye play," "playes," "comœdia," "plaing gere," "the stage in the hall," "the shewe in the gallery," "the playes in the chappell" throughout the sixteenth century. By the time Marlowe entered the university, its dramatic tradition was well established, though Corpus Christi had never been a leader in college theatricals. Its first known play was not given until 1576/7, when it is referred to in the accounts as "the Comœdye." ⁵¹

This presumably means a Latin comedy by Terence or Plautus or perhaps an original Latin play. Greek plays were rare at Cambridge. Latin dramas were looked on as instructive academic exercises and as such respectable, though English comedies were not unknown. *Gammer Gurton's Needle* had been produced at Christ's about 1553, and English plays were becoming more frequent and more popular about the time Marlowe entered. Corpus produced "comedyes" in 1578–79, just before Marlowe entered, and a "Comœdie" in 1581–82, a year afterwards. There were also "scenici ludi" at the college in February, 1582/3.

Marlowe may have seen productions at other colleges. These may have included "playes" at Trinity, February 6, 1580/1, 1582–83, 1583, and 1586/7; at St. John's in 1582, again on March 17, 1582/3, and in 1585–86. Plays whose names have been preserved include "*Persa* in Plautus" at St. John's at Christmas, 1583, and — more doubtfully — *Duns Furens* at Peterhouse and *Tarrarantantara* at Clare in 1585/6. It is probable that he saw Dr. Richard Legge's *Richardus Tertius*, his friend Nashe's *Terminus et Non Terminus*, and a Latin *Antigone* at St. John's. Various other performances of *Richardus Tertius* are mentioned, but these may not be Legge's play.

Plays satirizing townspeople and figures in the university itself were becoming popular. *Duns Furens* and *Tarrarantantara* are obviously satires of this sort. Nashe himself alludes to

anon.: "Latin Plays Acted before the University of Cambridge," *Retrospective Review*, 12: 1–42 (1825).
⁵¹ G. C. Moore Smith: *College Plays*, p. 61.

"*Pedantius,* that exquisite Comedie in *Trinitie Colledge,*" [52] which mercilessly satirized Gabriel Harvey, Marlowe's and Nashe's enemy. Harvey, said Nashe, was "full drawen & delineated from the soale of the foote to the crowne of his head." The players mimicked his mannerisms and even, it is said, used his gown as a costume, "the more to flout him." *Duns Furens* dealt with "the little Minnow his Brother," Richard, while *Tarrarantantara* ridiculed all three of the Harvey brothers, Gabriel, Richard, and John. The Cambridge citizens were also satirized at times.

It is easy to see why the plays frequently led to disorder. Richard Harvey expressed his disapproval of *Duns Furens.* "*Dick* came and broke the Colledge glasse windowes," says Nashe, and as a penalty was "set in the Stockes till the Shew was ended, and a great part of the night after." [53] The college halls were rarely able to accommodate all who sought admission. Those who were excluded relieved their feelings by smashing the windows, unless the colleges removed them entirely till the plays were over.

The accounts during Marlowe's student days are full of entries for the protection or replacement of glass. In 1582/3 Trinity paid "for lv foot of newe glasse in the hall after the playes." In 1586/7 the college took the precaution of "taking downe and setting vp the glasse wyndowes at the last playes." St. John's in 1578/9 paid "for nettes to hange before the windowes of ye Halle," and in 1585/6 "for taking downe and setting vpp the windowes." [54]

"Stage-keepers," sometimes armed, and often with visors or steel caps, tried to keep order, with very slight success. A letter written in December, 1579, recounts the turbulence of one Punter, who

vncased (as they call it) one of the stagekeepers of Caius colledge pluckinge of his visor; and at the first playes . . . at Trinitie Colledge had violently pressed to come into ye colledge, euen against ye wills of such Maysters of Arts as were there appointed to see good order kept, insomuch that he had almost set that house and S. Johns together by ye eares; and afterwards to reuenge himselfe for ye

[52] McKerrow's Nashe, III. 80.
[53] McKerrow's Nashe, III. 80–81.
[54] G. C. Moore Smith: *College Plays,* pp. 45–46.

repulse there sustained had priuely crept into Benet [Corpus Christi] Colledge, & takinge vpon him yᵉ habit of a stage keper there, to yᵉ greate disturbaunce of the whole assembly, did assault one of Trinitie colledge.[55]

The plays were usually given at Christmas, or during the next three months. William Soone praises the excellence of the acting and production, saying that the classical dramatists would have been more pleased with these academic performances than with those of classical antiquity![56]

These were the general conditions of English university life in the sixteenth century. In it, we can trace Marlowe's individual career with fair completeness.

Marlowe entered Corpus Christi College in the mastership of Dr. Robert Norgate, a relative by marriage of Archbishop Parker, who in 1584 became vice-chancellor of the university. As Master of Corpus he had made special provision for the care of Archbishop Parker's books, housing them in the room where they remained until 1823.

Parker's will had laid down the general requirements for his scholarships, but on April 12, 1580, his son John Parker made them still more specific. He claimed the right to make the appointments himself during his lifetime, after which the college authorities were to do so. Marlowe, therefore, owed his appointment to John Parker, who required:

All which said schollers shall and must at the time of their election be so entred into the skill of song as that they shall at the first sight solf and sing plaine song And that they shalbe of the best and aptest schollers well instructed in their gramer and if it may be such as can make a verse.[57]

The scholars were not to be allowed more than a month's absence, but their stipends were to continue during illness and absence on college business. The Norwich scholarships had specifically required that they should be "disposed to enter by Gods grace in time to come into the ministery in that voca-

[55] G. C. Moore Smith: *College Plays*, p. 47.
[56] Georg Braun, or Bruin: *Civitates Orbis Terrarum*, lib. II, of vol. II, fol. 1.
[57] The documents relating to the scholarships are in a book marked *Statuta &c. &c.* This is not kept with the other records in the Estates Bursary strong room, but in the Spencer Room, in the personal custody of the master. See especially fols. 56–57. On the Norwich scholars, see fol. 35 and G. C. Moore Smith, MLR, 4: 171 (1909).

tion to serve God and his Churche." There is no such specific requirement in the case of the Canterbury scholars, though it may have been taken for granted.

The amount of the stipend, "xij d by the weeke for their Commons," had already been fixed for the Norwich scholars, and the new scholars on the last Parker foundation received the same amount. John Parker further specified that Corpus Christi was to

give to them reading in the hall within the said Colledge their barber and launder frely without any thing paying thērfore and shall use the said schollers in such convenient order and manner as other schollers.[58]

They were to be lodged in

that roome or chamber in the said Colledge late called a storehouse now repaired and finished for that purpose at the cost and charges of the said John Parker in accomplishment likewise of the will of the said most reverend father.

Most of this represents legal copying,[59] with appropriate changes, of earlier documents, and is for the most part based on the Archbishop's will.

The storehouse stood on the ground floor at the northwest angle of the quadrangle known in modern Cambridge as the Old Court.[60] The room which tradition says was Marlowe's had had a garret built over it about 1536. The garret, or *solarium*, had had its windows glazed and the wall below was plastered. All this "at the College expense, on the urgent request of Thomas Aleyn, fellow." The room on the ground floor, which Marlowe was later to occupy, continued in use as a storeroom, but in 1542 it was plastered by Andrew Pierson, a fellow, who added a chimney with two flues.

In this converted storeroom, as repaired by John Parker, the poet seems to have lived for six years, and here he must certainly have meditated his earliest attempts in verse. His

---

[58] Agreement dated April 12, 1580, in *Statuta &c. &c.*, fol. 57.

[59] Cf. I. 47–49.

[60] See Parker's will and Robert Willis and John Willis Clark: *Architectural History of the University of Cambridge*, vol. IV, map 10, and vol. I, p. 241. Cf. Josselin: *Historiola* (ed. Clark, 1880), p. 24. It has sometimes been suspected that Marlowe actually lived in the room across the hall from the room usually pointed out.

"chamber fellows" were Thomas Lewgar, who graduated with him, and Robert Thexton, who in the second quarter of 1581–82 gave place to Thomas Munday, who in turn was followed by William Cockman. Presumably Christopher Pashley, whom Marlowe succeeded as Canterbury scholar, also lived in these quarters. None of Marlowe's fellow-scholars achieved any particular distinction.

Though Marlowe was just past seventeen when he matriculated on March 17, 1580/1, he was already above the usual age for entrance, and indeed so old that he had probably been hurried away from the King's School. Students at that time entered the university at fifteen, sixteen, or even earlier. The regulations of student dress included [61] "white Hose for boys," and surviving furniture of the period indicates that many students were in stature hardly more than children. University Statutes of 1570 [62] provide an oath to be taken by students over fourteen, implying that a good many were even younger. Thomas Finneux, later to come strongly under the influence of Marlowe's writings while at Cambridge, entered at thirteen. Older students were not unknown, however, for Parker's Norwich scholars were to be "betwixt the ages of fourteene and twentie." [63]

The exact date of Marlowe's arrival in Cambridge, long a matter of doubt, can now be definitely established, by means of the newly discovered Buttery Book of Corpus Christi College. The first entry of the name "Marlen" is in the tenth week after Michaelmas (September 29), 1580. That is, Marlowe arrived at Corpus early in December, 1580. He was hungry — or more probably thirsty — and he spent one penny at the buttery. It was his only purchase for the week. Such is Corpus Christi's first record of its famous son! Probably he had arrived late in the week and had no time to spend more; for in the next week the new freshman spends 3s. 1½d., more than three times the amount of his scholarship. [64]

Further evidence of the date, if any were needed, is provided

[61] See I. 52.
[62] No. 50 in *Documents Relating to the Universities and Colleges of Cambridge*, I. 337.
[63] *Statuta &c. &c.*, fol. 35.
[64] *Buttery Book*. See reprint in John Bakeless: *Christopher Marlowe, the Man in His Time*, pp. 334–335.

by the bursar's scholarship accounts, which show that by Lady Day (March 25) Marlowe had received 12*s*. in scholarship money.[65] He had, therefore, been in receipt of his stipend for twelve weeks. Counting backward, this brings us into the last few days of December. Marlowe, therefore, arrived early in December and began to draw his stipend a week or two later.

The Admission Book of Corpus Christi carries the name "Marlin" next to the last in the year 1580 — that is, according to modern reckoning in the winter of 1580–81, some time before what we should today call March 25, 1581 (Lady Day), which was then regarded as the beginning of the new year. There is also record of his payment of 3*s*. 6*d*. "Pro introitu in Convictum m*agist*ri et socior*um* et scholar*ium*.[66] The manuscript of the Registrum Parvum — which is now bound with the *Liber Actorum*, the oldest college chapter book — places Marlowe in the list of pensioners, "Pensionarij in scholarium com*m*eatu."

Marlowe had now been admitted to Corpus Christi College, but he had not yet matriculated in the university, as every student was required to do within one month of his arrival in Cambridge. Under the system then and still in force, admission to a college is quite distinct from matriculation in the university. The first simply records the student's entrance into residence.

He appears in the University Registry's *Book of Matriculation* on March 17, 1580/1:

Coll corp. x^r Chr̄of Marlen

in the *Convictus secundus*, a list of the matriculated students who were neither fellow-commoners nor sizars — the "pensioners," who constituted the majority of the students, and among whom Corpus Christi had already listed him.

Here is a puzzle. In 1579, only a year before, a regulation had been passed requiring all students to matriculate within a month of their arrival.[67] But Marlowe, though not yet formally

[65] *Audit Books*, CCC. Transcribed by G. C. Moore Smith: "Marlowe at Cambridge," *MLR*, 4: 173 Ja 1909; Brooke: *Life*, 27–28.
[66] *Audits*, *1580–81*; Brooke: *Life*, 22–23.
[67] MS. *Matriculation Book* (University Registry), fol. 319; G. C. Moore Smith: "Marlowe at Cambridge," *MLR*, 4: 168 Ja 1909; John Ingram: *Marlowe and His*

elected a scholar, had nevertheless received a scholar's stipend
— and must therefore have been in residence for nearly three
months. How? Why? There is no certainty; but it is reasonable to suppose that again some official stretched a point; and
that young Marlowe, who was certainly not very wealthy, was
given his stipend immediately after nomination to his scholarship without waiting for the formal election. Within less than
two months, his position had been made perfectly regular by
his election as a scholar in place of Christopher Pashley or
Pashlie.

Another entry, in the *Registrum Parvum* at Corpus Christi,
headed *Nomina Scholasticorum*, runs:

1581. Maii 7. Marlin electus et admissus in locum dni Pashley.[68]

a confirmation of the previous record.

As the scholarships were tenable for only six years at the
utmost, and as Pashley had entered June 15, 1575, his term
had expired. For this expiration, Marlowe had evidently been
waiting. Pashley received his M.A. degree a year later.

Presumably Marlowe took the oath usually required of students of mature age, under the statute of 1544, which first
established formal matriculation:

The Chancellor and Vicechancellor of the university of Cambridge
so far forth as is lawful and right, and according to the rank in which
I shall be as long as I shall dwell in this republic, I will courteously
obey. The laws, statutes, approved customs and privileges of the
university, as much as in me is, I will observe. The advancement
of piety and good letters, and the state, honour, and dignity of this
university I will maintain as long as I live, and with my suffrage and
counsel, asked and unasked, will defend.

So Help me God and the Holy Gospels of God.[69]

Poetry, pp. 18–19; Ingram: *Christopher Marlowe and His Associates*, pp. 55–56; Brooke:
Life, pp. 22–24; James Heywood and T. Wright: *University Transactions*, I. 222.

[68] This entry was first discovered by G. C. Moore Smith and published in the *Modern
Language Review* (4: 168 Ja 1909). Moore Smith's work establishes Marlowe's exact
position in the university and dates it. Previously this was not understood, and Dr.
Henry Paine Stokes in his history of Corpus Christi (p. 84) hazards the conjecture,
which we can now see to be erroneous, that Marlowe went to Cambridge "perhaps as
the first holder of the Canterbury scholarship which John Parker had just founded in
the name of his late father, the Archbishop." Actually, Marlowe followed another
scholar in regular succession. Pashley is definitely described as "ex fundacione Matthei
Archiepiscopi Cantuarensis." See Moore Smith, *op. cit.*, p. 170.

[69] J. B. Mullinger: *University of Cambridge*, II. 63; Cooper: *Annals*, I. 414; Josselin's

Marlowe took his first degree in a little more than three years. This had been made possible by a decree of February 15, 1578/9:

Whereas the statute concerning the aforesaid degree requireth *quadriennium completum*, it was and is by the same authority defined, orderd, interpreted, and decreed, the day and year abovesaid, that all and singular persons so enrolled as is aforesaid, before, at, or upon the day when the ordinary sermon *ad clerum* is or ought to be made in the beginning of Easter term, shall be reputed and accounted to have wholly and fully satisfied the statute, if he shall proceed in the 4th Lent next following the said sermon; but after that day of the said sermon *ad clerum*, if any shall come, then he shall not proceed in the 4th Lent following.[70]

Having entered before the date specified, in 1581, Marlowe was able to claim a *quadriennium completum* in Lent, 1584.

To qualify for the bachelor's degree, students were required to keep two "Acts" or "Responsions" and two "Opponencies" in the public schools. A student appearing as a respondent announced three philosophical propositions which he was prepared to defend, and students from other colleges were then selected as opponents. Marlowe is referring to this combat of wits when he makes the First Scholar in *Doctor Faustus* allude to "*Faustus*, that was wont to make our schooles ring with *sic probo*." [71] "The Schools" is a building still well known to Cambridge.

The "Acts" took place before an audience of graduates under the general direction of a Master of Arts. The respondent read a Latin thesis on whichever of his propositions had been selected, and then suffered the ordeal of three separate refutations, also in Latin, by each of the Opponents. The presiding Master of Arts ended the "Act" with his own comments. University statutes required "that all and singular bachelors and questionists, shall come from their several colleges at all publick disputations and other scholastical exercises in their habits and hoods." [72]

Historiola, Parker MSS. 488, 489.3, and ed. by J. W. Clark for Cambridge Antiquarian Society, 1880; also *Statuta Collegii corporis Christ et beatae Mariae virginis Cantabrigiae*, Parker MS. 489.

[70] James Heywood and T. Wright: *University Transactions*, I. 221–223.

[71] *Doctor Faustus*, ll. 196–197.

[72] Cooper: *Annals*, II. 430 (1586–87); *Stat. Acad. Cantab.*, p. 467.

Having thus twice demonstrated his argumentative skill, the candidate was examined by his college. If he succeeded, he was "sent up" for the B.A., the granting of degrees being the exclusive function of the university. The university examinations, given by the proctor and other officials, usually just before Ash Wednesday, lasted for three days, after which the successful candidates were given *supplicats* in which they prayed admission *ad respondendum quaestioni* of the vice-chancellor and senate. The *Quaestio* consisted of an examination in Aristotle's *Prior Analytics*. Marlowe is thinking of this when Faustus exclaims:

> Sweete *Analutikes* tis thou hast rauisht me,
> *Bene disserere est finis logices.* [34–35]

Having passed this examination, the candidates became "determiners," and after other formalities at length attained the baccalaureate on Palm Sunday.

The rigor of this preparation for the B.A. makes it easy to understand why many students left the university after a year or two, without attempting to take degrees. The Canterbury cobbler's son had achieved a good deal when, in 1584, he passed this appalling series of tests and when, as the *Grace Book* records,[73] "Xrōf. Marlyn" was admitted to his degree. His formal supplicat, which is still preserved in the university *Register*, runs:

Coll.   Supplicat reuerentijs vestris Christopherus Marlin, vt
Corp.   duo*decim* termini completi, in quibus ordinarias lectiones
Christj.   audiuit (lice*t non omnino* secundum formam statuti) una
            cum omnibus oppositionibus, *responsionibus* cæterisque
            exercitijs, per statuta regia requisitis, sufficiant ei *ad respon-*
            dendum quæstioni.

                               Thomas Harrjs: pr*aelector* [74]

The praelector was himself a former pensioner of Corpus and, since he received his M.A. in 1580, can have been very little older than Marlowe himself.

---

73 MS. *Grace Book* Δ, fol. 142*v*; Venn's printed transcript, pp. 372–373; Ingram, p. 80 and n. 68. Americans will be interested to find a Washington on the same page.

74 *Supplicats* (*MS*) *1583/4*, no. 199. There is no folio number. Marlowe's supplicat has been torn on the right margin, but as the formula is plentifully reproduced in other examples, the missing letters are easily restored.

Marlowe was one of a group of Elizabethan literary figures who were at Cambridge together. These included Marlowe's bitter enemies, Gabriel Harvey and Robert Greene, and Thomas Nashe, who was a friend of both Marlowe and Greene. Richard Harvey, Gabriel's brother, entered the university after Marlowe was gone, but Marlowe knew him and held him in contempt. Thomas Heywood, asserted by a doubtful tradition to have studied at Peterhouse, may also have been in Cambridge at this time, and a John Fletcher, probably the dramatist, entered Corpus in 1590.

Greene had taken his B.A. in 1579/80 as a member of St. John's College, Cambridge, and his M.A. as a member of Magdalene in 1583/4,[75] later taking an M.A. at Oxford also. Thomas Nashe, who was Marlowe's collaborator in writing *Dido* and who is said to have written an obituary poem on him, received his degree in 1585/6 as a student of St. John's but did not take an M.A.[76]

Two sets of documents make it possible to follow Marlowe's career, week by week, through his six and a half years at the university. One is the series of quarterly Audits of Corpus Christi College, which record all scholarship payments. Since these were paid at the rate of one shilling a week, for actual residence only, it is possible to tell how many weeks in each term a student spent in residence.

The other document is the Buttery Book of the college, which records what each man spent for food and drink. Since this is also kept weekly, one can tell exactly when a student is in residence and when he is absent. The Audits for the year 1585–86 have been lost, but the gap is filled by the Buttery Book, which continues until the second week after Michaelmas, 1586. There are no Buttery Book entries for Marlowe's last year, 1586–87, but this gap is in turn filled by the Audits for 1586–87, which have been preserved. By combining the two records, one can work out with fair accuracy the general outline of Marlowe's daily life as a student.

Marlowe's name first appears in the Audits in a mistaken entry in the first trimester, or term. Since he had arrived at the

75 MS. *Grace Book* Δ, fols. 129v and 143v; Venn's printed transcript, pp. 328, 377.
76 MS. *Grace Book* Δ, fol. 148, *r* and *v*; Venn's printed transcript, pp. 395–396.

college during the trimester, and was to become one of the Canterbury scholars, the bursar put down his name. Then, seeing his error, he crossed it out and substituted that of "Pashlye," who was still drawing a Canterbury scholar's stipend. Once his predecessor has departed, Marlowe's name appears regularly, beginning with the second trimester and running on consistently except for the "lost year" of 1585–86.[77]

For the first year we have:

1580–81

in 1ᵃ Trim.	2ᵃ Trim.	3ᵃ Trim.	4ᵃ Trim.
Dˢ Thexton xiijˢ	Dˢ Thexton xiijˢ	Dˢ Thexton xˢ
Leugar xiijˢ	Leugar xiijˢ	Leugar iijˢ
Marlin xiiˢ	Marlin xiijˢ	Marlin xijˢ

Marlowe has, therefore, been in constant residence from the beginning of the year until Michaelmas, 1581, probably with a short holiday in the last quarter, since some other scholars receive one shilling more than he. Presumably they were one week longer in residence.

The Buttery Book for this period shows Marlowe in constant residence, spending totals of 3s. 2d.; 19s. 5d.; apparently 5s. 4d.; and 17s. 5½d. as the totals for the four terms. It is worth noting that in the second and third trimesters he spends several shillings more than the total of his scholarship.

In the following year, 1581–82, the Audits indicate a prolonged absence in the fourth, or summer, trimester:

1581–82:

in 1ᵃ Trim.	2ᵃ Trim.
Dˢ Thexton xijˢ	Dˢ Thexton ⎫ xijˢ
	Mondey ⎭
Lewger xiijˢ	Lewger xiijˢ
Marlin xiijˢ	Marlin xiijˢ

3ᵃ Trim.	4ᵃ Trim.
Mondey ijˢ	Monday xiiijˢ
Lewger viijˢ	Lewger ijˢ
Marlin xiijˢ	Marlin vijˢ

This is confirmed by the Buttery Book, which has no entry for seven consecutive weeks during July and most of August.

---

[77] See G. C. Moore Smith, MLR, 4: 167–177 (1909); Brooke: *Life*, p. 27. Both writers are accurate as to the amounts paid Marlowe. The accounts are in the book labeled

In the following year he is again absent for seven weeks, but this time in the third, or Easter term. This is shown by the scholarship accounts in the Audits for 1582–83:

1582–83:
	in 1ᵃ Trim.	2ᵃ Trim.
	Munday xijˢ	Munday xjˢ
	Lewgar iiijˢ	Lewgar xiijˢ
	Malyn xijˢ	Marlin xiijˢ
	3ᵃ Trim.	4ᵃ Trim.
	Munday iijˢ	Munday xiˢ vjᵈ
	Lewgar ixˢ	Lewgar xiˢ
	Marlin vjˢ	Marlin xiiijˢ

The reduction in his scholarship payment in the third trimester is accounted for by an absence of seven weeks in May and June, as shown in the Buttery Book. The next set of scholarship payments are:

1583–84
	in 1ᵃ Trim.	2ᵃ Trim..
	D Munday xijˢ	D Monday xˢ vjᵈ
	D· Lewgar xijˢ	D Lewgar viijˢ
	D· Marlyn xijˢ	D Marlin xiijˢ
	3ᵃ Trim.	4ᵃ Trim.
	D· Monday iiiˢ	Cokman iiijˢ
	D Lewgar viijˢ	D Lewgar xiijˢ
	D Marlyn xiijˢ	D Marlin xjˢ vjᵈ

In this year Marlowe, having become a Bachelor of Arts, receives the honorific "D." or "Ds.," for "Dominus" in both sets of accounts, and by a blunder on the bursar's part his baccalaureate is antedated by an entire term. He is called "Dominus" in the first term, though he did not actually receive his degree until July. This probably happened because the bursar was slow in making up his accounts, and when he finally did so thought of Marlowe in his new academic rank. At the very end of the summer, Marlowe is absent for three weeks before Michaelmas, an absence which continues during almost the entire Michaelmas term. He is back at Corpus the week before Christmas, 1584, and then is absent again five weeks more. The effect on his scholarship payments is shown in the Audit:

Audits 1578 to 90, in the strong room of the Estates Bursary at Corpus Christi. They run for a year at a time, from Michaelmas to Michaelmas.

1584-85

in 1ª Trim.	2ª Trim.
Dˢ Lewgar	Dˢ Lewgar
Dˢ Marlin iijˢ	Dˢ Marlin vijˢ vjᵈ
Cockman xijˢ	Cockman xiijˢ

3ª Trim.	4ª Trim.
Dˢ Lewgar	Dˢ Lewgar
Dˢ Marlin iiijˢ	Dˢ Marlin vˢ
Cockman iijˢ	Cockman xiiijˢ

These absences continue throughout the year. He returns to Corpus about the end of January, 1585, and is in residence until the middle of April, when he disappears again until the very end of the term.

During the year 1585–86, which is lacking from the Audits, he is more faithful in his attendance. He is absent for two weeks in the middle of the Michaelmas Term. Then he is in the Buttery Book again weekly until March, 1585/6, when he disappears until June, 1586.

Marlowe's absence for two weeks in the Michaelmas term of 1585 is explained by documents discovered in 1939 by Frank W. Tyler, Esq. In the autumn of that year Mistress Catherine Benchkyn, of Canterbury, made her will, and young Christopher Marlowe, then visiting his family in Canterbury, witnessed it. His signature, thus preserved, is the only scrap of his unquestioned handwriting that has survived.

In October, 1586, John Marlowe, also a witness, was called to testify when the will was proved and described the circumstances in detail:

Aboute a twelmonethes agon or moe as this deponent remembreth and vppon a Sonday aboute the same day as this deponent remembreth . . . he this deponent, beeing requested by John Benchkin to come to the howse of his mother Catherine Benchkin scituat in St Michaels parishe in Canterburye went thither accompanied with Thomas Arthur his precontest and coming thether they fownde there this deponentes Soonne Christofer Marley and John Moore, this deponentes Soonne in Lawe and preconteste, and beeing there altogether the testatrix Catherine Benchkin towlde them that she had sent for them to bee witnesses to her will and thervppon she tooke the will will [sic] whervppon this deponentes Soonne requested him to reade the same which beeing by him soe read the saide testatrix acknowledged the same to bee her laste will and testament, and alsoe

Caste into the ffire one other owlde will which she said she had beefore tyme made and Burnt the same, and she vtterlie disownded the other wills and testaments by her beefore made and subscribed her hand and marke and set her seale vnto the saide will whervppon this deponent is now examined, and alsoe requested this deponent and other the precontestes afforenamed to subscribe their names to the same as witnesses vnto yt which they did accordinglie.[78]

This corresponds to Marlowe's absence from Corpus in the sixth and seventh weeks after Michaelmas, 1585, or the latter part of November. His father's deposition, dated October 5, 1586, sets the time as about a year before.

After June, 1586, Marlowe is in constant attendance until the Michaelmas term, in the third week of which this volume of the Buttery Book closes. The following volumes are lost and the series does not begin again until 1721, so that we have no record of his purchases during his last year in Cambridge.

The Audits for 1586–87 show that he was at Corpus for nine weeks in the Michaelmas term, 1586, and for five and a half weeks in the Christmas term, after which he received his M.A. and appears in the books of Corpus no more. These last accounts stand thus:

1586–87	in 1ª Trim.	2ª Trim.
	Dˢ Lewgar	Dˢ Lewgar ijˢ
	Dˢ Marly ixˢ	Dˢ Marlye vˢ vjᵈ
	Dˢ Cockman xiijˢ	Dˢ Cockman xjˢ

Thereafter his name disappears entirely. Marlowe, no longer a student, is off to secret service, London, and the theatre. His successor is duly elected in November, 1587.

What was Marlowe doing in these long absences from the university? The summer absences were probably vacations and nothing more, though many students spent the entire summer at the university, as Marlowe himself frequently did. At least one brief absence, as already stated, represents a visit to his home in Canterbury. But why the other absences? Unless they represent illness, they far exceed the month's absence which was all the Canterbury scholars were permitted.

Marlowe's nineteenth-century editor, Lieutenant-Colonel Francis Cunningham, believed that "he was trailing a pike or

[78] The original deposition is in the Public Record Office, Canterbury, 39/11, fol. 237. The Benchkyn will is in the Public Record Office, Canterbury, 16/86.

managing a charger with the English force" in Flanders.[79] He
argued that Marlowe's plays show a familiarity with military
terms, and added — with a lamentable lack of humor — that
"in the rough school of the march and the leaguer he was more
likely to have acquired the habit of using profane oaths and
appealing to the dagger than in the quiet halls on the banks of
the Cam." Colonel Cunningham might have added that at
least one later Elizabethan dramatist, Ben Jonson, actually did
join the army and saw some very active service.

Cunningham's arguments were never very convincing, even
before the Buttery Book and other documents were discovered.
Such familiarity with military terms as Marlowe's plays show
was natural enough to any Elizabethan in the years before the
Armada. All England was preparing for war. Since there was
no regular army, any man might be a soldier, or at least a
member of the trained bands. In any case, the most striking
example of Marlowe's military knowledge is simply "read up"
from Paul Ive's book on fortification, from which the poet
quotes copiously in *Tamburlaine*.[80] As for readiness with the
dagger or the language of unrighteousness, there was plenty of
both among the theatrical and literary men who became his
London associates. Moreover, both the Audits and the Buttery
Book, which Cunningham never saw, show that Marlowe was
never absent long enough, at any one time, to have seen service
as a soldier.

There is, however, another and a far more interesting story
behind Marlowe's achievement of the master's degree and his
departure from the university, which a series of documents
unearthed since 1925 have done much to clear up. Though
there is still — and perhaps always will be — a good deal of
mystery about his last student years, certain facts are now
clear: (1) Marlowe was in some kind of confidential government
service, either as a secret agent or as a confidential messenger;
(2) his frequent absences and mysterious journeys had brought
him into bad odor among a powerful group of academic authorities; (3) he was strongly suspected of Catholicism; (4) it was
proposed to deny him his degree; and (5) he finally secured it

[79] Cunningham's ed., pp. ix–x.
[80] See I. 210–211.

only by the direct intervention of Her Majesty's Privy Council.

Though the granting of the degree was most irregular, Marlowe's first steps toward it were regular enough. The supplicat follows the usual form:

Coll: Supplicat reverentijs Vestris Christopherus Marley, vt nonem
Corp. termini completi (post finalem eius determinationem) in
Chri: quibus lectiones ordinarias audiuit (licet non omnino secundum formam statuti) una cum omnibus oppositionibus responsionibus caeterisque exercitijs per statuta regia requisitis sufficiant ei ad incipiendum in artibus.

Robertus Norgate
Henricus Ruse prælector.[81]

The Grace Book contains the official record of his candidacy, "ultimo Martii, 1587," in the usual form.[82] But in April, May, or very early June of 1587 it was proposed to deny the degree entirely.

The circumstances under which Marlowe finally received his M.A. are partly explained by the discovery that the Privy Council itself wrote to the university, June 29, 1587, ordering that Marlowe's degree should be conferred as usual, in July. Though the original letter cannot now be found in the Cambridge University archives, the entry in the *Acts of the Privy Council* is clear enough. As an example of governmental interference in academic affairs, this document is remarkable even for the sixteenth century. It runs as follows:

Whereas it was reported that Christopher Morley was determined to have gone beyond the seas to Reames [Rheims] and there to remaine Their Lordships thought good to certefie that he had no such intent but that in all his accons [actions] he had behauved him selfe orderlie and discreetelie wherebie he had done her majestie good service, and deserued to be rewarded for his faithfull dealinge: Their Lordships' request was that the rumor thereof should be allaied by all possible meanes, and that he should be furthered in the degree he was to take this next Commencement: Because it was not her majestie's pleasure that anie one emploied as he had been in matters touching the benefitt of his Countrie should be defamed by those that are ignorant in th'affaires he went about [83]

---

[81] *Supplicats, 1586/7*, no. 65. University Registry, Cambridge.

[82] Marlowe's name is in *MS. Grace Book Δ*, fol. 152r; Venn's printed transcript, p. 410.

[83] MS. *Acts of the Privy Council*, vol. VI, June 29, 1587. Dasent: *Acts of the Privy Council*, XV. 141, prints an inaccurate version. This was first recognized as referring

Marlowe was perhaps thinking of this episode when he wrote in *The Massacre at Paris*:

> Did he not draw a sorte of English priestes
> From Doway to the Seminary at Remes,
> To hatch forth treason gainst their naturall Queene?

[1042–1044]

Immediately after Dr. John Leslie Hotson first identified the "Christopher Morley" of the document just quoted with Christopher Marlowe, question arose whether the identification was correct. It is now possible by a process of elimination to say definitely that the Privy Council's letter does actually refer to the dramatist.

There were at the time three Cambridge men to whom the name "Christopher Morley" might possibly refer. One was the dramatist of Corpus Christi to whom it actually did refer. The second was Christopher Morley, a Trinity College man who matriculated in Cambridge University in 1578, and proceeded M.A. in 1586, a year before Marlowe and a year before the letter directing the university to award the degree was written.[84]

The third was another Trinity man, John Matthew, called "Matheus" in the Latin records. He was born in Cambridge, studied at Westminster School, and matriculated in Cambridge University as a pensioner from Trinity at Michaelmas, 1588. He received his B.A. in 1592–93 and his M.A. in 1596. He is thus plainly out of the picture, for when the Privy Council's letter was written he was still a schoolboy in London.

Confusion arises after Matthew has been converted to Catholicism by Father Thomas Wright ("Writus" in the Latin records) and received into the Church by Father Henry Garnett, S.J., who has by some scholars been identified with the equivocator in *Macbeth*, "that could swear in both the scales against either scale."[85] Matthew used the alias "Chris-

---

to Marlowe by Dr. John Leslie Hotson in his *Death of Christopher Marlowe*, pp. 58–59. It is reprinted by C. F. Tucker Brooke: *Life*, pp. 32–33. The transcription here is directly from the original.

[84] John Venn: *Grace Book* Δ, p. 517; *Alumni Cantabrigienses*, III. 142; J. B. Whitmore: "The Other Marlowe," London *Times*, July 24, 1925, p. 10 b.

[85] II. iii. 9–10.

topher Marlor," and his activities may possibly have led contemporaries to the same confusion with the genuine Christopher
Marlowe — even after Marlowe's death — that they have produced in modern times. On May 30, 1599, Matthew was admitted to St. Albans, the English college at Valladolid. Before
leaving England, he had been imprisoned in the Clink for
fifteen days and had then reached the Continent via St. Omer.
He took the oath February 2, 1600, and was consecrated priest
in September, 1602, being sent back to England in 1603.[86]

Matthew is Number 160 in the old students' lists and the
entries concerning him run as follows:

[1]   Joannes Matheus alias Christopherus Marlerus Cantabrigiensis
      admissus est in hoc Collegium die 30 Maii anno 1599 fecit
      iuramentum die 2° februarii anno 1600.

[2]   factus est sacerdos ab episcopo hujus ciuitatis mense Septembri
      anni 1602 missus est in Angliam anno 1603 primo vere.

In the Douay Diary [87] there is an entry under December 10,
1604, on the return to England of a lately exiled priest, John
Mathewes, "dictus Mallonus" — a conjectural reading which
should probably be "Marlerus," as the original is interlined and
corrected at this point and therefore difficult to decipher. The
entry reads:

Die 10 Decembris redierunt in Angliam D. Lionellus Woodwardus et
D. Joannes Mathewes, hic dictus Mallonus, sacerdotes, nuper in
exilium deportati.

In the *Liber Primi Examinis* at Valladolid there is a full
history of Matthews:

Joannes Matheus, ["alias Christopherus Marlerus" inserted in right
margin in different but contemporary hand] Cantabrigiensis ortu et
educatione venit ad hoc Collegium 30 Maii annos natus viginti septem
venit missus Audomaropoli [88] cum aliis duobus sociis, fuit Collegialis
Collegii Sanctissimae [sc. Trinitatis] in Cantabrigia per septem annos

[86] Canon Edwin Henson (ed.): *Registers of the English College at Valladolid, 1589–1862*, vol. XXX, 6n, 57; J. B. Whitmore, *op. cit.*; Hotson, *op. cit.*, pp. 59 ff.; Brooke: *Life*, p. 33n; letters in the London *Times*, June 23, 24, 1925; *Liber Alumnorum* of the English College (MS), no. 160; and *Liber Primi Examinis*, 88.
[87] *Publications of the Catholic Record Society, The Douay College Diaries*, X. 63. See also originals in Archives of the Roman Catholic Diocese of Westminster, Cod. 34.
[88] The modern St. Omer. See *Dict. de géographie ancienne et moderne* (1870).

ibique factus est baccalaureus et magister in artibus reductus est ad agnitionem et professionem fidei Catholicae per Presbyterem Thomam Writum et postea receptus in vnitatem ecclesiae per Presbyterem Hugonis tunc in Carcere Clinch detentum quindecim dies antequam egressus est Anglia et per Presbyterem Garnetum societatis Jesu cum literis commendatitiis missus Audomaropolim, humiliter petiit admitti in hoc Collegium vt fieret sacerdos et mitteretur ad opus domini in Angliam.[89]

Matthew is specifically described in a letter from William Vaughan to the Privy Council. In his *Golden Grove* (1600), Vaughan had given an account of Marlowe's death. In 1602, while in Pisa, he learned of certain Jesuit plans, which he promptly reported:

WILLIAM VAUGHAN to the ARCHBISHOP OF CANTERBURY, SIR THOMAS EGERTON, SIR ROBERT CECIL, and the rest of the Council.

1602, July $\frac{4}{14}$. — I thought it the part of her Majesty's loyal subject in these my travels to forewarn the Council of certain caterpillars, I mean Jesuits and seminary priests, who, as I am credibly informed by two several men, whose names, under your pardon, according to promise, instantly I conceal, are to be sent from the English seminary at Valladolid, in the kingdom of Castile in Spain, to pervert and withdraw her Majesty's loyal subjects from their due obedience to her. I have therefore sent notice to some of you from Calais in France of some such persons, and of their dealing. . . .

In the said seminary there is . . . one Christopher Marlor (as he will be called), but yet for certainty his name is Christopher, sometime master in arts of Trinity College in Cambridge, of very low stature, well set, of a black round beard, not yet priest, but to come over in the mission of the next year ensuing. . . .[90]
Pisa, 14 July

After Matthew returned to England, he was soon in prison again, for an entry regarding him appears in the original bills [91] rendered by the Keepers of the Gatehouse Prison, Westminster, for the diet, laundry, and other needs of their charges in 1604: [92]

---

[89] Henson, *loc. cit.*

[90] *Hist. MSS. Commission, Salisbury MSS. XII. 211–212 (1910).* See also Henson, *op. cit.*, p. 46; Hotson, *op. cit.*, pp. 60–61. By a curious coincidence, several of Marlowe's early editions appear in the collection of Sir Thomas Egerton. See Seymour De Ricci: *English Collectors*, pp. 17–19.

[91] Reprinted in the London *Times* by Sir Israel Gollancz, June 23, 1925, p. 17e. The originals, which were at that time in the possession of Messrs. P. J. and A. E. Dobell, are now in the British Museum, Addit. MSS. 41257.

[92] See Henson, *loc. cit.*

| Comitted by my Lorde Cheife Justice. | Christopher Marlowe *alias* Mathews, a. seminary preist oweth for his dyet and lodging for 7 weeks, and two days being close prisoner at the rate of 14^s the weeke $5^{li}\ 2^s$
 For washing $2^s\ 4^d$ .. $5^{li}\ 4^s\ 4^d$ |

With all this detail regarding the other men, it is clear enough that the Privy Council's letter cannot refer to any of them and that it does refer to Christopher Marlowe, the dramatist. Christopher Morley, of Trinity College, had left the university before it was written. John Matthew, alias Christopher Marlerus, or Marlor, or Marlowe, had not yet matriculated.

The name Christopher Marlowe, or Morley, was indeed remarkably common in Elizabethan times, though it is usually possible to distinguish the men bearing it. Mr. Mark Eccles [93] has been able to list six additional contemporary Christopher Morleys who lived in London about the time of the dramatist. Needless to say, none of these could have been the subject of the Privy Council's letter, but to avoid confusion it is well to list them and have done, once for all. We thus have in all eight men using Marlowe's name or names closely resembling it — seven of them legitimately and one as an alias — without counting the author of *Tamburlaine*, who makes a ninth! There is Christopher Morley of St. Vedast's parish, Foster Lane, London, servant to one William Beale, who was buried September 12, 1593. In St. James's Parish, Clerkenwell, lived another Christopher Morley, whose son Thomas was christened in 1571, and another Christopher Morley who was married in 1594.

The name reappears after the dramatist's death. A carpenter named Christopher Morley, of St. Sepulchre's without Newgate, was indicted for felony in 1602. Christopher Morley, of the parish of St. Dunstan's, London, makes his will in 1603. Still another Christopher Morley, of Clement's Inn, died at Reading in 1610. Thomas Morley, the famous musician, had a son Christopher; but he was not even christened until 1599, six years after the poet's death. None of these can be confused with the man who was candidate for a Cambridge M.A. The early Canterbury and Cambridge documents cannot possibly refer to them. Later documents usually identify the dramatist

[93] *Christopher Marlowe in London* pp. 108 ff.

as "gentleman," and conveniently add his known friends and associates to make assurance still greater.

Marlowe received the disputed degree immediately after the Privy Council's letter was written. Neither college fellows nor the vice-chancellor cared to argue with Queen Elizabeth's Privy Council, especially when the chancellor of the university, Lord Burghley, was also a privy councillor.

This triumph over his academic seniors enabled the poet to attain a degree in which its holders felt a very keen pride. It was a proverb that "a Royston horse, and a Cambridge Master of Arts, are a couple of creatures that will give way to nobody." [94] Royston was a village near Cambridge, reputed for its malt, which was carried up to London on heavily burdened horses, which could not readily yield the road — hence the point of the proverb. The university itself officially recognized the dignity of a master, requiring "that no bachelor or scholar shall presume to sit by any master of art in any church at sermons, or at any lectures in the schools." [95] That explains Robert Greene's eagerness to boast that he is "Master of Arts in both Universities," and Ben Jonson's satisfaction in reflecting that he, too, was a master "in both ye Universities by y^r favour not his studie." [96]

There does not seem to have been any purely academic reason for denying Marlowe his degree, except for his frequent absences. He was a competent, though not a brilliant, student. In the *Ordo Senioritatis* of the bachelors, he ranks one hundred and ninety-ninth among 231. Three years later, he is sixty-fifth among masters, though only two of the seven M.A.'s from Corpus rank ahead of him. [97]

The implications of the incident are clear enough. The future

[94] ". . . Vt iam in prouerbij locum venerit, equum Roystonium (est autem pagus Roystonum, vnde Londinum hordeum coctum, equis impositum peruehitur) & magistrum Cantabrigensem, duo esse animalium genera, quæ nemini de via cedant." William Soone in George Braun or Bruin: *Civitates Orbis Terrarum*, lib. II of vol. II, fol. 1. The book is also referred to as *De Praecipuis, Totius Vniversi Vrbibus*. The passage is translated in Cooper: *Annals*, II. 329 (1575).
[95] *Ibid.*, II. 430 (1586–7); Stat. Acad. Cantab., p. 467.
[96] *Conversations with Drummond of Hawthornden* (ed. G. B. Harrison, 1923), p. 11.
[97] On the *Ordo*, see Venn: *Alumni Cantabrigienses*, I. vii. The annual records are given with the degrees in the *Grace Book*.

dramatist's frequent absences during his last year at the university were due to confidential government work of some sort. They gave offense at the university, and the offense may have been further aggravated by Marlowe's failure to take the holy orders for which his scholarship had probably been primarily established.

That there had been trouble of some sort about the degree is further shown by the omission of his name as the last previous holder of the scholarship when his successor is appointed. Normally, both men should be named in these entries. Perhaps there is a further trace of ill-feeling in the curious fact that his last scholarship payment is for five and one-half weeks — the only fractional payment made to him. It is almost as if either Marlowe or the bursar had insisted on that last sixpence as a kind of evidence that all scores had now been settled, with petulant exactness.

There is not much doubt as to the nature of Marlowe's government employment. His patron's relative, Sir Francis Walsingham, had about this time received a grant of three thousand pounds for secret service, and the inference is natural that Marlowe was engaged in some kind of espionage or confidential secret service, either at home or abroad. He may actually have gone to Rheims, where an English Catholic seminary existed from 1578 to 1593. Until the execution of Mary Queen of Scots, in 1587, this was a center of conspiracy against Elizabeth's government.

It is easy to see why the master and fellows of puritanical Corpus Christi looked with disfavor on a scholar suspected of journeys thither. Their suspicions were natural for two reasons. Candidates for the priesthood and converts to Catholicism frequently went abroad for ordination just before receiving the master's degree. In January of this very year, a preacher at St. Mary's, Cambridge, had hinted in a sermon that members of the university were spying for the Catholics both in Rome and in Rheims.[98]

There is nothing inherently improbable in the idea that Marlowe was employed in secret service of some kind. At least one other Cambridge student, James Welsh, of Magdalene, had

[98] Cooper: *Annals*, II. 429 (1586/7), quoting Baker MS. XXX. 294.

turned spy; and various other poets and playwrights had taken the same course. Among them were the Scotch poet, William Fowler — uncle of Drummond of Hawthornden — who spied for Walsingham; Anthony Munday, who served as an intelligence agent watching the English Catholics at Rome; William Vaughan, who spied in Italy; Ben Jonson, who, in 1605 tried to supply secret information about the Gunpowder Plot; and perhaps Marlowe's friend, Matthew Roydon.[99]

The circumstances of Marlowe's death in 1593 and the presence of two known government spies also lend color to the view that he had in some way become involved in a web of secret-service intrigue from which he was never able to extricate himself.

Mr. Tucker Brooke, however, suggests that Marlowe was more probably engaged in the secret peace negotiations then in progress with the Duke of Parma.[100] At the very least, he may have been a confidential messenger carrying secret dispatches of importance, like young Robert Cecil, Burghley's son, Marlowe's contemporary at Cambridge, who on April 26, 1588, is paid "for bringinge *lettres* in post, for her ma*jestes* affaires, from her highnes Commissioners at Ostend." [101] A letter to Lord Burghley from Utrecht, in October, 1587, mentions "Mr. Morley" as one of Burghley's messengers,[102] and a "Mr Marlin" is a messenger for Sir Henry Unton, the English ambassador who accompanied Henry of Navarre in the wars of 1591–92.[103] Thomas Walsingham, Marlowe's patron, was also engaged in secret business for the crown in 1588.[104]

The whole episode of the disputed M.A. may represent a silent struggle between Thomas Norgate, Master of Corpus, on

[99] A. K. Gray, PMLA, 43: 687, 690 (1928); Ethel Seaton, RES, 5: 273–267 (1929); *Cal. State Papers, Domestic, 1581–90*, CLXX, no. 44; Conyers Read: *Sir Francis Walsingham*, II. 323n; Anthony Munday: *English Romayne Life* (ed. G. B. Harrison, 1925), pp. 2, 6; Herford and Simpson: *Ben Jonson*, I. 202–203; Mark Eccles, RES, 13: 393 (1937). See also I. 80 of the present work.

[100] See Tucker Brooke: *Life*, p. 36. For the circumstances of Marlowe's death, see chap. VI.

[101] PRO, Declared Accounts, E 351/542, fol. 110.

[102] *Cal. State Papers, Domestic, Elizabeth. Additional, 1580–1625*, p. 217. The original is in vol. XXX, no. 43, fol. 100, October 2, 1587. SP 15/30.

[103] Joseph Stevenson: *Correspondence of Sir Henry Unton, Knt.*, Roxburghe Club, no. 64, p. 388; Ethel Seaton: "Robert Poley's Ciphers," RES, 7: 146 (1931).

[104] PRO, Declared Accounts, E 351/342, fol. 125v.

the one hand, and Marlowe on the other, supported by Lord Burghley and John Copcot, who succeeded Norgate as Master of Corpus in this very year. Norgate tried to adopt a conciliatory attitude toward Burghley, but did not hesitate to oppose him when he thought it necessary. Copcot, on the contrary, was practically Burghley's personal representative at Cambridge.

Though he went through the form of signing the supplicat, Norgate may have opposed Marlowe's candidacy for the degree on account of the irregularity which so many long absences involved. Burghley, perhaps prompted by Copcot, would not have been the less inclined to interfere on Marlowe's behalf because of Norgate, with whom he had already had friction. In November, 1587, Norgate died, and Copcot became master of Corpus. But by this time Marlowe was already beginning to make a name for himself in London and *Tamburlaine* was probably already on the stage.

CHAPTER IV

LONDON: THE LIFE OF LETTERS

Bright Marlowe, brave as winds that brave the sea
When sundawn bids their bliss in battle be,
Lit England first along the ways whereon
Song brighter far than sunlight soared and shone.
SWINBURNE: Afterglow of Shakespeare

THE BEGINNING of Christopher Marlowe's literary career probably dates from those last years of intermittent graduate study at Cambridge. He now had behind him all the rigorous training of the schools and before him the comparative leisure and increased liberty of the graduate.

It was a time when the youthful poet must have been asking of himself many of those agonizing questions in the first scene of *Doctor Faustus* — for Marlowe's Faustus is no German *Gelehrter*, but a Cambridge man whose speech bewrayeth him. He has uttered but two lines upon the stage when he uses the word "commenced" in the curious and unusual sense peculiar to an English university. At Cambridge "to commence" is to receive a new degree — a sense still partially reflected in the American academic vocabulary with its modern "Commencements." Faustus, as we have seen, makes other allusions to Cambridge and its life.

Law, medicine, divinity — for which Marlowe was probably still in training, at least ostensibly — must all have hovered in the restless head of the young Cambridge graduate, just as they hover in the head of Faustus, musing in his cell.

"Still climing after knowledge infinite," this was no ordinary mind, but one which felt itself at length constrained to "sound the depth" of what it would profess. When, after three years, the master's degree was attained at length, it broke away from all recognized and conventional occupations of the scholar, abandoned the ecclesiastical career, and flung itself into the strange, new, fascinating craft of letters, into the whirl of splendor stained with sordid vice, poverty, and misery which was literary London, the capital of the Virgin Queen.

It was the step which all the "University Wits" were taking or were soon to take — men like John Lyly, who had forsaken scholastic pursuits and gone to London to commence author under the patronage of Sir Robert Cecil, just as Marlowe seems to have done with Thomas Walsingham as patron. All these young men are like the hero of Greene's *Neuer Too Late* — "for hee being a Scholler, and nurst vp in the Vniuersities, resolued rather to liue by his wit, than any way to be pinched with want." [1] Alas, too many of them *were* pinched with want all their lives!

Cambridge tradition declares that *Tamburlaine* was written in "Marlowe's room" at Corpus Christi, and though the tradition is obviously beyond proof, none has better claim to credence in view of its inherent probability. My own suspicion is that the germs, at least, of several of Marlowe's plays and poems were thought out in this room. *Tamburlaine* was being acted very early in Marlowe's literary career.[2] The first part, therefore, was probably written at Corpus Christi, though the second, which is frankly a hasty effort to follow up a first success, may have been dashed off in London lodgings; or again, both the *Second Part of Tamburlaine* and the first draft of *Faustus* may go back to the dramatist's browsings in the Corpus Christi Library.

A second work, the translation of the *Helenae Raptus* of Coluthus — now lost — was probably written in the same year that saw the M.A. attained and *Tamburlaine* produced.[3] To it may be added three other classical works, which might just as well be lost like the Coluthus, for all the good they are likely to do Marlowe's reputation, either as poet or scholar. These are the translations of Lucan's *Pharsalia* and Ovid's *Elegies*, and the play of *Dido*, all of which may quite possibly belong to this period.

The London to which the young Cambridge scholar jour-

---

[1] Grosart's Greene, VIII. 64.
[2] See I. 198–200.
[3] See II. 293–294.

neyed was not yet the London of Shakespeare. That talented young bumpkin, having married and become the father of three children while Marlowe was still a Cambridge student, may already have been forced to leave Stratford to better his fortunes, but he had not yet achieved a reputation. He may have been holding horses outside the Theatre, or even venturing upon the boards, about the time of Marlowe's arrival in Elizabeth's capital.

London had as yet but two playhouses — *the* Theatre, which James Burbage had erected in Finsbury Fields, north of the city, eleven years before; and the Curtain, which emulous rivals had built in imitation, not far away. The stage had caught the fancy of both the artistic and amusement-seeking portions of the Elizabethan public already, and had begun to alarm the godly years before. The Puritans were to be thorns in the players' flesh for years to come. But in spite of their protests, more new theatres were to spring up, even in Marlowe's lifetime, and many of the famous inns were practically theatres already.

In international politics, it was a time of anxiety for the English. Philip of Spain's Armada was known to be building. His beard had been singed by Drake at Cadiz, and the friendly intervention of Genoese bankers had been enough to delay him once. The English were still in negotiation with Philip's general, the Duke of Parma; but every apprentice in Queen Bess's London knew that Spain would not be held off a second time by anything save oaken walls. In April, 1588, less than a year after Marlowe had left the university, the town of Cambridge raised two thousand pounds for defense against the Spaniards,[4] and it was proposed to raise troops within the university itself. Marlowe's England knew that she might be fighting for her life at any moment.

It was a dramatic moment in history. It was also a pregnant moment in English literature.

Several centuries of miracle, mystery, and morality plays had trained Elizabethan audiences to a taste for the stage. The crude vigor of the popular theatre had been refined by the

[4] Cooper: *Annals*, II. 451–453. Cf. *Names of the Nobility, Gentry, and Others, Who Contributed ... at the Time of the Spanish Invasion* (London, 1798).

delicate though somewhat inane plays of Lyly. It had also received from them a little of that sense of form which it so badly needed. Here were audiences, companies of actors, theatres. Plays were the thing now required — not the halting, clumsy makeshifts in an intolerably heavy verse or affected rhyme or even duller prose that had hitherto done duty with the public; not the polite but rather bloodless dramas of the court, either. They might be fit for elegant amateurs, perhaps, but they were caviare to the play-hungry London mob.

Where was the dramatist who should give the illusion of life, the rush and splendor and horror which were the very stuff of drama as Elizabethans understood it? And where was the dramatist who could do all this and at the same time put into the actors' mouths the living and poetic word which should atone for the bare crudeness of the stage?

It was not the hour for Shakespeare yet. He was not for an age but for all time. At this precise moment the Elizabethan theatre required a poet who was the age's very essence. Such a poet was Christopher Marlowe, the Cambridge scholar, who in his supreme moments is as truly for all time as Shakespeare himself, but who, in the less inspired passages of his fumbling technique, experimental characterization, and humorless rant, becomes merely the earliest of the Elizabethan playwrights — and Shakespeare's schoolmaster in stagecraft.

At such a time the young scholar, after living six years at least theoretically withdrawn from the world at Cambridge, supported by the archbishop's scholarship, came up to London — probably with *Tamburlaine* and a few translations in his pocket, perhaps with other plays that we can only guess at — and cast about for means of livelihood.

He did not come into an entirely strange or foreign environment. His secret missions for the government had certainly drawn him occasionally to London. Anthony Marlowe, a prosperous merchant of Deptford,[5] is supposed to have been a kinsman. Richard Boyle, who had studied in the King's

---

[5] On Anthony Marlowe, see W. W. Greg: *Henslowe Papers*, p. 51; Joseph Lemuel Chester (ed. J. Foster): *London Marriage Licenses, 1521–1869*, p. 887; *Publications* of the Harleian Society, XXV. 83 (1887); *Cal. State Papers, Foreign, Eliz., 1584–1585*, p. 132; *Cal. State Papers, Dom., Eliz., 1591–1594*, pp. 396–397. His will is at Somerset House.

School and who had been at Cambridge in 1583, while Marlowe was still in residence, had abandoned the law to become a clerk in the service of Sir Roger Manwood, Lord Chief Baron of the Exchequer, a Kentishman with whom Marlowe certainly had some sort of acquaintance,[6] and for whom he composed a Latin epitaph. Nashe, Marlowe's contemporary at the university and his collaborator in writing *Dido*, may have come to London already, though there is no trace of him till later. Greene, another Cambridge man, was an enemy, or was soon to become one.

At some stage in his career, perhaps in childhood, more probably while at the university or in London, Marlowe seems to have made the acquaintance of Thomas Walsingham, a second cousin of the eminent contemporary statesman, head of the government secret service, Sir Francis Walsingham. Two pieces of evidence make it perfectly clear that Marlowe was on intimate terms with Thomas Walsingham. One is the fact that the Privy Council in 1593 specifically directs its constable to seek out Marlowe at his estate.[7] The other is Edward Blount's dedication of *Hero and Leander* — in rather involved and obscure language — to Sir Thomas Walsingham, who had by that time been knighted.

"I suppose my selfe executor to the vnhappily deceased author of this Poem," says Blount, "vpon whom knowing that in his life time you bestowed many kind fauors, entertaining the parts of reckoning and woorth which you found in him, with good countenance and liberall affection: I cannot but see so far into the will of him dead, that whatsoeuer issue of his brain should chance to come abroad, that the first breath it should take might be the gentle aire of your liking: for since his selfe had ben accustomed thervnto, it would prooue more agreeable and thriuing to his right children, than any other foster countenance whatsoeuer."

Thomas Walsingham was the fourth of that name in a family which had settled in Chislehurst, Kent, in the reign of Edward III. He was the second son of the third Sir Thomas, who had been first cousin to Sir Francis Walsingham. The third Sir

6 See II. 161–163.
7 See I. 109, 138.

Thomas had died in 1583, while Marlowe was at Cambridge. The fourth, Marlowe's patron, succeeded to the estate on the death of his brother Edmund in 1589. His epitaph describes him as "most famous for a liberal hospitality towards all." [8] His son, the fifth Sir Thomas, married the daughter of Peter Manwood (d. 1625), of St. Stephen's near Canterbury, son of Sir Roger Manwood.

Though overshadowed by his more famous kinsman, Sir Francis, the fourth Sir Thomas Walsingham spent much time at court, where he was especially favored by Queen Elizabeth, who visited him at Scadbury, Chislehurst, in 1597. He was, therefore, an influential friend who could be — and apparently was — useful to a rising dramatist, and who numbered among his other protégés the poets George Chapman and Thomas Watson, Marlowe's friends, and his acquaintances Ingram Friser and Robert Poley.

Sir Thomas Walsingham's relations with Sir Francis Walsingham do not seem to have been close; but second cousins, both of whom were frequently at court, could not fail to know each other. The third Sir Thomas had bought land at Chislehurst from Sir Francis, and the appearance of a Francis Walsingham among the children of the fifth Sir Thomas, son of Marlowe's patron, suggests that family relations were of at least normal cordiality.[9] The records of the Privy Council show that on at least one occasion Sir Thomas benefited "by mediacion of [the] late Mr. Secretary Walsingham," [10] and Robert Poley writes in one of his letters that he had "attended Mr. Thomas Walsingham for my secret recourse to Mr. Secretary." [11] It was natural that he should do so, for Thomas Walsingham had also done government business which was too secret to be specified in the accounts except as "speciall services for Her Majestie wherewith her Highnes was acquainted."[12] It is not hard to guess how and why Marlowe became involved in the secret service.

[8] Webb, Miller, and Beckwith: *History of Chislehurst*, p. 137.

[9] Owen Manning and William Bray: *History and Antiquities of . . . Surrey, passim*; Webb, Miller, and Beckwith: *History of Chislehurst*, pp. 135–142.

[10] J. R. Dasent: *Acts of the Privy Council*, XIX. 153–154, May 24, 1590.

[11] Poley to Earl of Leicester, February (?) 1587, in PRO, France XVII. 26 bis. See also *Cal. State Papers, Foreign Series, Elizabeth, 1586–1588*, pt. I (General), p. 229.

[12] Declared Accounts, E 351/542, fol. 125v, February 12, 1588, PRO.

Presumably, Marlowe moved also among the cultivated circles of Kent, including the Manwood family at St. Stephen's and perhaps the Oxindens at Barham. Sir Roger Manwood, who rose to be Chief Baron of the Exchequer, was a cynical lawyer, more than once accused of political corruption, and author of a *mot* still current, to the effect that corporations have no bodies to kick and no souls to damn. He was not, however, remarkably corrupt for that age of corruption, and he was noted for good works in an age not particularly so inclined. He helped to found the grammar school at Sandwich and built the house of correction in Westgate, Canterbury, not far from Marlowe's home.

At least once Marlowe appeared in court while Manwood was on the bench,[13] and the praise showered on Sir Roger in the epitaph attributed to Marlowe may be due to the court's leniency on that occasion. The Manwoods were related by marriage to both the Walsinghams and the Sidneys, and there had been a Sidney at King's School in Marlowe's time. All these circumstances are trifles, but they all help to make it probable that Marlowe was acquainted with the Manwood family, who possessed a library of contemporary books and manuscripts.

There is no clear evidence that Marlowe was also acquainted with the Oxindens, who owned one of the early collections of quartos,[14] but the fact that he was on intimate terms with other gentry, and that half a century later Henry Oxinden possessed Marlowe's books and much intimate information about him, suggests as much. He may also have had some acquaintance with the Finneux family, also well known in Kent. Elizabeth's England was after all a small bit of earth.

The general picture that we get of Marlowe at this time is that of a university man, known to be of humble origin, whose talents have made him a reputation, who is ordinarily referred to as "Christopher Marlowe, gentleman," and who is accepted as a friend by people of rank and station.

It is entirely possible that, like Shakespeare, the youthful Marlowe may for a short period have been an actor. It is, however, impossible to make any definite statement to that effect,

[13] See I. 100.
[14] W. C. Hazlitt: *Shakespeare: The Man and His Work*, p. 211.

especially as acting does not seem to have run in Marlowe's head as it did in Shakespeare's. Several of Shakespeare's most familiar metaphors are drawn from the stage; Marlowe uses practically none.

Worse still, the only manuscript that refers to Marlowe as an actor is an undoubted forgery. John Payne Collier produced as evidence for his belief that Marlowe once trod the stage [15] a ballad called "The Atheist's Tragedie," which recounts Marlowe's supposed adventures under the transparent anagram of Wormall. This ballad contains the stanzas:

> A poet was he of repute
>   And wrote full many a playe
> Now strutting in a silken sute
>   Then begging by the way
>
> He had alsoe a player beene
>   Vpon the curtaine stage
> But brake his leg in one lewd scene
>   When in his earlie age

The story, not in itself improbable, is accepted by Dyce, Bullen, and Cunningham, all of whom reprint the ballad, Dyce giving as his source "a manuscript copy in the possession of Mr. J. P. Collier." This manuscript is now regarded as fraudulent, presumably forged by Collier himself, the handwriting being patently modern. C. M. Ingleby wrote in 1876: "I have no hesitation whatever in branding this ballad as a contemptible forgery of the present century. The incidents narrated are derived from well-known sources, with the exception of what is narrated in the fifth and sixth verses [quoted above].

"The ballad appears to have been fabricated to furnish the desiderated evidence of Marlowe having been an actor before he was a playwright." [16] Ingram calls it a "pseudo-antique ballad," and Tucker Brooke "preposterous."

The ballad is not the only evidence, however, that Marlowe was on the stage; and while Collier's forgery certainly does not

---

[15] *New Particulars* (1836), pp. 47–48. The original MS. is in the British Museum, Addit. MS. 32380. It has been reprinted by Dyce, III. 349–352; Bullen, III. 303–307; Cunningham, pp. 369–370.

[16] *Academy*, 9: 313, 1 Ap 1876. Cf. E. M. Thompson, *Academy*, 27: 170, 7 Mr 1885; Ingram, *Christopher Marlowe*, p. 226; Tucker Brooke: *Life*, p. 38n.

prove that Marlowe ever was an actor, neither does it prove the contrary. Indeed, it proves nothing at all, except that Collier wanted to believe in Marlowe's stage experience.

There are three genuine allusions to Marlowe as an actor, dating from the century immediately following his death. In 1675 Edward Phillips, in the *Theatrum Poetarum*, remarks that Marlowe "rose from an Actor to be a maker of Plays." In 1687 William Winstanley, apparently echoing this passage, says that he "rose from an Actor, to be a maker of Comedies and Tragedies." [17] In 1691–92 Anthony à Wood says that after writing *Tamburlaine* Marlowe was "first an actor on the stage, then (as Shakespear, whose contemporary he was), a maker of plays."

The story was generally accepted by eighteenth-century critics, finds its way into the third edition of the *Encyclopædia Britannica* (1797), and is accepted by Malone in annotating his copy of Langbaine.

It is lamentably obvious that the later writers [18] are quoting each other, but there is nothing inherently improbable in the story itself, which persists as late as the *Biographica Dramatica* published in 1812.[19] This account declares that Marlowe "was not only an author but an actor also, being very considerable in both capacities."

[17] Phillips, II. 24; Winstanley: *Lives of the English Poets*, p. 134; Anthony à Wood: *Ath. Oxon.* (ed. 1815), II. col. 7.

[18] William Oldys (1696–1761) observes in a manuscript note in his copy of the 1691 Langbaine, now in the British Museum, that Marlowe was "educated at Cambridge, afterwards an Actor and then a writer of plays." Giles Jacob wrote in 1723 that Marlowe "was Fellow-Actor with *Heywood*" (*Poetical Register*, II. 171). In 1748 Bishop Tanner, probably quoting Anthony à Wood, to whom he acknowledges a debt, says that the dramatist had been "actor scenicus" (*Bibliotheca Britannico-Hibernica*, p. 512). William Rufus Chetwood, or Chetwode, asserted in 1752 that "this Author was both a Poet and a Player" (*British Theatre*, p. 8). The *Lives of the Poets* (1753), attributed to Theophilus Cibber, though probably written by Robert Shiels, repeats in the following year that Marlowe was "a player on the same stage with the incomparable Shakespear" (I. 85).

John Berkenhout, in 1777, says that Marlowe "settled in London, and went upon the Stage. What were his peculiar talents as an actor, are not recorded." (*Biographia Literaria*, p. 357.) He quotes Langbaine who "says in general terms, that he trodd the Stage with applause," a bit of information that disappears from Langbaine's later editions. Berkenhout cites Oldys and Tanner as authorities.

In 1797, the third edition of the *Encyclopaedia Britannica* (X. 576) says that "turning player, he trode the same stage with the inimitable Shakespeare," but this is not repeated in later editions. Malone's manuscript annotations are in his Langbaine, numbered Malone 131 at the Bodleian.   [19] Vol. I, pt. II, pp. 491–493.

The skepticism with which more recent authorities have regarded the tale is largely due to Collier's forged ballad; but a view may be correct even if Collier did support it with fraudulent evidence. After all, Collier also forged evidence to show that Marlowe was the author of *Tamburlaine*,[20] an attribution which is today universally accepted.

If Marlowe was ever on the stage at all, he probably did not remain there long, for success as a writer came swiftly. The *First Part of Tamburlaine* was so popular that the players demanded more. The prologue to the second part opens with plain allusion to this success:

> The generall welcomes Tamburlain receiu'd,
> When he arriued last vpon our stage,
> Hath made our Poet pen his second part.
> [2317–2319]

Marlowe apparently worked hard and fast, for the second part, though not lacking in power, shows plain signs of having been hastily put together; and this successful play — consisting really of two separate successes — was speedily followed by the equally popular and far greater *Doctor Faustus*. By commercial standards, which measure dramatic values in terms of popularity and the large audiences that result, *Tamburlaine* and *Faustus* at once established Marlowe as the dramatist of the hour. The literature of the period, even many years after the early performances, teems with allusions to these plays and quotations from them,[21] which leave no doubt that almost every play-going Londoner intimately knew them both and, consequently, must have seen or read them often. It is easy to understand why *Tamburlaine* went through seven editions and *Faustus* through ten.

It is also significant that attacks by the jealous Greene began just at this time. Marlowe's first triumphs were bitter gall to him, as were Shakespeare's first successes, which began a few years later. His earliest ridicule is directed against Marlowe in the pamphlet called *Perimedes*, published in 1588 — perhaps before *Doctor Faustus* had appeared, for the satire is all against *Tamburlaine*. Greene explains the failure of a play from his own pen because "I could not make my verses jet upon the

[20] See I. 196.   [21] See I. 238 ff., 306 ff.

stage in tragical buskins, every word filling the mouth like a fa-burden of Bow-bells, daring God out of heaven with that atheist Tamburlaine." The allusion is obviously to the line:

What daring God torments my body thus? [22]

As if this were not pointed enough, Greene alludes specifically to "such mad and scoffing poets that have poetical spirits, as bred of Merlin's race, if there be any in England, that set the end of scholarism in an English blank verse." The allusion to "Merlin's race" — the e being pronounced as a, as in modern English "clerk" — deserves note.[23] It suggests that Greene had been personally acquainted with Marlowe while they were both at Cambridge, for the play that he makes on the name of the magician, Merlin, is intelligible only to those who know Marlowe as "Marlin." This form of the name occurs only in college and university records, where — as Marlyn, Marlin, Marlen, or Malyn — it is the sole form used until his last year of residence. In Canterbury the poet was Marley; in London he was either Marley, Marlo, Morley, or Marlowe, the name that has found its way into literary history.

The increased bitterness with which Greene returned to the attack in his *Menaphon*, published the next year, suggests that Marlowe's popularity was growing. Sneeringly alluding to a love passage as a "Canterbury tale," Greene explains that it was told by a "propheticall full mouth that as he were a Cobbler's eldest sonne, would by the laste tell where another's shoe wrings." Marlowe *was* a Canterbury cobbler's eldest son. Greene's allusion to his rival's humble parentage, though his own was probably no better, may be due to the fact that Marlowe, a Cambridge scholar, was now regarded as a "gentleman."

Curiously enough, the one current pamphlet attributed to Greene whose title seems to point most clearly at Marlowe does not allude to him at all and is probably not by Greene. This is *The Cobler of Canterburie* (1590), which in spite of its date and title turns out to be merely a popular tale, without personal or

[22] II. *Tamb.* 4434.
[23] The burial record of Marlowe's father (see I. 28) actually uses the spelling "clarke." Otto Jespersen says specifically (*Modern English Grammar*, I. 197, sec. 641) that this combination was sounded *ar* in the Elizabethan period, and he is confirmed by H. C. Wyld (*Short History of English*, p. 151), who says that the pronunciation persisted to the end of the eighteenth century.

satirical implications. Greene denied writing it and intimated that he had been "wronged with suspition." [24]

Elsewhere, Greene, in his eagerness to wound, makes use of any weapon, and in 1591 his *Farewell to Folly* hints that the sales of the first quarto of *Tamburlaine*, published a year before, had been so bad that the sheets were used as wrapping paper. A peddler, he says, seeking Greene's *Mourning Garment*, "founde them too deare for his packe, that he was faine to bargain for the life of Tomliuclin [Tamburlaine] to wrappe vp his sweete powders in those vnsauorie papers." [25] This fresh outburst of spleen may herald the success of *The Jew of Malta*. More probably, the mere publication of *Tamburlaine* sufficed to provoke the sneers. The next year, Greene is attacking the young man from Stratford, who also was rising too rapidly to please the envious pamphleteer, and who may have been associated with Marlowe about this period. [26]

Not even the approach of death could quiet Greene's malignant heart. Shortly before he died on September 3, 1592, he returned to the attack in his *Groatsworth of Witte*. Marlowe and Shakespeare were both victims of the malice displayed in this venomous little pamphlet, but they were not the only ones. Greene pours it out upon Nashe and Peele almost as plentifully. Greene's spite now takes — as spite is very likely to do — the form of piety, and masks itself as a sincere desire for the sinner's repentance. Harping again on the old, familiar charge of atheism, he exhorts Marlowe: "Wonder not, (for with thee wil I first begin), thou famous gracer of Tragedians, that *Greene*, who hath said with thee like the foole in his heart, There is no God, should now giue glorie vnto his greatnesse: for penitrating is his power, his hand lies heauie vpon me, he hath spoken vnto me with a voice of thunder, and I haue felt he is a God that can punish enimies." [27] Among God's enemies, by implication, Christopher Marlowe is one.

Three hundred years later all this malice serves but to aid a few admiring students to follow the growth of Marlowe's literary reputation.

[24] There is a copy of the 1590 edition, STC 4579, at the Bodleian. It is reprinted in *Shakespeare Society Publications*, vol. XIII. For Greene's denial, see *Greene's Vision*, Grosart's Greene, XII. 197.   [26] See I. 104.
[25] Grosart's Greene, IX. 230.   [27] Grosart's Greene, XII. 141–142.

About this time, while they were probably living as neighbors,[28] Marlowe and Shakespeare must have had their first meeting — an event pregnant with significance for English literature. Shakespeare may have been in London as early as 1584, or he may have arrived in the capital in 1588, just as the peril of the Armada hung closest over the nation, or a little later, when the London burghers, relieved of danger from abroad, were ready to lend their minds to the fascination of the strange new play, *Tamburlaine*. In the relation of master and apprentice, the two may even then have been busy revising the two earlier plays which were to become the Second and Third Parts of *Henry VI*.[29]

At the very height of his triumphs, however, Marlowe suddenly found himself afoul of the law. In some way he had made the acquaintance of the poet and dramatist, Thomas Watson, also a protégé of Thomas Walsingham's. It was perhaps through Watson's influence that Marlowe was brought into Walsingham's circle, though as to that we can only conjecture. Watson had an enemy, one William Bradley, a Londoner living in Holborn near Gray's Inn, the son of an innkeeper, who had already been involved in several affrays. It is possible that he may have been the same William Bradley who had been a Cambridge student in Marlowe's day.[30]

Some time in the summer of 1589, Bradley went before a justice of the Queen's Bench, alleging that he was in fear of death from Hugh Swyft, John Allen, and Thomas Watson. The document which conveys this interesting information has been preserved:

Anglia ss   Willelmus Bradley petit securitates pacis versus Hugonem Swyft & Johannem Allen & Thomam Watson ob metum mortis &c.

      Attachiamentum vicecomiti Middlesex retornabile XVe martini.[31]

---

[28] See I. 104.

[29] But see II. 221–241.

[30] See *Alumni Cantabrigienses*. The Thomas Watson who was also a fellow-student, and whose supplicat for the B.A. still stands on the same page as Marlowe's, was a quite different person who cannot possibly be identified with the poet Watson.

[31] Original in Queen's Bench Controlment Rolls, K. B. 29/226, PRO. Discovered by Dr. John Leslie Hotson and first published by Mark Eccles: *Christopher Marlowe in London*, p. 57.

This was equivalent to instructing the sheriff to cause these three men to appear at Westminster Hall and give suitable security. The date set was the fifteenth of St. Martin, or November 25, 1589.

Bradley had good reason for his fears, but unfortunately for him, he had petitioned too late. On September 18 [32] he met Christopher Marlowe in Hog Lane in the Parish of St. Giles without Cripplegate. This was just north of the city wall, not far from Finsbury Field and near the Curtain Theatre. It was near Marlowe's lodgings in Norton Folgate and the two men may have met by appointment. They were certainly acquainted and with equal certainty they were on bad terms, so that a prearranged duel would not have been impossible.

At any rate, in the report of the Gaol Delivery, which repeats the phrasing of the coroner's inquest on the unfortunate Bradley, we find "will*elmu*s Bradley et quidam *Christ*oferus Morley, nup*er* de London gen*erosus* . . . insimul pugnantes." Presumably, it was a battle in the usual Elizabethan style — sword in the right hand, dagger in the left. Why Marlowe was involved, we do not know and in all probability never shall. Bradley may have attacked him simply because he was Watson's friend; or we may have here proof of Thomas Kyd's assertion that Marlowe was given to "rashnes in attempting soden pryvie iniuries to men." [33]

Watson, arriving upon the scene of combat, drew his sword to separate the fighters — or so he told the coroner. Marlowe dropped his point and drew off, or, as the Latin record has it, "Morley seip*su*m retraxit & a pugnand*o* desistit." But Bradley, whose blood was up, greeted his new enemy with a shout, the exact words of which — the only English in the document except for place names — the official scribe has carefully preserved.

---

[32] The date is erroneously given as September 28, 1589, in the coroner's inquest, and the Chancery record of pardons gives the day of the inquest itself as September 29. The numerals in these records are Roman, and a scribe apparently added an "x" too many. The record of Bradley's burial gives September 19 as the date. A daily record of this sort, confirmed by preceding and following dates, cannot very well be in error, whereas the routine official reports are very likely to contain clerical slips. The burial record is confirmed by the Middlesex Sessions Roll, 284, which says that Marlowe was jailed September 18. Cf. Eccles, *op. cit.*, pp. 34, 36.

[33] British Museum, Harleian MS. 6848, fol. 154. Reprinted by Ford K. Brown, TLS, 20: 355, 2 Je 1921, and Brooke: *Life*, pp. 107–108.

"Arte thowe nowe come then I will haue a boute with thee,"
he yelled, deliberately using the familiar and insulting "thou"
and "thee." There was probably more bad language (the
coroner says primly, "insultum fecit") before he threw himself
on Watson with sword and dagger and "then and there smote
him, wounded him, and ill-treated him." The swords clashed,
and Watson defended himself, retreating until he had his back
against a ditch. Then, seeing that there was no escape and
being hard pressed, he ran his sword (worth three shillings,
fourpence, according to the meticulous officials) through Bradley's right breast near the nipple. The wound was six inches
deep and one inch wide. Bradley died on the spot; Marlowe
and Watson were both arrested for murder.

The two were taken before the lieutenant of the Tower, who
committed them to Newgate Prison. On December 3, 1589,
they came before the justices at the Old Bailey, which is still
the Central Criminal Court. Among Her Majesty's judges then
on the bench was that very Sir Roger Manwood whose epitaph
Marlowe was later to write. The judges apparently accepted
Watson's story, and he was returned to jail to await pardon.
In other words, he had proved that he had killed only in self-
defense, after making every effort to escape, and was therefore
in no danger from the law; but the killing nevertheless required
a pardon, which would take time. Ingram Friser, who killed
Marlowe four years later, waited only thirteen days; but Watson had to wait until February 10, 1589/90 before he was finally
pardoned and set free.

As Marlowe had not killed Bradley — nor even wounded
him, so far as the records show — his case was less serious, and
the records are less precise as to what happened to him. We
have, however, the Middlesex Sessions Roll, which notes his
arrival in Newgate Prison:

Thomas Watson nuper de Norton ffowlgate in Comitatu Middlesex generosus & Christoferus Marlowe nuper de Eadem yoman qui ducti fuerunt Gaole xviij° die Septembris per Stephanum wyld Constabularium ibidem pro Suspicione Murdri viz pro Morte [blank] et Commissi fuerunt per Owinum Hopton Militem.[34]

---

[34] Middlesex Sessions Roll, 284, no. 12, now in the Middlesex Guildhall, London. Printed by Eccles, *op. cit.*, p. 34.

A marginal note opposite Watson's name says that he was "balliat*us*," that is, "bailed," and another opposite Marlowe's says that he was "del*iberatus* p*er* proclam*acionem*," that is, "released on proclamation." His imprisonment is especially interesting because of the charges made in the Baines Libel some years later that Marlowe "was aquainted wth one Poole a prisoner in newgate" who had taught him counterfeiting. It was long suspected that this was Robert Poley, Walsingham's spy, who was present when Marlowe was assassinated; but there is no record that Poley's chequered career ever included a term in Newgate. Marlowe was almost certainly referring to one John Poole, a prisoner in the prison at this very time, who boasted of his methods of passing counterfeit coin: "Hee said he had a man that Coigned halfe pence who putt away many of them to beggers to whom he would geue an halfpeny but not vnles they had a greater peece of money as vj[d] viij[d] or xij[d] & so would take the greate peece and would geue all halfe pence for it." [35]

Marlowe was released on recognizance of forty pounds on October 1, after spending only thirteen days in jail. The document recording his release has been known since 1894, but has always been a mystery, since there was nothing to show why the poet was in jail at all, until Mr. Mark Eccles made his brilliant discovery of the new documents which tell the story of the fatal duel and Marlowe's subsequent imprisonment.

In the crabbed legal Latin of the Middlesex Sessions Roll, the recognizance recounts:

Mid*dlesex* ss M*emorandum* q*uo*d primo die octobris Anno regni *domi*ne *no*st*r*e Elizabethe R*egi*ne nunc Etc. Tricesimo primo Ric*hard*us Kytchine de Clyffordes Jnne gen*erosus* et Humfridus Rowland de East Smythfeilde in Com*itatu* p*re*dicto horner venerunt coram me Willmo ffletewoode Servien*ti* ad legem et Recordatore Ciuit*atis* London vno Justic*iarium domi*ne *no*st*r*e R*egi*ne in Com*itatu* p*re*dicto assign*atorum* Etc et manucep*er*unt p*ro* xpoforo Marley de London gen*er*oso: vizt vter*que* manucaptor*um* p*re*dic*torum* sub pena vigin*ti* libr*arum* et ip*s*e p*re*dic*tus* xpoforus Marley assumpsit p*ro* sei*p*so sub pena quadragin*ta* libr*arum* de bonis Catall*is* terr*is* et tene-

---

[35] "The speeches vsed by John Pole in Newgate to [John] Gunstone." See State Papers, Domestic, vol. CCLXXIII, no. 103. *Cal. State Papers, Domestic 1598–1601*, pp. 372–373; Mark Eccles: "Marlowe in Newgate," TLS, 33: 604, 6 S 1934. Gunstone's paper is dated July 25, 1587.

mentis suis et eorum cuiuslibet ad opus et usum dicte Domine Regine levandarum sub Condicione quod si ipse predictus xpoforus personalliter comparebit ad proximam Sessionem de Newgate ad respondendum ad omnia ea que ex parte dicte Domine Regine versus eum obiecientur et non discedet absque Licencia Curie Quod tunc Etc Aut alioquin Etc.[36]

It is worth noting that the cobbler's son is here styled "gentleman" as a matter of course. The Newgate Prison records call him only "yoman."

Most interesting of all is the fact that William Fleetwood, the Recorder of London, before whom this remarkable prisoner appeared, took an early opportunity to buy his works. Fleetwood owned a large library of plays which remained intact until they were disposed of by sale in 1774. Among them is listed "*The conquests of* Tamburlaine *the Scythian Shepheard*, 2 Plays, B.L. both imperfect at the Beginning." [37] The description fits the rare 1590 edition at the Bodleian, which may have been Fleetwood's own copy. If he did not buy this edition the year after Marlowe appeared before him, he must have bought the 1592 edition, the last that appeared before his own death in 1594, a year after Marlowe had been killed.

Marlowe's sureties were average respectable citizens.[38] Though Richard Kitchen was himself indicted for an assault with a dagger in 1594, he lived to be at least seventy, owned a house and lands, and was a member of Clifford's Inn. There are numerous records of his appearances in the courts, which suggest a prosperous attorney in active practice, and he is repeatedly described as "gentleman."

"Humphrey Rowland, horner," the other surety, was a less prosperous person — his trade was the preparation of horn for lanterns and knife handles—but he, too, was intensely respectable. Lord Burghley had described him as "a very honest poore

[36] Middlesex Sessions Roll, 284, no. 1, now at the Middlesex Guildhall. *Middlesex Sessions Records* (I. 189) print an abstract; Brooke (*Life*, pp. 96–97) gives an accurate transcript. It is quoted by Sir Sidney Lee in the *Athenaeum*, no. 3486: 235–236, 18 Ag 1894; by H. F. Westlake in the London *Times*, June 24, 1925, p. 17d; and by Dr. J. L. Hotson in an independent translation in the *Atlantic Monthly*, 138: 40 Jy 1926.

[37] *Bibliotheca Monastica-Fletewodiana*, no. 1351, p. 76. The Bodleian Library has several copies.

[38] J. L. Hotson in *Atlantic Monthly*, 138: 37–44 Jy 1926; Mark Eccles: *Christopher Marlowe in London*, pp. 69 ff.

man," [39] in 1583; and he had been a churchwarden of St. Botolph, Aldgate, in 1586. He was occasionally in legal difficulties, but they do not seem to have been serious, and he was frequently surety for others, as he was for Marlowe. He may have been a professional bondsman, like Marlowe's father, but his name hardly appears frequently enough in the records to justify the idea.

That these two reputable businessmen were willing to be sureties for the godless playwright speaks fairly well for his character; and that so poor a bondsman as Rowland was acceptable to the authorities at all may mean either that they regarded Marlowe himself as prosperous enough to make possible a levy of forty pounds; or else that they did not regard the murder charge very seriously; or even that official influences were again at work on Marlowe's behalf.

Watson languished in prison until February 10, 1589/90, when he received the royal pardon, which again rehearses the circumstances of the fight.

Not the least important aspect of this affair for the student of today is the fact that it fixes Marlowe's place of residence in London. He was, says Middlesex Sessions Roll 284, living in Norton Folgate. This may have been the main street so named, leading from London Bridge north through London, a short stretch of which was known by that name. Much more probably it was the liberty of Norton Folgate, which extended to the west, south of Hog Lane, the scene of the duel, and far enough east to include the site of St. Mary's Hospital, better known as the "Spital." Stowe asserted that "in place of this Hospitall, and neare adioyning, are now many faire houses builded, for receipt and lodging of worshipfull persons." [40]

A liberty was a good residence for anyone connected with the Elizabethan theatre, because it was not technically a part of the city. It had its own officers of the peace, who were responsible not to the puritanically inclined and theatre-hating Lord Mayor but to the justices of Middlesex, who were more amenable to the influence of the theatre-loving court. The proprietors

[39] Letter to the Lord Mayor, first noted by Eccles, *op. cit.*, p. 91. Cf. Remembrancia, I, nos. 505, 516 (ff. 256, 262), and W. H. and H. C. Overall: *Analytical Index to the Series of Records Known as the Remembrancia* (1878), p. 154.

[40] *Survey of London* (ed. Charles Lethbridge Kingsford, 1908), I. 167.

of the Rose, the Globe, and the Hope theatres were careful tó
build in the liberty of the Clink. A further advantage of
Norton Folgate as a lodging for Marlowe was its proximity to
the theatres. Quite probably he had William Shakespeare as a
fairly close neighbor, for Aubrey's *Brief Lives* [41] record the
statement of William Beeston that Shakespeare "lived in
Shoreditch," which is close to Norton Folgate. Beeston himself had lived in Shoreditch and, when he talked with Aubrey,
was living "at Hoglane within 6 dores — Norton-Folgate."

About this time — certainly by early 1591 — Shoreditch had
a more sinister resident, none other than the government spy
who in 1593 stood by while Marlowe was being murdered. He
is described in a deposition as "Rob. Poley, of Shoreditch." [42]

Three years after the duel, Marlowe was once more in difficulties. Two constables of Holywell Street, Shoreditch, appealed to the courts for protection against the redoubtable
playwright. The Dogberries of Shoreditch who went in terror of
their lives because of the poet were Allen Nichols, constable of
Holywell Street, and Nicholas Helliott, subconstable. On
May 9, 1592, these two went before Sir Owen Hopton at Middlesex Sessions, and demanded that Marlowe be bound over to
keep the peace toward all the Queen's people and particularly
toward themselves. One gets an idea of the liveliness of the
quarter in which Marlowe lived from this incident and from the
binding over of two of Marlowe's neighbors to keep the peace
on October 2 of the same year. Both Norton Folgate and
Shoreditch make frequent appearances of this sort in the
records.

There is no document to tell what ultimately resulted from
the constables' appeal, but the appeal itself still remains:

Midd*lesex* ss M*emorandum* qu*od* ix*no* die Maij 1592 Annoq*ue* Regni
d*omi*ne n*os*tre Elizabethe Nunc &c xxxiiij*to* Venit cora*m* me Owino
Hopton Milite vno Justic*iariorum* di*c*t*e* d*omi*ne R*eg*ine ad pace*m* in
com*itatu* pr*edicto* Conservand*am* assignat*orum* Christopherus Marle
de Lond*on* gener*osus* et recognovit se debere di*c*t*e* d*omi*ne Regine
xx*li* bone et legalis monete Anglie: Sub Condici*one* qu*od* personal*iter*
comp*arebit* ad pr*oximam* gener*alem* Sessione*m* pac*is* in et pr*o* com*itatu*

    [41] Aubrey MS. 8, fol. 45*v*; E. K. Chambers: *Shakespeare*, II. 252.
    [42] *Cal. State Papers, Dom. Elizabeth, 1591–1594,* p. 35, vol. CCXXXVIII, no. 140,
Ap? 1591. See also I. 178 of the present work.

predicto tenend*am*: et interim geret pacem versus cunct*um* populu*m*
dic*te* do*m*ine Regine et *pre*cipue versu*s* Allenu*m* Nicholls Constabu-
lari*um* de Hollowellstreet in co*m*itatu predic*to* et Nicholau*m* Helliott
subconstabulari*um* de eadem:/ Quam sum*m*am pred*i*ctam concessit
de bonis et Cattallis terris atque ten*e*ment*is* suis ad vsum *d*ic*te*
do*m*ine Regine p*er* formam Recognici*o*nis levari Si defecerit in
premiss*is* &c.[43]

His difficulties with the law do not seem to have interfered
with Marlowe's literary productiveness.

Once he had begun producing, he turned off play after play,
though at a speed much less than the average theatrical hack's
in that day. *The Jew of Malta* reached the stage in 1589,
played by Lord Strange's Company, who had defied the city
fathers and were acting at the Cross-Keys Inn. There follows
a lull in Marlowe's writing, and then in 1591 or thereabouts we
have the last of the great plays, *Edward the Second*, which, to be
sure, was not entered in the *Stationers' Register* until 1593, but
which there is good reason to believe was finished and produced two years earlier. Almost simultaneously, Marlowe must
have been working on *The Massacre at Paris* — a trivial, made-
to-order melodrama with some history thrown in, which adds
nothing to his reputation — and probably also on the first two
books of *Hero and Leander*, those exquisite lines never quite
equaled in their kind until two hundred years later John Keats
was born, another whom, like Marlowe, the gods loved too well.

For a time at least (we have Kyd's word for it) Marlowe and
Thomas Kyd had shared a room and were "wrytinge in one
chamber." [44] This must have been about 1591, since Kyd in
1593 dated it "twoe yeares synce."

Marlowe's other associates included many of the most brilliant and best of Queen Bess's subjects — Sir Walter Raleigh,
Thomas Harriot, mathematician and astronomer, either Walter
Warner, the mathematician, or William Warner, the poet,[45]
Robert Hues, the mathematician, George Chapman, the poet,
who asserted that he received Marlowe's dying charge to complete *Hero and Leander*,[46] and Shakespeare himself, who in

[43] Middlesex Sessions Roll, 309, no. 13. Discovered by Mark Eccles and first printed
in his *Christopher Marlowe in London*, p. 105.
[44] Kyd's letter to Sir John Puckering, Harleian MS. 6849, fol. 218.
[45] See I. 136–137. [46] See II. 482–487.

As You Like It [47] alludes with a note of unmistakable tenderness to the "dead shepherd." Marlowe was also on familiar terms, not only with the Kentish gentry, but also with an unnamed Lord, to whom Kyd alludes in his letter to Sir John Puckering, presently to be discussed. [48]

Now, when Marlowe is at the very height of his fame, when he has become a man of importance in literary, intellectual, social, and official circles, there falls a succession of misfortunes, terminating in his death. These misfortunes were of such a nature that, even had the poet's hand been able to turn aside the fatal dagger and save his life in the brawl at Deptford, it might have preserved him only for a more ignominious end upon the scaffold.

But this is speculation, and speculation — even two hundred years after an event that never happened — is rarely safe. At least, however, we know that the clouds were lowering about Marlowe when Ingram Friser's dagger thrust stilled that restless and unhappy heart forever.

[47] III. v. 81–82. See also II. 208–209 of the present work.
[48] Harleian MS. 6849, fol. 218; Brooke; *Life*, p. 104.

CHAPTER V

"MARLOWES MONSTRUOUS OPINIONS"

Discontent run into regions farre.
Hero and Leander, I. 478

MARLOWE HAD FALLEN into doubtful and dangerous company. However the careless roistering of his Bohemian fellows in the playhouse may have scandalized the godly burghers of Elizabeth's London and the cathedral town of Canterbury, it could never have brought him in peril of his life. Even if, like Thomas Watson and Ben Jonson, he had ended a fight by killing his man, Marlowe was scholar enough to read his "neck verse" and claim benefit of clergy, a potent stimulus to scholarship in a violent age.

There was a far graver suspicion afloat. Marlowe was rumored to be a freethinker. Worse still — or rather, in Elizabethan eyes, very much the same thing — he was said to have spoken well of the Roman Catholic faith. This was an offense which the government of a queen whose legitimacy and title to the throne Rome denied could scarcely ignore. The spies and informers, whose reports upon the dramatist are still extant, translated the freedom of that fiery spirit into flat "atheism" — and to be in the least degree unorthodox when church and state were closely linked into one was to be an enemy of the state.

Discovery of the Buttery Book of Corpus Christi somewhat strengthens the idea that Marlowe may have become infected with unorthodox religious ideas during his university days. Corpus Christi itself was a stronghold of Puritanism, but among its fellows was Francis Kett, later burnt as a heretic. Early students of Elizabethan literature suspected that Marlowe's unorthodox views might have been stimulated by Kett's teaching. Later scholars pointed out that there was no proof of Marlowe's arrival in Cambridge until 1581, and that Kett gave up his scholarship in 1580.

The earlier scholars were right, however, in believing that
Marlowe and Kett had been in residence at Corpus at the same
time. Even poets and heretics must eat and drink, and the Buttery Book thus settles the question. Kett undoubtedly ceased
to be a fellow in 1580, but he continued in residence until the
eleventh week of the Easter term in 1581, months after Marlowe's arrival. Indeed, the bursar keeps his name on the books
— though without any charges — until the end of July, 1581,
when he is marked "non co" [no commons], and disappears forever. During all this period Marlowe's name stands on the list.
The heretic, soon to be burnt for his views on the divinity of
Christ, and the future "atheist" poet were both getting food
and drink from the same buttery, eating in the same hall.

It is strange to read these prosaic entries, or to see the brisk,
businesslike signature, "F. Kett," in another account book, and
then picture the fate that overtook him in the castle moat at
Norwich, a few years later, when he was dragged to the stake
crying "nothing but blessed bee god," and so continuing
"vntill the fire had consumed all his neather partes, and vntill
he was stifled with the smoke."

In spite of this new evidence, however, it is not possible to
attribute Marlowe's unorthodoxy unhesitatingly to Kett. That
saintly theologian might be charged with instigating Marlowe's
anti-Trinitarian doctrines, for he held that Christ was "not
God, but a good man," who would "be made God after his second resurration." William Burton (d. 1616) in *Dauid's Evidence* says that Kett had "the sacred Bible almost neuer out
of his handes, himselfe alwayes in prayer" — obviously a different person from the madcap scoffer of Norton Folgate and the
Bankside playhouses.[1] Kett had certainly nothing to do with the
blasphemous obscenities in which Marlowe plainly delighted;
and it is doubtful whether he had even developed his unitarian
ideas before leaving Cambridge. That he had some kind of
influence on the young Marlowe's impressionable mind remains,
nevertheless, at least a possibility.

It will not do to take the accusation of "atheism" against

[1] William Burton: *Dauids Evidence* (ed. 1596), pp. 124 ff. The Harmsworth copy of
this book is now in the Folger Library. The title is actually *Dauids Evidenece*, an
obvious misprint. See also Alexander Gordon: article "Kett, Francis," DNB, XI. 74.

Marlowe too seriously. The word was bandied about loosely, much as words like "red," "radical," "liberal" are used today and with quite as vague a meaning. Atheism meant almost any religious view of which the speaker disapproved. Queen Elizabeth herself [2] was charged with it by a disgruntled Englishman in Germany, as her vigilant secret service promptly informed her government.

This charitable view of Marlowe's alleged irreligion was suggested long ago by David Erskine Baker, who in his *Companion to the Playhouse* (1764) wrote:

Allowing that Mr. *Marloe* might be inclinable to Free-thinking, yet that he could not run to the unhappy Lengths he is reported to have done, especially as the Time he lived in was a Period of Bigotry; and that even, in these calmer Times of Controversy, we find a great Aptness in Persons, who differ in Opinion with Regard to the speculative Points of Religion, either wilfully or from the mistaking of Terms, to tax each other with Deism, Heresy, and even Atheism, on even the most trivial Tenets, which have the least Appearance of being unorthodox.[3]

Her Majesty's Privy Council was not so leniently inclined. On May 18, 1593, it issued "a warrant to Henry Maunder, one of the Messengers of her Majesty's Chamber, to repair to the house of Mr. Thomas Walsingham in Kent, or to anie other place where he shall understand Christofer Marlow to be remayning, and by vertue thereof to apprehend and bring him to the Court in his companie." [4]

Irreligion may not have been the only charge against Marlowe, but it was probably one of the charges, for it is perfectly clear that the government had been investigating his beliefs.

Precisely what those beliefs were, it is not possible to say. Although much has been written of Marlowe's "atheism" and his association with Sir Walter Raleigh's "School of Atheism," the whole subject of his religious beliefs remains obscure. Such evidence as remains is contained in the following documents:

---

[2] *Cal. State Papers, Dom. Eliz., 1601–1603*, p. 23.

[3] Ed. 1764, vol. II, sig. x2v; ed. 1782, I. 301.

[4] *Acts of the Privy Council*, ed. J. R. Dasent, XXIV. 244. The original is in Elizabeth XI (P.C. 2/20), PRO. Ingram (*Christopher Marlowe*, p. 237) gives the wrong reference. See also Brooke: *Life*, p. 58. Maunder was often employed on such errands. See Dasent, *op. cit.*, XXIV. 20, 24; XXV. 52, 58, 304. The warrant for Marlowe follows the usual form. See XXIV. 24.

1. The so-called "Baines libel," consisting of two separate documents. One is Harleian MS. 6648, fols. 185–186, formerly numbered 170–171. This is the spy's original note. A copy, presumably made for the Queen, is Harleian MS. 6853, fols. 307–308, formerly numbered 320–321.

2. Thomas Kyd's letter to Sir John Puckering, Lord Keeper of the Privy Seal, Harleian MS. 6849, fol. 218.

3. A second letter from Kyd to Sir John, Harleian MS. 6848, fol. 154.

4. Manuscript extracts from a Unitarian treatise, Harleian MS. 6848, fols. 187–189, formerly numbered 172–174. This is refuted in *The Fal of the Late Arrian* (1549), by John Proctour.

5. Manuscript notations in the Prideaux copy of the 1629 *Hero and Leander*, now in the hands of an unknown collector, but surviving in copies which appear to be reliable.

6. Commonplace Books of Henry Oxinden, of Barham, Kent, now in the British Museum and Folger Shakespeare Library, both of which are directly related to the preceding document.

7. Robert Greene's taunts in the *Groatsworth of Witte* (1592) and *Perimedes the Blacksmith* (1588).

8. Assertions of Puritan divines.

9. An allusion to an atheist in *The French Academie* (1594), which does not name Marlowe specifically but probably alludes to his views.

10. "Remembraunces of wordes and matters against Richard Cholmeley," Harleian MS. 6848, fol. 190, a government spy's report.

11. A second spy's report. Harleian MS. 6848, fol. 191.

12. Assertions of Gabriel Harvey.

13. Marlowe's known association with the Raleigh circle of freethinkers.

1. The two extant copies of the Baines libel do not agree textually in all respects, but the essence of their charges is the same and there is practical identity of mood.[5] The documents read like the jottings of a horrified and rather literal-minded listener to the rather wild conversation of a radical young man who took an intense pleasure in making his hearers' flesh creep, but who certainly had no idea that his assertions were being noted down. The opinions with which the documents charge Marlowe were sufficient to bring any subject in peril of his life. Among other things, Marlowe is said to have declared:

[5] The name is also spelled Bame, Bome, and Baine.

That the Jndians and many Authors of antiquity haue assuredly writen of aboue 16 thousand yeares agone wheras [Moyses] Adam is [said] proued to haue lived *within* 6 thowsand yeares. . . .[6]

That Moyses was but a Jugler, & that one Heriots being Sir W Raleighs man Can do more then he.

That the first beginning of Religioun was only to keep men in awe. . . .

That Christ was a bastard and his mother dishonest. . . .

That Crist deserved better to dy then Barrabas and that the Jewes made a good Choise though Barrabas were both a thief and a murtherer.

That if there be any god or any good Religion, then it is in the Papist*es* because the service of god is performed w*i*th more Cerimonies, as Elevation of the mass, organs singing men, Shaven Crownes, & cta. That all protestant*es* are Hypocriticall asses. . . .

That all the new testament is filthily written. . . .

That he had as good Right to Coine as the Queen of England, and that he was aquainted with one Poole a prisoner in Newgate who hath greate Skill in mixture of mettals and hauing learned some thing*es* of him he ment through help of a Cunni*n*ge stamp maker to Coin ffrench Crownes pistolet*es* and English shilling*es*. . . .

That the Angell Gabriell was baud to the holy ghost, because he brought the salutation to Mary.

That on Ric Cholmley [hath Cholmley] hath Confessed that he was perswaded by Marloe's Reasons to become an Atheist.

Few liberal Christians of our day would be very deeply shocked by Marlowe's alleged views on the chronology of Genesis, the quality of New Testament Greek prose, the origin of religion, or the virgin birth. But, even today, the rigidly orthodox would find such a document painful reading; and in the eyes of the Elizabethan secret service it was evidence of total depravity, especially as there is more in the same wild vein.

In *Christs Teares Over Ierusalem* Marlowe's friend, Thomas Nashe, condemns those who "persist in it, that the late discouered Indians are able to shew antiquities thousands [*sic*] before *Adam*." Of other unorthodox thinkers, he complains, "With *Cornelius Tacitus*, they make *Moyses* a wise prouident man, well seene in the Egiptian learning, but denie hee had any diuine assistance in the greatest of his miracles." He is equally

---

[6] Words in brackets are scored through in the original. "Heriots" is, of course, Thomas Harriot.

emphatic in his disapproval of efforts to use Biblical errors to reduce the Scriptures to mere legend.[7] As all of these are Marlowe's views, there is not much doubt at whom Nashe is glancing.

He does not, however, deal with Marlowe's still more extreme contentions. These include accusations of unnatural vice against Christ, scandalous assertions as to his relations with "the woman of Samaria & her sister," other tedious obscenities of the same sort, and the odd assertion that the Sacraments "would haue bin much better being administred in a Tobacco pipe."

The authenticity of this document has been questioned, not very convincingly, by Ingram,[8] who suggests that it is a mere transcript by the antiquary Thomas Baker and perhaps a forgery. Further doubt is cast on the document's authenticity by the much scored notation on the copy sent the Queen:

A note delivered on Whitsvn eve last of the most horreble blasphemes and damnable opinions vttered by *Christ*ofer Marly who within iij dayes after came to a soden & fearfull end of his life.

Whitsun Eve, 1593, fell on June 2, so that this is equivalent to dating the murder on June 5, four days after Marlowe had been buried. Slips of this sort, however, are not uncommon in Elizabethan official records, especially in copies.

The identity of Richard Baines remains a mystery. Mr. Tucker Brooke has shown that Queen Elizabeth had three subjects of this name, two of whom were living in 1593 and one of whom was certainly hanged at Tyburn [9] December 6, 1594. It would be pleasant to know that such a fate overtook the author of the charges against Marlowe, but for lack of evidence we are denied this comfortable belief.

The attacks on Marlowe's religion are far less serious in modern eyes than the charges against his morals. The whole episode throws into dark relief his unhealthy interest in unnatural vice.[10] Baines and Kyd both mention his curious accusation

[7] McKerrow's Nashe, II. 116; Grosart's Nashe, IV. 174–175.

[8] *Op. cit.*, Appendix B, pp. 257–263.

[9] A fact first discovered by Malone. See *Stationers' Register*, bk. B, p. 316. Cf. Cooper: *Athenae Cantab.*, II. 174; J. Peile: *Biographical Register of Christ's College*, I. 108; and Venn: *Alumni Cantabrigienses.* See also Brooke: *Life*, p. 103.

[10] Cf. Eugen Dühren [Pseudonym of Iwan Bloch]: *Englische Sittengeschichte*, II.

against Christ and St. John, and Baines asserts that Marlowe specifically defended homosexuality. This unfortunately accords with Marlowe's pretty obvious tendency to drag in allusions to unnatural vice wherever possible, notably in the first scene of *Dido*; in the scene between Neptune and Leander in *Hero and Leander*; and in *Edward the Second*.

On the other hand, it is easily possible to make far too much of the whole matter. In *Dido*, Nashe may be equally responsible with Marlowe. In *Edward the Second*, history and, in *Dido*, mythology both give authority for the material used. As for the charges against Marlowe by Kyd and Baines, both seem to have been persons likely to be easily shocked, and one strongly suspects Marlowe, perhaps after a little too much wine, of having deliberately set out to shock them. It is true that the Neptune episodes in *Hero and Leander* are deliberately dragged in, without any justification, from the Greek of Musaeus, which was the chief source; but they do not ill accord with the sensual atmosphere of the poem nor with other Greek myths. As witnesses, both Baines and Kyd command very little confidence, and the evidence is far too slight to justify conclusions as to Marlowe's personal morality.

2. In the spring of 1593 Thomas Kyd was arrested — "suspected for that Libell that concern'd the state."[11] London tradesmen had been engaged in riots against intruders. The royal government was disturbed by "certaine libelles latelie published by some disordered and factious persons in and about the cittie of London, shewinge an intente in the artyficers and others who holde themselves prejudiced in theire trades by strangers." The Privy Council ordered a group of gentlemen "to examine by secrete meanes who maie be authors of the saide libelles." They were given the right to interrogate anyone they thought fit. Others were to "search in anie the chambers, studies, chestes or other like places for al manner of writings or papers that may geve you light for the discoverie of the libellers."[12]

9–10, and Havelock Ellis: *Studies in Sexual Inversion*, p. 22. Every one of Dühren's statements about Marlowe's life is erroneous, so that his conclusions need not be taken very seriously.

[11] Harleian MS. 6849, fol. 218.

[12] *Acts of the Privy Council* (ed. J. R. Dasent), XXIV. 200–201, dated April 22, 1593. See also p. 222.

Kyd became involved in this investigation. It was found that he had in his possession papers expressing unorthodox religious views. After various "paines and vndeserved tortures," he attempted to save himself from the charge of irreligion by inculpating Marlowe and condemning his "monstruous opinions." This may not have been so base an act as it now seems. Kyd probably knew that his friend was dead before he himself sat down to write Sir John Puckering. One letter refers to Marlowe in the past tense. The other specifically refers to his death. Kyd may have felt justified in saving his own skin at Marlowe's expense, because Marlowe was already beyond earthly harm.

In the first letter Kyd tried to clear himself, as compared with Marlowe, "of being thought an Atheist, which some will sweare he was." He refers to Marlowe as "one so irreligious," and accuses him of being "intemperate & of a cruel hart." [13]

3. In his second letter, Kyd asserts that it was Marlowe's "custom when J knewe him first & as J heare saie he contynewd it in table talk or otherwise to iest at the devine scriptures gybe at praiers, & stryve in argument to frustrate & confute what hath byn spoke or wrytt by prophets & such holie men." [14] He then specifically repeats some of the Baines charges, including Marlowe's ridicule of St. Paul and his assertion that "things esteemed to be donn by devine power might haue aswell been don by observation of men." [15]

4. When Kyd was arrested, there was found among his other papers a document which develops a very dull argument, based on Scripture, to prove that Christ was not divine. Kyd attempted to clear himself by writing to Sir John Puckering that these notes merely happened to be lying "amongst those waste and idle papers (which J carde not for) & which vnaskt J did deliuer vp." He explained that they had been "shufled with some of myne (vnknown to me) by some occasion of our wryting in one chamber twoe yeares synce." Kyd's argument is at least plausible, though he is obviously in terror of his life

---

[13] Harleian MS. 6849, fol. 218.

[14] Harleian MS. 6848, fol. 154. Reprinted by F.-C. Danchin, *Revue germanique*, 9:567–570 n–D 1913.

[15] W. D. Briggs: "On a Document Concerning Christopher Marlowe," *Studies in Philology*, 20: 153–159 (1923).

and endeavoring to save himself by portraying the deceased Marlowe in the darkest possible colors.

The incriminating paper has an odd history, which has only in recent years been cleared up. In 1549 a Unitarian heretic was arrested. Archbishop Cranmer allowed him to state his heretical views in writing, and copies of his statement were made and handed about privately. The document with which Kyd was caught is one of these papers, still circulating in manuscript after forty years.

Mr. Tucker Brooke has pointed out that the handwriting closely resembles that of the Latin quotations in Kyd's own letters, which are in two separate handwritings. He has used the ordinary secretary scrawl for his own English, but has engrossed his Latin in a beautiful Roman scrivener's hand. This, however, is also the hand that Thomas Harriot frequently uses for extracts from books. It is quite as likely, therefore, that Harriot owned this copy; that he lent it to Marlowe; and that it really did get mixed up with Kyd's papers by accident. The handwriting is at least as much like Harriot's as Kyd's and might be almost any educated Elizabethan's, for this beautiful calligraphic hand was so completely stylized that it is often hard to tell one man's writing from another's.[16]

When the heretic's arguments were allowed to leak out, a copy came into the hands of one John Proctour, a staunch Trinitarian, who promptly and piously wrote a book about it.[17]

Thou shal [sic] vnderstand [he says] that I haue in the same confuted the opinion of a serten man who lately denyed Christ deuinitie and equalitie, with God the father, affirmynge that he was but a mere Creature, and a passible man only, not God. And this was Arrius opinion. . . . and as many as do holde that opinion, are called of Auncient writers, Arrians; and therfore I intitle my treactise: The fall of the late Arrian: not disclosing his name throughe oute my worke, but vnder the name of Arrian: whom I wold be lothe to displease, if he hath Recanted that blasphemous oppinion, as some saye that he hathe. This oure late Arrian therfore not long synce was before serten of the Counsell & dyuers other Learned men, for his opinion, by whose procurement I know not. And deliuered to the

16 For Harriot's use of this hand, see Addit. MSS. 6785, fol. 238; 6783, fol. 76; 6787, fols. 306, 312, 318, 377.
17 Fols. Div verso–Dv verso. There are copies of the book in the British Museum, Bodleian, and University Library, Cambridge.

same his opinion with his prouffes in writyng to the lord Archbishop
of Cau*n*terbury beyng therunto at length required, as in the be-
gynnung of his writyng he confesseth. Wherof dyuers copies came
into diuers mens ha*n*des: And one was sent to me.

The unitarian heretic has been at least tentatively identified
with the parish priest, John Assheton.[18] Three persons were
charged with unitarianism during this year: Michael Thombe,
a London tradesman; Joan Bocher, or Joan of Kent; and
Assheton. Thombe was accused chiefly of doubting the efficacy
of infant baptism. He recanted, but is not known to have
written anything. Joan Bocher cannot be considered, since
Proctour refers to the heretic as "he." Assheton, in recanting,
admitted that his heresies had been "presumptuously affirmed
by subscription of my proper handwriting," and describes
views similar to those set forth in the Marlowe-Kyd document.

Proctour's book reprints the arguments in the document
paragraph by paragraph and demolishes each of them. His
printed text of these heresies is almost verbatim that of the
document found in Kyd's possession, except that parts of the
manuscript have been torn off and the printed version is therefore more complete. In Harleian MS. 6848 the pages have been
placed in reverse order and must be read backwards to make
sense.

The incriminating paper is exactly the kind of thing that one
might expect the skeptical Marlowe to possess. Its tone is not,
however, the wild rant of his conversations as recorded by his
enemies, though that tone does not ill accord with various passages in the plays. The tone is rather that of sober theological
discussion.

5. Manuscript notations in the Prideaux copy of the 1629
edition of *Hero and Leander* tend to confirm the charge of
atheism. The notations are essentially the same as those in the
two Oxinden Commonplace Books now in the Folger Shakespeare Library and the British Museum. The first known
reference to these appears in the catalogue of the sale of the
books of Richard Heber, in 1834:

[18] See Lansdowne MS. 980, fol. 67, formerly numbered 70; Cranmer Register, fols.
73–74, at Lambeth Palace; John Strype: *Memorials of Archbishop Cranmer*, I. 257–258;
and George T. Buckley in MLN, 49: 502–503 (1934).

The MS. notes in this copy of Hero and Leander 1629, are very re-markable, with reference to the History of Marlow. In them we are told that he was an Atheist; that he was stabbed at about thirty, swearing; that he had a friend at Dover, whom he made an Atheist, but who was obliged to recant, &c. At the back of the title-page is a Latin Epitaph on Sir Roger Manwood, by Marlow, which has never been printed. At the end of the second Sestiad we are told in a MS. note that Marlow wrote no more upon the subject.[19]

This book had at one time probably belonged to Henry Oxinden, of Barham, near Canterbury, who probably bought it on publication. His library at length passed to his protégé and son-in-law, John Warly, then to his son, also named John Warly, and then to Lee Warly, son of the second John Warly.[20] In 1807 Lee Warly died, leaving his books to Elham Parish, Kent.

Thereafter the book appears in the Heber Sale, where it went to an unknown collector for ten shillings and for a time disap-peared. Its very existence was questioned by C. M. Ingleby in his Complete View of the Shakespeare Controversy,[21] published in 1861. Inquiries by Dr. Edward F. Rimbault, an early nine-teenth-century student of English literature, regarding its whereabouts, in 1850, led to no results.[22]

The mysterious purchaser at the Heber sale had actually been J. P. Collier, who admitted ownership in his own edition of the Heber Catalogue, published after the sale in 1834. No one seems to have noticed this, and as late as 1885 Colonel W. F. Prideaux still says only that "it came into Mr. Collier's possession many years ago." In the Bridgewater Catalogue (1837), Collier merely mentions its existence, without giving any clue to the ownership, and adds that it contains "some par-ticulars of Marlow, in the hand-writing of Gabriel Harvey" — the final statement being a very bad guess.[23] The book was sold

[19] Heber Catalogue, pt. IV, no. 1415, p. 183.
[20] Mark Eccles: "Marlowe in Kentish Tradition," N&Q, 169: 60–61, 27 Jy 1935. See also the MS. Catalogue of the Books of Lee Warly (1760), now among the books belonging to Elham Parish, Kent, preserved in the Howley Library, in care of the Cathedral Library, Canterbury (fol. 34).
[21] Page 314 n.
[22] "Ten Queries Concerning Poets and Poetry," N&Q, 1st ser., 1: 302, 9 Mr 1850.
[23] N&Q, 6th ser., 11: 305–306, 18 Ap 1885, and 385, 2 My 1885. See Collier: Cata-logue of Early English Literature (Bridgewater), pp. 189–190; Catalogue of Heber's Col-lection, p. 16 ("Notes and Prices"), p. 183.

with the library of F. Ouvry, president of the Society of Anti-
quaries, Collier's son-in-law, in April, 1882. Prideaux purchased
it "some time afterwards" from a "well-known London bookseller."

When the second portion of Colonel Prideaux's books were
sold at Sotheby's, February 14, 1917, his 1629 *Hero and Leander*
was sold to Dobell for twenty-six pounds. As it never appeared
in a Dobell catalogue, it must have been resold immediately,
but Mr. P. J. Dobell, formerly in general charge of the firm's
rare book business, does not know to whom. The inscriptions
were photographed for A. H. Bullen at one time, and there is
some reason to suppose that a print still exists in the files of
Messrs. Sidgwick & Jackson, who have many of Bullen's papers.
Efforts to discover it have, however, proved futile.[24]

At the Heber Sale in 1834 the book had attracted the attention of John William Burgon, later Dean of Chichester, who
copied part of the inscription, apparently without questioning
its authenticity. When Joseph Hunter was preparing the
manuscript of his *Chorus Vatum*, he consulted Burgon, who in
January, 1836, sent him as much of the note as he had been able
to make out.[25] The proper names and the word "Trinitie" had
been left in a cipher which Colonel Prideaux later described as
looking "like Greek bewitched." [26]

Collier published the inscription twice — completely in his
Bibliographical and Critical Account of the Rarest Books (1866)
and partially in the "History of the Stage" prefixed to his
Shakespeare. As his printed accounts did not agree with each
other and as his reputation was cloudy, doubts as to the authenticity of the documents soon arose.[27]

According to Collier, the first note, on the title page, read as
follows:

Feb. 10. 1640. Mr. —— said that Marloe was an Atheist and wrot a
booke against the Trinitie: how that it was all one mans making, and

[24] W. F. Prideaux: "Marlowe's Epitaph on Sir Roger Manwood," N&Q, 11th ser., 2:
24, 9 Jy 1910; letter of P. J. Dobell, Esq., January 4, 1933; oral information from
Arundell Esdaile, Esq., and Sidgwick & Jackson.
[25] *Chorus Vatum*, Addit. MS. 24488, fols. 207v–208; Brooke: *Life*, p. 78; Mark
Eccles in N&Q, 169: 22–23, 13 Jy 1935.
[26] N&Q, 6th ser., 11: 305, 18 Ap 1885. See also p. 352 of this volume of N&Q and
12: 15.
[27] *Bibliographical and Critical Account*, I. 313–314; *Shakespeare*, I, xliv.

would have printed it, but it would not be sufferd to be printed. Hee was a rare scholar and made excellent verses in Latine. Hee died aged about 30.

The second, which appeared at the end of the dedication, read:

Christopher Marloe, who wrot the 2 first sestiads of Hero and Leander was an acquaintanc of Mr. —— of Dover whom hee made become an —— so that hee was faine to make a recantation uppon this Text, 'The foole hath said in his heart there is no God.' —— would say (as Galen) that Man was a more excellent composition then a beast, and by reason thereof could speak; but affirmed that his soul dyed with his body, and as wee remember nothing before wee were borne, so wee shall remember nothing when wee are dead.

This——learned all Marloe by heart, and divers other bookes: he would never have above one book at a time, and when hee was perfect in it, hee would put it away and get another. Hee was a very good scholar: *teste* Mr. ——.

At the beginning of the poem, there was a marginal note: " 'Latet in muliere aliquid majus potentius omnibus aliis humanis voluptatibus.' Marloe was stabd with a dagger, and dyed swearing."

6. Subsequent discovery of the two Commonplace Books belonging to Henry Oxinden (1609–1670) confirms the authenticity of the inscription in the *Hero and Leander*. The one now in the Folger Library is a vellum-bound volume of folio manuscript, numbering 540 pages and lettered on the back, "Miscellany, 1617, MS. by H. O." Oxinden seems to have made entries in it from 1647 until his death in 1670, mingling verse, prose, and religion with licentiousness, and leaving many blank folios. The British Museum copy closely resembles it.

At least one book remained in the family for many years after Oxinden's death, for it bears the name of his great-grandson, "Lee Warly, Canterbury, 1764." Later it appeared in the Huth Library,[28] and it has now found a permanent home in the Folger Shakespeare Library. Although the Huth Catalogue specifically says that it contains anecdotes of Marlowe, no attention was paid them until the publication of Mr. Mark Eccles' articles. Both Commonplace Books were probably taken out of

[28] Pt. 6, no. 5508, p. 1569.

the Oxinden-Warly collection during the period when it was left open to the entire parish of Elham.

The Oxinden family had literary interests. W. C. Hazlitt credits them with "the first ascertained attempt to form a collection of the early quartos,"[29] which in Henry Oxinden's time included a 1594 *Dido* and a 1598 *Edward the Second*. Oxinden might thus easily have owned and annotated a 1629 *Hero and Leander*, a poem with which he was certainly acquainted, since he mentions it in the Folger Commonplace Book, on folios 42 and 56.

The book contains three passages relating to Marlowe. There are two copies of the epitaph on Sir Roger Manwood [30] with an entry attributing it to "that Marlo, who made the 2 first bookes of Hero & Leander, witnes Mr Alderich." On folio 54 is another note again quoting Mr. Ald[erich]:

Mr. Ald. sayd that Mr Fineoux of Douer was an Atheist & that hee woud go out at midnight into a wood, & fall downe uppon his knees & pray heartily that the Deuil woud come, that he might see him (for hee did not beleiue that there was a Deuil) Mr Ald: sayd that hee was a verie good scholler, but would neuer haue aboue one booke at a time, & when hee was perfect in it, he would sell it away and buy another: he learnd all Marlo by heart & diuers other bookes: Marlo made him an Atheist. This Fineaux was faine to make a speech uppon The foole hath said in his heart there is no God, so got his degree. Fineaux would say as Galen sayd that man was of a more excellent composition then a beast, and thereby could speak: but affirmed that his soule dyed with his body, & as we remember nothing before wee were borne, so we shall remember nothing after wee are dead.

The last reference to Marlowe is on folio 56:

he [i.e., Aldrich] said that Marlo who wrot Hero & Leander was an Atheist: & had wrot a booke against the Scriptur, how that it was al of one mans making, & would haue printed it but would not bee suffered: hee said that the sayd Marlo was an excellent scoller, & made excellent verses in latin he was stabd with a dagger & dyed swearing.

[29] W. C. Hazlitt: *Shakespear: Himself and His Work*, p. 211. On Oxinden himself, cf. DNB, XV. 11–12, article "Oxenden or Oxinden, Henry," by Thomas Seccombe; Giles E. Dawson: "Henry Oxinden," TLS, 32: 380 1 Je 1933; Dorothy Gardiner: "Henry Oxinden," TLS, 32:413 15 Je 1933; Dorothy Gardiner: *Oxinden Letters*. Many of Oxinden's books are now in the Elham Parish Library, stored in the Howley-Harrison Collection in care of the Cathedral Library, Canterbury.
[30] Fol. 42.

The other Commonplace Book, which was bought by the British Museum in 1869, has twenty-seven pages of Aldrich's remarks, which Oxinden carefully noted:

Feb. 10, 1640. He said that Marlo who wrot Hero & Leander was an Atheist & had writ a booke against the Scripture; how that it was all one man's making, & would haue printed it but could not be suffered. He was the son of a shomaker in Cant. He said hee was an excellent scholler & made excellent verses in Lattin & died aged about 30; he was stabd in the head with a dagger & dyed swearing. [31]

Aldrich also remarks that "Sir Walter Raleigh was an Atheist in his younger days."

On February 12, 1640/1, Aldrich tells the story of "Finis of Douer" in the words of the Folger Commonplace Book.

The close correspondence between the phraseology of the inscriptions in Prideaux's *Hero and Leander* and Oxinden's Commonplace Books clearly indicates a common authorship. If the *Hero and Leander* could now be rediscovered, comparison of the handwriting would probably strengthen this view, but the confirmation is hardly necessary. No two men would write independently: "He was stabd with a dagger & dyed swearing." The loss of the printed book is no longer serious, since the unquestionably authentic Commonplace Books provide the same data.

It seems probable that Prideaux's *Hero and Leander* was at one time in Oxinden's possession, and that he copied into it the information already entered in his Commonplace Books. He hesitated to use Fineux's and Aldrich's names in a printed book, which others might see, and therefore used the Greek cipher. He had no such compunctions about his own private notes in his Commonplace Books.

Oxinden's friend, "Mr. Alderich," is undoubtedly Simon Aldrich, of Canterbury, who was licensed to marry at St. George's Church, two years after the death of John Marlowe, the poet's father, and a year after the death of Katherine Marlowe, his mother. Living in the parish where the Marlowes lived and which immediately adjoined the parishes to which the Marlowes later moved, Simon Aldrich was probably personally acquainted with both the poet's parents.

[31] Addit. MS. 28012, fol. 505v–518. See especially fol. 514.

The erring Fineux, whom Marlowe "made an Atheist," was almost certainly Thomas, the son of "Thomas Fineuxe," christened in Hougham Parish, Kent, May 16, 1574.[32] Both Fineux and Aldrich seem to have been students at Cambridge about the time of Marlowe's death. Aldrich is named as a scholar of Trinity at Easter term, 1596, and as a fellow in 1599. He became Master of Arts in 1600 and Bachelor of Divinity in 1607.[33] Quite probably he was related to that Thomas Aldrich who had been master of Corpus from 1570 to 1573.

Thomas Fineux seems to have been a relative of Oxinden's and a collateral descendant of Sir John Fineux, chief justice of the King's Bench from 1495 to 1527, who leased lands to Richard and the first Christopher Marley.[34] Richard Fineux, younger brother of Sir John, was obviously the "second husband called Phineaux" who married Henry Oxinden's "grandmother Brooker," and became father of the older Thomas Fineux. Oxinden adds that he "was judge Phineaux his brother." [35]

Henry Oxinden's acquaintance with Fineux is further attested by a Latin poem, the manuscript of which is now in the Folger Library, addressed to "Affini meo dilecto Phineaux Armigero." Oxinden here describes him as "vir egregii ingenii" and "cultor*que* penitus Musarum." [36] A poem scribbled on the title page of Oxinden's *Anatomy of Melancholy* — "Hen: Oxinden Esqr: his Advice to an Atheist" — is doubtless also addressed to Fineux.[37]

Oxinden, who during the lonely years after his first wife's death had been living near Simon Aldrich, evidently sought consolation in his conversation. He frequently notes what "Mr. Aldrich said," both in his Commonplace Books and on the flyleaves of various volumes.[38]

---

[32] Register of Hougham Parish (transcript). Copy supplied by Frank W. Tyler, Esq., of the Kentish Archeological Society.

[33] *Alumni Cantabrigienses*, I. 14.

[34] Tucker Brooke: *Life*, p. 5 and n. See also the text of the wills.

[35] Oxinden's MS. note in *Select Epigrams of Martial* (1620), now no. 186 in the Elham Parish Library, stored for safekeeping in the Howley-Harrison Library, Cathedral Library, Canterbury.

[36] Oxinden MSS., Folger Library. "Oxinden Amici," fol. 33.

[37] No. 210 among the Elham Books.

[38] See the cover and p. 4 of Cartwright's *Epistel to the Churche of Englande*, no. 109 among the Elham books, and the twenty-seven pages of Aldrich's sayings in Addit. MS. 28012, fols. 505*v*-518.

In view of all this, it seems almost certain that Fineux must have known Marlowe personally. His admission to Corpus Christi College as "Phyney" is recorded in 1587,[39] and as "Pheneux" is repeated in the annual audit of the same year. The audits record him as paying a pensioner's fee, and the university *Matriculation Book* confirms this by placing him in the "convictus secundus,"[40] on June 23, 1587, as "Tho. fiñieux." Presumably he was in residence at Corpus while Marlowe was in the midst of the disputes regarding his master's degree.

The university records contain nothing to indicate that Fineux ever received a degree himself, but this is not surprising, since such records for the early 1590's are very scanty. Oxinden says quite clearly that he "got his degree."

We have thus a continuous series of unorthodox members of Corpus. Francis Kett was actually in residence during Marlowe's first year. Fineux's path a few years later crosses Marlowe's, precisely as Marlowe's had crossed Kett's.

7. Robert Greene's taunting reference to Marlowe's atheism is well known. It appears amid various exhortations to repentance in his *Groatsworth of Witte* (1592):

Wonder not, (for with thee wil I first begin), thou famous gracer of Tragedians, that *Greene*, who hath said with thee like the foole in his heart, There is no God, should now giue glorie vnto his greatnesse: . . . Why should thy excellent wit, his gift, be so blinded, that thou shouldst giue no glory to the giuer? Is it pestilent Machiuilian pollicie that thou hast studied?[41]

There is no doubt whom Greene means. At this period, before Shakespeare had turned to tragedy and when Marlowe was at the height of his fame, the "famous gracer of tragedians," especially if given to Machiavellian views, could only be the author of *Tamburlaine*, *Faustus*, and the Machiavellian *Jew of Malta*, not to mention *The Massacre at Paris*, to which Machiavelli speaks the prologue. Greene had, however, already made the allusion doubly clear by references in his "Epistle to the Gentlemen readers," prefixed to his *Perimedes The Blacke-Smith* (1588). He speaks here of "daring God out of heauen

39 Corpus Christi *Audit Books*; University *Matriculation Book*, p. 392.
40 *Alumni Cantabrigienses*, II. 139.
41 Grosart's Greene, XII. 141–142.

with that Atheist *Tamburlan*" and "impious instances of intollerable poetrie." [42] The accusation that Marlowe was an atheist
is plain enough, though it need not be taken very seriously.
Greene's malicious motives were fairly clear to his contemporaries. Even his friend Nashe calls the *Groatsworth of Witte* "a
scald triuial lying pamphlet." [43]

8. No greater weight need be attached to the charges of
atheism brought against Marlowe by such writers as Thomas
Beard, Edmund Rudierd, or William Vaughan. Puritan in
sympathies, these men were seeking to point a moral from
Marlowe's sudden death. A charge of atheism or heresy was
almost a necessity to them. They are plainly echoing common
report — eagerly, but without much, if any, first-hand knowledge of the dramatist's private life or opinions. Their attacks
are significant mainly as evidence of Marlowe's general reputation for unorthodox views, about the time of his death. He
must have indulged in much reckless talk of the sort these books
outline,[44] for their charges are closely akin to the Baines libel
and to Kyd's letters, both of which were at that time confidential government papers, unknown to the public.

9. Belonging to the same class, but of less weight — since it
does not specifically name Marlowe — is a passage which appears in the third (1594) edition of the Second Part of *The
French Academie,* by Pierre de la Primaudaye, translated by
"T. B." The author discusses a certain Ligneroles, a French
courtier and atheist, after which he denounces "students of
Machiauels principles." He then draws a parallel with an
unnamed individual of similar views in England:

This bad fellowe whose works are no lesse accounted of among his
followers, then were *Apollos* Oracles among the Heathen, nay then
the sacred Scriptures are among sound Christians, blusheth not to
belch out these horrible blasphemies against pure religion, and so
against God the Author thereof, namely, That the religio*n* of the
heathen made them stoute & courageous, whereas Christian religion
maketh the professors thereof base-minded, timerous, & fitte to become a pray to euery one: that since men fell from the religion of the

[42] Grosart's Greene, VII. 8.

[43] "Private Epistle to the Printer," prefixed to the second ed. (1592) of *Pierce
Penniless*. Grosart's Nashe, II. 7. McKerrow's Nashe, I. 154.

[44] See I. 144-147.

Heathen, they became so corrupt that they would beleeue neither
God nor the Deuill: that Moses so possessed the land of Iudæa, as
the Gothes did by strong hand vsurpe part of the Romane Empire.
These and such like positions are spued out by this hel-hound.[45]

While this passage might refer either to Raleigh or to
Marlowe, it is significant that it does not appear in the editions
of 1586 and 1589, but is inserted in the 1594 edition immediately after Marlowe's irreligious opinions had been bruited
about, and perhaps before news of his death reached the
printer.

"T. B.," who is named as translator, was once believed to
be Thomas Beard, but is now identified with Thomas Bowes,
whose name is signed to the first part of the book. A passage which follows that quoted above seems to refer to Robert
Greene (1560–1592), who was also dead when the book appeared.

10–11. The document headed "Remembraunces of wordes
& matter againste Richard Cholmeley"[46] is a government
spy's report, which mentions Marlowe only incidentally, just
as Cholmeley himself is mentioned in the Baines libel. This is
followed by the report of another unknown government agent-
provocateur,[47] also dealing with the atheism of Marlowe's
friend and alleged convert, Cholmeley, but not mentioning
Marlowe himself. In the first document, "Sʳ Walter Raliegh &
others" are linked with "one Marlowe," who "is able to shewe
more sounde reasons for Athiesme then any devine in Englande
is able to geve to prove devinitie." The words "Sʳ Walter
Raliegh & others" sound strangely like the "men of quallitie"
mentioned by Kyd. Cholmeley was eventually captured by
the government,[48] but nothing is known of his subsequent fate.

While it is not possible to identify him completely, he is
probably the Richard Cholmeley of the manor of Ingleton,
"within the hundred of wapentake of Yewcrosse," Yorkshire,
an estate which he had inherited from Sir Richard Cholmeley,

---

45 J. P. Collier: *Poetical Decameron*, II. 274–275; *Dictionary of Anonymous and
Pseudonymous English*, II. 333; R. Watt: *Bibliotheca Britannica*, II. 777. Primaudaye's
book is STC 15233–15341. The 1594 ed. is STC 15235. There are copies in the Bodleian, Huntington, and Folgar libraries. The reference here is b3v, in STC 15238 (Second
Part).

46 Harleian MS. 6848, fol. 190.

47 Harleian MS. 6848, fol. 191.   48 BM. Harleian MS. 7002, fols. 10–11.

knight, who died in or before 1583,[49] and who had at least occasionally rendered the government service in protecting the
coast against Scottish ships.

Like Marlowe, the younger Richard Cholmeley was in gov-
ernment service of some kind. In January, 1593, a certain Hugh
Cholmeley in letters to Sir Robert Cecil alludes to his brother,
Richard, who is apparently already in government service.[50]
There is no good reason for identifying him with Robert
Cholmeley, servant to the Earl of Leicester, or with the Chol-
meley who was servant to the Earl of Essex. The latter was,
however, in trouble of some kind in November, 1593.[51]

Richard Cholmeley had been in alternate favor and disfavor
with the Privy Council since early in 1591. In May of that year
a certain "Chomley" and others were ordered to appear and
answer "such things as shalbe objected against them." In
July, however, the Council ordered a payment to him for aid
in an arrest. By October the Council was ordering "Richard
Cholmley of Ingleton" to appear and give bond. In March of
1592/3 there was a warrant for his arrest, and another was
issued May 13, 1593. He was finally arrested June 28, 1593.[52]
Long afterward a Richard Cholmeley is arrested for breaking
into a dwelling house and stealing an iron chest and a hundred
pounds.[53]

12. Gabriel Harvey, in the "Glosse" upon the obscure
"Sonet" in his *New Letter of Notable Contents* (1593), has the
lines:

> He that nor feared God, nor dreaded Diu'll,
> Nor ought admired, but his wondrous selfe.[54]

---

[49] *Proceedings in Chancery in the Reign of Queen Elizabeth*, vol. H–K, nos. 47, 58, 72.
Cal. State Papers, Dom. Eliz., 1581–1590, p. 109, vol. CLX, no. 52.

[50] *Cal. State Papers, Dom. Eliz., 1591–1594*, p. 173, vol. CCXLI, no. 22, January 19,
1593. Cf. *Cal. State Papers, Irish, 1574–1585*, pp. 245, 270, 281, 552.

[51] *Cal. State Papers, Dom. Eliz., and James I., Addendum, 1580–1625*, p. 179, vol.
XXIX, no. 116, June 18, 1586; *Cal. State Papers, Foreign Series, 1586–1587*, pt. II,
Holland and Flanders, p. 84 (July 12, 1586), p. 209 (October 29, 1586), p. 243. *Hist.
MSS. Comm. 4th Report*, p. 330, November 15, 1593. See Hatfield (Salisbury) MSS.
(Hist. MSS. Comm.), pt. I, p. 338, no. 1113.

[52] Harleian MS. 7002, fol. 10. *Acts of the Privy Council* (ed. J. R. Dasent) under
dates indicated. Various suits in which a Richard Cholmeley is engaged are listed in
Proceedings in Chancery in the Reign of Queen Elizabeth, PRO. See especially H. h. 10,
nos. 58, 72; I. i, 6, no. 47; P. p. 10, no. 1.

[53] Middlesex Session Roll, 28 Jan. 42, Eliz. See also F.-C. Danchin in *Revue germanique*, 10: 51–68 Ja–F 1914; F. S. Boas: *Marlowe and His Circle*, pp. 79 ff.

[54] *Works of Gabriel Harvey* (ed. Alexander B. Grosart, 1884), I. 297.

In the prose text of the *New Letter*, Harvey twice compares Marlowe to Lucian (ca. 125–200 A.D.), the second-century Hellenistic satirist, an uncompromising skeptic who had ridiculed the Greco-Roman deities in his *Dialogues of the Gods*, *Dialogues of the Dead*, and other works. Some of these Marlowe knew, since he borrows an idea from the *Dialogues of the Dead* in the "thousand ships" passage of *Faustus*.[55] Harvey's other allusions to Marlowe plainly imply atheism:

Though *Greene* were a Iulian, and *Marlow* a Lucian: yet I would be loth, *He* [Nashe] should be an Aretin.

He is even plainer in another passage:

Plinyes, and *Lucians* religion may ruffle, and scoffe awhile: but extreme *Vanitie* is the best beginning of that brauery, and extreme *Miserie* the best end of that felicity. *Greene*, and Marlow might admonish others to aduise themselues.[56]

About the same time, in *Pierce's Supererogation* (1593), Harvey refers to "no religion but precise Marlowisme." Harvey's malice against Marlowe and Greene is so well known, however, and his joy in their deaths so ghoulish, that, even were all these passages specific in their charges, they need not be taken literally. As they stand, however, they certainly imply a general charge of extreme unorthodoxy.

13. Much has been made, on rather slender evidence, of Marlowe's association with Sir Walter Raleigh's "School of Atheism." Sir Sidney Lee, for example, says that Marlowe and Raleigh "debated together the evidences of Christianity, and reached the perilous conclusion that they were founded on sand." [57] He also says that they were in "confidential relations." [58] Both views are probably sound enough but as yet wholly beyond proof.

There are only two bits of evidence definitely linking Raleigh and Marlowe. One is the answer to the "Passionate Shepherd," attributed to Sir Walter. The other is the assertion, attributed to Cholmeley, "that Marloe tolde him that hee hath read the

---

[55] See I. 291–292.
[56] *New Letter of Notable Contents*, sig. D1, D2. In Grosart's Harvey, I. 289, 292.
[57] *Great Englishmen of the Sixteenth Century*, p. 135.
[58] Article "Ralegh," DNB, XVI. 635.

Atheist lecture to Sr Walter Raliegh & others." [59] Baines probably refers to this episode when he says that Marlowe "hath
quoted a number of Contrarieties oute of the Scripture which
he hath given to some great men who in Convenient time shalbe
named." [60] Unfortunately Baines never fulfilled this promise,
or if he did the document has been lost.

Confirming Cholmeley's assertion — according to the spy —
of Marlowe's association with Raleigh are three facts: first,
that Marlowe's associates, frequently named in the government
documents of the period, are usually the same as Raleigh's; second, that Raleigh was closely associated with Sir Francis
Walsingham, a relative of Marlowe's patron; [61] third, that the
general tenor of Raleigh's and Marlowe's theological questioning is about the same, although Raleigh seems to have been a
gravely philosophic thinker who ended as a believer, whereas
Marlowe's wild rant, even though exaggerated by its reporters,
appears to have been mainly intended to shock somebody,
and to have been based on complete, or almost complete,
skepticism.

As further evidence of a sort, it is interesting to note that Sir
Walter Raleigh also uses the odd and unusual word "contrarieties" in his book, *The Skeptic*. It is almost as if one friend
had picked up the other's word.[62]

Even Marlowe's enthusiasm for tobacco, on which the
Baines libel dwells so grotesquely, suggests Marlowe's relations
with Raleigh and with Harriot, the latter just back from Virginia as Marlowe came up to London from the university. The
habit of smoking was not at all common in England during
Marlowe's lifetime, though it became common enough soon
after his death. The first pipe had been brought back from
Virginia in 1586 and given to Raleigh. The Baines libel in 1593,
a scant seven years later, puts two allusions to tobacco in
Marlowe's mouth, though the *New English Dictionary* is able
to find only two allusions to the weed before 1597.

[59] Harleian MS. 6848, fol. 190.
[60] Harleian MS. 6848, fols. 185v–186. In the copy, Harleian MS. 6853, fols. 307–
308, this passage has been crossed out.
[61] Henry Stevens: *Thomas Hariot* (1900), pp. 36, 42, 54.
[62] Raleigh: *Works*, VIII. 554. The parallel was first detected by Miss M. C. Bradbrook: *School of Night*, pp. 17–18.

Our knowledge of Raleigh's circle and their discussions is based on the following documents:

1. *Advertisement written to a Secretarie of my L. Treasvrers of Ingland* [Cecil of Burghley] ... 1592. [A summary which apparently preceded no. 2 in England.]
2. *Responsio ad Elizabethae Reginae edictum contra Catholicos*, by the Jesuit, Robert Parsons or Persons. (1592, 1593.)[63]
3. The investigation at Cerne Abbas, undertaken by direction of the Court of High Commission.
4. Records of Raleigh's trial.

Giordano Bruno, during his visit to England in 1583–85, while Marlowe was at Cambridge, encouraged speculation of an atheistical nature. Bruno was for a time at Oxford and was received at court, where he made a marked impression. Sir Philip Sidney and Sir Fulke Greville were among the friends with whom he discussed "philosophical and metaphysical subjects of a nice and delicate nature." And, says his biographer, "the doors of the apartments in which they met were kept shut." [64]

Whether Marlowe, then a student, and Raleigh, then at court, were affected by Bruno's teaching, there is no means of knowing. But it seems probable that the Italian philosopher's visit helped produce a general atmosphere of religious speculation which both Marlowe and Raleigh found congenial. "There is little doubt," says Sir Sidney Lee, "that Ralegh, Harriot, and Marlowe, and some other personal friends, including Ralegh's brother Carew, were all in 1592 and 1593 members of a select coterie which frequently debated religious topics with perilous freedom." [65]

The group was probably the subject of gossip from the beginning; but the first known public allusion to it is in *An advertisement written to a Secretarie of my L. Treasvrers of Ingland, by an Inglishe Intelligencer ... Concerninge An other Booke ...* (1592). In this, the anonymous author, who is obviously the Jesuit, Robert Parsons, or Persons, complains

---

[63] This title does not exactly correspond with the unmanageably long form on the title page.

[64] Thomas Zouch: *Memoirs of Sir Philip Sidney* (2nd ed. 1809), pp. 339–340n.

[65] Article "Ralegh," DNB, XVI. 635.

Of Sir VValter Rauleys schoole of Atheisme by the waye, and of the Coniurer that is M. thereof [Harriot?], and of the diligence vsed to get young gentlemen to this schoole, where in both Moyses, and our Sauior; the olde and new Testamente are iested at, and the schollers taught amonge other thinges, to spell God backwarde.[66]

The "other booke" was Parsons' Latin *Responsio ad Elizabethae Reginae edictum contra Catholicos*, then in press, for which the *Advertisement* seems to have been merely advance publicity. In this work, which appeared in 1592 and ran through four editions by the end of 1593, the same charges are rehearsed at greater length:

43. Et certè si Gualteri quoque Raulæi schola frequens de Atheismo paulò longiùs processerit, (quam modò ita notam et publicam suis in ædibus habere dicitur. Astronomo quodam Nicromanceo praeceptore, vt iuuentutis nobilioris non exiguæ turmæ tam Moysis legem veterem, quàm nouam Christi Domini, ingeniosis quibusdam facetijs ac dicterijs eludere, ac in circulis suis irridere didicerint) si hæc inquam schola radices ac robur acceperit, & ipse Raulæus in Senatum delectus fuerit, quò Reip. quoque negotijs præsideat (quod omnes non sine summa ratione expectant, cùm primas apud Reginam post Dudlæum & Hattonum teneat, & ex gregario propè hyberniæ milite virum principem, ac potentem, Reginæ sola gratia, nullis præcedentibus meritis effectum videant) quid (inquam) erit expectandum aliud, nisi vt aliquando edictum aliquod à mago illo Epicuro Raulæi præceptore conscriptum, Reginæ nomine euulgatum cernamus, quo planè omnis diuinitas, omnis animæ immortalitas, & alterius vitæ expectatio, dilucidè, clarè, breuiter, & citrà ambages denegetur, & læsæ maiestatis accusentur tanquàm Reipub. perturbatores, qui contra istiusmodi doctrinam tam placidam, & carnalibus hominibus adeò suauem, scrupulos, cuiquam aut molestias moueant? [67]

Aubrey in his Lives [68] says of Raleigh: "He was scandalizd with atheisme; but he was a bold man, and would venture at discourse which was unpleasant to the church-men. I remem-

---

[66] Page 18. Copies in NYPL and BM. Cf. William Oldys: *Life of Sir Walter Ralegh* (1750), I. xxiv–xxv.

[67] Chap. 43, pp. 49–50, sig Dᴵ, recto and verso, of the Latin edition in the Pierpont Morgan Library; pp. 34–35 of the German edition of the same year in the same library. No other copies appear to be in the United States. The British Museum has several other editions. Father Parsons used various pseudonyms, including Andrea Philopater and Ihon Philopater. Cf. Sidney Lee, *op. cit.*, and J. M. Stone: "Atheism under Elizabeth and James I," *The Month*, 81:179 Je 1894.

[68] John Collier's ed., p. 38. Aubrey MS. 6, fol. 77v. John Aubrey: *Brief Lives* (ed. Andrew Clark, 1898), II. 188.

ber first Lord Scudamour sayd "twas basely sayd of Sir W. R., to talke of *the anagramme of Dog.*' "

By the following year, gossip seems to have become more open, and on March 21, 1593/4, ten months after Marlowe's death, an official investigation was undertaken at Cerne Abbas, near Sherborne, Dorset, where Raleigh was living. The special commission was specifically instructed to examine Sir Walter Raleigh, his older brother Carew, "Mr. Thynne of Wiltshire," and "one Heryott of Sir Walter Raleigh's house." [69]

"Mr. Thynne of Wiltshire" was undoubtedly John Thynne, of Longleat, Wilts. Carew Raleigh was for a time his "gentleman of the horse" and later married his widow.[70]

In the interrogatory which the commission was directed to employ, these were some of the questions:

1. Inprimis whome doe you knowe, or have harde to be susspected of Atheisme; or Apostacye? And in what manner doe you knowe or have harde the same? And what other notice can you geive therof?

2. Item whome doe you knowe, or have harde, that have argued, or spoken againste? or as doubtinge, the beinge of anye God? Or what or where God is? Or to sweare by god, addinge if there be a god, or such like; and when & where was the same? And what other notice can you geive of anye such offender?

3. Item whome doe you knowe or have harde that hath spoken against god his providence ouer the worlde? or of the worldes beginninge or endinge? or of predestinacon? or of heaven or of hell? or of the Resurreccon in doubtfull or contenciouse manner? when & where was the same? And what other notice can you geive of anye such offender?

4. Item whome doe you knowe or have harde that hath spoken againste the truth of god his holye worde revealed to vs in the scriptures of the oulde & newe testament? or of some places therof? or have sayde those scriptures ar not to be beleived & defended by her majestie for doctrine, & faith, and salvacon, but onlye of policye, or Civell gouernment, and when & where was the same? And what other notice can you geive of anye such offender? [71]

The questions were evidently drawn up by someone who had

---

[69] Harleian MS. 7042, fol. 401. See also DNB, XVI. 636.

[70] Aubrey MS. 6, fol. 47, also numbered 75. John Aubrey: *Brief Lives* (ed. Andrew Clark, 1898), II. 178. On the Thynne family, see *Athenae Oxonienses* (ed. Bliss, 1815), II. 107; *Handbook . . . Wilts, and Dorset* (London: Murray, 1899), col. 378; Beriah Bitfield: *Stemmata Botevilliana* (Westminster: J. B. Nichols, 1858), pp. clxxx and 59.

[71] Harleian MS. 6849, fol. 183. First printed in *The Month*, 81:179–180 Je 1894. For complete transcript see G. B. Harrison's ed. of *Willobie His Avisa.*

a pretty clear knowledge of the discussions of the Raleigh circle. Perhaps this was Sir Ralph Horsey, one of the investigators who had actually been present — and apparently very much horrified — at a discussion in the summer of 1593, just after Marlowe's death. Perhaps it was the Rev. Ralph Ironside, "Minister of Winterbourne," who had also been present, since some of the depositions are in his handwriting.[72]

The views inquired about are closely akin to those in other documents relating to Marlowe. The idea that man's soul is identical with that of a beast is very close to the opinion of Marlowe's alleged convert to atheism, Mr. Fineux, of Dover. The sixth question was obviously framed with exact knowledge of the answer that would have to be given. One witness testified from hearsay that Thomas Allen, Lieutenant of Portland Castle and one of Raleigh's retinue, "when he was like to dye, beinge perswaded to make himselfe reddye to God for his soule," replied blasphemously that "he would carrye his soule vp to the topp of an hill, and runne God, runne Devill, fetch it that will have it" — almost in the exact language of the interrogatory.

The testimony of Ralph Ironside, minister of Winterbourne, gives a fair idea of the discussions of the Raleigh circle: "Wednesdaye sevenight before the Assises summer Laste I came to Sr George Trenchardes in the afternone accompayned with a ffellowe minister, & frinde of myne Mr Whittle Viccar of fforthington. There were then with the Knight, Sr Walter Rawleigh, Sr Raulfe Horsey Mr Carewe Rawleigh Mr John ffitziames, &c."

The discussion which followed seems extremely bold when one considers that both Sir Ralph Horsey and Sir George Trenchard were deputy lieutenants of the county — the Privy Council having decided early in 1593 that "Sir Mathewe Arrundell and Sir Georg Trenchard, being themselves aged and subjecte to sickenes, should be holpen and assisted in the service by the addition of Sir Ralf Horsey."[73] Ironside and the two

---

[72] G. B. Harrison, *op. cit.*, p. 255.
[73] *Acts of the Privy Council* (ed. J. R. Dasent), XXIV. 40, 306. The Council is in fairly steady correspondence with Trenchard and Horsey. See pp. 345, 354–355, 395–396, and XXV. 23. On Trenchard's appointment, see *Cal. State Papers, Dom.*

deputy lieutenants were evidently gravely disapproving audi-
tors of a discussion thus described:

> Towardes the end of supper some loose speeches of Mʳ Carewe
> Rawleighes beinge gentlye reproved by Sʳ Raulfe Horsey in these
> wordes Colloquia prava corrumpunt bones [sic] mores. Mʳ Rawleigh
> demaundes of me, what daunger he might incurr by such speeches?
> whervnto I aunswered, the wages of sinn is death. and he makinge
> leight of death as beinge common to all sinner & reightuous; I inferred
> further, that as that liffe which is the gifte of god through Jesus
> Christ, is liffe eternall: soe that death which is properlye the wages of
> sinne, is death eternall, both of the bodye, and of the soule alsoe.
> Soule quoth Mʳ Carewe Rawleigh, what is that? better it were (sayed
> I) that we would be carefull howe the Soules might be saved, then to
> be curiouse in findinge out ther essence.⁷⁴

Sir Walter presently observed that "heithervnto in this
pointe (to witt what the reasonable soule of man is) have I
not by anye benne resolved." Ironside quoted Aristotle and
attempted an analogy from the nature of God, "Marrye quoth
Sʳ Walter these 2 be like for neither coulde I lerne heitherto
what god is." Yet at the close of this impious dialogue, Raleigh
"wished that grace might be sayed; for that quoth he is better
then this disputacon."

It is noteworthy that no witnesses charge the Raleigh circle
with immoral practices or impugn their loyalty to the Crown,
though Raleigh was at this time in disgrace at court because of
his marriage. Both he and his brother continued their philosophical interests after the investigation, and as late as 1603
Sir John Harington wrote of Sir Walter that "in religion he
hath shown in private talk great depth and good reading, as I
once experienced at his own house before many learned men." ⁷⁵
In June, 1594, Raleigh spent a whole night discussing religion
with the Jesuit, John Cornelius (1557–1594), then under arrest
at Wolverton.⁷⁶ Although accusations of atheism were renewed
at his trial, Raleigh seems to have died a believer.

Mr. F. S. Boas writes of the Raleigh circle: "Clearly the

Eliz. 1581–1590, p. 647. The original is dated February 8, 1590, and is in vol. CCXXX, no. 65, PRO.
⁷⁴ Harleian MS. 6849, fol. 185ᵥ. Transcribed by G. B. Harrison in Willobie His Avisa (Bodley Head Quartos, no. 15), pp. 265–266.
⁷⁵ Nugae Antiquae, II. 132, as quoted in DNB.
⁷⁶ DNB, XVI. 636; Henry Foley: Jesuits, III. 461–462.

scholars who gathered there, stirred by the Renaissance speculative impulse, were wont to prove all things — to test by
stringent dialectic the most sacred conceptions. The 'Atheist
lecture' read by Marlowe to Raleigh was thus probably a
closely reasoned discussion in scholastic form of first principles." [77] Marlowe was dead at the time of the Cerne Abbas
investigation, but the testimony suggests the kind of speculative discourse which he probably joined in his more serious and
less noisy skeptical moods.

Marlowe was also associated with the mathematician and
astronomer, Thomas Harriot (1560–1621), said to have been
called "that devil Harriot" at Raleigh's trial; with Walter
Warner (fl. 1600), also a mathematical scholar; and with
Matthew Roydon (fl. 1580–1622), a very minor poet. We know
this from Kyd's remark in his first note to Sir John Puckering [78]
that "Harriot, Warner, Royden, and some stationers in Paules
churchyard" were "such as he [Marlowe] conversed withall."

Probably Robert Hues, or Hughes (1553–1632), was also an
associate, since he, Harriot, and Warner were constantly in
company with Raleigh and his friend, the Earl of Northumberland. They are mentioned together by Aubrey, who says that
when Raleigh was imprisoned "the earle of Northumberland
was prisoner at the same time, who was patrone to Mr. . . .
Harriot and Mr. Warner, two of the best mathematicians then
in the world, as also Mr. Hues." [79]

Marlowe's association with Harriot would follow inevitably
from his association with Raleigh. Raleigh had engaged Harriot
as a mathematical tutor in 1580, had sent him to Virginia in
1585 with his other colonists (to be rescued by Sir Francis
Drake the following year), and had later introduced him to the
Earl of Northumberland, who gave him an annual pension of
three hundred pounds.

That Marlowe and Harriot were acquainted is at least suggested by two or three odd memoranda preserved among the
4,000 folios of Harriot's mathematical and other scientific papers, preserved in the British Museum. [80] These are for the most

[77] "New Light on Sir Walter Raleigh," *Literature*, 7: 113, 18 Ag 1900.
[78] Harleian MS. 6849, fol. 218.
[79] MS. Aubrey 6, fol. 77; John Aubrey: *Brief Lives* (ed. Andrew Clark, 1898), II. 188.
[80] Addit. MSS. 6782–6789.

part a wild mixture of tables, calculations, notes on reading, notes on fortification, notes on navigation, and plans for colonization. But Harriot had a curious habit of mingling personal notes with his scientific papers, and to this we owe three foolscap sheets that may refer to Marlowe. One is a shopping list in which Harriot includes "my garkin," pipes, tobacco, shoestrings, and "a horse for Kit." [81] Another is a strange note, at least partly mathematical:

In the plain sphere of Gemma Frisius which is called catholicke as the outmost quarter of the meridian is 90. the next is 89. & the next is 88 &c. so that that of 45 is is [sic] half of the outmost &c also of the parallelles. This Morly told me to consider what benefit followeth.[82]

"Morly," or "Marly" — it might be either in this hastily scrawled note — is, of course, a familiar variant of the name Marlowe. It is at least worth observing that Archbishop Parker's Library, at Corpus Christi, possessed an astronomical work by the Dutch scholar, Gemma Frisius, which might conceivably have interested the poet in him.[83]

A third folio contains some logarithms and a short list of names, including "Mr. Hues, Mr. Alisbury, Mr. Throperly, Mr. Marlo." [84]

At first sight, all these notes seem to refer to the dramatist. But Miss Ethel Seaton has pointed out [85] that Harriot had two servants whose first names were Christopher, to either of whom he would naturally refer as "Kit." The other two notes may well be references to Captain Edmund Marlowe, with whom Harriot was also acquainted. This is particularly probable in the last entry. Thomas Ailesbury did not take his B.A. until 1602 and can therefore hardly be associated with Christopher Marlowe.

Harriot was one of the most brilliant scientific minds England ever produced. He was the first surveyor of Virginia; he advanced algebra; he anticipated Descartes in analytic geometry; he applied the telescope to astronomy as early as Galileo; he

[81] Addit. MS. 6789, fol. 514r.
[82] Addit. MS. 6786, fol. 491r. The word "Frisius" looks as if Harriot had first begun to write "Parisius" and had corrected himself.
[83] Rough List of Parker Books, CCC, no. 180.
[84] Addit. MS. 6786, fol. 182.
[85] TLS, 36: 428, 5 Je 1937.

corresponded with Kepler on optics; and he was one of the first observers of comets and sunspots.[86]

His studies were naturally misunderstood and gave rise to rumors of atheism. Nashe presumably alludes to him in *Pierce Penniless* (1592), when he writes: "I heare say there be Mathematitions abroad that will prooue men before *Adam*." [87] In the Baines libel, Marlowe is accused of just this statement. He might easily have picked up this (in modern view) far from heterodox opinion directly from Harriot, whose manuscripts are filled with calculations of Biblical chronology.[88]

Anthony à Wood says of Harriot that "notwithstanding his great Skill in Mathematics, he had strange thoughts of the Scripture, and always undervalued the old Story of the Creation of the World, and could never believe that trite Position, *Ex nihilo nihil fit*. He made a *Philosophical Theology*, wherein he cast off the *Old Testament*, so that consequently the *New* would have no foundation." [89]

At the Cerne Abbas investigation, one Nicholas Jeffreys, parson of Weeke Regis, testified from hearsay that Harriot had been "convented before the Lordes of the Counsell for denyinge the resurreccon of the bodye." [90] Like Marlowe, Harriot was associated with Chapman, who calls the mathematician "my worthy and most learned friend, . . . whose iudgement and knowledge in all kinds I know to be incomparable and bottomlesse; yea, to be admired as much, as his most blameles life, and the right sacred expence of his time, is to be honoured and reuerenced." [91]

If he knew Harriot, as he certainly did, Marlowe would also know Walter Warner and Robert Hues,[92] who with Harriot

[86] Agnes Mary Clarke: article "Hariot, Thomas," in DNB, VIII. 1322–1323; D. E. Smith: *History of Mathematics*, I. 388–389, II. 322; H. Stevens: *Thomas Harriot and His Associates*, p. 75; John Aubrey: *Brief Lives* (ed. Andrew Clark, 1898), I. 284–287 and *passim*.

[87] McKerrow's Nashe, I. 172.

[88] Addit. MSS. 6782, fol. 31; 6788, fols. 508–510; 6789, fols. 474, 493.

[89] *Athenae Oxonienses* (ed. 1721), I. 460.

[90] Harleian MS. 6849, fol. 185. See G. B. Harrison's ed. of *Willobie His Avisa*, pp. 255–260.

[91] Preface to Chapman's Homer. See J. E. Spingarn: *Critical Essays of the Seventeenth Century*, I. 69–70.

[92] The documents say merely "Warner." Certain writers, including Sir Sidney Lee, have assumed this to be William Warner, the poet, but there is no evidence to link him with the Raleigh circle. The spelling "Hues" is used in the DNB.

were known as Northumberland's "three magi." Hues likewise was acquainted with Chapman, who calls him his "learned,
honest, and entirely loued friend." [93] All these men were under
suspicion of free thought, as was the poet, Matthew Roydon,[94]
who is supposed to have been the author of "An Elegie or
Friends Passion for his Astrophell" [Sir Philip Sidney], the
first piece in *The Phoenix Nest*, reprinted with Spenser's *Colin
Clout* in 1595.[95] He was intimate with Sidney, Spenser, Chapman, and Lodge. Nashe includes him in a list of "most able
men, to reuiue Poetrie," who were "extant about *London*." [96]

All were probably acquaintances of Marlowe's. Sidney, related to the Walsinghams by marriage, was a friend of Raleigh's.
Spenser's lines appear repeatedly in *Tamburlaine*. Chapman
finished *Hero and Leander*. Lodge was well known to all
literary London.

In addition to his other charges, Kyd asserted that Marlowe
and Roydon were disloyal to the Crown. At a time when any
relations with James VI of Scotland were almost equivalent to
treason, Kyd was writing to Sir John Puckering that Marlowe
"wold perswade with men of quallitie to goe vnto the K of
Scotts whether J heare Royden is gon and where if he [Marlowe]
had liud he told me when J sawe him last he meant to be." [97]
There is no further evidence for this charge.

Since no record is preserved, there is no way of telling the
outcome of the Cerne Abbas investigation. At least it indicates clearly the difficulties that beset Marlowe's friends about
this time and thus, presumably, the difficulties which led the
Privy Council to issue its warrant for his arrest by Henry
Maunder. Raleigh seems to have suffered little from the investigation, though his banishment from court continued; and
it is possible that Marlowe, had he lived, might likewise have
extricated himself.

He is supposed to have gone down to Thomas Walsingham's
country seat at Chislehurst, Kent, to escape the plague, which

[93] Spingarn, *loc. cit.*
[94] DNB, XVII. 374. Harleian MS. 7042, fol. 206.
[95] W. C. Hazlitt: *Collection and Notes* (first ser.), 1867–76, p. 367.
[96] "Epistle to the Gentlemen Readers," prefixed to *Menaphon.* Cf. Chambers,
Elizabethan Stage, IV. 235–236.
[97] Harleian MS. 6848, fol. 154.

had broken out in London. It was a natural refuge for a literary man of Kentish origin. Master Henry Maunder evidently had little difficulty in finding his man, for an entry in the *Acts of the Privy Council* dated May 20, 1593, two days after the order for Marlowe's arrest, records that:

This day *Christ*ofer Marley of London gent*leman*, being sent for by warrant from their L*ordshi*ps, hath entered his appearance accordinglie for his Jndemnity therein, and is commaunded to give his daily attendaunce on their L*ordshi*ps untill he shalbe lycensed to the contrary.[98]

With these tantalizing hints the whole affair vanishes from the records and Marlowe's name never reappears. Possibly this was because the charges against him, whatever they may have been, were never pushed but were quietly allowed to drop, as not infrequently happened. Indeed, it is not by any means certain that any action against Marlowe himself was ever contemplated. He may merely have been wanted as an essential witness.

The Council's summons was not necessarily a serious matter. Dr. William Coale, president of Corpus Christi, Oxford, for example, was required to appear on April 21, but seems to have been put to no further inconvenience. A certain Mrs. Anne Rolles, having been summoned before their lordships in a dispute over an estate, is excused on the simple ground that her brother "alledgeth that the said Mistres Rolles, his syster, was not well at ease, and thereby (thoughe she was in towne) not in case to repair hether, he did undertake that uppon her recovery she should as well attende uppon theire Lordships, as that [she] shuld not depart till leave were graunted unto her."[99]

Sir Thomas Walsingham's house, whither the Queen's messenger was directed, still stands at Scadbury, Chislehurst. Richard Harvey, author of *The Lamb of God* (1590) and brother of the malignant rhetorician, Gabriel Harvey, was then rector of Chislehurst.[100] Of him, according to Nashe, "*Kit Marloe* was wont to say that he was an asse, good for nothing but to

---

[98] The original is in PRO, P.C. 2/20. See *Acts of the Privy Council* (ed. J. R. Dasent), XXIV. 244. Cf. the case of Thomas Lodge, June 27, 1581 (Dasent, *op. cit.*).

[99] *Acts of the Privy Council* (ed. J. R. Dasent), XXIV. 118. See also pp. 128, 137, 144, 277.

[100] Thomas Nashe: *Have With You to Saffron-Walden*; McKerrow's Nashe, III. 85.

preach of the Iron Age."[101] However discourteous Marlowe's judgment of this unfortunate clergyman may have been, it is at least supported by Robert Greene, an author who certainly would not go out of his way to confirm Marlowe's opinions. In a suppressed[102] passage of his *Quip for an Upstart Courtier* (1592), Greene remarks: "The one sir [Richard Harvey] is a Deuine to comfort my soule; & he indeed though he be a vaine glorious asse, as diuers of his age bee, is well giuen to the shew of the world."

Gabriel Harvey's hatred of Marlowe is shown clearly enough in his comment on Marlowe's death[103] and in various passages whose venom attracted comment even in that age of bitter pamphleteering. Nashe observes of Harvey: "How he hath handled *Greene* and *Marloe* since their deaths, those that read his Bookes may iudge."[104]

Marlowe's friends seem to have shared his quarrel with the Harveys, for Nashe records with evident relish the verses which Thomas Watson wrote of the elder brother:

But, o, what newes of that good *Gabriell Haruey*,
Knowne to the world for a foole and clapt in the Fleet for a Rimer?[105]

The point here is that Marlowe's arrest, which must have taken place at Scadbury, was so quietly managed that no least hint of it ever reached the eager ears of the Harveys. Gabriel Harvey, at least, would have rejoiced at the chance to use the news to Marlowe's hurt — perhaps because he resented his bitter tongue, perhaps because he held him partly responsible for attacks by Nashe and Watson.

All this mass of evidence as to Marlowe's unorthodoxy is no doubt rather confused and sometimes contradictory, but it is possible to elicit from it pretty clear general ideas of Marlowe's

---

[101] Nashe, *op. cit.*, McKerrow's Nashe, III. 85; *Athenae Oxonienses* (ed. 1691), I. 174; (ed. 1721), I. 217; (ed. 1815), II. 500.

[102] The passage appears only in the Bridgewater copy, now in the Huntington Library. Cf. *Papers of the Bibliographical Society of America*, XIV. 7-8, pt. I.

[103] See I. 143.

[104] *Op. cit.*, McKerrow's Nashe, III. 132.

[105] *Op. cit.*, McKerrow's Nashe, III. 127. Cf. I. 300 and G. Gregory Smith: *Elizabethan Critical Essays*, II. 241. The verses are here attributed to "Maister *Butler* of Cambridge."

religious beliefs. Plainly he is not an orthodox and unquestioning Protestant. He questions Trinitarianism, doubts the historical accuracy of Holy Writ, prefers Catholicism to Protestantism, and dabbles in unitarian views. He enjoys theological speculation and takes an interest in the early stages of the "conflict between science and religion," probably as a result of discussions with his friends Harriot and Warner. He is a part of the Raleigh circle, where — as the Cerne Abbas testimony shows — religious views were subject to cold philosophical scrutiny which, to the average mind of that day or this, would have seemed flatly atheistic.

There is, however, no clear evidence to show that Marlowe was an atheist in the technical, theological meaning of the term — that is, one who denies the existence of a deity of any kind. Perhaps he was. Some of his recorded utterances obviously point that way. But many of them also indicate an impish delight in shocking, a tendency to talk for the talk's effect on unctuously pious listeners. That leaves one doubtful of the talker's sincere opinions.

One thinks of the horror of the last scene in *Doctor Faustus*, the intensely felt poetry of that frantic wretch's appeals to God for mercy, and it is hard to regard them merely as an author's devices to end a play with a climax. True, the best poetry is the most feigning, especially dramatic poetry; but true also that Marlowe is the least adept of dramatists in concealing himself. All his characters are Marlowe, as all Shaw's characters are Shaw.

Surely in that last scene of *Faustus*, the finest that Marlowe ever wrote, there lingers at least an echo of the boyish faith of a meditative lad, wondering and growing up in the dim, religious atmosphere of ancient Canterbury, the first foothold of Christianity on English soil, the chief center of the Faith in England.

CHAPTER VI

MARLOWE'S DEATH

And on his grave, though there no stone may stand,
The flower it shows was laid by Shakespeare's hand.
SWINBURNE: *Prologue to Doctor Faustus*

IT MAY BE that the real reason why arrest was not followed by prosecution lies in no leniency of the Privy Council, but in Marlowe's sudden death, which followed hard upon the Council's summons. Compelled to remain within call of the Privy Council, Marlowe naturally sought to leave plague-stricken London and yet to find a residence close at hand. His bond required him to be near enough to the capital "to give his daily attendaunce on their Lordships," and as a man of the theatre he could not afford to go very far in any case. London was still the center for actors and playwrights, who, though they wandered in the provinces in time of plague, regarded the capital as their base, whether the theatres were open or not. Chislehurst was doubtless open to him, but it was too far away, and it is not hard to understand his reluctance to return to his patron's country seat, whence he had probably been taken under arrest only two days before.

He could not take refuge in Canterbury, either, for the plague was raging there as well as in London. The Canterbury accounts show the danger in two eloquent entries: "Gave to Goodman Eccles for watching at Anthony Howe's Door in the Morning after the Watch was broken up when his House was first infected with the plague. 2^d. Abel Payne for watching at several other Doors on the like cause." [1]

Marlowe may have turned to Anthony Marlowe, wealthy merchant of Deptford, supposed to have been his kinsman, representative of the Muscovy Company and contractor to the Admiralty, whose influence with the government would have

[1] Bunce MSS., I. 127.

been useful.[2] A draper named Thomas Morley had owned a house actually in Deptford Strand, though he was living in London when he died in 1566.[3] A certain James Morley lived in East Smithfield but describes himself as of Greenwich.[4]

In any case, Deptford was a natural place to go, far enough from the London of those days to escape the plague, yet close enough for easy return, and very much in the public eye at the moment. Sir Francis Drake's vessel, the *Golden Hind*, in which that intrepid if somewhat piratical explorer had circumnavigated the globe, was at this time lying off the town. People came from far and near to see it. The Queen herself was magnificently entertained aboard and, ever susceptible to flattery or good cheer, knighted Drake before departing — not altogether to the pleasure of some of her subjects. The *Golden Hind* now became more popular than ever as a pleasure resort, and so numerous were the visitors that her cabin was made over into a refreshment saloon.

"Wee'll haue our prouided Supper brought a bord Sir *Francis Drakes* Ship, that hath compast the world:" exclaims Sir Petronel Flash in *Eastward Hoe*, "where with full Cupps, and Banquets we will doe sacrifice for a prosperous voyage." [5]

To Deptford, then, went Marlowe; and there in a brawl he fell. The poet's career ends with a single mournful note in the Burial Register of the Church of St. Nicholas, Deptford.

Contemporary accounts of Marlowe's death, several of which appeared in the next few years, correspond with tradition (partly because tradition is based on them); but they are unsatisfactory and untrustworthy sources because they are all either written by hostile writers or borrowed from hostile writers.[6] The "moral" lessons to be drawn from the tragic end

[2] *Cal. State Papers, Foreign,* 1584–1585, p. 132; *Dom. Eliz.,* 1591–1594, p. 396.

[3] London Inq. P.M. Brit. Rec. Soc., II. 65–66; PCC Wills, 6 Stonarde; de Kalb 24; Burial Reg. of St. Olave, Hart St., London. Harl. Soc. Pub. See also Hasted's *Kent* (1886), pt. I, p. 8; Dew's *Hist. of Deptford.*

[4] PCC Wills, 72 Harrington; de Kalb 25. He died 1592.

[5] Ll. 1639–1642 of the edition by Dr. Julia Hamlet Harris (1926). (Yale Studies in English, LXXIII.)

[6] Aubrey MS. 6, fol. 118, now at the Bodleian, contains on its upper left margin a late note about Marlowe's death. This is an error due to confusion with Ben Jonson's killing of Gabriel Spencer: "He [Jonson] killed Mʳ . . . Marlow yᵉ Poet on Bunhill, comeing from the Green-curtain playhouse — from Sʳ Ed. Shirburn." See C. H. Herford and Percy Simpson: *Ben Jonson,* I. 178n.

of the irreligious playwright were too tempting for the Puritan
divines and Marlowe's other enemies to miss; but in their eagerness to point out the awful warning conveyed by his death, they
played fast and loose with such facts as were known, besides
contradicting each other.

In that unintelligible farrago, the *New Letter of Notable Contents* (1593), Gabriel Harvey makes unseemly haste to gloat
over his foe's death — less than three months after the assassination, since the book was finished by September, 1593, and must
have been written during the summer months. Harvey is too
hurried to make sure of his facts and — having apparently
heard no news except that Marlowe was dead, and having there-
upon jumped to the agreeable conclusion that he was a victim
of the plague — scribbles only a cryptic poem which contains
the line:

Weepe Powles, thy Tamberlaine *voutsafes to dye.*[7]

Obscure though it is, this unquestionably alludes to Marlowe,
for it names his most famous play and also St. Paul's Cathedral,
one of his haunts, as we know from Kyd's letter to Sir John
Puckering, which refers to "some stationers in Paules churchyard" as being "such as he conversd withall." [8] Harvey had
actually been in London for nearly a year, engaged upon some
legal business, at the time of Marlowe's death.[9]

With the publication in 1597 of Thomas Beard's *Theatre of
Gods Iudgements*,[10] the Puritan pack is off in full cry. Beard —
Oliver Cromwell's schoolmaster and later his fellow justice of
the peace — was a clergyman noted for the Puritan zeal with
which, according to a contemporary, he "painfully preached the
word of God." He was deliberately writing to discredit the
Papacy, the stage, and all anti-Puritans. Such religious leanings as Marlowe had were very likely Roman — certainly he

[7] Grosart's Harvey, I. 295.
[8] Harleian MS. 6849, fol. 218. Cf. Brooke: *Life*, p. 105.
[9] McKerrow's Nashe, V. 80–81.
[10] Thomas Beard, D.D., was educated at Cambridge and became rector of Hengrave,
Suffolk, on January 21, 1597/8. He was later master of Huntington Hospital and
Grammar School and was prebendary of Lincoln, 1612–32. He is said to have flogged
Cromwell. Cf. DNB, II. 15; Benjamin Brook: *Lives of the Puritans*, II. 396; Carlyle's
Cromwell, VII. 67 of the *Works* (New York, 1897); and Hunter's *Chorus Vatum*.

was no Puritan. He was a scoffer, a poet, a playwright, very possibly an actor, and as such fair game for the parson.

The Theatre of Gods Iudgements is simply a collection of horrific examples, largely translated from the French, with about three hundred additional instances gathered up, hit or miss, from books uncritically scanned or from simple hearsay. Beard recounts the incredible iniquities — including atheistic opinions — of sundry popes, and describes the deathbed of Rabelais much as one of his modern congeners might describe that other revivalistic classic, the deathbed of Voltaire. For such an author, Marlowe's murder — somewhat embroidered after four years of bandying from mouth to mouth — fell admirably into place among the moral tales of poets whose folly in writing verses had led them to bad ends.

The book was popular enough to run through four editions, the last as late as 1648,[11] for Beard had at least the saving merit of a feeling for the picturesque, though he was quite untroubled by any scrupulousness as to fact. He thus describes the poet's death:

Not inferiour to any of the former in Atheisme & impiety, and equall to all in maner of punishment was one of our own nation, of fresh and late memory, called *Marlin*, by profession a scholler, brought vp from his youth in the Vniuersitie of Cambridge, but by practise a play-maker, and a Poet of scurrilitie, who by giuing too large a swinge to his owne wit, and suffering his lust to haue the full raines, fell (not without iust desert) to that outrage and extremitie, that hee denied God and his sonne Christ, and not only in word blasphemed the trinitie, but also (as it is credibly reported) wrote bookes against it, affirming our Sauiour to be but a deceiuer, and *Moses* to be but a coniurer and seducer of the people, and the holy Bible to be but vaine and idle stories, and all religion but a deuice of pollicie. But see what a hooke the Lord put in the nosthrils of this barking dogge:[12] It so fell out, that in London streets as he purposed to stab one whome hee ought a grudge vnto with his dagger, the other party perceiuing so auoided the stroke, that withall catching hold of his wrest, he stabbed his owne dagger into his owne head, in such sort, that notwithstanding all the meanes of surgerie that could be wrought, hee shortly after died thereof. The manner of his death being so terrible (for hee euen cursed and blasphemed to his last gaspe, and togither with his breath

[11] STC, 1659–61. The last ed. lies outside the period of the STC.
[12] It is interesting to find the same epithet applied to the American atheist, Robert Green Ingersoll. See *American Mercury*, 3: 109 S 1924.

an oth flew out of his mouth) that it was not only a manifest signe of Gods iudgement, but also an horrible and fearefull terrour to all that beheld him. But herein did the iustice of God most notably appeare, in that hee compelled his owne hand which had written those blasphemies to be the instrument to punish him, and that in his braine, which had deuised the same. I would to God (and I pray it from my heart) that all Atheists in this realme, and in all the world beside, would by the remembrance and consideration of this example, either forsake their horrible impietie, or that they might in like manner come to destruction: and so that abominable sinne which so flourisheth amongst men of greatest name, might either be quite extinguished and rooted out, or at least smothered and kept vnder, that it durst not shew it[s] head any more in the worlds eye.[13]

Since Marlowe had been killed in Deptford, Beard's phrase "in London streets" was a puzzle until Dr. John Leslie Hotson showed, in 1925, that there was a thoroughfare called London Street in Greenwich, which adjoins Deptford not far from the scene of Marlowe's death.[14] This is probably what led Beard astray, though he may also have been confused by the previous duel with Bradley,[15] which really was a London street brawl. The second edition of his book drops the words, probably because Beard had discovered his own mistake.

In 1618 Edmund Rudierd, in his *Thunderbolt of Gods Wrath* — which, as the author admits on his title page, follows but abridges *The Theatre of Gods Iudgements* — reproduces Beard's story, even to the phrase "in London streets," now transformed to "a streete in London." Rudierd writes:

We read of one *Marlin*, a *Cambridge* Scholler, who was a Poet, and a filthy Play-maker, this wretch accounted that meeke seruant of God *Moses* to be but a Coniurer, and our sweete Sauiour but a seducer and deceiuer of the people. But harken yee braine-sicke and prophane Poets, and Players, that bewitch idle eares with foolish vanities: what fell vpon this prophane wretch, hauing a quarrell against one whom he met in a streete in London, and would haue stabd him: But the partie perceiuing his villainy preuented him with catching his hand, and turning his owne dagger into his braines, and so blaspheming and cursing, he yeelded vp his stinking breath: marke this yee Players, that liue by making fooles laugh at sinne and wickednesse.[16]

---

[13] Ed. of 1597, pp. 147-148, BM copy. The misprint "remembranee" has been silently corrected.
[14] *Death of Christopher Marlowe*, p. 39.
[15] See I. 98 ff.
[16] Chap. XXII, p. 29. Copies at BM, Bodleian, University Library, Cambridge.

Essentially the same story is told by another divine, Samuel Clark, or Clarke, (1599–1683), minister of St. Bennet Fink, London, in his *Mirrour, or Looking-Glaſs both for Saints and Sinners*, which appeared in March of 1645/6 and in later editions of 1654, 1657, and 1671. Clarke, who was the author of a *Life of Tamerlane the Great* which may have given him a special interest in Marlowe, devotes the ninth chapter of his first volume to "Examples of Gods judgments upon Atheiſts," and (openly acknowledging Beard as his source) describes Marlowe's death as follows:

There was in our own Nation, one *Marlin*, somtimes a Student in the University of Cambridg, but afterwards a maker of Stage-Playes, and a notorious Atheist, denying God, and his Son Christ, and not only in word blasphemed the Holy Trinity, but also wrote books against it, affirming our Saviour to be a deceiver, and *Moses* to be a Conjurer, and a Seducer of the people, and the Sacred Scriptures to be vain and idle stories, and all Religion but a Politick device: But God suffered not such prophanenesse to go long unpunished; for this man upon a quarrel intending to have stabbed another, the other party perceiving it, to avoid the stroke, caught hold on his wrist, and forced him to stab his own dagger into his head, which wound could not be cured by Surgery, so that he lay cursing, swearing, and blaspheming, and together with an oath breathed forth his accursed soul: Gods justice notably appearing, in that his own hand that had written those Blasphemies, was an instrument to wound his head that had devised them. *Beards Theat.*[17]

Beard's influence, which is plain enough in all these accounts, is also perpetuated by one "R. B." — believed to be either Richard or Robert Burton — in his *Wonderful Prodigies*, published in 1682 and again in 1762. This quotes Beard at length in a section treating of "Judgements on Athiests" [*sic*].[18]

Other accounts of the murder seem to owe less to Beard. William Vaughan, in his *Golden Grove*, gives the murderer's name as "one Ingram," a chance remark which provided the clue by which Dr. John Leslie Hotson eventually cleared up the mystery surrounding Marlowe's death. One or two turns

---

[17] Vol. I, pp. 41–42, of the 1671 ed. Copies exist in NYPL and LC. On Clarke himself, see Leslie Stephen's article in DNB, X. 441–442. The British Museum has all editions.

[18] BM copy, pp. 2–3 (1682), quotes Beard with credit. Tentative identification of the author is from the BM catalogue. Authorship has also been assigned to a certain Nathaniel Crouch.

of Vaughan's phraseology suggest that he is drawing facts from
Beard, but he does not confine himself to a mere repetition.
As he introduces two new and correct details when he gives the
Christian name of the murderer and the place of the murder,
he may be an independent witness. The story, as Vaughan tells
it, runs as follows:

> Not inferiour to these was one Christopher Marlow by profession
> a play-maker, who, as it is reported, about 7. yeeres a-goe wrote a
> booke against the Trinitie: but see the effects of Gods iustice; it so
> hapned, that at Detford, a litle village about three miles distant
> from London, as he meant to stab with his ponyard one named
> Ingram, that had inuited him thither to a feast, and was then playing
> at tables, he quickly perceyuing it, so auoyded the thrust, that withall
> drawing out his dagger for his defence, hee stabd this Marlow into the
> eye, in such sort, that his braines comming out at the daggers point,
> hee shortlie after dyed.[19]

For many years this passage and the fact of Marlowe's burial
at Deptford were the only reasons for supposing him to have
been killed there.

Various other allusions, or possible allusions, to the murder
exist. The anonymous author of *The Returne from Pernassus*
— published in 1601 but probably written not long after Marlowe's death and produced at St. John's College, Cambridge [20]
— so evidently manifests dislike for the whole school of University Wits that it is not surprising to find him echoing the
Puritan view of Marlowe:

> *Marlowe* was happy in his buskine muse,
> Alas vnhappy in his life and end,
> Pitty it is, that wit so ill should dwell
> Wit lent from heauen, but vices sent from hell.[21]

Edward Phillips, in his *Theatrum Poetarum* (licensed 1674),
contents himself with the statement that Marlowe "in some
riotous Fray came to an untimely and violent End." [22]
In his *Wit's Treasury* (1598) Francis Meres had added to

[19] Editions of 1600 and 1608, sigs. C4v and C5 respectively. There is a copy of the
1600 ed. in the Huntington Library.
[20] See title page of the BM copy.
[21] Arber's reprint (English Scholar's Library, no. 6), pp. 12–13.
[22] In "Modern Poets" section, p. 25. The arrangement is alphabetical by first
names.

Beard's account a salacious detail of his own which, though without the slightest foundation in fact, was destined to have a life of over three centuries. Meres wrote:

> As Iodelle, a French tragical poet, beeing an epicure and an atheist, made a pitifull end: so our tragicall poet Marlow for his Epicurisme and Atheisme had a tragical death. You may read of this Marlow more at large in the *Theatre of God's judgments.* . . .
> As the poet Lycophron was shot to death by a certain riual of his: so Christopher Marlow was stabd to death by a bawdy Servingman, a riual of his in his lewde loue.[23]

In the light of subsequent discoveries, it is clear that Meres was inventing the "lewde loue" in order to perfect his comparison to Lycophron, who according to Ovid [24] was killed while on the stage, by a rival lover. The failure of the Puritan divines to lay hold on so edifying a morsel of scandal is sufficient reason for doubting Meres. He had, however, started a story that other writers were quick to take up. John Lane may be referring to it in *Tom Tel-troth's Message* (1600), though Marlowe is not named and the place of the murder is given as Smithfield:

> Wrath is the cause that men in Smith-field meete,
> (Which may be called smite-field properly)
> Wrath is the cause that maketh euery streete
> A shambles, and a bloodie butcherie,
> > Where roysting ruffins quarrell for their drabs,
> > And for sleight causes one the other stabs.[25]

John Earle's *Micro-Cosmographie* (1628) may also be describing Marlowe's death:

Sitting in a Baudy-house, hee writes Gods Iudgements. Hee ends at last in some obscure painted Cloth, to which himselfe made the Verses, and his life like a Canne too full spils vpon the bench. He leaues twenty shillings on the score, which my Hostesse looses.[26]

Both these passages, however, are probably mere descriptions of the brawls common in Elizabethan London. They are chiefly valuable as showing that the quarrels in which Marlowe en-

---

[23] G. Gregory Smith: *Elizabethan Critical Essays*, II. 324.
[24] *Ibis*, ll. 531–532.
[25] Quotation verified from the Huntington copy. The book is STC 15190. Cf. Collier: *Bibliographical Decameron*, I. 448; F. J. F[urnivall], N&Q, 5th ser., 3:224 20 Mr 1875.
[26] Character 24 in Arber's reprint. The text here corresponds to that in the first of the three 1628 editions, a copy of which is in the Folger Library.

gaged were not especially remarkable. Four years prior to Marlowe's death, Thomas Nashe — perhaps with an eye on the Bradley killing — had written of "dagger drunkennesse" and of

> ... the blacke pot; which makes our Poets vndermeale Muses so mutinous, as euerie stanzo they pen after dinner is full poynted with a stabbe.[27]

In 1691 Anthony à Wood revives the story of Marlowe and his erring lady in the *Athenae Oxonienses*:

> But in the end, so it was, that this *Marlo* giving too large a swing to his own wit, and suffering his lust to have the full reins, fell to outrage and extremity, as *Jodelle* a French tragicall Poet did, (being an Epicure and an Atheist,) that he denied God and his Son Christ, and not only in word blasphemed the *Trinity*, but also (as 'twas credibly reported) wrote divers discourses against it, affirming our *Saviour* to be a deceiuer, and Moses to be a conjurer: the holy Bible also to contain only vain and idle stories, and all religion but a device of policy. But see the end of this person, which was noted by all, especially the Precisian[s]. For so it fell out, that he being deeply in love with a certain Woman, had for his rival a bawdy serving man, one rather fit to be a Pimp, than an ingenious *Amoretto* as *Marlo* conceived himself to be. Whereupon *Marlo* taking it to be a high affront, rush'd in upon, to stab, him, with his dagger: But the serving man being very quick, so avoided the stroke, that with all catching hold of *Marlo*'s wrist, he stab'd his own dagger into his own head, in such sort, that notwithstanding all the means of surgery that could be wrought, he shortly after died of his wound, before the year 1593.[28]

It will be noted that some of this is very like the language of the Baines libel, and of Beard.

Meres's original slander has had a life of three centuries, being quoted by one "authority" after another and making an appearance in print as late as 1938.[29] A whole series of indus-

---

[27] "To the Gentlemen Students," prefixed to Greene's *Menaphon* (1589). Grosart's Greene, VI. 23.

[28] *Athenae Oxonienses* (ed. 1691), I. 288–289; (ed. 1721), p. 218; (ed. 1815), II. 9.

[29] The erring lady, for whose existence there has never been the slightest shred of real evidence, simply will not die. The story of Marlowe's illicit love affair is rehearsed with entertaining new additions and the wrong date in *The British Theatre* by William Rufus Chetwode, or Chetwood. His version runs: "Having an intrigue with a loose woman, he came unexpectedly into her Chamber, and caught her in the Embraces of another Gallant. This so much enraged him, that he drew his Dagger and attempted to Stab him; but in the Struggle, the Paramour seized Marlow, turnd the Point into his Head, and killed him on the spot in 1592" (p. 8). J. P. Kemble noted in his copy of

trious chroniclers of the English stage, without producing any new facts and — to tell the truth — without any very critical weighing of the old ones, have gone placidly on echoing these Puritan attacks adown the years. The accepted opinion of Marlowe as a man has therefore been based chiefly on the things that his enemies, the Puritan foes of the stage, wrote about him. These statements his too credulous biographers — with the exception of John H. Ingram, who o'erleaps himself and falls on the other side of idolatry — have generally accepted.

There was always a strong temptation to credit the Puritans because they were so definite in their charges and so picturesque in stating them; whereas the quite different picture of the dramatist which can be drawn from the casual but usually friendly references of his contemporaries in literary and theatrical London is less arresting. From them we get the same picture of brilliant and impassioned youth that is so clearly implicit in the plays and poems. Though it is dangerous to seek anything save the most general outlines of a dramatist's opinions and personality in his work — since the best dramatist is he who most entirely veils himself in the characters he creates — such a general impression is at least no bad confirmation of the verdict of his fellows. Marlowe's fellows in the Elizabethan theatre usually describe for us a winning, talented, impetuous youth.

The Theatrical Intelligencer (1788), now preserved in the Folger Shakespeare Library, that Marlowe "died about 1592 of a wound received in a brothel from his own sword being forced upon him," and referred to Warton's *History of English Poetry.*

Collier repeats the story in the *Poetical Decameron* (I. 128) in 1820. David Erskine Baker echoes Anthony à Wood in 1764 and again in 1782. (*Companion to the Playhouse,* ed. 1764, sig. X2*r*; ed. 1782, I. 301.)

The lady reappears in Taine's *History of English Literature* (Edinburgh, 1872, I. 238) as a "drab"; in the work of the Brothers Didot as "une fille de basse condition" (*Nouvelle Biographie Générale,* XXXIII. 860–863); and as "a low girl" in the third edition of the *Britannica* (1797, X. 576). She becomes a "Soldatendirne" for no particular reason in Iwan Bloch's *Englische Sittengeschichte* in 1912 (II. 10) and makes another appearance — final, I once hoped — in 1917 in a modern article on "Marlowe and the Heavy Wrath of God" (F. Paul in *American Catholic Quarterly Review,* 42: 584–588 O 1917).

This last author still adheres to the notion that Marlowe's death was due to "a clandestine love affair of an illicit nature," and avers that he died "stabbed amid a swarm of outcast knaves . . . in a quarrel over a disreputable wench." He adds that "the evils of Marlowe's chief characters were also Marlowe's own, and he, like these characters, fell to be plagued in hell."

The legend lingers on to 1938, when Mr. Oliver St. John Gogarty, in *I Follow Saint Patrick,* p. 32, without a shadow of evidence, refers to Dame Eleanor Bull's tavern as "half brothel, half public house."

The Puritans' plainly prejudiced and contradictory accounts were the sole authorities for the circumstances of Marlowe's death until 1925, when Dr. John Leslie Hotson published his sensational discovery of the original official copies of the coroner's investigation and the pardon granted to Ingram Friser, who stabbed Marlowe to death.

It is too much to say that this remarkable find made the circumstances of Marlowe's death absolutely clear. There is some doubt as to the complete truthfulness of the documents, and they are at best open to several interpretations. Nevertheless, there is no possible doubt that we have here, officially stated, the main facts of Marlowe's death — the exact time and place, the events which led up to it, and the circumstances of the killing, which, though perhaps colored in Friser's favor, are certainly correct in most particulars and never in the least contradict what we know of Marlowe's life and associates.

Marlowe's death had been a puzzle for a little over a century, largely because of an initial mistake in the burial register in the Church of St. Nicholas, Deptford, plus subsequent persistent misreading. In 1820 the literary antiquary, James Broughton, after studying Vaughan's account of Marlowe's death, wrote the vicar of St. Nicholas, inquiring whether there was a record of Marlowe's burial — a practical step which earlier investigators had omitted. He received the following reply:

In the Register of Burials at the Church of St. Nicholas, Deptford appears the following: — 1st. June, 1593. Christopher Marlowe, slain by Francis Archer.[30]

The vicar of St. Nicholas must not be too greatly blamed for his error. Although Dr. Hotson describes the entry as made in "a very plain Elizabethan hand," it is certainly obscure to the paleographically inexpert eye.[31] The "ff" which does duty for a capital in Friser's name looks marvelously like a capital "A," though no more so than the "ff" in "ffrancis," which the vicar read almost correctly. The effect of the clergy-

[30] First published in Thomas Kenrick's *British Stage and Literary Cabinet*, 5: 23 Ja 1821. It is signed "Dangle, Jun.," probably a pseudonym of Broughton himself. Cf. Hotson: *Death of Christopher Marlowe*, p. 17; Brooke: *Life*, p. 77; *Gentleman's Magazine*, (OS) 100 (NS) 23: 6 Ja 1830.
[31] Hotson, *op. cit.*, p. 21.

man's blunder, however, was to set scholars searching after a nonexistent Francis Archer all through the next century.

John H. Ingram, writing the first full-length biography of Marlowe, copied the vicar's errors and added a few of his own. He read the entry:

Christopher Marlowe, slain by ffrancis Archer, sepultus I. of June.[32]

The correct reading, in which Hotson, Brooke, and Boas concur, and which the adjoining facsimile confirms, is:

Christopher Marlow slaine by ffrancis ffrezer; the · 1 · of June.[33]

Correct reading of the burial entry by no means solves the puzzle, however, since it merely substitutes for a nonexistent Francis Archer an almost equally mythical Francis Frezer. Strange to say, there really were two Francis Frisers, though there is ample documentary evidence to show that neither could have had anything to do with the murder.[34]

In fact, the correct reading of the name did not have to wait for Dr. Hotson.[35] Sir Sidney Lee says, in his *Dictionary of National Biography* article on Marlowe, that Halliwell-Phillips read the name "Frezer." The Rev. W. Chandler, another of those Deptford clergymen who began with an erroneous reading in the sixteenth century and have persisted in misreading ever since, gave the name as "Frazer," after examining the record for W. G. Zeigler.[36] Sir Sidney Lee hesitated to decide between the two names.

In *The Golden Grove*, however, Vaughan, the only contem-

---

[32] *Christopher Marlowe and His Associates*, Plate XXVI, facing p. 245.

[33] Hotson, *op. cit.*, p. 21; Brooke: *Life*, p. 77; Boas: *Marlowe and His Circle*, p. 99.

[34] The will of Francis Fawconer, of Kingsclere, Hants, proved May 21, 1663, mentions "Francis Friser, of Kingscleare, the elder." (P.C.C. Wills, 60 Juxon; H. F. Waters: *Genealogical Gleanings in England*, I. 98.) The marriage of "Frauncis Friser" to John Paull at St. Dionis Backchurch, London, was discovered by Miss de Kalb. The bride is said to have come from Eltham, Essex, but since there is no such village in that county, she may possibly be a relative of the Friser family of Eltham, Kent. (*Reiester Booke of Saynte De'nis Back church*, Harleian Society Publications, *Registers*, III. 18; de Kalb, *op. cit.*, p. 67.)

[35] Correct reading of the name and the later identification of Ingram Friser as the murderer has by no means laid the ghost of Francis Archer-Friser. He continues to appear in the writings of authors who have had every opportunity to learn better. See "Old Fag" in *John O'London's Weekly*, 35: 874, 19 S 1936; George Rylands: *Elizabethan Tragedy* (1933), p. 3; Burton Rascoe: *Titans of Literature* (1932), p. 268. The latter shows clearly that he has read Dr. Hotson, but continues in the old blunder.

[36] W. G. Zeigler: *It Was Marlowe*, p. 300.

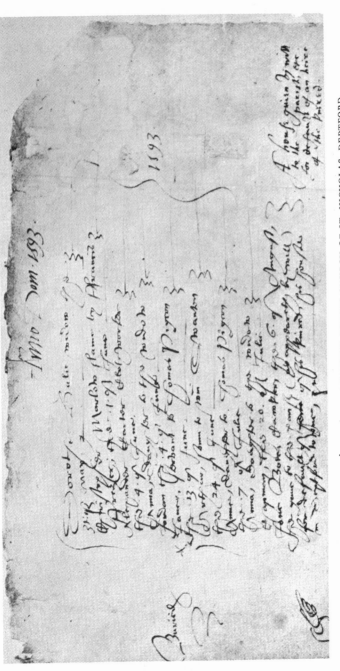

RECORD OF MARLOWE'S BURIAL.   REGISTER OF THE CHURCH OF ST. NICHOLAS, DEPTFORD
(Third line from top)

porary who actually named the murderer, had unwittingly provided a clue. He described him as "one named Ingram," using the Christian name only, as Elizabethans often did. In the Hotson documents, for example, Friser is called "the said Ingram," and Marlowe "the said Christopher." Gabriel Spencer, killed by Ben Jonson, is elsewhere described merely as "one Gabriel,"[37] and Archbishop Parker is described as "predictus Mattheus" in the history of Corpus Christi written by his own direction.[38] Scholars, however, regarded Ingram as a surname, and were all the more puzzled by the discrepancy in names shown by comparison with the Deptford record of burial.

Bearing these facts in mind, Dr. Hotson instantly suspected the truth when, while examining Elizabethan documents in the Public Record Office, he stumbled upon the name "Ingram Frizer" in the Calendar of Close Rolls. The paper in which he found it had nothing to do with Marlowe, but it suggested the true name of the man who killed him. After examining the "Inquisitiones Post Mortem" and the court records in vain for any mention of either Marlowe or Frizer, Dr. Hotson turned to the list of pardons in the Patent Rolls of Chancery, 35 Elizabeth (1593), and there found the entry:

Regina xxviij° die Junij concessit Ingramo ffrisar perdonam de se defendendo,[39]

dated just four weeks and a day after Marlowe's murder on the thirtieth day of May.

At this moment the Public Record Office closed, and the discoverer was compelled to remain on the verge of his discovery one whole — and very long — night. Returning in the morning, he found the two documents — the coroner's investigation and the pardon — which told the whole story in minute legal detail.

At the same time, another investigator, Miss Eugénie de Kalb, was searching the records of the southeastern counties for the coroner's inquest, which she felt sure must exist. She was just about to turn to the Public Record Office, where the

---

[37] The Jonson indictment is preserved in a special binding at the Middlesex Guildhall, London.
[38] Corpus Christi College, Parker MS. no 489, no. 4, fol. 73. (Joscelyn's *Historiola*.)
[39] Patent Rolls, 35 Eliz.; Hotson, *op. cit.*, p. 24.

documents really lay hidden, when Dr. Hotson's discovery was announced.[40]

From the Hotson documents, it is possible to reconstruct the last day of Marlowe's life, almost hour by hour. He arrived at the house in Deptford Strand owned by Eleanor Bull, widow, at about ten o'clock on the morning of May 30, 1593. This has been called a tavern by many writers and may well have been one; but there is no good evidence that it was anything more than a private house.

With the poet were three doubtful characters: Ingram Friser, who was to slay Marlowe a few hours later, a sharper whose wiles kept him in perpetual litigation; Nicholas Skeres, decoy for Friser in his swindling schemes; and Robert Poley, a government secret agent of unsavory reputation. The first two are described in the documents as "late of London, Gentleman." Poley is "of London aforesaid, Gentleman." This probably means that Poley, who had just returned from abroad, had not had time to change his lodgings, while Friser and Skeres had left London at the first sign of the plague.

The four "met together in a room in the house of a certain Eleanor Bull, widow; & there passed the time together & dined & after dinner were in quiet sort together there & walked in the garden belonging to the said house until the sixth hour after noon of the same day & then returned from the said garden to the room aforesaid & there together and in company supped." [41]

Obviously, this was an important conference. It required practically an entire day. Obviously also, it was confidential. The quartet shunned the tavern ordinary — if the house really was a tavern — took two meals privately, conversed in private, and walked privately in the garden. All except Friser (and perhaps Friser, too, though evidence is lacking) had been concerned in minor matters of state which were at least confidential.[42] Whatever his capacity, Friser was well known to many government agents.

---

[40] De Kalb, *op. cit.*, p. 11.

[41] Hotson's translation. Practically nothing is known of Eleanor Bull. Miss de Kalb surmises that she was the wife of Richard Bull, gentleman, who was buried at St. Nicholas, April 9, 1590. She may be the "Mistress Bull" buried there March 19, 1595, according to the parish register. See de Kalb, *op. cit.*, p. 124, for other possibilities.

[42] See I. 158–182.

Probably all four had, with their two meals and during the afternoon and evening, consumed a fair quantity of wine. After supper in their private room, Marlowe lay down on a bed, while the other three sat side by side at a table in front of him. They were sitting on a bench, chairs being rarely used in Elizabethan taverns, and with their knees under the table, so that they could not rise suddenly. Marlowe was presumably Friser's guest. At least, Vaughan says that Friser "had inuited him thither to a feast, and was then playing at tables." [43]

A dispute arose. Friser and Marlowe "were in speech & uttered one to the other divers malicious words for the reason that they could not be at one nor agree about the payment of the sum of pence, that is, *le recknynge* there." Kyd had accused Marlowe in one letter to Sir John Puckering of being "intemperate & of a cruel hart," and in the other had referred to his "rashnes in attempting soden pryvie iniuries to men." [44] Of the latter quality, Marlowe now gave evidence.

Like most Elizabethans, Friser was wearing a dagger. In its sheath, it hung from his belt over the back of the bench on which he sat. Perhaps he had hitched it around to sit down more comfortably — everyone who has worn a bayonet knows the difficulty of sitting down with sidearms.

This weapon swung within easy reach of the infuriated Marlowe, who snatched it from the sheath and "maliciously gave the aforesaid Ingram two wounds on his head of the length of two inches & of the depth of a quarter of an inch." It is hard to believe that wounds so slight were inflicted by an angry man striking downward with a steel blade, if he was really striking to kill. Marlowe may have followed the common Elizabethan practice of reversing the dagger and beating his opponent's head with the heavy hilt, trying to "knock him out," without

---

[43] "Tables" was the Elizabethan name for backgammon, the name being derived from the table-like leaves of the backgammon board. Chaucer refers to "playe either at chesse or tables" in the *Book of the Duchess* (l. 51); and Shakespeare in *Love's Labour's Lost* (V. ii. 326), a play of about this period, alludes to

> Monsieur the nice,
> That, when he plays at tables, chides the dice.

It was the common game of taverns; and Frizer, his business done, might naturally have been thus occupied, though the official report omits so trivial a detail.

[44] Harleian MS. 6849, fol. 218; Harleian MS. 6848, fol. 154.

fatal injury. Such blows would cause scalp wounds without penetrating the skull. They would also leave the blade of the dagger pointing upward and backward, so that when Frizer turned and seized Marlowe's hand, he would drive the point back into the angry face above him.[45]

This is apparently what happened. In the words of the coroner's report, Friser

in his own defence & for the saving of his life, then & there struggled with the said Christopher Morley to get back from him his dagger aforesaid; in which affray the same Ingram could not get away from the said Christopher Morley; and so it befell in that affray that the said Ingram, in defence of his life, with the dagger aforesaid of the value of 12 d. gave the said Christopher then & there a mortal wound over his right eye of the depth of two inches & of the width of one inch; of which mortal wound the aforesaid Christopher Morley then & there instantly died.

The murder committed, Friser "neither fled nor withdrew himself" — since that would have been a confession of guilt. Like Marlowe's friend, Thomas Watson, in the Bradley killing four years earlier, he stood his ground in anticipation of pardon.

The technical Elizabethan legal phrasing needs a little explanation. Under English law, then as now, a plea of self-defense is of no avail in a murder charge unless the defendant can show that he had no means of escape, so that to save his own life he had to kill his opponent. He must also give clear proof that his own life was actually in danger. The value of the weapon which had committed a felony, and was therefore forfeit to the Crown, was usually given in Elizabethan times and later, as shown by the indictment of George Browne in *A Warning for Faire Women*.

It was also usual to give the dimensions and exact location of the wound, as had been done in the Bradley killing. These are of importance to modern students, since they raise a doubt. No medical man will believe that penetration of the frontal lobe of the brain to the depth stated could possibly cause immediate death.[46] Instead it should cause coma, as in the case

[45] William Poel: "Death of Marlowe," TLS, 24:352, 21 My 1925.
[46] Samuel A. Tannenbaum: *Assassination of Christopher Marlowe*, Appendix. All medical testimony confirms this view.

of one James Feake, killed by the actor Gabriel Spencer, whom Ben Jonson, in turn, killed a little while later.[47] Spencer saw Feake "having in his hand a certain candelabrum of copper called a candlestick worth sixpence, which he then and there had in his right hand, and held with the intention to throw it at the said Gabriel Spencer, having a sword called a rapier of iron and steel of the price of five shillings, being in the scabbard." Seeing his danger Spencer struck instantly "with the sword being in the aforesaid scabberd," and inflicted "a mortal wound, six inches deep and two inches wide, on the face, that is to say, between the pupil of the right eye, called the ball of the eye, and the eyebrowes, penetrating to the brain." With such an injury, Feake "languished & lived in languor, 3 days." This is the normal result of such a wound.

Either, therefore, Friser, Poley, and Skeres mistook Marlowe's coma for death, or they deliberately lied to the coroner's jury. This doubt gives rise to several other questions, of which more presently.

Queen Elizabeth happened to be near enough to bring Deptford "within the verge," a twelve-mile circle surrounding the person of the sovereign, wherever she moved.[48] The case thus came directly under the jurisdiction of the court, superseding the local authorities of Deptford.

Friser seems to have had little difficulty. William Danby, the royal coroner, took charge of the investigation. The inquest was held Friday, June 1, and Marlowe was buried in Deptford Church the same day, presumably by the Rev.

[47] John Cory Jeaffreson: *Middlesex Records*, I. xlv–xlvii. The original documents are at the Middlesex Guildhall.

[48] Dr. Hotson (*Death of Christopher Marlowe*, p. 75, n. 6) defines the verge as "an area of twelve miles round the body of the sovereign." Miss de Kalb (*op. cit.*, p. 44) thinks that "in the time of Elizabeth, its bounds were not so rigidly enjoined." As it was twelve miles both before and after Elizabeth, Dr. Hotson is probably right. Stat. 13 Richard II, cap. III, says: "Item accordez est & assentuz qe la court de seneschall & mareschall de hostiell du Roy ne la jurisdiction dycelle ne passe lespace de dousze lewes a counters entour le tenell du Roi." (*Statutes at Large*, Cambridge, 1763, II. 311.) M. S. Giuseppi (*Guide to the Public Records*, II. 135) renders "lewes" as "miles." By Stat. 27 Henry VIII, cap. 24, s. 12, the King's coroner had authority within the verge. (*Statutes at Large*, Cambridge, 1763, IV. 384–385.) By Letters Patent of 9 James I, the Curiae Virgae Palatii Dominis Regis dealt with trespasses within twelve miles of the Royal Residence. (Giuseppi, *op. cit.*, I. 217.)

Friser's pardon states that the Queen was then at Kewe. Presumably she was also there at the time of the murder, but E. K. Chambers (*Elizabethan Stage*, IV. 108) does not give the location of the court at this time.

Thomas Macander, then vicar. The Chancery issued a writ of certiorari Friday, June 15. Friser was pardoned at Kewe, Thursday, June 28. He probably owed his easy escape to his friends, the Walsinghams, for whom he was transacting business the very next day!

Marlowe's grave is entirely unknown and unmarked, though in 1919 an unknown admirer placed a brass tablet on the north wall of the church:

To the Immortal Memory of
Christopher Marlowe   M. A.
The Founder of Grandiloquent Blank Verse
Who Met a Tragic Death near This Spot
On 1st June 1593 Aged 29 Years

"Cut Is the Branch That Might Have Grown Full Straight"

This Tablet Is Placed to Remedy the Omission of
Past Years by One Who Valued His Writings
1919

The date of death is, of course, here confused with the date of burial.

Deptford legend differs as to the place of burial. According to one story, Marlowe's grave is near the old tower, which is all that remains of the original church. According to another, he is buried near the present site of the tablet, which prior to 1640 would have been outside the church. The churchyard itself is so crowded with the graves of parishioners that it is said to contain three separate levels of burials. It was obviously selected for Marlowe's grave solely because it was only a few hundred yards from the tavern where he was killed.

Dr. Hotson's brilliant discovery of the documents relating to Marlowe's death raises almost as many questions as it answers; but, to understand them, it is necessary to know more of the Walsingham family and of Marlowe's three companions on that fatal day at Deptford. Investigation following Dr. Hotson has supplied a good deal of information about Sir Thomas and Lady Audrey Walsingham. It has also revealed a good deal about all three of Marlowe's companions at Dame Eleanor Bull's, and practically nothing that has been discovered is to the credit of any one of them, except that Friser eventually became a churchwarden.

Marlowe, Thomas Walsingham, Robert Poley, and Nicholas Skeres had all at one time or another been part of the far-reaching network of "forraine Espialls and Intelligences"[49] set up by Sir Francis Walsingham, Secretary of State. As a young man, Sir Francis had revealed a special talent for intelligence work;[50] and by 1581 he had begun to build up that network of espionage and counterespionage which soon reached as far afield as Turkey. Acting on his favorite maxim, "knowledge is never too dear," he supplemented the government secret service funds out of his own private purse. He had, declares Sir Robert Naunton, "secret wayes of intelligence above the rest." William Camden refers to him as "a most subtle searcher of hidden secrets."[51] "Dexterous he was in finding a secret," says David Lloyd.[52]

The Yelverton Manuscript — attributed with good reason to his brother-in-law, Robert Beale — says that "Mr. Secretarie Walsinghame, with her Majestie's allowance and his owne purse, entertained [spies] in above fortie severall places. In the time of the Ambassages of Mr. La Mott and Mr. Mauvesier he had some of his Secretaries that bewrayed the secretts both of the French and Scottish dealinges. In Scotlande he was well beloved of many of the Nobilitie, Ministers and others, whom he releived when they weare banished into England; with moneye he corrupted Preists, Jesuits and Traitors to bewraye the practises against this Realme."

Another writer[53] says that at one time Walsingham had fifty-three private agents in foreign courts and eighteen spies. A list of "forren places, from whence Mr. Secretary Walsingham was wont to receive his advertisements" contains thirteen

---

[49] Yelverton MSS., vol. CLXII, fols. 1 ff., now in possession of Lady Calthorpe, 38 Grosvenor Square, London. Reproduced in Conyers Read: *Mr. Secretary Walsingham and the Policy of Queen Elizabeth*, I. 423–443. Signed "R. B.," this is undoubtedly written by Robert Beale, Walsingham's brother-in-law and secretary, who was also clerk of the Privy Council.

[50] Conyers Read: *Mr. Secretary Walsingham*, II. 340–341.

[51] *Fragmenta Regalia* (ed. 1641), p. 22; Arber's Reprint, p. 36; Camden: *Annales* (ed. 1627), pt. IV, p. 25; (ed. 1635), p. 394; Conyers Read, *op. cit.*, II. 340. For a general study of Walsingham's intelligence system, see Read, II. 314–341, and *passim*.

[52] *State-Worthies* (ed. 1766), I. 398.

[53] David Lloyd: *State-Worthies* (ed. 1766), I. 400.

towns in France, seven in the Low Countries, nine in Germany, five in Italy, five in Spain, three in the United Provinces, and three in Turkey.[54] "He had all the private papers of Europe: few letters escaped his hands, whose contents he could read and not touch the seals. . . . He would cherish a plot some years together, admitting the conspirators to his own and the queen's presence familiarly, but dogging them out watchfully: his spies waited on some men every hour, for three years." Yet, well aware that paid secret agents tend to invent "toyes and matters of their owne invencon," Sir Francis was at pains to test and verify their information.[55] Finally, "lest they could not keep council, he dispatched them to forraign parts, taking in new servants." [56] Marlowe's sinister acquaintance, Robert Poley, for instance, was kept moving from one secret assignment to another in precisely this way. In his espionage, Walsingham had the aid of Thomas Phelippes, as spy-master and cipher expert.

In the absence of newspapers — the newsbooks being very inadequate substitutes — he necessarily depended largely on these confidential reports. Such a system as his demanded swift and secret communication, and the Declared Accounts are full of payments to messengers, who were sometimes also spies. It is often obvious that the accounts contain just as little information as the Lord Treasurer would accept as a basis for payment. Highly secret matters were probably paid for by Walsingham himself and so do not appear in the accounts at all.

His messengers seem to have been of two sorts — young gentlemen of good family with their ways to make and men of humbler birth who by breeding and education could be regarded as gentlemen. Thomas Walsingham, Francis Bacon, Walter Raleigh, Richard Hakluyt, and Robert Cecil were of the first class. In the second were men like Marlowe, Poley, and Skeres.[57] The system created, as Miss de Kalb remarks, "many secrets in common between men of position and gentlemen blackguards."

[54] John William Burgon: *Life and Times of Sir Thomas Gresham*, I. 95n. See also DNB, LIX. 234.
[55] Yelverton MSS., *loc. cit.*; Read, *op. cit.*, I. 437.   [56] Lloyd, *op. cit.*, I. 401.
[57] See PRO, E. 351/452, fols. 32v, 65r; 107v; E. 351/541, fol. 222v; de Kalb, *op. cit.*, p. 34.

Thomas Walsingham

Although there were several generations of Thomas Walsinghams, there is no doubt as to the identity of Marlowe's patron. He was the fourth Thomas Walsingham, of Scadbury, Chislehurst, Kent, son of the Thomas Walsingham who died in 1584.[58] His eldest brother, Guldeford, predeceased their father,[59] and his second brother, Edmund, died in 1589, leaving Thomas heir to the estate, "then aged 26 years and more." In London and Surrey he held property worth £40 6s. 8d. per annum.

On appointment by Sir Francis Walsingham and others, Guldeford Walsingham had been employed in military intelligence abroad during 1578.[60] His younger brother Thomas found similar employment after 1580, when he became a government courier and later a confidential agent, traveling back and forth with official correspondence. On October 13, 1580, he brought letters from France to the court and on November 11 carried others back. He is similarly employed on several occasions in the following year. November 12, 1581, he is seized by wandering soldiers but on showing "Monsieur's packet" is released. His companion on this occasion was one "Skeggs," who sounds suspiciously like Nicholas Skeres.[61] Young Thomas Walsingham is again employed as a courier in the latter part of 1582. Thereafter he seems to have remained in France until early in 1582/3, when he is again carrying letters.[62] In 1583/4 Lord Cobham begs Sir Francis to supply funds to Thomas Walsingham, who has been serving as a messenger.[63] In 1586 he is turning information over to Sir Francis' intelligence system.[64]

[58] *London Inquests Post Mortem*, British Record Society, 36: 73; Chancery Inquests Post Mortem, 26 Eliz., vol. CCIV, no. 138.

[59] *Visitations of Surrey*, 1530, 1572, 1563, containing the Walsingham pedigrees. *Harleian Society Publications*, XLIII. 10–11; *London Inquests Post Mortem*, British Record Society, 36: 36, 150–151; Chancery Inquests Post Mortem, ser. 2, vol. CCVI, no. 181, London, C. 142/226.

[60] *Cal. State Papers, Foreign, 1578–1579*, nos. 58 and 59, pp. 44–45.

[61] On these errands, see PRO, E. 351/542, fols. 19v, 20, 21, 23r; *Cal. State Papers, Foreign, 1579–1580*, p. 491; ibid., *1581–1582*, p. 365; de Kalb, *op. cit.*, pp. 53 ff.

[62] PRO, E. 351/542, fol. 43v; *Cal. State Papers, Foreign, 1583, and Addenda*, p. 12; PRO, E. 351/542, fol. 45r.

[63] *Cal. State Papers, Foreign, 1583, and Addenda*, p. 142.

[64] *Cal. State Papers Relating to Scotland and Mary, Queen of Scots*, VIII. 627. The "Fole" here referred to may be Robert Poley.

Doubtless Marlowe's friend, Thomas Watson, is thinking of this stay in France when in his poem, *Melibœus*, dated 1590, he refers to himself and Walsingham's being in Paris together "of yoare." [65] The Latin version of this poem is dedicated to Thomas Walsingham, who is represented by the character Tityrus, while Sir Francis himself is Melibœus. Since Thomas Kyd remarks that Marlowe was a friend of the stationers at St. Paul's, the deposition of one William Smith, on November 12, 1582, is interesting. He says that he has lived for nine years in the churchyard and is well known to Thomas Walsingham.[66]

During the Babington conspiracy, Thomas Walsingham was acquainted with the government spy, Robert Poley. In the summer of 1586 young Walsingham was in Poley's lodgings, where he received messages from Sir Francis, through Poley. He actually met the Catholic conspirator Ballard here, just before the latter's arrest.[67] A letter of Poley's, probably written in February, 1587/8, shows Walsingham as a kind of go-between for the spy and Sir Francis.[68] This is about the period when the young Cambridge master, Christopher Marlowe, was becoming involved in secret service.

In 1588/9 Thomas Walsingham is paid a hundred shillings for fifteen days spent in special services to the Queen.[69]

After this, payments to Walsingham stop, either because he left the service when he inherited his estate in 1589, or because his subsequent activities were too confidential to be mentioned in accounts.

In later life he is completely overshadowed at court by his wife. He appears in the records again in November, 1596, when he is named as one of a group of "captains" engaged in coast defense.[70] In 1597 he is given the manor of Dartford for twenty-one years,[71] and is also associated with Peter Manwood in defense measures.[72] Elizabeth visited his country seat, Scadbury,

[65] *Melibœus* (Arber's reprint), p. 157. See also DNB, LIX. 239.
[66] *Cal. State Papers, Domestic, Addenda, 1580–1625*, p. 79.
[67] *Cal. State Papers Relating to Scotland and Mary, Queen of Scots*, VIII. 602.
[68] PRO, State Papers, France, XVII. 26-bis. The MS. was placed in this volume as late as 1925. See also *Cal. State Papers, Foreign, 1586–1588*, p. 229.
[69] PRO, E. 351/542, fol. 125v.
[70] *Cal. State Papers, Domestic, 1595–1597*, pp. 305–306.
[71] Aug. Off. Ind., Roll 9, fol. 5, 40 Eliz. no. 156, PRO, E. 310/file 67.
[72] *Acts of the Privy Council* (ed. J. R. Dasent), XXVII. 109, 298, 308.

Chislehurst, and knighted him there in 1597.[73] In 1598 he is granted a house at the lower end of the tiltyard, Whitehall, which he still holds in 1620.[74] He also receives the reversion of the keepership of the royal park at Eltham, Kent, where Ingram Friser settled.[75]

LADY AUDREY WALSINGHAM

Since Ingram Friser's chief employer seems to have been Lady Audrey Walsingham, some knowledge of her life is essential to an understanding of the tragedy at Deptford.[76] Audrey Shelton was the youngest daughter of Sir Ralph Shelton, knight, of Norfolk, by his first wife, whose maiden name was Mary Woodhouse. She was born June 10, 1568. There is no record of her marriage, but it presumably took place about 1589, when his second brother's death made Thomas Walsingham an eligible match.[77] It is noteworthy that we first find mention of Ingram Friser about this time.

Practically all that can be learned about Lady Walsingham is of a date later than Marlowe's death. All facts tend to show, however, that Ingram Friser was frequently engaged as her business agent; that during the last decade of Elizabeth's reign she was engaged in political intrigue, probably concerned with James's accession to the throne; and that after James ascended the throne she enjoyed a quite inexplicable favor. All this has a distinct relation to the murder.

It is certainly interesting that Marlowe, just before his assassination, remarked that his friend Roydon had already gone to the King of Scots and that he himself intended following Roydon. It is at least conceivable that Marlowe was killed because he knew too much about affairs of state in which Lady Walsingham was guiltily involved. But this view cannot be

---

[73] *Cal. State Papers, Domestic, 1595–1597*, p. 473; *Acts of the Privy Council* (ed. J. R. Dasent), XXVII. 308.

[74] John Nichols: *Progresses . . . of Queen Elizabeth*, III. 591–592.

[75] *Cal. State Papers, Domestic, 1598–1601*, p. 341; de Kalb, *op. cit.*, p. 70a.

[76] The only thorough study of Lady Walsingham is Miss de Kalb's dissertation. Unfortunately, this occasionally confuses Lady Audrey with others. See especially pp. 81–109.

[77] Francis Blomefield: *Essay towards a topographical history of . . . Norfolk*, V. 268. [Avery Library, Columbia.]

intelligently discussed without a more detailed knowledge of her career at court.

Under Queen Elizabeth, Lady Walsingham was made a lady of the bedchamber,[78] and she enjoyed much favor from Elizabeth during the ageing Queen's last years. At New Year's, 1599/1600, both she and her husband gave the Queen gifts of clothing. In return, the Queen gave each some gilt plate. In July, 1600, the Queen gave Lady Audrey a purse of gold, and at the next New Year's another purse valued at £20 12s. 8d.[79] Richard Baker asserts in his *Chronicles* that Lady Walsingham was concerned with the care of King James's children, Prince Henry and Princess Elizabeth, in 1603; and Miss de Kalb suspects that some years earlier she had gone to Scotland to attend on them.[80]

As early as September, 1599, a Lady Walsingham — who may be Lady Audrey — was so deeply involved in a political intrigue of some kind that Rowland Whyte, steward of Sir Robert Sidney, asked his master to assign a cipher symbol to her.[81] Presumably this had something to do with the intrigues for the succession of James to the English throne. This was the main subject for intrigue at the time, and Sir Robert was an old friend of the Scottish king. In 1604 Lady Walsingham is specifically referred to as one of Cecil's three favorites.[82] In 1610 there is evidence of how far his favor went. In a document dated April 10, 1610, Sir Jasper Crofts petitions that he may not lose the grant of a recusant's forfeited estate which has already been promised to him. He fears a claim by Lady Walsingham. On May 2 his fears are realized. Lady Walsingham already has the estate, or so the indignant Sir Jasper understands.[83]

The favor of James I is still more remarkable, and is most plausibly explained by the theory that Lady Audrey had rendered him special services prior to his accession. When in 1603

---

[78] Hist. MSS. Commission, Rutland Papers, IV. 430.

[79] John Nichols: *Progresses and Public Processions of Queen Elizabeth*, III. 453, 454, 463, and 591, n. 2. Rutland Papers, IV. 430, 431; de Kalb, *op. cit.*, p. 88.

[80] Richard Baker: *Chronicles* (ed. 1730), p. 403; de Kalb, *op. cit.*, pp. 99–101.

[81] Arthur Collins: *Letters and Memorials of State*, II. 126.

[82] Diary of Lady Anne Clifford, quoted in John Nichols: *Progresses, Processions, and Magnificent Festivities of King James the First*, I. 174.

[83] *Cal. State Papers, Domestic, 1603–1610*, pp. 599, 606.

Lady Walsingham went with others to escort Queen Anne from Berwick to London, the Queen refused to admit her to the Privy Chamber. This may have been because Lady Walsingham had been in charge of the royal children. Queen Anne was notoriously jealous of attendants assigned to her children by the King. In this instance, James personally intervenes to secure Lady Walsingham's admission.[84] On July 26, 1603, when she was formally admitted to the Privy Chamber, the Queen made her guardian and keeper of the robes, at forty marks a year, an office which she shared with her husband after 1607.[85] In this capacity, Lady Walsingham controlled the Queen's purchases of gold, silver, tinsel, and silk stuffs from tailors, embroiderers, and haberdashers, and directed the cutting.

In May, 1604, she is granted a life pension of two hundred pounds a year for attendance on the Queen.[86] On December 28, 1604, the King grants a lease to Ingram Friser for the use of Lady Walsingham. This is granted on the extraordinary ground of her good and faithful service to Queen Elizabeth [87] — probably a convenient way of disguising early service to James himself. She is probably the Lady Walsingham who on December 15, 1609, is granted precedence over a certain Lady Hoby, or any other lady of her rank, and who in 1619 is granted precedence over the wives of baronets at the Queen's funeral.[88]

In 1616 Lady Walsingham is His Majesty's valentine, and receives a gift of plate.[89] Leases in reversion, usually through the agency of Ingram Friser, are numerous.[90] The royal favor showers almost equally upon her son, the fifth Sir Thomas.[91]

[84] John Nichols: *Progresses . . . of King James*, I. 161–162, 167.
[85] *Cal. State Papers, Domestic, Addenda, 1580–1625*, p. 427; *Cal. State Papers, Domestic, 1603–1610*, p. 420.
[86] *Cal. State Papers, Domestic, 1603–1610*, p. 113.
[87] Duchy of Lancaster, Leases in Reversion, 14/19, no. 55; de Kalb, *op. cit.*, p. 108.
[88] *Cal. State Papers, Domestic, 1603–1610*, p. 573; John Nichols: *Progresses . . . of King James*, III. 541.
[89] *Cal. State Papers, Domestic, 1611–1618*, p. 380; *1619–1623*, p. 472; Abstract of the present state of his Majesties Revenew, p. 35. (Catalogued in BM under James I.)
[90] Eugénie de Kalb, *op. cit.*; PRO, Duchy of Lancaster. Particulars of Leases, Bundle 63; Index 6801, p. 49; Duchy of Lancaster Miscellanea, 1–12, James I, Bundle XV, no. 1; S. P. D. 1604, Docquet 7; Duchy of Lancaster, Leases in Reversion, Bundle 79, no. 23.
[91] Book of Establishment of Prince Henry, Duchy of Cornwall, Office, 10 Buckingham Gate, London; *Parliamentary Returns*, 1586–1620; de Kalb, *op. cit.*, p. 96 and n.; State Papers, Domestic, vol. CLXXXI, no. 48.

It is interesting to note that Lady Walsingham is named as one of the friends of Mrs. John Thornborough, wife of the Bishop of Bristol. The so-called "Thornborough Commonplace Book," now in the Folger Library, which contains a manuscript version of Marlowe's poem, "Come, Live with Me," has been regarded as Bishop Thornborough's, though on somewhat doubtful authority.[92]

INGRAM FRISER

Most of our knowledge of Ingram Friser[93] is based on records of the litigation, frequently shady, in which he was constantly involved, and on his activities as a business agent for Thomas and Audrey Walsingham. He had been associated with Thomas Walsingham at the time of Marlowe's death. Through the early seventeenth century he constantly appears in the official records as an agent for Lady Walsingham.

Nothing is known of Friser's origin and early life. Miss Eugénie de Kalb, whose researches have provided most of our knowledge of the man's career, conjectures that he may have come from Kingsclere, Hants, where there were many Frisers and where the Christian name Ingram was frequent, though there is no trace of an Ingram Friser.[94] The Hampshire parish registers for this period also include a number of Marlowes and Marlens, and also the name of Skyres.

Miss de Kalb's view of Friser's origin is supported by two facts: One is the existence of a John Ffryxor, of Basingstoke Extra, Hants, who may have been Ingram Friser's father.[95] A second is the fact that Ingram Friser's first appearance in legal records is at Basingstoke itself, not far southeast of Kingsclere. On October 9, 1589, he purchases the Angel Inn, Basingstoke, for a hundred and twenty pounds. This was an important house on the post road known as "London Street." Two years later he sells it to a London draper.[96]

---

[92] *Cal. State Papers, Domestic, 1611–1618*, p. 338. On the Thornborough Commonplace Book, now Folger MS. 297.3, see Chap. XIV.

[93] In his surviving signatures, Friser spells his name in this way, except on two occasions when he shifts to "Frizer." See de Kalb, *op. cit.*, p. 70 and n.

[94] De Kalb, *op. cit.*, p. 68.

[95] Lay Subsidy Rolls, Hundred of Basingstoke Extra, 13 Eliz., PRO, E. 179, 174/386; de Kalb, *op. cit.*, p. 70.

[96] PRO, Close Rolls, 1339; Hotson, *op. cit.*, p. 42; de Kalb, *op. cit.*, p. 70.

At the time of the purchase Thomas Bostock, one of the sellers, incurred a debt to Friser of two hundred and forty pounds. He delayed payment. Friser brought suit [97] and, after the usual legal delay, secured judgment at the Easter term, 1592. Apparently Bostock still delayed payment, for Friser secures execution against him on May 30, 1595, and with this the record closes.[98]

On June 28, 1594, Friser rents a house in St. Saviour's parish, Southwark, near the south end of London Bridge. The lease was to run from June 24, 1594. On July 4, however, one Edmund Ballard drives him out. October 17, 1594, Friser sues Ballard for recovery of the house and forty pounds damages. The Court gives Friser the house but cuts the damages down to five pounds with sixpence costs.[99]

Almost exactly a month after Marlowe's death, while the ink was hardly dry upon the pardon for the murder, Friser and Skeres, with the support of Thomas Walsingham, became involved in one of the most questionable of Friser's business transactions. The victim was Drew Woodleff, or Woodlief, of Peterley, Bucks, son of the widow Anne Woodleff, of Aylesbury, Bucks.[100] Though not blood relatives, the Woodleffs were distantly connected with both the Walsinghams and with the Sheltons, Lady Walsingham's family.[101]

About 1593 Robert Woodleff, of Peterley, Bucks, had died, leaving property to Drew Woodleff, presumably his son.[102] Young Woodleff asserts in a suit of 1595 that he was much in debt and owed bonds to divers men. In these, or similar, financial difficulties he appealed to Nicholas Skeres for help. Skeres brought him to Friser, who induced the incautious young heir to sign a bond for sixty pounds. In lieu of cash, he was persuaded to accept "a certayne nomber of gunnes or

[97] PRO, Exchequer Plea Rolls, 394; Hotson, *op. cit.*, p. 42.

[98] Exchequer Plea Rolls, 396; Hotson, *op. cit.*, p. 45.

[99] Exchequer Plea Rolls, 394; Hotson, *op. cit.*, p. 45.

[100] PRO, Chancery Proceedings, Eliz., Bundle 25, no. 43; London *Times*, June 6, 1925, p. 8g; Hotson, *op. cit.*, pp. 69–73; de Kalb, *op. cit.*, pp. 72 ff. Quotations from the documents follow Hotson's transcription, which Miss de Kalb acknowledges to be accurate except in minor matters.

[101] De Kalb, *op. cit.*, pp. 75–76, 82–83.

[102] PRO, Chancery Proceedings, Eliz. D. d. 7/6, records a suit to protect this property, discovered by Miss de Kalb, *op. cit.*, pp. 71–72. The suit is brought in 1595, and Robert Woodleff had died about two years before.

greate Iron peeces." What property rights Friser had in this ordnance, which would naturally be government property, no one inquired.

When Woodleff asked Friser to turn the artillery into cash for him, Friser brought him thirty pounds and protested he could get no more; whereas "in truthe the saide peeces or gunnes were his owne and the xxx[li] he broughte his owne and never offered them to be soulde at all but lett them remayne uppon Tower Hill." Woodleff had simply been tricked into accepting thirty pounds after having given sixty.

The stupid fellow was now mulcted again. He was persuaded that Skeres owed Friser twenty marks, and on behalf of Skeres signed a second bond to Friser. Then, finding that he could not pay, Woodleff was led in his "unwarie age" — and very "unwarie" it seems to have been — to sign a bond for two hundred pounds. This transaction is important because the bond was given to Sir Thomas Walsingham, who is described as Friser's "Maister." Whether Sir Thomas was aware of the fraudulent nature of these transactions is not clear. He bore a high reputation in his own day, but Elizabethan standards of honor were in some respects rather mixed.

At a date not earlier than June, 1598, long after the actual transaction, Anne Woodleff complained to the Lord Keeper of these frauds, which had taken place "about fyve yeres" then past — that is, in 1593. The bond is "a statute of CC[li] vnto a gentleman of good worshipp . . . the saide Fryser his then Maister." An allusion to this very paper was discovered by Dr. Hotson in a collection of entry books of bonds of recognizance among the Lord Chamberlain's papers at the Public Record office:

June 29, 1593. Drew Woodleff of Peterley, Bucks, gentleman, bound in the sum of two hundred pounds to Thomas Walsingham of Chislehurst, Kent, esquire.[103]

This was to be paid on July 25, 1593, and when young Woodleff defaulted, the case went to Chancery.

On April 30, 1596, the Woodleffs, who at that time had appar-

---

[103] PRO, L. C. 4/192, p. 267; Hotson, *op. cit.*, p. 48; also *Atlantic Monthly*, 138: 39 Jy 1926.

ently not yet lost confidence in Friser, sold him two houses and thirty acres, which he resold.[104]

When, in 1598 or thereabouts, the Woodleffs brought charges against him, Friser made no effort to contradict them. Instead, he took refuge in the plea that they were outlawed. This was, in effect, an admission that they were true.

A deed of sale dated June, 1602, shows that Friser had about that time gone to Eltham, Kent, and there made his permanent home. He is described as "late of London yoman and nowe dwellinge at Eltham in the Countye of Kente."[105] As already stated, Sir Thomas Walsingham had about this time received the reversion of the keepership of the royal park at Eltham.[106]

A jotting in the old vicar's hand on the leaves of the Eltham Parish Register records that, in this same year, the vicar granted Friser leave to dig a well in the corner of his close. This was to provide water for Friser's brewing at his house, near by. Like most others who had dealings with Friser, however, the old clergyman never received any return; and his note leaves continuance of the privilege to the discretion of his successors.[107]

In spite of this episode, Friser remained in sufficiently good odor to be a churchwarden in 1605, and his experience in real estate was used in the measuring of church lands.[108] Thomas Walsingham signs the assessment lists in these books of the churchwardens. In 1611 Friser is a certified assessor of the parish and is himself taxed on a small land holding.[109] In 1625 there is a surprising payment "for putten forth of Sheeres Childe." This may indicate a late association with Nicholas Skeeres. A "Mrs. Ingreram," perhaps Friser's wife, is buried August 25, 1616.[110]

On July 16, 1622, as "Ingram Feezer," he is one of sixteen

[104] PRO, Close Rolls, 1578; C. P. 25, 40 Eliz., Easter, Bucks; Patent Rolls, 1506; Hotson, *loc. cit.*, de Kalb, *op. cit.*, p. 71.

[105] PRO, Close Rolls, 1711; Hotson: *Death of Christopher Marlowe*, p. 50; *Atlantic Monthly*, 138: 39 Jy 1927; de Kalb, *op. cit.*, p. 62.

[106] *Cal. State Papers, Domestic, 1598–1601*, p. 341.

[107] Transcribed by Miss de Kalb, *op. cit.*, p. 65.

[108] Books of the churchwardens, Eltham Parish, discovered by Miss de Kalb, *op. cit.*, p. 65.

[109] PRO, Subsidies 127/566; Hotson: *Death*, p. 51; de Kalb, *op. cit.*, pp. 62–63, and TLS, 24: 351, 21 My 1925.

[110] Eltham Parish Register; de Kalb, *op. cit.*, p. 64n.

"good and lawful men of the county," whose oath is accepted by a commission which included the Bishop of Rochester, Dr. Samuel Page, then vicar of the church at Deptford where Friser's victim lay buried, and "Sir Thomas Walsingham, the elder," that is, Marlowe's former patron.[111] He was prosperous enough to keep a servant, for there is a reference to "Marget Ingeram freesers maid" in the register for October, 1616. In 1625 the children of his daughter, Alice Dixon, were buried "from Ingeram's house" and are described as "Londiners."

James I grants a series of leases in reversion of crown lands to Lady Audrey Walsingham or to Ingram Friser for the use of Lady Audrey Walsingham. Even when the lease is to Friser himself, one suspects that Lady Walsingham in some way profited. It is likely that in all these cases Lady Walsingham exerted the necessary influence on the King. Friser then took over the leases, paying Lady Walsingham their value and thereafter making what he could out of them by the sale of grazing rights and the like.

A lease as early as 1603 is noted as the second, so that James must have begun these grants almost as soon as he was on the throne. Together with this is a note stating that His Majesty wishes Friser to have the use of land worth £40 to his own use for forty years. On December 23, 1604, there is a lease of £15 19s. 4d. worth of lands in the Duchy of Lancaster lands to Ingram Friser on surrender of other parcels to Lady Audrey Walsingham. The lease of December 28, 1604, to Ingram Friser has already been mentioned. It seems to have been as late as 1613 when the King directs that it must no longer be delayed, in spite of an entail.[112]

It is startling to find Friser doing business for Thomas Walsingham the day after his pardon for Marlowe's murder. It is still more startling to find him obviously still doing business for Lady Walsingham twenty years later. Neither the mur-

[111] John Kimbell: *Account of the Legacies . . . appertaining to St. Alphège, Greenwich* (1816), pp. 54 ff.; J. W. Kirby, TLS, 29: 592, 17 Jy 1930; F. S. Boas: *Marlowe and His Circle* (ed. 1931), p. 157. Kimbell states that the original document is still "in the chest at the church."

[112] Practically all of these were discovered by Miss de Kalb. See *op. cit.*, pp. 92 ff.; PRO, Duchy of Lancaster, Particulars of leases, Bundle 63; *Cal. State Papers, Domestic, 1603–1610*, p. 179; *Addenda, 1580–1625*, p. 536.

der of Marlowe nor the fleecing of the Woodleffs could shake the Walsinghams' faith in him. It may, however, be significant that he is clearly in the service of Lady Walsingham rather than her husband, except in the earlier records.

Miss de Kalb's researches show that Friser was buried at Eltham, Kent, August 14, 1627. With poetic justice, there was legal trouble over his estate. Relatives tried to show that a nuncupative will existed, but the court decided he had died intestate. The "sentence," or decision, shows that he was still living in Eltham at the time of his death. He left a daughter, Alice Dixon, and a grandson, John Banckes, by another daughter who is not named. It is possible that a wife, perhaps a second wife, survived him.[113]

"A Verie Bad Felow"

Robert Poley, whose name is also spelled "Polly," "Poly," "Poole," "Pole," and in various other ways, was an Elizabethan spy of long experience, a shady character involved in various disreputable affairs and occasionally suspected of spying for two sides at once. He may be identical with the Robert Pollye who was at Clare College, Cambridge, in 1568 and who became a chorister of King's in 1564. As a Cambridge man, some years older than Marlowe, he might readily strike up an acquaintance with him.[114]

He is first identifiable in official records when Sir Francis Walsingham commits him to Marshalsea prison.[115] Thereafter he is in and out of prison with fair regularity every year or two, sometimes serving as an intelligence agent on the other prisoners. He remains in the Marshalsea until the tenth of May,

---

[113] The will is in 99 Skynner, Somerset House. See also Admon-Act Book, 1627, October, fol. 175; Eltham Parish Register; de Kalb, *op. cit.*, p. 63; TLS, 24: 351, 21 My 1925. Hasted's *Kent* (1886), p. 212, gives the death of Mrs. Friser on the same day as her husband's, but this is presumably due to misreading of the register, which records the remarriage of William Friser's widow in January 1627/8. This may be an error for Ingram Friser, as there was no other Friser in the parish.

[114] *Alumni Cantabrigienses*, III. 380. See Ethel Seaton in RES, 7: 147 (1931).

[115] State Papers, Domestic, Elizabeth, vol. CCXXII, nos. 13 and 14, January 7, 1588/9, contain the examination of William Yeomans and others before William Fleetwood, Recorder of London. The original is SP 12/222. First noted by Sir E. K. Chambers in MLR, 21: 84–85 Ja 1926. See Ethel Seaton in RES, 5: 280 Jy 1929; Boas, *op. cit.*, p. 32.

either in 1583 or 1584, half the time a close prisoner, the rest of the time enjoying the liberty of the house.

Poley had been married to the daughter of a certain Watson by a seminary priest, and it is probable that Anne, daughter of Robert Pollye, who was baptized at St. Helen's, Bishopsgate, August 22, 1583, was his daughter.[116]

He was, however, engaged in an intrigue about this time and for some years afterward with Mistress Joan Yeomans, wife of a London cutler, William Yeomans. The record of this sordid affair is rather full, for in January 1588/9 Poley became involved in a suit for the alienation of the lady's affections and many depositions were taken. Among the deponents was Richard Ede, a keeper at the Marshalsea prison [117] while Poley was imprisoned there. At some time in 1583 Poley was committed to Marshalsea by Sir Francis Walsingham, where he remained until May 10, 1584, part of the time a close prisoner and part of the time enjoying the liberty of the house, with the privilege of entertaining his paramour at "fine bankets." Meantime, he refused to see his own wife, though she often tried to see him.

At some time after his release, Poley went to lodge at the home of Mistress Browne, mother of Joan Yeomans. This made the meetings of the lovers easy and natural, especially as Mistress Browne knew nothing of her daughter's amours.

About 1585, however, Mistress Browne found her daughter "sittinge vppon the said Polleys knees the sight thereof did soe stryke to her hart that she shoulde never recover yt." Indeed, she testified, she "prayed God to cutt her of verie quickly or ells she feared she shoulde be a bawde vnto her owne daughter." [118] As a matter of fact, the old lady did die almost immediately.

Meantime, Poley entered the Catholic plots to free Mary, Queen of Scots. Presumably he was a government agent from the very beginning, and the plotters at first received him with suspicion, but he soon won them over. Poley was apparently chosen by Christopher Blunt, or Blount, a younger brother of

---

[116] The original is in Register A (Parchment), 1575–1649. See Harleian Society Publications, *Registers*, XXXI. 3, p. 3; de Kalb, *op. cit.*, p. 42.

[117] Identified as such in E. 351/542.

[118] State Papers, Domestic, Elizabeth, vol. CCXXII, no. 12. PRO, SP 12/222.

William Blunt, seventh Lord Mountjoy. A letter from Thomas
Morgan, one of the Scottish queen's agents abroad, refers to
Poley's carrying letters for Blunt,[119] July 10, 1585. Morgan was
then in the Bastille, and his friends were inclined to fear that
Poley had come to assassinate him. After meeting him, Morgan
concluded that Poley was a good Catholic and meant well, but
he was careful not to trust him with letters. Instead, he sent
word that Blunt should hear from him by another channel. A
letter from Poley to Blunt was intercepted by the Council, but
in spite of this slip, which may not have been accidental, the
conspirators trusted him. Early in 1586 Blunt "placed him to
be Sir Phillipp Sidney's man," [120] piously hoping that Poley
might "quietlye live a Christian life vnder the sayd Sydney."
Sidney had married the daughter of Sir Francis Walsingham,
head of the secret service, three years before and was at this
time living in his house. Poley was "therebye able to picke
owt many things" for the Catholic party — or so they thought.
By 1586 Poley had worked his way into the confidence of
Anthony Babington himself.

Babington was for a time suspicious and wrote to Nawe,
Mary's secretary:

I would gladlie understand what opinione you hould of one Robert
Pooley whome I find to haue intelligence with her Ma*jes*tyes occasions I am private with the man and by the meanes thereof knowe
some whate but suspect more, I pray you deliuer yor opinione of him[121]

Eventually, Babington tried to use Poley's influence to secure
a passport from Walsingham, and proposed to pay Poley's expenses on the Continent.[122] On August 2, 1586, Babington and a
group of his supporters were in London and supped in Poley's
garden, a fact which Thomas Phelippes, the spy-master, was
able to report to Sir Francis Walsingham the very next day.[123]

[119] Cal. State Papers, Scotland, II. 973; Cal. State Papers Relating to Scotland and Mary,
Queen of Scots, VIII. 12.
[120] Letter of Morgan, dated January 18, 1586, PRO, SP 53/16, no. 17, fol. 449; Cal.
State Papers Relating to Scotland and Mary, Queen of Scots, VIII. 25–26; Boas: Marlowe
and His Circle, p. 39; Boas: Christopher Marlowe, pp. 120–121.
[121] Bodleian, Ashmolean MS. 830, fol. 4r; also in BM, Cottonian MSS., Calig. B. V.
art. 22, fol. 170r; Calig. C. IX. art. 154–7, fol. 303r, formerly fol. 240r.
[122] State Papers, Scotland, vol. XIX. no. 26, PRO, SP 53. Cal. State Papers Relating
to Scotland and Mary, Queen of Scots, VIII. 695–696.
[123] Cal. State Papers Relating to Scotland and Mary, Queen of Scots, VIII. 584; Cal.
State Papers, Scotland, II. 1003.

When all the evidence was in its hands, Elizabeth's government struck. Babington fled, writing Poley a pathetic letter which shows at once his suspicions and his unwillingness to entertain them:

ffarewell sweet Robyn, if as I take the, true to me. If not Adieu, *omnium bipedum nequissimus* Retorne me thyne answer for my satisfaction and my dyamond & what els thow wilt. The fornace is prepared wherin our faith muste be tryed. ffarewell till we mete, which god knowes when.[124]

Father John Ballard, the priest who had encouraged Babington, was arrested in Poley's very lodgings on August 4, 1586.[125] Poley himself was thrown into the Tower on August 18 and remained there till late September. He was again in the Tower from late in 1587 till March 25, 1588, and again from June 24 to September 29, 1588.

It is by no means certain just why Poley went to prison. The age-old device of "planting" an ostensible prisoner as a spy was well known to Elizabeth's government, and the betrayed Catholics soon became suspicious. A secret service report from "II to Walsingham," dated September 19, 1586, shows that the government knew of these suspicions. The report states: "There is one Roberte Poole, alias Polley, the Papists gyve out to be the broacher of the last treason," and "his commytting to the Tower was but to blynd the worlde. Also he hath reveyled Babbington and his complices." The back is endorsed "From II Secret Intelligence." Comparison of handwritings suggests that "II" was Maliverny Catlyn, one of Walsingham's four leading spies.[126] On November 25, 1587, Poley wrote to Sir Francis Walsingham about a certain fellow prisoner who might give information about the Jesuits: "mee thinkes it requisite, eyther se the Paquet, els heare me speake, ere you discharge him." [127]

---

[124] BM, Lansdowne MS. 49, no. 25, fol. 63.

[125] *Cal. State Papers Relating to Scotland and Mary, Queen of Scots*, VIII. 602.

[126] The original is in State Papers, Domestic, vol. CXCIII, no. 52, PRO, SP 12/193. There is no adequate foliation of this volume. *Cal. State Papers, Domestic, Elizabeth, 1581–1590*, p. 354, wrongly gives the signature as the Greek letter II. Dr. Conyers Read, in *Mr. Secretary Walsingham*, II. 323n, identifies Catlyn.

[127] State Papers, Domestic, vol. CCV, item 49; *Cal. State Papers, Domestic, 1581–1590*, p. 439; Ethel Seaton in RES, 7:148 (1931).

The Jesuit, Robert Southwell, charged in so many words that
"*Poolie* being Sir *F. Walsinghams* man, and throughly seasoned
to his Maisters tooth, was the chiefe instrument to contriue &
prosecute the matter, to draw into the net such greene wittes,
as (fearing the generall oppression, and partly angled with
golden hookes) might easilie be ouer wrought by M. Secr. sub-
tile & sifting wit." And, he added, "though none were so deepe
in the very bottome of that conspiracy as *Poolie* himselfe, yet
was hee not so much as indited of any crime, but after a little
large imprisonment (more for pollicy then for any punishment)
set at liberty, & is in more credit then euer he was before." [128]

During the summer of 1586 the government was nearly as
suspicious of Poley as the Catholics themselves. There still
exists a memorandum endorsed "Articles uppon w*hi*ch Pooley
is to be examined." Intended merely to aid the examiner's
memory, it is now unintelligible, but it makes the official suspicion clear enough. It notes "that he had conference wi*th*
Bab*ington* a part a lyttle before his departure"; "that Pooley
payd for the supper" — which is more than Ingram Friser was
willing to do; that "yt was well neere twelve of the clocke before Pooley came to Jhon ffuryers"; "that Pooley wrote bothe
the letters." There is also the question, "What Pooley dyd
after he departed from Jhon ffuriars." [129]

During the Yeomans affair the injured husband testified on
January 7, 1589, that about three years earlier Sir Francis
Walsingham had examined Poley for two hours with regard
to a book written against the Earl of Leicester. This was
presumably *Leycesters Commonwealth*, published in 1584 and
banned by the Privy Council, June 28, 1585. After Leicester's
marriage to Lettice, Countess of Essex, September 21, 1578,
Lord North had told "his trusty Pooly" that he would "sinke
or swimme with my Lord of *Leycester*." Poley repeated this to
Sir Robert Jermine. This is presumably Robert Poley the spy,
as he later writes to the Earl of Leicester on terms of complete
acquaintance. [130]

[128] *Humble Supplication to Her Maiestie.*
[129] State Papers, Scotland, Mary Queen of Scots, 1586, Aug.–Sept., vol. XIX, no. 26.
PRO, SP 53/19. *Cal. State Papers Relating to Scotland and Mary, Queen of Scots*, VIII.
595.
[130] Ed. of 1641, p. 86. See Boas, *op. cit*, p. 45.

Walsingham handled Poley severely. He was famous for the skill and harshness with which he conducted examinations of this sort. "He would so beset men with Questions," says David Lloyd, "and draw them on, & pick it out of them by piece-meals, that they discovered themselves whether they answered or were silent."[131] Poley later remarked that "Mr. Secretary did vse him very cruelly." This has been interpreted as sug-gesting torture, but it more probably refers to the severity of this two-hour examination. For once Sir Francis had met his match, however. Poley "saied that he putt Mr. Secretary into that heate that he looked out of his wyndoe and grynned like a dogge." [132] This was unusual, for according to Lloyd, "so patient was this wise man, *Chiselhurst* never saw him angry, *Cambridge* never passionate, and the Court never discomposed." [133]

Poley himself describes this episode in an autograph letter to Leicester, probably written in February, 1587:

Mr. Secretary in my late examynation dyd charge mee as Justly [irony for unjustly] to bee suspected by your honour, and him, as procurenge, or knowinge the procurers of sertain lybels, against her Majesty, the State, and other persons of honour published: J humbly and dutifully proteste that J am who/ly innocent, and in no cyr-cumstance to bee tuchte, eyther in any such trayterous lybelinge, or other undutifull practyce [?] against her Majesty, or the State what-soeuer: neyther is ther any dependence, or conformytie Right Hon-ourable; that J havenge taryed iij or iiij yeeres intente to serve the State in lyke discoueryes, and moste instantly labouringe myne admyttance, and dyrection in the same for x: or xij continuall monethes laste paste, should eyther in the meane tyme my selfe comytt any offence of lyke quallitye: or knowinge of others procurenge should conceale the same.

Like Kyd, Poley insists that the suspected books in his pos-session belonged to a friend. He had merely been "receayuenge, and keepenge of a feawe purposeles Book*es* from the sayd Norres" — a priest then in Marshalsea prison.

When Poley finally emerged from the Tower, a free man, he went back to the Yeomans house to live, sorely to the distress of the suspicious husband. He apparently was one of those

[131] David Lloyd: *State-Worthies*, ed. 1665, p. 327; ed. 1679, p. 514; ed. 1766, I. 399.
[132] Yeomans inquiry, previously cited.
[133] Lloyd, *op. cit.*, ed. 1665, p. 328; ed. 1679, p. 516; ed. 1766, I. 401.

rare spies who can make espionage pay, for he was able on this occasion to spend forty pounds "att the least" on furnishing his rooms. His yearly income was about eighty pounds,[134] and on one occasion he was able to give Mistress Yeomans a hundred and ten pounds of "good gould."

"Had not I good lucke to gett owt of the Tower?" he asked Yeomans, explaining that he owed his release to Sir Francis Walsingham.

"You are greatlie beholdinge vnto Mr. Secretaries," said Yeomans.

"Naye," boasted Poley, "he is more beholdinge vnto me then I am vnto him for there are further matters betwene hym & me then all the world shall knowe of."

This evidence of official favor did not, however, cheer the unfortunate Yeomans. He took his friend Ede "into his nether room and made very great mone that Poley was come to lodge." Ede urged Yeomans to get rid of his boarder, who was certain to "beguile him either of his wife or of his life." Ede proved only too correct. By November, Poley had managed to get Yeomans committed to Marshalsea prison, charged with disregarding a warrant issued by Sir Thomas Heneage. Ede procured his release. When the poor man's return made her intrigue with Poley difficult, Mistress Yeomans set off for market one day and, instead of returning, eloped with Poley.

By December, Poley was again in official favor. Between this period and Marlowe's death he is steadily engaged in confidential messenger service or outright espionage. In December, 1588, upon Sir Francis Walsingham's authority, he is paid for bringing letters from Denmark.[135] The marriage of King James of Scotland to Anne of Denmark was then in the air, but this was probably not Poley's first trip to Denmark. Three years earlier a certain "Pooley" had been in "Hellsingnore" (Elsinore), ostensibly in the Danish service.

[134] Ethel Seaton in RES, 7: 148n (1931), based on rough quarterly payments noted on Cipher 105A in State Papers 106. An Italian spy, in 1596, drew a hundred pounds a year.

[135] These entries are carefully transcribed in an appendix to the dissertation by Miss de Kalb, who discovered most of them. See PRO, E. 351/542, fols. 124v, 129r, 141v, 144r, 154v, 156r, 159r, 167v, 169r, 170v, 171v, 180, r and v, 181, r and v; Cal. State Papers, Foreign, 1585–1586, p. 89; State Papers, Domestic, CCXXXVIII. 140; Hist. MSS. Comm., Salisbury MSS. (Hatfield MSS.), IV. 142, 156, 200, 466; VIII. 26.

In July, 1589, Poley is paid for a trip to and from Holland. In February, 1589/90, he makes a trip to Berwick, on the Scottish border. In July and December he goes to the Low Countries. He is back in Berwick again in May and December, 1591. In March, 1591/2, he is off to Brussels. In June, 1592, he is again off to Berwick. In September, 1592, he goes to Antwerp, which Marlowe specifically mentions in *Faustus*, and to other places in the Low Countries. In September, 1592, he goes to Dover. In late 1592 he is again off to Scotland, where he stays two months, "rydeinge in sondrye places within that province," returning by December 14. For this journey he received forty-three pounds. In January, 1592/3, he is off to Scotland again, and in March of the same year he makes another trip on "her heighnes speciall and secret afayres of greate importance," returning on the twenty-third. Shortly after this trip there is a series of arrests. In May, 1593, Poley goes to The Hague, returning on the very day of Marlowe's murder, but delaying until June 8 before presenting his dispatches.[136]

Poley appears in 1591 in a deposition by Robert Rutkin, a broker, who "saieth that his neighbor menc*i*oned in the *lette*re [which is otherwise unknown] is one Robt Poolye and that hee deliu*e*reth him *lette*res for S*i*r Thom*a*s Henneage & sendeth *lette*res to him from S*i*r Thom*a*s Henneage." This looks as if Rutkin served as what in modern espionage is known as a "letter-box," or "cover address," receiving and forwarding reports from the spy and instructions to him. Rutkin also adds that "the said Rob*er*t Poolye lyv*e*th in Shorditch," near Marlowe's lodgings in Norton Folgate. "Hee was sent ou*er* by S*i*r Thom*a*s Henneage w*i*th *lette*res to diuers p*er*sons about a yeare past." [137] Henneage had apparently taken over the intelligence service after Sir Francis Walsingham's death, in April, 1590.[138] In 1592 Sir Robert Cecil is inquiring of Heneage about both "Rutkyn," Poley, and seditious books.[139] A year later,

---

[136] PRO, E. 351/542, fol. 182*v*; Eugénie de Kalb, *op. cit.*, Appendix, and TLS, 24: 351, 21 My 1925.

[137] *State Papers, Domestic, Elizabeth*, vol. CCXXXVIII, no. 140, fol. 140, PRO, SP 238. See *Cal. State Papers, Domestic, 1591–1594*, p. 35, for summary; Boas: *Marlowe and His Circle*, pp. 112–113; Boas: *Christopher Marlowe*, pp. 267–268.

[138] Ethel Seaton in RES, 5: 282 Jy 1929.

[139] Hist. MSS. Commission, Salisbury MSS. (Hatfield MSS.), IV. 200. See also pp. 142, 156.

again writing to Heneage, he remarks: "I have spoken with Poly & find him no Foole." [140]

Like Friser, Poley suffers no loss of his employers' confidence after Marlowe's killing, though on other occasions they were ready enough to suspect him. In July, 1593, he is sent to meet an English agent in France. He continues in service from 1593 to 1596 and returns to service in 1598.[141] A group of cipher keys dating from 1596, still surviving in the Public Record Office, are designated for his use, and their completeness suggests the importance of his investigations. One of them has three symbols for each letter, besides numbers up to three thousand "and so forwards," and special symbols for the Queen, "K. Scotts," Poley himself, and various other figures in international affairs. The system even includes "nullities" — the "nulls" of modern intelligence ciphers — that is, symbols without any meaning whatever, intended to prevent possible deciphering by unauthorized persons. Various secret "cover addresses" for the transmission of the secret letters are also arranged.[142]

Poley's absence from the accounts during 1597 may have meant that he was engaged in some special service for which he was paid in some other way. During the famous conversations, Ben Jonson told Drummond of Hawthornden that while he was in close imprisonment the authorities "placed two damn'd Villans to catch advantage of him, with him, but he was advertised [i.e., warned] by his Keeper." Jonson added that "of the Spies he hath ane Epigrame." If this should refer to Jonson's imprisonment for his share in *The Isle of Dogs* from early August until October 8, 1597, it would fall within the very period in which Poley is not otherwise accounted for. Furthermore, the epigram referred to is not necessarily Jonson's "On Spies," but may be another on "Inviting a Friend to Supper," in which occurs the line:

And we will haue no *Pooly'* or *Parrot* by.

---

[140] *State Papers, Domestic, Elizabeth,* vol. CCXLII, no. 25; *Cal. State Papers, Domestic, 1591-1594,* p. 222.
[141] PRO, E. 351/542, fols. 183r, 196v, 207v, E. 351/543, fols. 13r, 39v, 58v, 68r, 70, r and v.
[142] PRO, State Papers, 106, vol. I (index); vol. II, nos. 105, 105A, 105B. Described by Ethel Seaton, RES, 7: 137-150 (1931).

Possibly, then, Poley was one of the two "damn'd Villans." The description fits him exactly, especially as he is known to have served as an informer in prisons. Parrot is reported as an informer in Newgate prison in the following year.[143]

About 1599 or 1600, Poley again fell into official disfavor. In a letter to Sir Robert Cecil, dated December 17, 1600, he complains of his dismissal from Cecil's service and offers help in ferreting out Jesuit plots. He made only one trip in 1599, so far as the accounts show, but he carried letters in June and December, 1600, and again in August and September, 1601. In July of this year he tried to smuggle back into England a young cousin who had been illegally studying at St. Omers. He was detected. But Lord Cobham suggested in a letter to Sir Robert Cecil that he be let off with a reprimand and taken back into service.[144]

Sir Robert may not have been quite so forgiving as Lord Cobham wished, for on July 18, 1602, Poley writes that he has made no further offer of service because of a petulant remark. Cecil had complained that Poley brought no good intelligence and that his service was worthless.[145] Poley, however, now volunteers some further information with regard to the Jesuits.

Thereafter he drops out of official records, unless he is the "well beloued Subiect, R. P." who is made a yeoman waiter at the Tower.[146] It is just possible that he is identical with Robert Pooley, citizen and haberdasher of London, whose will is proved in 1626.[147] If so, age had sobered that intriguing, unscrupulous, adventurous spirit.

Nicholas Skeres

Less is known of Nicholas Skeres than of the other two men present when Marlowe was killed; and what we do know of him is, if possible, even less respectable. He was probably the son of Nicholas Skeres, of the Merchant Taylors' Company, citizen

---

[143] Discovered by Mark Eccles, RES, 13: 385–397 (1937); Boas: *Christopher Marlowe*, p. 289. See also E. K. Chambers: *Elizabethan Stage,* II. 420. Jonson's epigrams are LIX and CI.

[144] Hist. MSS. Commission, Salisbury MSS. (Hatfield MSS.), XI. 216, 278, 302.

[145] *Ibid.*, XII. 230.

[146] Warrant Book, Elizabeth, I. 41.

[147] 97 Hele, Somerset House.

of London and parishioner of Allhallows the Less,[148] who was assessed at £10 10s. od. in 1563/4. His family was probably connected with the Skyres family, of Skyres Hall, Wentworth, Yorkshire,[149] or with a family named "Skiers," settled near Doncaster, Yorkshire.[150] In both families the name Nicholas occurs at least once. There is also a reference to a Nicholas Skyers, gentleman, who is concerned in a sale of Yorkshire land in 1601.[151]

The will of Nicholas Skeres the elder, proved in 1566,[152] leaves a good deal of property to his children, Jerome and Nicholas. This bequest makes it practically certain that we are dealing with the man that Marlowe knew to his cost, for in January, 1581/2, "Jeronimus Skyers de Ciuitate London generosus & Nicholaus Skyers de ffurnyvalls Jnne in Holborne predict. generosus" sign a bond of forty pounds in company with "Matheus Royden de Davyes Inne in holborne in Com. Midd. generosus." [153] Obviously we have here the two Skeres brothers dealing with one of Marlowe's known associates.

Nicholas Skeres next appears in official records on July 7, 1585, when the recorder of London, William Fleetwood, writes a letter to Lord Burghley, in which he refers to the man as one of the "Maisterles men and Cutpurses whose practice is to robbe Gentelmen's Chambers and Artificers' shoppes in & about London."[154]

Shortly after this, Skeres is involved in some way in the Babington conspiracy, in which both Thomas Walsingham and Poley had been concerned. Walsingham's aid, Francis Mylles, reporting on the conspirators, lists "Babington, Dunn, Skyrres

---

[148] De Kalb, op. cit., p. 47; P. C. C. Wills, 33 Crymes.

[149] Robert Glover: Visitation of Yorkshire, 1584/5 and 1612, p. 355; de Kalb, op. cit., p. 49.

[150] Joseph Hunter: South Yorkshire, II. 101.

[151] Feet of Fines, pt. IV, Record Series, VIII. 170 (Yorkshire Archaeological and Topographical Association); de Kalb, op. cit., p. 53.

[152] P. C. C. Wills, 33 Crymes, discovered by Miss de Kalb.

[153] PRO, Close Rolls 1144 (24 Elizabeth, pt. 24), discovered by G. C. Moore Smith, MLR, 9: 97–98 (1914). Furnival's Inn was an Inn of Court on the north side of Holborn between Leather Lane and Brooke Street. See E. H. Sugden: Topographical Dictionary, p. 211.

[154] Lansdowne MS. 44, no. 38, fol. 115, BM. First noted by Sir E. K. Chambers, TLS, 24: 352, 21 My 1925. See also F. S. Boas: Marlowe and His Circle, pp. 96–97; T. Wright: Queen Elizabeth and Her Times, II. 248; Eugénie de Kalb, op. cit., pp. 46 ff.

and others of this crew." [155] Skeres was probably a government spy, for in July, 1589, Sir Francis Walsingham authorizes payment to him for bearing letters between the Earl of Essex and the Queen.[156]

He appears twice in 1593, once as Friser's decoy in the Woodleff swindling case, and again as a witness of Marlowe's murder. On March 13, 1594/5, he is arrested by Sir Richard Martin, alderman, in "very dangerous company," at the house of one Edmund Williamson, perhaps identical with the prisoner who made a deposition regarding Poley. Skeres, as a result, is imprisoned in the Counter. He is described as "Nicholas Kyrse, *alias* Skeeres, seruant to the Earl of Essex." [157] In 1601, he is imprisoned after the Essex uprising. July 31, 1601, the Privy Council sends a warrant to the keeper at Newgate authorizing him to transfer Nicholas "Skiers," then in his custody, to Bridewell. Another warrant to the keeper of Bridewell authorizes his confinement there.[158] After 1601 Skeres fades into the half-light of the Elizabethan underworld and is heard of no more.

One might describe our knowledge of Christopher Marlowe's death as consisting of facts, doubts — and theories which have a sound basis in fact. Marlowe was undoubtedly killed at Dame Eleanor Bull's house, Deptford Strand, on the night of May 30, 1593. Ingram Friser undoubtedly killed him. Robert Poley and Nicholas Skeres were certainly witnesses. Marlowe was unquestionably stabbed in or near the eye.

Beyond that point, however, doubts persistently arise; and some scholars have been inclined to question the truthfulness of the coroner's report. There is something queer about the whole episode. Dr. Samuel A. Tannenbaum, himself a physician, has produced medical evidence to show that a "wound over his

[155] The name is misprinted "Ekyeres" in *Cal. State Papers Relating to Scotland and Mary, Queen of Scots*, VIII. 584. The original is in PRO, Mary Queen of Scots Papers, vol. XIX, item 4, p. 2. Milles made the letters "E" and "S" very much alike. See Ethel Seaton, RES, 5: 280–281 (1929).

[156] PRO, E. 351/542, fol. 129; de Kalb, *op. cit.*, p. 47.

[157] Hist. MSS. Commission, Salisbury MSS. (Hatfield MSS.), V. 139; Hotson, *op. cit.*, p. 51; de Kalb, *op. cit.*, p. 46.

[158] *Acts of the Privy Council* (ed. J. R. Dasent), XXXII. 130.

right eye of the depth of two inches and of the width of one inch"
could hardly have killed Marlowe "then & there instantly."
Friser's own wounds are strangely slight if Marlowe, armed
with a dagger, really sprang at the seated and helpless man
from behind, as the inquest states. It is also a little hard to believe that Friser sat with his back to an angry opponent while
they disputed "le recknynge."

Neither Poley nor Skeres seems to have tried to separate the
struggling men or to call help. Why? It is also still to be explained why these four men — three precious scoundrels and a
poet who had been involved in confidential government affairs
— had business together so important that it required a whole
day's private conversation. The fact that Marlowe was at this
time held by the Privy Council, very probably as a witness
against someone, makes matters still more suspicious.

Poley, Friser, and Marlowe had been either friends or confidential agents, or both, for either Sir Francis or Sir Thomas
Walsingham. Friser was a swindler by whose schemes Sir
Thomas seems at least once to have profited. Poley was an
adulterer and a spy. Skeres seems to have been a jackal for
both. Where we find records of one we frequently find another
of the three associated with him. Is it not odd that they should
all be together at Marlowe's death? Is it not odd that there is
nothing to explain why three men could not overpower Marlowe
without killing him? Is it not stranger still that the Walsinghams so frequently appear in connection with Poley and
Friser? And is it not strangest of all that they remained on
friendly terms with the man who had killed their friend?

The Puritans say that Marlowe was killed in a quarrel over
a lewd wench. The official records — presumably based on the
testimony of the perjurer Poley, the cutpurse Skeres, and the
swindler Friser — say that Marlowe was killed in a quarrel
over a tavern bill. One wonders whether he may not have been
killed deliberately because some powerful personage wanted
him out of the way. It was, and is, an established method in
international espionage.

There is no real evidence that this was the case, nor is there
any definite ground for naming the individual responsible.
Dr. Tannenbaum asserts that Sir Walter Raleigh procured the

murder.[159] He argues that Raleigh was already under the suspicion of atheism which culminated in the Cerne Abbas investigation. Kyd, then under arrest, was hinting that he could name "men of quallitie" who shared Marlowe's atheism. Presumably these were members of the Raleigh group. Kyd had shown that he could and would hold his tongue; but Marlowe was at liberty, was in the hands of the Privy Council, and had to be silenced. He was therefore lured to a private room, plied with drink, and killed out of hand, after which the killers concocted a plausible, but medically impossible, story. Influence was then brought to bear to persuade the coroner to hush the whole matter up.

The difficulty with Dr. Tannenbaum's view is that Raleigh seems to have been in no particular danger and emerged unscathed from the Cerne Abbas investigation; that there is no real evidence that Marlowe was dangerous to Raleigh's circle; that anyone desperate enough to have Marlowe murdered would also have made sure of secrecy by murdering Kyd, too; and finally that medical opinions as to the nature of the wound are not very important, for it does not really matter whether Marlowe died instantly or not.

A more credible explanation is suggested by Miss de Kalb.[160] She has shown, with at least a high degree of plausibility, that Lady Audrey Walsingham was involved in the Scottish intrigues. She has also shown that Poley's return from Scotland was followed by a series of arrests. She has demonstrated clearly that Friser was a confidential agent for Lady Walsingham. It is therefore reasonable to believe that Marlowe possessed information dangerous to Lady Walsingham, and that her agent Friser was encouraged to silence him at any cost.

All this suggests that Francis Meres's account of the tragedy is more accurate than has hitherto been believed. Marlowe may not have been "stabd to death by a bawdy Servingman, a riual of his in his lewde loue." But he was stabbed to death by a servingman, who was in a sense his rival in the Walsinghams' employ. There is no evidence of a "lewde loue," but there was at least a lady in the case.

---

[159] *Assassination of Christopher Marlowe, passim.*
[160] Eugénie de Kalb, *op. cit.*, pp. 97 ff.

A final puzzle is when and why Marlowe asked George Chapman to complete his poem, *Hero and Leander*. Chapman can hardly have talked to Marlowe after the stabbing; but if the dramatist knew that his life was in danger, he may have asked his friend to complete this especially cherished poem in the event of his own sudden death, which he had reason to fear.

Contemporaries in the Elizabethan theatre, who were wont to gibe at one another as bitterly as any men that ever lived, usually kept a special note of admiration and tenderness for Marlowe after his death, and even before it. Greene, Harvey, and Chettle are practically the only writers who speak ill of him; and Greene was jealous, Harvey peculiarly malignant, and Chettle trying to help the sale of a book. Kyd attacked his recently murdered friend's reputation in his letters to Sir John Puckering; but he was at that time trying to clear himself of serious charges and may have felt that Marlowe was beyond harm, and his own life more important than a dead man's reputation.

Greene's and Harvey's attacks have already been quoted.[161] Harvey also makes one allusion to "Marlowe's brauados." Henry Chettle, in his *Kind-Harts Dreame* (1592), says that Greene's advice in the *Groatsworth of Witte* "to diuers play makers, is offensively by one or two of them taken." Greene has "about three moneths since died," and their indignations "light on me." One of these two indignant dramatists is obviously Marlowe and the other Shakespeare. "With neither of them that take offence was I acquainted, and with one of them I care not if I neuer be." That, of course, is Marlowe, for an apology to Shakespeare follows immediately. Chettle then returns to "the first, whose learning I reuerence." He has, Chettle continues, "at the perusing of *Greenes* Booke, stroke out what then in conscience I thought he in some displeasure writ: or had it beene true, yet to publish it, was intollerable: him I would wish to vse me no worse than I deserve." [162]

Two other allusions have been regarded as hostile to Marlowe, but their exact meaning is doubtful. Thomas Nashe in *Strange Newes of the Intercepting Certaine Letters* (1593) refers to the

---

[161] See I. 95–97, 126–127.
[162] Pp. 5–6 of G. B. Harrison's ed. (Bodley Head Quartos).

obscure poet Thomas Churchyard (1520?–1604) as one whose muse "may well be grand-mother to our grandeloquentest Poets at this present." [163] As Marlowe had borrowed from Churchyard,[164] this has been regarded as an allusion to him. The epithet "grandeloquent" may have been a sneer — it is at least ambiguous,[165] and it may not refer to Marlowe at all.

It has also been assumed that John Marston's character Tubrio in *The Scourge of Villanie* (1598) represents Marlowe, but this is guesswork at best.[166]

The preponderance of Elizabethan comment is all in Marlowe's favor and remains so for years after his death, until his reputation gradually sinks into forgetfulness before and after 1700. Francis Meres in *Palladis Tamia* (1598) compared him to Homer, Euripides, Virgil, Ovid, and other great classical poets, while ranking him with the greatest writers of his own day:

> As the Greeke tongue is made famous and eloquent by Homer, Hesiod, Euripedes, Æschylus, Sophocles, Pindarus, Phocylides, and Aristophanes; and the Latine tongue by Virgill, Ouid, Horace, Silius Italicus, Lucanus, Lucretius, Ausonius, and Claudianus: so the English tongue is mightily enriched and gorgeously inuested in rare ornaments and resplendent abiliments by Sir Philip Sydney, Spencer, Daniel, Drayton, Warner, Shakespeare, Marlow, and Chapman.[167]

Subsequently Meres lists Marlowe as among "our best for Tragedie," his name being again linked with Shakespeare's.

The publisher, Edward Blunt, dedicating the posthumous *Hero and Leander* to Sir Thomas Walsingham, calls Marlowe "our friend . . . the man that hath been deare unto us." [168] To Chapman, Marlowe is a "diuine wit." [169] To the publisher Thomas Thorpe, he is "that pure Elementall wit *Chr. Marlow.*" [170] To Nashe, in *Christs Teares Over Ierusalem,*[171] written in the very year of Marlowe's death, he is "poore deceassed *Kit Marlow.*" To George Peele, writing the prologue

[163] McKerrow's Nashe, I. 309.
[164] See I. 293.
[165] Alwin Thaler, MLN, 38: 91 F 1923.
[166] Cazamian and Legouis: *Hist. Eng. Lit.* I. 207.
[167] G. Gregory Smith: *Elizabethan Critical Essays*, II. 315, 319.
[168] Brooke's ed., p. 491.
[169] Brooke's ed., p. 513.
[170] Brooke's ed., p. 647.
[171] "To the Reader." McKerrow's Nashe, II. 180.

to his *Honour of the Garter* (dated June 26, 1593), a month after Marlowe had been killed, he is "Marley the Muses' darling." Shakespeare's allusion to the "dead shepherd" in *As You Like It* [172] has a distinct tone of personal regret. Chapman, in his continuation of *Hero and Leander*, bids a "strangely-intellectual fire" to seek out Marlowe, now a

> free soule, whose liuing subiect stood
> Vp to the chin in the Pyerean flood. [173]

Other contemporaries make more specific allusions. To the obscure Henry Petowe, who also attempted to finish *Hero and Leander*, [174] Marlowe is

> that king of poets,
> Marlo admired, whose honney-flowing vaine
> No English writer can as yet attaine;
> Whose name in fame's immortall treasurie
> Truth shall record to endless memorie,

— lines in which the poet may not be equal to his subject, but in which his admiration is none the less apparent.

To the mysterious "J. M." — who may have been John Marston or Jervis [Gervase] Markham — he was "kynde Kit Marlowe." [175] "J. M." even attempts, with a crude tangle of tenses, to praise his unfinished poem. Alluding to Hero, he says that Marlowe

> if death not prevent-him
> Shall write her story, love such art hath lent-him.

Thomas Dekker, in *A Knights Conjuring*, draws an attractive picture of a group of Elizabethan poets in another world:

These were likewise carowsing to one another at the holy well, some of them singing Pæans to Apollo, som of them hymnes to the rest of the goddes, whil'st Marlow, Greene, and Peele had got vnder the shades of a large vyne, laughing to see Nash (that was but newly come to their colledge,) still haunted with the sharpe and satyricall spirit that followed him here vpon earth. [176]

[172] III. v. 81–82. For other echoes of Marlowe in Shakespeare, see Ch. XVI.
[173] III. 183–190.
[174] See II. 109–111.
[175] In *The Newe Metamorphosis* (1600–15). BM Additional MS. 14824, vol. I, pt. I, fol. 39. See John Henry Hobart Lyon: *Study of the Newe Metamorphosis* (Columbia University Press, 1919), p. 62.
[176] Quarto 1607, sig. L; Percy Society reprint (1842), p. 76.

More than thirty years after Marlowe's death, Michael Drayton still remembered him, and in his "Elegie to my most dearely-loued friend Henery Reynolds Esquire of Poets and Poesie" (1627) wrote:

> Neat Marlow, bathed in Thespian springs
> Had in him those braue translunary things,
> That the first Poets had, his raptures were,
> All ayre, and fire, which made his verses cleere,
> For that fine madness still he did retaine,
> Which rightly should possesse a Poets braine.[177]

In his *Hierarchie of the blessed Angells* (1635) Thomas Heywood, commenting on the nicknames given to the English poets, observes:

> *Marlo*, renown'd for his rare art and wit,
> Could ne're attaine beyond the name of *Kit*;
> Although his *Hero* and *Leander* did
> Merit addition rather.[178]

Ben Jonson alludes to "Marlowe's mighty line" in the verses prefatory to the First Folio, and appears to have used the phrase habitually in conversation.[179]

But Christopher Marlowe wrote, unaware, his own best epitaph, as his admirers long ago were quick to see, in the last lines of the epilogue to *Doctor Faustus*:

> Cut is the branch that might haue growne ful straight,
> And burned is *Apolloes* Laurel bough.

Not until 1891 was a memorial to Marlowe erected in Canterbury. On September 16, 1891, Sir Henry Irving unveiled the present monument, which then stood in the Butter Market, just outside Christ Church Gate, where the war memorial now stands. The monument was the work of Onslow Ford and was designed to include four bronze statuettes of Marlowe's chief characters. As originally unveiled, however, it contained only

---

[177] The final couplet is erroneously attributed to "a copy of verses" by Ben Jonson, called "A Censure of the Poets," which does not appear in his works now extant. See Giles Jacob (1723), I. 172.

[178] Page 206. See Dyce's Marlowe (1850), I. xxxviii, and Halliwell-Phillips: *Life of Shakespeare*, p. 190.

[179] George Saintsbury: *Minor Poets of the Caroline Period*, II. 527, and II. 175–176 of the present work.

the Tamburlaine statuette, the other three being added in 1928. J. W. Mackail was president of the Marlowe Memorial Committee, which included Browning, Tennyson, and Swinburne, with Sir Sidney Lee as a leading spirit. The original proposal to place the memorial in Westminster Abbey was dampened by the Dean's request for a fee of two hundred and fifty pounds, [180] and there was some opposition to any memorial on account of "Marlowe's acknowledged life and expressions." [181] Ellen Terry remarked in a personal letter [182] that she and Sir Henry Irving had actually been the chief contributors.

In the summer of 1921 the memorial was moved from the Butter Market to the Dane John.

In 1924 it was proposed at a dinner of the Elizabethan Literary Society, at which Sir Sidney Lee presided, to complete the memorial. Charles Hartwell, R.A., a pupil of the original sculptor, made the remaining statuettes of Faustus, for which Sir Johnston Forbes-Robertson was the model; of Barabas, which was taken from a portrait of Edward Alleyn; and of Edward II, which was taken from a photograph of James K. Hackett. The original idea of these statuettes seems to have been due to Swinburne's suggestion [183] of "a series of medallions representing the principal figures of his works." The three statuettes were unveiled November 1, 1928, by Sir Hugh Walpole, like Marlowe a graduate of the King's School.[184] The chief figure in the memorial represents Erato, the lyric muse — appropriately enough, since Marlowe's gift was primarily lyric rather than dramatic.

[180] Letter of Swinburne to Sir Sidney Lee, December 13, 1888, now in the Bodleian.
[181] Letter in Sir Sidney Lee's correspondence, no. 185, April 6, 1889, now in the Bodleian.
[182] *Kentish Gazette and Canterbury Press*, 253: 7, 3 November 1928. (File in the Royal Museum and Public Library, Canterbury.)
[183] Letter to Sir Sidney Lee, August 15, 1888, now at the Bodleian.
[184] *Kentish Gazette and Canterbury Press*, 211: 8, 19 S 1891; 253: 2, 27 O 1928; 253: 7, 3 N 1928.

CHAPTER VII

TAMBURLAINE

Threatning the world with high astounding tearms.
Prologue to *Tamburlaine*, 5

THE TWO PARTS of *Tamburlaine* may reasonably be regarded as Marlowe's first work. Certain critics would have us believe that *Dido, Queen of Carthage* deserves this honor; while others hold that *Hero and Leander* and the translations, if not his earliest attempt, at least belong with *Dido* to Cambridge days. But these matters are in dispute. There is good reason for assigning these posthumously published works, at least in their present form, to his later days; whereas there is no doubt at all that *Tamburlaine* was the first play that made the unknown young university man at a single bound the foremost dramatist of his day, a rank which he retained for the four, five, or six years that remained of his short life. Even if we admit that other works preceded it, *Tamburlaine* remains the first significant landmark in Marlowe's literary career.

The popular estimate of Marlowe, in his own day as in ours, is based largely on this one play, or rather pair of plays. His rant, his purple patches, his exquisite verse, his faulty structure, his lack of all humor save his own grim kind, his failure to produce credible feminine characters, his soaring ambition, his daring religious unorthodoxy are all clearly marked in this first work. To think of Marlowe is to think of *Tamburlaine*. Indeed, this, his first great success, so completely established his reputation that from the sixteenth to the twentieth century most readers and many critics have overlooked the plainly marked development that seems to have been going on in his later plays and have judged him by *Tamburlaine* alone.

AUTHORSHIP

It is, therefore, odd to find that there is no satisfactory evidence of Marlowe's authorship outside of the play itself. All of the early editions appear without his name upon the title page, and as late as Edward Phillips' *Theatrum Poetarum*[1] *Tamburlaine* was still being attributed to Thomas Newton. Farmer and Malone, in the eighteenth century, suggested that "*Tamburlaine* was either written wholly or in part by Nash,"[2] and Robinson in his 1826 Pickering edition, though he included the play, added that it seemed "probable that Nash was the author" and that "Tamburlaine cannot be laid to Marlowe's charge."[3] Hallam[4] regards Nashe as Marlowe's collaborator in the play, and C. H. Cooper[5] assigns it to Nashe entirely.

The only possible reason for this extraordinary blunder is a passage in Thomas Middleton's *Blacke Booke*, alluding to Nashe:

the Spindle-shanke Spyders which showd like great Leachers with little legges, went stalking ouer his head, as if they had bene conning of *Tamburlayne*.[6]

This certainly does not prove Nashe's authorship, and probably means only that the spiders stalked like an actor playing Tamburlaine. Hall's *Satires* also ridicule "the stalking steps of his great personage."[7]

In a manuscript note in his copy of Langbaine, dated February 28, 1811, Malone also asserted his belief that *Tamburlaine* was written by Nicholas Breton, whom he regarded as author of *The Three Bold Beauchams*. He apparently based this idea on a passage in Sir John Suckling's *The Goblins*:

> But here's he that writ *Tamerlane*.
> *Poet.* I beseech you bring me to him.
> There's something in his Scene
> Between the Empress[es] a little high and Cloudy.
> I wou'd resolve myself.
> *1 Thie[f].* You shall, Sir.
> Let me see — the Author of the *bold Beauchams*,
> And *England's Joy*.[8]

[1] II. 182. (Arranged according to authors' Christian names.)
[2] Robinson's (1826) ed., I. xxii. Cf. Malone's annotation opposite p. 344 of his Langbaine, now in the Bodleian (Malone 131).
[3] Robinson's (1826) ed., I. xxiii.
[4] *Introduction to the Literature of Europe* (1843), II. 169.
[5] *Athenae Cantab.*, II. 306–309.
[6] Sig. D1r of the Huntington copy. See also Dyce's ed., V. 526; Bullen's ed., VIII. 25.
[7] Joseph Hall's *Satires*, bk. I, satire III, p. 10 of the ed. by Thomas Wharton, expanded by Samuel Weller Singer (1824).
[8] Act IV, sc. i, p. 330 of the 1766 Dublin ed.; IV. iv. 49–55, p. 198 of A. Hamilton Thompson's (1910) ed. See also Dodsley (1826), X. 141–142. The texts vary.

This passage can undoubtedly be so read as to identify the author of *The Bold Beauchams* with the author of *Tamburlaine*; but it is more reasonable to suppose that the dash indicates a break in which the actor impersonating the thief goes on to the next piece on his list — presumably by a different author.

Sir William D'Avenant, in his *Play-house to be Let* (ca. 1662), also couples

> the times of mighty *Tamberlane*,
> Of conjuring *Faustus*, and the *Beauchamps* bold.[9]

In any case, the authorship of *The Bold Beauchams* is uncertain. Chambers [10] does not mention it. Ward [11] believes it is Heywood's; and, as the play is lost, it may for all we know be Marlowe's.[12]

Though no one today doubts Marlowe's authorship of *Tamburlaine*, it is certainly desirable to clear up this question at the very start. No other author is ever named by Elizabethans. On the other hand, there are numerous contemporary allusions which, though vague, certainly apply to Marlowe, and equally certainly do not apply to any other known figure of the day. Unfortunately, the phraseology, intended to be understood by contemporaries and not by scholars three centuries later, is never specific and does not supply adequate evidence now, though doubtless it was entirely clear in the sixteenth and early seventeenth centuries.

Phillips may have attributed the play to Thomas Newton because of Newton's writings on the Near East, which contain allusions to Tamburlaine; but it is more probable that he was misled by Kirkman's list of plays. Here *Tamburlaine* is marked as anonymous, but stands next to Newton's *Thebais*.[13] The blunder is fortunate, since it was later specifically corrected by two writers on Newton and thus provides the two earliest definite attributions of the play to Marlowe. These, made

---

[9] The 1673 folio of D'Avenant's *Works* is paged in three sections. The quotation here is on p. 76, ll. 20–21, of the second group. See also the 1873 Edinburgh ed., IV. 31.
[10] *Eliz. Stage*, IV. 236.
[11] *Hist. Eng. Dram. Lit.* (1899), II. 583.
[12] See Ellis-Fermor's ed. of *Tamburlaine*, p. 14. Dyce's Peele, II. 170n; Gifford's Jonson, VIII. 330.
[13] First pointed out by W. W. Greg. Cf. *Year's Work in English Studies* (1923), III. 88.

within a century of his death, show pretty clearly that his authorship was already generally accepted and had probably never been in doubt, though obscured by the impression made by the actor Alleyn's impersonation of Tamburlaine, to which allusions abound.

There are five seventeenth-century lists of plays which purport to include all printed. Richard Rogers and William Ley, booksellers, published one list with their 1656 edition of the *Careles Shepherdess*.[14] Edward Archer, another bookseller, published a second in the same year with his edition of *The Old Law*,[15] by Massinger, Middleton, and Rowley. Francis Kirkman published two, one in 1661 as an appendix to *Tom Tyler and his Wife*,[16] the other in 1671. Gerard Langbaine began his series of lists with *Momus Triumphans* in 1688, though he refers obscurely to an earlier list of 1680.

The two lists of 1656 and Kirkman's first list, of 1661, omit the author's name in listing *Tamburlaine*; but in 1671 Kirkman specifically names Marlowe as the author, a view which Langbaine echoes in *Momus Triumphans*.[17] When he brought out his account of the *English Dramatick Poets* (1691), he said clearly: "I know not how Mr. *Philips* came to ascribe *Tamburlaine the Great* to this Author [Thomas Newton]; for tho' *Marloe*'s Name be not printed in the Title-page, yet both in Mr. *Kirkman*'s and my former Catalogue printed [in] 1680. his Name is prefix'd." [18] Still later, his *Lives and Characters* (1699) again contradicts Phillips' assertion of Newton's authorship, asserting that *Tamburlaine* was "none of his but Marlo's." [19] He based his attribution on Heywood's prologue to the 1633 edition of *The Jew of Malta*. This runs:

> We know not how our Play may passe this Stage,
> But by the best of Poets in that age
> The *Malta Jew* had being, and was made;
> And He, then by the best of Actors play'd:

[14] Copy in British Museum, 644.e.21.
[15] Also in British Museum, 644.e.86.
[16] Both in British Museum, 643.d.63 and 643.d.75.
[17] See p. 17. The first three lists are printed as Appendix II to W. W. Greg's *List of Masques, Pageants, &c.* There is a facsimile of Kirkman's 1671 list in *Old English Drama. Student's Facsimile Edition.* Mention of *Tamburlaine* is on p. 15.
[18] See pp. 394–395, 344.
[19] See p. 106, under Newton.

In *Hero* and *Leander*, one did gaine
A lasting memorie; in *Tamberlaine*,
This *Jew*, with others many: th'other wan
The Attribute of peerelesse.

Printed marginal notes identify "the best of Poets" with "Marlo," and "the best of Actors" with "Allin." Malone [20] in 1811 asserted that "Langbaine's assertion that Heywood attributes Tamburlaine to Marlowe in his prologue to the 'Jew of Malta' is founded in a mistake and a false punctuation. Heywood only asserts that Alleyn was famous in the part of Tamburlaine, not that Marlowe wrote the play."

E. G. Robinson, in his 1826 Pickering edition,[21] questioned "whether this play has not been attributed to Marlowe under a misconception of Heywood's meaning." Broughton, writing four years later, agreed with him [22] and his proposal to re-punctuate so that the lines would read:

In 'Hero and Leander' one did gain
A lasting memory: in 'Tamburlaine,'
This 'Jew,' with others many, th'other wan
The attribute of peerless.

This would mean only that Marlowe wrote *Hero and Leander* and that Alleyn acted in *Tamburlaine* — which nobody has ever doubted.

The language is so obscure that no definite conclusion can be drawn; but Heywood seems to associate *Tamburlaine* with two other works by Marlowe. Langbaine first identified the play as Marlowe's with the cautious proviso, "Had I not Mr. *Heywood*'s Word for it, In the foremention'd Prologue, I should not believe this Play to be his." In later editions, however, he omits these words.[23]

Marlowe's authorship is confirmed by Anthony à Wood, who in the *Athenae Oxonienses*, published in the same year (1691), observes that Newton "was author, as a certain writer [Phillips] saith, of two tragedies, viz. of the first and second parts of *Tamerline the great Scythian Emperor*, but false. For in Tho.

[20] MS. note dated February 28, 1811, in his Langbaine, now at the Bodleian.
[21] I. xx.
[22] *Gentleman's Magazine* (NS), 100: 596, Je (1830). See "Supplement."
[23] *Account of the English Dramatick Poets*, p. 344.

Newton's time the said two parts were performed by Christop. Marlo, sometimes a student in Cambridge." [24]

The admittedly vague contemporary evidence for Marlowe's authorship begins with Robert Greene's allusion in *Perimedes the Blacksmith* (licensed March 29, 1588). Greene had been ridiculed "for that I could not make my verses iet vpon the stage in tragicall buskins, euerie worde filling the mouth like the faburden of Bo-Bell, daring God out of heauen with that Atheist *Tamburlan*." Then follows his allusion to "*Merlins* race." Since "Merlin" was pronounced "Marlin" in Elizabethan times [25] and since Marlowe's verse is clearly described, this pretty plainly connects Marlowe with *Tamburlaine*. In his *Farewell to Folly* (1591) [26] Greene alludes to "the life of Tomliuclin" — by which he presumably means *Tamburlaine*, though he names no author. His attitude in this passage, however, is the same attitude of hostility that he always took toward Marlowe.

Supplementary evidence is to be found in a "Sonet" affixed to Gabriel Harvey's *New Letter of Notable Contents* (1593) entitled "*Gorgon*, or the Wonderfull yeare," a production in itself quite as wonderful as the year it purports to describe. Harvey follows up the line already quoted, "thy Tamerlaine voutsafes to dye," [27] with an equally obscure "glosse" which tells how death, "smiling at his Tamberlaine contempt . . . sternely struck home the peremptory stroke." Since the *New Letter* appeared in 1593, this must be the "Wonderfull yeare," and it can hardly be coincidence that this is also the year of Marlowe's death. Here, then, is a second contemporary writer associating *Tamburlaine* with Marlowe.

Finally, there is the well-known passage, already quoted, in Nashe's epistle "To the Gentlemen Students of both Vniuersities," contributed as a preface to Greene's *Menaphon*.[28] Nashe here ridicules "idiote art-masters" who are "mounted on the stage of arrogance" and who commit "the digestion of their cholerick incumbrances, to the spacious volubilitie of a drumming decasillabon."

---

[24] Ed. 1815, II. 7. See under "Newton."
[25] Grosart's Greene, VII. 7–8. See also I. 96–97 of the present work.
[26] Grosart's Greene, IX. 230.   [27] See I. 143.   [28] Grosart's Greene, VI. 10.

This, though it does not mean very much, at best, and though it does not name either dramatist or play, nevertheless looks very much like a reference to *Tamburlaine*. At this time, the "drumming decasillabon" was peculiarly Marlowe's own, and the words "idiote art-masters" (Nashe was never one to mince his words) applies especially to Marlowe, who had taken his degree in 1587. The extant edition of *Menaphon* is dated 1589, but an earlier one may have appeared in 1587 — either date is close enough to the time of Marlowe's degree and the first production of *Tamburlaine* to give the reference the cutting application that Nashe appears to intend,[29] and too early to apply to other plays written in the "mighty line."

There is an entry in *Henslowe's Diary*[30] which would establish Marlowe's authorship definitely, had it not long since been shown to be a forgery, probably the handiwork of John Payne Collier.[31] It has been inserted in a conveniently blank space among the genuine entries, and reads:

pd vnto Thomas dickers the 20 of Desembr 1597 for ⎫
adycyons to ffostus twentie shellinges and fyve shellinges more ⎪
for a prolog to Marloes tambelan so in all J saye payde ⎬ xxv s.
twentye five shellinges . . . ⎭

The *Diary*, originally sent to Dulwich with Alleyn's papers, was lost until about 1790. It was then lent to Malone, who made certain notes, in which this passage does not appear.[32] After Malone's death the manuscript was returned to Dulwich, whither Malone's extracts also found their way. Collier used the *Diary* in writing his *History of Dramatic Poetry* (1831), in which he describes the forged entry as providing the "most conclusive" proof of Marlowe's authorship of *Tamburlaine*.[33] In his own edition of the *Diary*, Collier makes no comment whatever on this entry.

[29] But see I. 95.
[30] Fol. 19, ll. 13–16; Collier's ed., p. 71; Greg's ed., I. 38.
[31] C. M. Ingleby: "Spurious ballads, &c., affecting Shakspere and Marlowe," *Academy*, 9: 313, 1 Ap 1876; C. M. Ingleby: "Henslowe's Diary," N&Q, 6th ser., 4: 103–104, S Ap 1881; G. F. Warner: *Catalogue*, p. xlv and pp. 157–163; Greg's ed. of the *Diary*, pp. xxxvi–xlv; G. F. Warner: article "Collier, John Payne," DNB, IV. 804–809.
[32] Appendix to *History of the Stage*, vol. I, pt. ii, p. 288.
[33] HEDP, III. 113.

In September, 1868, C. M. Ingleby examined the manuscript and concluded "that some dishonest person had taken advantage of the blanks, not infrequently left by Henslowe, for the purpose of inserting pseudo-antique entries, evidently with the view of supporting unauthorized statements by adducing the purport of those false entries." [34] In 1876, in the *Academy*, he specifically denounced the *Tamburlaine* entry.

In 1881 Sir George Frederic Warner, of the British Museum staff, in his catalogue of the Dulwich Manuscripts, listed five forgeries, of which the *Tamburlaine* entry was one. "The whole entry," he asserted, "is evidently a forgery, written in clumsy imitation of Henslowe's hand." The forger was particularly clever at this point, taking advantage of a genuine blot in the original to give authenticity to his handiwork. He ran the letters "ll" up to the blot, then continued the loops above it, so that the modern interpolation seemed to pass under the sixteenth-century ink. The fraud is, however, apparent enough under a glass. Later investigation has increased the list of forgeries known to have been inserted in the *Diary*, but none of these more recently discovered frauds relate to Marlowe. No one, today, doubts Collier's guilt. [35]

The other contemporary allusions are of unquestioned authenticity and, though obscure, gain weight by their number. The close association of Alleyn's name with the part of Tamburlaine and of his company with the play itself point to Marlowe's authorship, since we know that Marlowe wrote for this group of actors.

The clearest evidence, however, is the play itself. It has the right tone of Marlowe, as we learn to know it in the later plays. It fits in accurately at the bottom of the curve of literary development shown by his later plays. It has several clear examples of Marlowe's characteristic trick of echoing his own lines. The verse, the style, but most of all the impetuous unrest, the aching struggle for the eternally unattainable, the flaming glory of the words, are Marlowe's very essence.

[34] N&Q, 6th ser., 4: 103, 6 Ag 1881.
[35] Warner, *op. cit.*, p. 160; Greg's ed., I. xxxix. See also I. 294 of the present work.

DATE

The First Part of *Tamburlaine* is usually supposed to have been written during the winter of 1587–88. The Second Part would then have been written immediately afterward, presumably some time during the latter part of 1588. The passage in Greene's *Perimedes* (1588) is pretty clear evidence that the play was already so familiar to the play-going public that allusion to it would be clear to the average reader. Greene's allusion, moreover, is probably to the second part of the tragedy, since most of the passages "daring God out of heaven" appear there. Greene was thinking of passages like

> Now *Mahomet*, if thou haue any power,
> Come downe thy selfe and worke a myracle.
>   [II *Tamb.* 4298–4299]
> What daring God torments my body thus,
> And seeks to conquer mighty *Tamburlaine?* . . .
> Come let vs march against the powers of heauen,
> And set blacke streamers in the firmament,
> To signifie the slaughter of the Gods.
>   [II *Tamb.* 4434–4442]

There is no specific challenge to the Christian deity anywhere in the play. Instead, there are some surprisingly edifying passages. But defiances of deity in general are frequent enough in Part Two to give clear application to Greene's gibe, and both passages contain the words "daring God."

Harvey's "Sonet" in the *New Letter of Notable Contents* opens with the lines

> *St. Fame* dispos'd to cunnycatch the world,
> Vprear'd a wonderment of *Eighty Eight.* . . .
> The wonder was, no wonder fell that yeare.[36]

This is obscure enough to mean anything; but there is specific mention of *Tamburlaine* in a later line, and the "Postscript" and "Glosse" which follow seem to be hostile references to Marlowe: "Sir Rodomont . . . Gargantua minde . . . sky-surmounting breath . . . that taught the Tempany to swell . . . hawty man . . . tamberlaine contempt . . ."

> He that nor feared God, nor dreaded Diu'll,
> Nor ought admired, but his wondrous selfe.

[36] Grosart's Harvey, I. 295.

Gabriel Harvey's meaning is, perhaps, that *Tamburlaine*, first produced in 1588, was the wonder of the year, but after all not a very wonderful play. This would agree with the date indicated by *Perimedes*.[37]

In 1930 Sir Edmund K. Chambers published in the *Times Literary Supplement* [38] a note which he believed settled the date of *Tamburlaine* once for all. Though not quite beyond question, his discovery assuredly deserves serious consideration. It consists of a letter from Philip Gawdy (1562–1617), a Norfolk gentleman resident in London, written to his father November 16, 1587:

My L. Admyrall his men and players having a devyse in ther playe to tye one of their fellowes to a poste and so to shoote him to deathe, having borrowed their Callyvers one of the players handes swerved his peece being charged with bullett missed the fellowe he aymed at and killed a chyld, and a woman great with chyld forthwith, and hurt an other man in the head very soore.[39]

Sir Edmund identified this scene with the execution of the Governor of Babylon in the fifth act of *Tamburlaine*, Part II; and it is certainly true that there is a close similarity between the scene which Gawdy describes and that in *Tamburlaine*. It is also true that *Tamburlaine* was acted by the Admiral's Company, as the title page of 1590 testifies.

On the other hand the scene, as Gawdy describes it, is not exactly like that in Marlowe's text (4196, 4220–4221). Tamburlaine directs that the unfortunate governor shall be hanged from the city walls and there shot to death. Nothing is said about tying him to a stake. Gawdy, however, says specifically that he did not actually see the incident: "thoughe my self no wyttnesse thereof, yet I may be bold to veryfye it for an assured trothe." Hence it is possible to assume that the scene on the stage accorded exactly with the text, and was merely garbled by word-of-mouth accounts. If we make this assumption, it is absolutely certain that both parts of *Tamburlaine* had been finished within a short time after Marlowe left Cambridge, or while he was actually at the university.

[37] F. G. Hubbard: "Date of *Tamburlaine*," PMLA, 33: 436–443 (1918).
[38] TLS, 29: 683, 28 Ag 1930; *Eliz. Stage*, II. 135.
[39] BM, Egerton MS. 2804, fol. 35; Isaac Herbert Jeayes: *Letters of Philip Gawdy* (London: J. B. Nichols and Sons, 1906), p. 23.

If this is true, it is hard to explain the play's quotation from Paul Ive's *Practise of Fortification*,[40] which was published in 1589. It is possible, of course, that there was an earlier edition of which we know nothing — since military handbooks wear out quickly under service conditions. Marlowe may, also, have seen the manuscript; and finally, since Ive was a mere compiler, Marlowe may be quoting the same passage that Ive quoted from some earlier work, still unknown.

The play cannot be later than 1590. The entry in the *Stationers Register*, August 14, 1590,[41] to Richard Jones of "*The twooe commicall discourses of* TOMBERLEIN *the Cithian shepparde*" and the appearance of two editions in the same year definitely fix a *terminus ad quem*. The Cambridge tradition that *Tamburlaine* was written in Marlowe's room at Corpus Christi has no evidence to support it, but is not improbable. If it is correct, Marlowe may have begun the play as early as 1586, since he was rarely in residence during 1587 and probably had little leisure to write.[42]

[40] See I. 210–211.

[41] Arber's Reprint, II. 262.

[42] Dates assigned by Marlowe's editors and critics are as follows:

1826. E. G. Robinson: No opinion.

1831. J. P. Collier: "Acted anterior to 1587." [HEDP, III. 112]

1850. Alexander Dyce: Quotes Collier approvingly. [I. viii]

1854. Tycho Mommsen: "Dieser Umschlag [the blank verse of *Tamburlaine*] geschah 1586 bis 1587." [Eisenach Programm]

1865. H. Ulrici: "Es kaum einem Zweifel unterliegen kann, dass sein *Tamburlaine the Great*, wahrscheinlich sein erstes dramatisches Werk, bereits 1586–7 aufgefuhrt wurde." (*Jahrb*. I. 60 [1865])

1870. Francis Cunningham: "Both parts . . . had been publicly performed in London at least as early as 1587." [p. x]

1881–86. Nikolai Il'ich Storojenko: "Put on the stage in 1586." [Grosart's Greene, I. 169]

1885. A. H. Bullen: "Presented on the stage in or before 1588 (probably in 1587)." [I. xviii]

1885. A. Wagner: Quotes Mommsen approvingly. [pp. iii–iv]

1887. Ernest Faligan: "Verisimilior mihi videtur . . . (1587)." [*De Marlovianis Fabulis*, p. 100]

1899. A. W. Ward: "On the stage as early as 1588; probably . . . as Mr. Fleay says, . . . 'as early as 1587.'" [HEDL, I. 321]

1901. Wolfgang Keller: "Um das Jahr 1587 Marlowes Tamerlan auf der Londoner Bühne erschien." [*Jahrb*. 37: 1 (1901)]

1901. E. Hübener: "Das Erscheinungsjahr des Tamb. wohl ohne Zweifel 1586/87 ist." [*Einfluss von Marlowe's Tamburlaine*, p. 4]

1903. Erich Kroneberg: "'Tamburlaine' höchstwahrscheinlich schon 1586 aufgeführt wurde." [George Peele's "Edward the First," p. 71]

1904. John H. Ingram: "Produced by 1587." [*Christopher Marlowe and His Associates*, p. 102]

Stage History

There is no evidence of stage production earlier than Henslowe's note of a performance of "Tamberlan" by the Admiral's Company, August 30, 1594; but a multitude of contemporary allusions show that the play had long been familiar, and also that it was excessively popular. The haste with which Marlowe wrote Part Two indicates the same thing. Thomas Coryat, the traveler, wrote that Tamburlaine was probably "not altogether so famous in his own Country of *Tartaria*, as in *England*." Henslowe marks the 1594 production "j" but probably means the First Part rather than the first production.[43]

The Elizabethan stage productions were evidently as sumptuous as they could be made. The inventory of the stage properties owned by the Admiral's men, made in 1598, includes "Tamberlyne brydell," which was evidently used for the captive kings, and "j cage," doubtless for the accommodation of Bajazeth. The costumes include "Tamberlynes cotte, with

---

1905. Churton Collins: "Produced in or about 1587." [*Life and Works of Robert Greene*, I. 75]
1908. Greg: "The first part at least was almost certainly acted in 1587." [*Henslowe's Diary*, II. 168]
1910. Tucker Brooke: "The two parts of *Tamburlaine* are commonly ascribed to the years 1587 and 1588 respectively, and these dates are almost certainly correct." [*Works*, p. 1]
1912. W. L. Phelps: "It is assumed that Marlowe's play was acted in 1588 or 1589; but, as a matter of fact, nobody knows." [pp. 12-13]
1916. A. F. Hopkinson: "Acted by the Admiral's men in 1587." [*Selimus*, p. xxx]
1918. F. G. Hubbard: "1588 is the date of the first appearance of *Tamburlaine* upon the stage." [PMLA, 33: 440 Je 1918]
1922. Tucker Brooke: "Part one can hardly have been written later than the beginning of 1587." [PMLA, 37: 391 S 1922]
1923. E. K. Chambers: "Greene's *Perimedes* reference suggests 1587 or 1588 as the probable date of *Tamburlaine*." [*Eliz. Stage*, III. 422]
1927. U. M. Ellis-Fermor: "In the absence of definite evidence, we must conjecture the date, and the latter part of 1588, or the earlier part of 1589 is that generally accepted." [*Christopher Marlowe*, p. 4]
1931. J. M. Robertson: "Produced in 1587." [*Marlowe*, p. 41]
1931. U. M. Ellis-Fermor: "The date which has been generally accepted for the completion of the first part of *Tamburlaine* and its first performance is the winter of 1587/8 and that for the second part very shortly afterwards, the spring or early summer of 1588." [*Tamburlaine*, p. 6]
1936. Rupert Taylor: "Produced before the publication of Greene's *Perimides*" [1588]. [PMLA, 51: 660 S 1936]

43 See MLR, IV. 408; John Taylor: *Works* (1630), p. 85.

coper lace," and "Tamberlanes breches of crymson vellvet." [44]

The frequency of allusions to *Tamburlaine* during the seventeenth century, however, suggests that there must have been at least occasional performances. When eventually the rage for "improvement" and adaptation of the older drama began, Marlowe was forgotten and only the adaptations of Nicholas Rowe and Charles Saunders held the stage.[45]

There is no further record of performances until a revival by the Yale Dramatic Association in 1919. This was followed by performances at Rosemary Hall in 1925 and at Worcester College, Oxford, by the Buskins Society, June 12, 13, and 14, 1933.[46] The National Broadcasting Company gave a radio production March 19, 1938.

Henslowe's records show *Tamburlaine*, presumably the First Part, performed August 28, 1594, with takings of £3 11*s*. Other performances were:

Date	Takings
Sept. 12, 1594	45s.
Sept. 28, 1594	31s.
Oct. 15, 1594	28s.
Oct. 17, 1594	40s.
Nov. 4, 1594	39s.
Nov. 27, 1594	22s.
Dec. 17, 1594	31s.
Dec. 30, 1594	22s.
Jan. 27, 1594/5	30s.
Feb. 17, 1594/5	30s.
Mar. 11, 1594/5	30s.
May 21, 1595	22s.
Sept. 15, 1595	21s.
Nov. 12, 1595	18s.

The Second Part is first recorded December 19, 1594, two days after a performance of "tamberlen," and the takings are 45*s*. Thereafter the two parts usually appear within a day or two of each other. Performances of the Second Part are listed by Henslowe as follows:

[44] *Henslowe Papers*, ed. W. W. Greg, pp. 116, 117, 119, 120. *Diary of Philip Henslowe*, ed. Collier (1845), pp. 273–275.
[45] See I. 244, 270–273.
[46] TLS, 32: 364, 25 My 1933.

Date	Takings
Dec. 19, 1594	46s.
Jan. 1, 1594/5	£3 2s.
Jan. 29, 1594/5	47s.
Feb. 18, 1594/5	36s.
Mar. 12, 1594/5	22s.
May 22, 1595	25s.
Nov. 13, 1595	32s.

Though there are no definite records of specific performances, *Tamburlaine* seems to have been revived fairly frequently under Charles I, if we may judge from a contemporary allusion by Edmund Gayton (1608–1666), one of Ben Jonson's adopted sons:

I have known upon one of these *Festivals*, but especially at *Shrove-tide*, where the Players have been appointed, notwithstanding their bils to the contrary, to act what the major part of the company had a mind to; sometimes *Tamerlane*, sometimes *Jugurth*, sometimes the Jew of *Malta*, and sometimes parts of all these, and at last, none of the three taking, they were forc'd to undresse and put off their Tragick habits, and conclude the day with the merry milk-maides.[47]

Unless the players thus complied with the wishes of the audience, Gayton concludes, "the Benches, the tiles, the laths, the stones, Oranges, Apples, Nuts, flew about most liberally." The old plays had by this time apparently reached the limit of their popularity, though there is a reference to roaring "like Tamerlin at the Bull" Theatre in Cowley's *Guardian*.[48] Cowley's play, according to the title page, was "Acted before Prince CHARL[E]S His HIGHNESS at Trinity-Colledg in *Cambridge*, upon the twelfth of *March*, 1641." Bullen, in the introduction to his edition,[49] and Sir Sidney Lee, in the *Dictionary of National Biography*,[50] are apparently thinking of this allusion when they refer to a production of *Tamburlaine* at the Bull Theatre about 1650. Cowley's play was published in that year, but the events alluded to must antedate the production of 1641.

---

[47] *Pleasant Notes upon Don Quixot*, ed. 1654, p. 271. Passage omitted in ed. 1768. The book is also referred to as *Festivous Notes upon Don Quixot*.

[48] *Guardian*, III. vi, ed. 1650, sig. C3v. The allusion also appears in *Cutter of Coleman Street* (III. vii), the revised version of *The Guardian*.

[49] I. xxii.

[50] Article "Marlowe." DNB, XXXVI. 182.

Sources

The study of Marlowe's sources for *Tamburlaine* is of particular importance because it definitely reverses the view of his mind and character which has been generally accepted for three centuries. Detailed, minute, even trifling though the necessary investigation may be, it is rewarded in the end by a new understanding of the mind of a very great poet. It shows Marlowe as something more than an impetuous youth with a gift for poetry. It shows him as a careful writer who bases work of the purest poetic beauty on an elaborate and careful study of all available materials.

It has long been the commonly received opinion that Marlowe drew his material for *Tamburlaine* from two main sources: first, the life of Tamburlaine contained in Pedro Mexia's *Silva de varia leción*, published at Seville in 1544 and more or less inaccurately translated as *The Foreste* by Thomas Fortescue in 1576, while Marlowe was still a boy; [51] and second, the *Vita magni Tamerlanis* by Petrus Perondinus, published at Florence in 1551, and reprinted in a collection of *Turkish Histories* edited by Conrad Clausser and published at Basel in 1556. Marlowe might have taken most of the material in *The Foreste* from George Whetstone's *The English Mirror* (1586), which reproduces many of Mexia's details upon which the dramatist seized. He might have taken most of the material in Perondinus from *Beautiful Blossoms Gathered by John Bysshup*, which had borrowed heavily from the *Vita*.

The view that Marlowe borrowed — directly or indirectly — from Mexia and Perondinus only, though generally accepted until recently, is not wholly justified in itself, and is at best an incomplete statement of the true facts. Although Marlowe probably consulted Mexia, the order of whose incidents he follows closely, and though he may have made use of Perondinus as well, it is by no means certain that he used either of them; whereas it is perfectly certain that, whether he used these two authors or not, he did not confine himself to them. In addition to these books, Marlowe read the *Elogia virorum bellica virtute*

---

[51] Other editions, Lione, 1556; Venice, 1565; Paris, 1572.

illustrium of Paulus Jovius, Bishop of Nocera; the *De Dictis factisque memorabilibus collectanea* of Baptista Folgotius,[52] and probably *The Turkish Affaires* of the Florentine, Andrea Cambine, translated by John Shute in 1562 — three books from which he might have learned everything given by Mexia. It is probable, however, that he discovered them by following up the bibliography given by Mexia. He also read Philip Lonicer's *Chronicorum Turcicorum tomi duo* (1578 and 1584).

Besides these, Marlowe seems to have had access, in some unexplained way, to a group of facts about the historical Timur contained in Oriental works, none of which were translated during his lifetime. He drew practically all his geography from the *Theatrum Orbis Terrarum* of the German geographer, Ortelius, which was already at Corpus Christi, among the Parker books, when Marlowe arrived from Canterbury, and which Bishop Richard Barnes presented to the university library, July 7, 1581, a few months later.[53]

There is also a group of minor sources, on which Marlowe can be shown to have drawn in very slight degree, and which for convenience should be discussed first. These are the classic writers Herodotus, Xenophon, and Euripides; Spenser; Paul Ive's *Practise of Fortification* (1589); and Ariosto's *Orlando Furioso*.

Marlowe's best-known borrowing from Spenser is the simile of the almond tree:

> Ile ride in golden armour like the Sun,
> And in my helme a triple plume shal spring,
> Spangled with Diamonds dancing in the aire,
> To note me Emperour of the three fold world,
> Like to an almond tree ymounted high,
> Vpon the lofty and celestiall mount,
> Of euer greene *Selinus* queintly dect
> With bloomes more white than *Hericinas* browes,
> Whose tender blossoms tremble euery one,
> At euery little breath that thorow heauen is blowen.
> [II *Tamb.* 4094–4103]

---

[52] Reprinted in 1578 as *Factorum dictorumque memorabilium, Libri IX.*
[53] *Rough List of Parker Books*, at Corpus; *Catalogus Librorum MS*, p. 21, University Library; C. Sayle: *Cambridge University Library Annals*, p. 52.

There can be no question of the relationship of these lines to
Spenser's

> Vpon the top of all his loftie crest,
> A bunch of haires discoloured diuersly,
> With sprincled pearle, and gold full richly drest,
> Did shake, and seem'd to daunce for iollity,
> Like to an Almond tree ymounted hye
> On top of greene *Selinis* all alone,
> With blossomes braue bedecked daintily;
> Whose tender locks do tremble euery one
> At euery little breath, that vnder heauen is blowne.
> [FQ. I. vii. 32]

Marlowe had not yet done, however, with his borrowing from
the *Faerie Queene*. The rest of his passage in *Tamburlaine* comes
from another part of Spenser's poem.[54] Marlowe continues:

> Then *in my coach* like *Saturnes* royal son,
> Mounted his *shining chariot, gilt with fire*,
> And *drawen with princely Eagles* through the path,
> Pau'd *with bright Christall*, and enchac'd with starres,
> When *all the Gods stand gazing* at his pomp.
> So will I ride through *Samarcanda* streets.
> [II *Tamb.* 4104–4109]

This is freely adapted from Spenser's

> So forth she comes, and *to her coche* does clyme,
> *Adorned all with gold*, and girlonds gay,
> That seemd as fresh as *Flora* in her prime,
> And stroue to match, in royall rich array,
> Great *Iunoes* golden chaire, the which they say
> *The Gods stand gazing on*, when she does ride
> To *Ioues* high house through *heauens bras-paued way*
> Drawne of faire Pecocks.
> [FQ. I. iv. 17]

There are several other unmistakable borrowings from the
Faerie Queene in *Tamburlaine*, notably:

> Ile make ye roare, that earth may eccho foorth
> The far resounding torments ye sustaine,
> As when an *heard of lusty Cymbrian Buls*,
> Run mourning round about *the Femals misse*,

---

[54] A parallel first noted by Charles Crawford: *Collectanea*, I. 78–79 (1906). Georg
Schoeneich: *Der litterarische Einfluss Spensers auf Marlowe* (1907) lists other parallels.

And stung with furie of their following,
Fill all the aire with troublous bellowing.
[II *Tamb.* 3860–3865]
He loudly brayd with beastly yelling sound,
That all the fields rebellowed againe;
As great a noyse, as when *in Cymbrian plaine*
An heard of Bulles, whom kindly rage doth sting,
Do for *the milkie mothers want* complaine,
And *fill the fields with troublous bellowing.*
[FQ. I. viii. 11]

Enrolde in flames and fiery smoldering mistes.
[I *Tamb.* 618]
Enrold in flames, and smouldring dreriment.
[FQ. I. viii. 9]

Engyrt with tempests wrapt in pitchy clouds.
[I *Tamb.* 2076]
Enwrapt in coleblacke clouds and filthy smoke.
[FQ. I. xi. 44]

Then let the stony dart of sencelesse colde,
Pierce through the center of my withered heart,
And make a passage for my loathed life.
[I *Tamb.* 2083–2085]
Now let the stony dart of senselesse cold
Perce to my hart, and pas through euery side,
And let eternall night so sad sight fro me hide.
[FQ. I. vii. 22]

So from the East vnto the furthest West,
Shall *Tamburlain* extend his puisant arme.
[I *Tamb.* 1344–1345]
Stretching your conquering armes from east to west.
[II *Tamb.* 2666]
Their scepters stretcht from East to Westerne shore.
[FQ. I. i. 5]

O highest Lamp of euerliuing *Ioue,*
Accursed day. . . .
[I *Tamb.* 2071–2072]
O lightsome day, the lampe of highest *Ioue.*
[FQ. I. vii. 23]

The golden balle of heauens eternal fire,
That danc'd with glorie on the siluer waues.
[II *Tamb.* 2970–2971]

> . . . as the Sunny beames do glaunce and glide
> Vpon the trembling waue. . . .
>
> [FQ. II. v. 2]

When Tamburlaine warns the virgins of Damascus, showing then his sword's point,

> For there sits Death, there sits imperious Death,
> [I *Tamb.* 1892]

he is again echoing the *Faerie Queene*:

> For death sate on the point of that enchaunted speare.
> [FQ. III. i. 9]

The well-known opening lines of *Tamburlaine*,

> From iygging vaines of riming mother wits,
> And such conceits as clownage keepes in pay,
> Weele lead you to the stately tent of War,

are probably based on a passage in Spenser's October Aeglogue in *The Shepherd's Calendar*:

> Abandon then the base and viler clowne, . . .
> And sing of bloody Mars, of wars, of giusts.

Marlowe was probably also acquainted with Spenser's version of Bellay's *Rvuines of Rome*, from which he seems to borrow.[55] In stanza ten of his translation, Spenser tells the story of Cadmus. Marlowe (I *Tamb.* 570–575) repeats the story, adding, "So Poets say, my Lord." It is possible also that the captured Zenocrate's distress in *Tamburlaine* owes something to distressed damsels in the *Faerie Queene*.

Both the First and Second Parts of *Tamburlaine* were printed in 1590, the same year in which the first three books of the *Faerie Queene* appeared. But since *Tamburlaine* had certainly been played before this time, it is probable that Marlowe had access to Spenser's poems circulating in manuscript in the Walsingham and Raleigh circles, to which both poets belonged. This practice we know to have been common in Elizabethan days — so common, indeed, that the poems of Sir Philip Sidney, Walsingham's son-in-law, were never published at all during

<hr>

55 Cf. Charles Crawford: *Collectanea*, I. 66 ff.

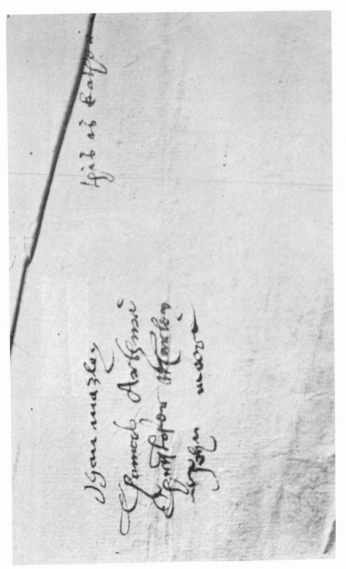

MARLOWE'S SIGNATURE. WILL OF KATHERINE BENCHKYN

(Third from top)

his lifetime. Spenser dedicated the poem to Marlowe's friend, Sir Walter Raleigh, with whom he had returned from Ireland in 1589, while Marlowe was in London. The first three books of the *Faerie Queene* are supposed to have been part of Raleigh's effort to recover Queen Elizabeth's favor,[56] and it is noticeable that Marlowe quotes only from these.[57]

There seems no possible doubt that in the Marlowe-Spenser parallels Marlowe is the borrower. In the first place, the almond tree simile [58] is in Spenserian rhyme scheme and still retains a telltale alexandrine. In the second place, as already stated, the parallels are all with the early books of the *Faerie Queene*, written during the early part of Marlowe's career and available just as he was at work on *Tamburlaine*. Moreover, Spenser (1552–1599) was older than Marlowe, and therefore likely to exercise an influence.

ORLANDO FURIOSO

In the Second Part of *Tamburlaine* a whole scene is taken from Ludovico Ariosto's (1474–1533) *Orlando Furioso*, probably through the medium of Sir John Harington's (1561–1612) translation. This is the scene in which Olympia, wife of a slaughtered captain of Basora, or Balsora (the modern Basra), saves her honor from the lust of Theridamas by pretending to anoint her throat with a magic ointment in order to make it proof against steel, and then inviting the amorous but not very intelligent chieftain to test its efficacy by striking at her with his dagger. This is a mere paraphrase of a story in the twenty-ninth book of *Orlando Furioso*, where Isabella saves her virtue from Rodomont by the same rather transparent stratagem.[59]

Olympia's killing of her child is not in Ariosto's version of the story, but appears in *De Bello Rhodio* (1556), by Jacobus Fontanus, and in Belleforest's *Cosmographie Universelle* (1575), which is, at least in part, translated from Sebastian Muenster's *Cosmographey*. According to Belleforest's version, the heroine of Rhodes:

[56] Janet Spens: *The Faerie Queene*, chap. I; M. C. Bradbrook: *School of Night*, p. 5.
[57] See I. 205–208.
[58] See I. 205.
[59] II *Tamb.*, 3882–3999. The parallel was first pointed out by Collier: *English Dramatic Poets and Annals of the Stage*, II. 496 (1879).

dés qu'eut entẽdu que ce sien seigneur & amy estoit mort en com-
batant vaillamment, comme aussi il estoit fort homme de bien: prit
ses deux enfants qu'ell auoit eu de ce seigneur, & les baisant & em-
brassant, leur empraignit le signe de la croix au front, puis leur coupa
la gorge, & les ietta au feu, disant qu'il n'estoit pas raison que ces
enfants tant beaux, & sortie d'vn pere tant illustre, seruissait aux
plaisirs infames des Barbares.[60]

PAUL IVE

Tamburlaine's lecture on the art of war, delivered to his sons
(II *Tamb.* 3253–3268), is obviously related to an obscure work
on military engineering, *The Practise of Fortification*, by one
Paul Ive.[61] Both extant editions of this work were printed in
1589, the latest date usually assigned to *Tamburlaine*; but
since the existing editions are very rare it is likely that earlier
ones may have vanished entirely.[62]

The Marlowe lines which most obviously come from Ive's
book are:

> Then next, the way to *fortifie* your men,
> *In champion grounds*, what *figure* serues you best,
> For which the *quinque*-angle fourme is meet,
> Because the corners there may *fall more flat*:
> Whereas the Fort may fittest be assailde,
> And sharpest where th'assault is desperate.
> The *ditches must be deepe*, the Counterscarps
> Narrow and steepe, the *wals made high* and broad,
> *The Bulwarks and the rampiers large and strong*,
> *With Caualieros* and thicke counterforts,
> And roome within to *lodge sixe thousand men*
> *It must haue priuy ditches, countermines,*
> *And secret issuings to defend the ditch.*
> *It must haue high Argins* and couered waies
> *To keep the bulwark fronts* from battery,
> And Parapets to hide the Muscatters:
> *Casemates* to place the great Artillery.

---

[60] II. 750. The book, curiously enough, has *two* "second" volumes. The work of
Fontanus is bound up with Clauserus: *Laonici Chalcondylae Atheniensis, de origine et
rebus gestis Turcorum Libri Decem* (1556), pp. 481 ff.

[61] There is a copy in the British Museum. Though published by F.-C. Danchin in
1912, this source has eluded most writers. See Danchin's "Études critiques sur
Christophe Marlowe," *Revue germanique*, 8: 23–33 Ja–F 1912, and U. M. Ellis-Fermor:
Tamburlaine, pp. 45, 224–226.

[62] See I. 200.

In Ive's work this runs:

Who so shall *fortifie in playne ground*, may make the Fort he pre-
tendeth of what forme or figure he will, and therefore he may with
lesse compasse of wall enclose a more superficies of ground, then where
that scope may not be had. Also it may be the perfecter, because
the angles that do happen in it, may be made the *flatter* or sharper.
... a Fort scituated in a dry playne, must haue *deepe ditches, high
walles, great bulwarks, large ramparts*, and caualieroes; besides, it must
be great *to lodge fiue or sixe thousand men*, and haue great place in it
for them to fight, ranked in battaile. *It must also haue countermines,
priuie ditches, secret issuings out to defende the ditche, casmats* in the
ditch, *couered ·wayes* round about it, and an *argine* or banke to
empeache the approach.[63]

The word "cynqueangle," equivalent to Marlowe's "*quinque-
angle*," appears in the next chapter.[64] Ive himself may have
been the Paul Ive who entered Corpus Christi, Cambridge,[65] in
1560; and he has a further possible connection with Marlowe,
since Sir Francis Walsingham is one of the dignitaries to whom
the book is dedicated.

Ive, like Marlowe, was in Queen Elizabeth's secret service,
or at least in the confidential messenger service.[66] He is described as "*Paul Ive* (an Ingeneere)" in 1601, and he built at
least two English fortifications in Ireland.[67]

PHILIP LONICER

The queer word "zoacum" comes from Philip Lonicer's
Chronicorum Turcicorum tomi duo.[68] Marlowe wrote:

Now scaldes his soule in the Tartarian streames,
And feeds vpon the banefull tree of hell,
That *zoacum*, that fruit of bytternesse,
That.in the midst of fire is ingraft,
Yet flourisheth as *Flora* in her pride,
With apples like the heads of damned Feends,

[63] II *Tamb.* 3252–3268; Paul Ive: *Practise of Fortification*, chap. II, pp. 2, 3.
[64] *Ibid.*, p. 6.
[65] Charles Henry Cooper and Thompson Cooper: *Athenae Cantabrigienses*, II. 550;
Alumni Cantabrigienses, II. 452.
[66] PRO, Declared Accounts, E 351/542, August 23, 1587, fol. 86, r and v; E 351/543,
August 18, 1600, fol. 59v.
[67] *Pacata Hibernia* (1633), lib. 2, chap. XXV, p. 252. Copy in Yale Library.
[68] Ed. 1578, fol. 64v, tom. I, lib. II (secundo pars), chap. xxiii; ed. 1584, tom. I, p. 122.
[CUL]

> The Dyuils there in chaines of quencelesse flame,
> Shall lead his soule through *Orcus* burning gulfe:
> From paine to paine, whose change shal neuer end.
>
> [II *Tamb.* 2939–2947]

Lonicer's account runs:

Credunt [sc. the Turks] praeterea arborem, quam vocant *Zoacum
agacci*, hoc est, amaritudinis, in medio inferni, licet igni quasi infixam,
florere, cuius singula poma diabolorum capitibus sint similia. Fructi-
bus arboris istius damnati vescuntur, sperantes inde refrigerationem
aliquam se percepturos. Verum non solum nihil inde refrigerationis
percipiunt, sed amaro venenatuque sapore magis magisque excru-
ciantur, grauioribusque inde mortis torminibus afficiuntur, tum etiam
diaboli ipsi ignitis eos catenis constrictos (ne una poenarum tor-
mentorumque sit facies) assidue volutant.

The passage had originally appeared in *Cinque Libri de la Legge
de Turchi* (Venice, 1548), by Giovanni Manavino, and had been
copied thence in a *Turkische Chronica* by one Müller.[69] Both
these writers, however, spell the word with two *c*'s and describe
the demons' heads before naming the tree. Marlowe and
Lonicer agree on these points, and there is also reason to suppose that Marlowe took other spellings from Lonicer.[70]

The "Humors" Theory

The character of Tamburlaine himself, brave, violent, cruel,
passionate, "hastily vengeable," is presumably an early but
entirely conscious example of the "comedy of humors," later
developed by Ben Jonson. Marlowe was familiar with the
theory of the four humors, as shown by his lines on

> Nature that fram'd vs of foure Elements,
> Warring within our breasts for regiment.
>
> [I *Tamb.* 869–870]

He develops in Tamburlaine the characteristics that a predominance of choler over other humors was supposed to produce.[71]

These, however, are mere subsidiary sources, which show us
only the origin of incidental details of the story of Tamburlaine

[69] Ed. 1577, bk. II, fol. 26v.
[70] See I. 211, 225.
[71] Carroll Camden, Jr.: "Tamburlaine: The Choleric Man," MLN, 44: 430–435 N
1929.

and his captains as Marlowe presents it. Whence comes the play itself? Which one of the numerous Latin and English accounts of Tamburlaine's life did Marlowe draw upon? Writers upon the stage from Gerard Langbaine in 1691 to Marlowe's most recent editors in the twentieth century express very different opinions. In the first (1691) edition of his *English Dramatick Poets*, Langbaine bids his readers, "For the Story, see those that have writ his Life in particular, as *Pietro Perondini*, M. *St. Sanctyon, Du Bec*, &c. and those that have treated of the Affairs of *Turks* and *Tartars* in general, in the Reigns of *Bajazet* and *Tamerlane*, as *Laonicus, Chalcocondylas, Pet. Bizarus, Knolles*, &c." [72]

It is interesting to find Perondinus suggested as a source so early. It is perhaps equally interesting that neither Mexia nor his translator, Fortescue, is mentioned; and it is well to note that there is no mention of Fulgotius, Paulus Jovius, or Cambine, of whom more presently.

In 1764 D. E. Baker asserts in his *Biographia Dramatica*: "The plot is taken from the Life of Tamerlane, as related by Knolles and other historians of the Turkish affairs" [73] — a quite erroneous statement so far as Knolles is concerned, for his *Historie of the Turkes* was not published until 1603, long after the play of *Tamburlaine* was familiar to every 'prentice in London and its author in his grave. [74]

Now follow a series of writers who trouble themselves not at all about sources: Thomas Hawkins in his *Origin of the English Drama* (1773), and four successive editors, W. Oxberry (1818-20), E. G. Robinson (1826), Dyce (1850), and Cunningham (1870).

In 1865 John Payne Collier suggested that "possibly" a passage in Thomas Newton's *Notable Historie of the Saracens* (1575) might be the source of *Tamburlaine*. [75] Fourteen years later, in the 1879 edition of his *History of English Dramatic Poetry*, he stated without qualification that "Marlow's [sic] play was printed in 1590, and was founded upon the account in Newton's

---

[72] *Account of the English Dramatick Poets* (1691), p. 345.

[73] II. 362.

[74] Yet Miss Ethel Seaton apparently falls into a similar error in TLS, 20: 388, 16 Je 1921.

[75] *Bibliographical Account of Rare Books*, II. 30.

Notable Historie of the Saracens." [76] Even a casual examination of this supposed source, however, is sufficient to show its utter inadequacy.[77] It consists merely of a note tucked into "A Summarie or breefe Chro*nicle of Saracens and Turkes,*" which Newton placed at the back of his book; [78] but it is at best one of a hundred lives of Tamburlaine afloat at this period, is far less closely related to Marlowe's play than either Mexia or Perondinus, and contains nothing not to be found in them, except a few proper names and inadequate references to the defeat of Sigismund, which patently come from other sources. Yet, with incredible carelessness, Milton's not very intelligent nephew, Edward Phillips, in his *Theatrum Poetarum* (1675) actually credits Newton with the authorship of the play.[79]

MEXIA AND PERONDINUS

In 1883 Professor A. Wagner and Professor C. H. Herford published in the London *Academy* [80] an article which stood for years as the final authority on the sources of *Tamburlaine*. Practically all editors and critics of later date were content to accept this masterly treatment of the subject, which reviews a wide range of facts and pronounces Mexia to be the main source, with Perondinus as a useful supplement. Among those who have accepted the results of this study are A. H. Bullen (1885),[81] Havelock Ellis (1887),[82] Ernest Faligan (1887),[83] Thomas Seccombe (1891),[84] F. S. Boas (1896),[85] A. W. Ward (1899),[86] John H. Ingram (1904),[87] Sir Sidney Lee (1909),[88] Tucker

---

[76] For some reason, this edition is rare in American libraries, but there are copies in the Folger, LC, and NYU. See II. 492n.

[77] Tucker Brooke dissents from this view, believing it probable that Newton "furnished Marlowe with a number of proper names and suggested the story of Sigismund in Part II." Proper names, perhaps, but not the story of Sigismund. Since Mr. Brooke wrote (*Works*, 1910, p. 4), Miss Ethel Seaton has published an investigation throwing new light on the whole matter. See I. 232–236.

[78] Page 129, under the year 1397 of the chronological table.   [79] See I. 191–193.

[80] *Academy*, 24: 265–266, 20 O 1883.

[81] *Works*, I. xxi–xxiv.

[82] *Best Plays of Christopher Marlowe* (Mermaid ed.), p. xxxiii.

[83] *De Marlovianis Fabulis*, pp. 114–115.

[84] *Encyclopædia Britannica*, article "Marlowe."

[85] *Shakespeare and His Predecessors*, p. 41.

[86] *Hist. Eng. Dram. Lit.*, I. 322–323. Ward casually refers to other sources, "at which his eye may have glanced," but gives no further information.

[87] *Christopher Marlowe and His Associates*, p. 105.

[88] DNB, article "Marlowe."

Brooke (1910),[89] William Lyon Phelps (1912-14),[90] and the *New International Encyclopedia* (1916). Professor Wagner reiterated, in his Heilbronn edition of Tamburlaine in 1885, the ideas that he had expressed with Professor Herford in the *Academy* two years before.

An article that can exert such influence over such scholars for so long a period deserves serious consideration. Wagner and Herford trace the stages by which, during the fifteenth and sixteenth centuries, the story of Tamburlaine reached Western Europe. They point out that Mexia and Perondinus sum up "all that Europe — in the middle of the sixteenth century — knew or imagined about Timur"; but they also draw up a formidable list of other authors discussing the conqueror: Cuspinian, Cambinus, Paulus Jovius (who were all among Mexia's own admitted sources, though Wagner and Herford fail to note that Marlowe went behind Mexia and drew on these authors); the Byzantine historians, Chalcocondylas, Ducas, and Phratzes; and the two Europeans who actually met the conqueror in person, the Bavarian Schiltberger and the Spaniard Ruy Gonzalez de Clavijo.

So far as dates of publication are concerned, Marlowe might have perused all of these in print, except the last two; and their manuscripts were in existence while he was working on *Tamburlaine*.

Just before Marlowe's birth, Turkish sources began to reach Western Europe. In 1551 the *Annals of the Turks*, written in Turkish, was brought from the East and translated, first into German and then (1588) into Latin, by a certain Leunclavius. This account agrees substantially with the Byzantine writers. In 1595, too late for Marlowe, came Jean du Bec's biography of Timur, followed in 1603 by Knolles's *Historie of the Turkes*, and finally, in 1653, by Clark's *Life*.

After this survey Wagner and Herford develop the case for Mexia and Perondinus. Both books were available to Marlowe in languages that he could read. Both books follow practically the same order of events, which is partly unhistorical and therefore cannot be due to a mere fidelity to the same facts in each

[89] *Works*, p. 3.
[90] *Christopher Marlowe*, p. 7.

case; Marlowe follows essentially this order. In the two sources and the play the principal incidents — according to Wagner and Herford — are: (1) the intrigues by which Tamburlaine attains the throne of Persia; (2) the overthrow of Bajazeth; and (3) the fall of Damascus. Strictly speaking, it is not true that these are the "principal incidents," since it is Tamburlaine's love for Zenocrate that gives the play what unity it possesses and is the link that binds the otherwise unrelated series of events together. There is nothing else to unite the episodes save the central figure of Tamburlaine himself. Wagner and Herford ignore this.

The first incident is quite unhistorical and gives Marlowe his first two acts. The resemblances to Mexia and Perondinus are at first sight startlingly close, for they extend even to the exact number of horsemen sent out by the Persian king against Marlowe's hero. The number is specifically stated four times in the course of two scenes:

> Your Grace hath taken order by *Theridimas*,
> Chardg'd with *a thousand horse*, to apprehend
> And bring him Captiue to your Highnesse throne,
> [I *Tamb.* 54–56]

says Meander to the effeminate Persian king. When Tamburlaine receives the news the number is thrice repeated. A soldier enters, crying:

> *A thousand Persean horsmen* are at hand,
> Sent from the King to ouercome vs all.
> [I *Tamb.* 307–308]

Tamburlaine repeats the number twice:

> Such hope, such fortune haue the *thousand horse*.
> Soft ye my Lords and sweet *Zenocrate*.
> You must be forced from me ere you goe:
> *A thousand horsmen?* We *fiue hundred foote?*
> [I *Tamb.* 314–317]

Mexia, describing the desertion of Theridamas to the robber band whom he was sent to capture, says that the King

sent forth vnder the conducte of one, of his capitaines, *a thousande horses* well appointed to apprehende and take hym: at whose commyng, he so well knewe in this matter howe to beare hym, that of his enimie he soone had made hym, his assured frende, and companion: in suche sorte that they ioigned both their companies together.[91]

Perondinus tells how the Persian king

ducem quem sibi fidũ ac strenuum putabat Tamerlanẽ captivatũ misit *cum mille equitibus* [92]

and gives the rest of the story essentially as Mexia and Marlowe give it. One enormously significant trifle that Wagner and Herford overlooked may be mentioned here. Although neither Mexia nor Perondinus gives the number of Tamburlaine's followers at this stage of his career, Marlowe is specific on this point: "We fiue hundred foote." As this detail appears elsewhere, Marlowe obviously was not content with Mexia and Perondinus alone.

The incidents of Bajazeth's captivity are given in Mexia and Perondinus much as in Marlowe — the cage, the feeding "as he had been a Dog," according to Mexia, and the use of Bajazeth as a mounting block — much, indeed, as they are also given in many other books and popular traditions, where they often bulk large enough to exclude everything else.

Here again we may note another small but significant detail. Tamburlaine in Marlowe's play specifically calls Bajazeth a "footstool." [93] Mexia omits this detail altogether. Perondinus recounts the manner of the Turkish Sultan's humiliation but does not use the word "footstool." Instead he says: "Eo [Bajazeth] procumbente, non sine ludibrio eius tergo pedem imponens, [Tamburlaine] solitus erat equu*m* conscendere." [94] But this detail does appear in other books which actually use the word "scabellum," or footstool.

Marlowe agrees with Perondinus in describing Bajazeth as beating out his brains against the bars of his cage and in describing the ignominy with which Bajazeth's queen is treated. Finally, Perondinus describes the person of Tamburlaine in terms which Marlowe practically duplicates; but, as we shall

---

[91] *The Foreste* (1576), chap. XIV, fol. 83*v*, HCL copy. There are no italics in the original.

[92] Perondinus (ed. 1556), p. 236. There are no italics in the original.

[93] "Bring out my foot-stoole." I *Tamb.* 1445.

[94] Perondinus (1556), p. 242.

presently see, quite another interpretation may be placed upon this coincidence.

The third and last incident, the siege of Damascus with the white-red-black tents or banners and the deputation of virgins with olive branches, is given in both Mexia and Perondinus, though these picturesque details, which the dramatist seizes upon with an unerring eye for effect, are not, in the supposed sources, connected with the city of Damascus. These same stories are also contained in Andrew Cambine's *Turkish Affaires*, which had been "Englished" by John Shute in 1562 and was therefore available to Marlowe. It was bound with an account of Scanderbeg, the Albanian hero on whom Marlowe is supposed to have written a play,[95] as *Two Notable Commentaries*.

"So much," observe Wagner and Herford, "for the correspondences, which obviously cover the whole framework of the drama." They then proceed to discuss two modifications in the story introduced by Marlowe. One of these is the omission of all reference to Tamburlaine's lameness — which Perondinus describes,[96] as do many other writers — in order to make his hero an imposing and terrible figure. The other is the introduction of feminine characters. The wife of Tamburlaine is dismissed with a casual line in Perondinus and passed over in silence by Mexia. It is with regard to the sources from which the Zenocrate episodes are derived and the relation which they bear to the play that the conclusions of the present study differ most widely from the generally accepted theory of its sources.

Exhaustive, laborious, and highly suggestive as were the investigations of these two brilliant scholars, their conclusions are not entirely valid. It is highly probable that Marlowe may have used either Mexia or Perondinus; but it is by no means certain that he used both; and it is even possible that he used neither. It can be definitely established that Marlowe had recourse to other material, adhering to the facts of the historical Timur's career very closely, though perhaps without realizing that he was doing anything more than follow tradition, in entire indifference to historical exactness.

[95] See II. 284–285.
[96] "Integra valetudine, excepto altero pede, quo non perinde valebat, ut inde claudi-

This conclusion is supported by three facts:

1. Many of the details in Marlowe's *Tamburlaine* which do not appear in either Mexia or Perondinus do appear in other sources, presenting such close similarities that a relation of some kind to Marlowe's version of the story cannot be reasonably questioned.

2. If we lay aside Mexia and Perondinus entirely, practically every incident in the play can be duplicated from a source known to have been printed in a language comprehensible to Marlowe prior to the first performance of *Tamburlaine* in 1587 or thereabouts.

3. The love story of Tamburlaine and Zenocrate, though it does not exist in any known European source available to Marlowe, did exist in Oriental documents written before the middle of the sixteenth century, and the historical account presents unmistakable kinship with the drama.

The two details — lacking in Mexia and Perondinus but present in the play and in other sources — which are most convincing are the number of Tamburlaine's own troops and the use of Bajazeth as a footstool. These appear in other accounts of Marlowe's hero which are earlier in date than either Mexia or Perondinus and therefore available to Marlowe while working on his play.

Much has been made of the way in which Marlowe reproduces the numbers of troops sent against Tamburlaine, as reported in the supposed sources. Just as Marlowe takes a curious delight in giving a realistic touch to his romantic drama by painstaking (though not always exact) enumeration of high-sounding place names, so he delights in specifying the number of troops in a combat, dispatched on an expedition, or killed in battle. Correspondences between source and play in minute particulars of this sort are highly convincing; they evidently cannot be accidental. We have already seen that in the first two scenes of *Tamburlaine* Marlowe begins by specifying, no less than four times, the number of horsemen sent against him by King Mycetes. We have also seen that, although both Mexia and Perondinus give the number of horsemen sent

care ac deformiter incedere prospiceretur" (Perondinus, 1556 ed., p. 246 [wrongly numbered 244]).

against Tamburlaine, neither states the number of Tamburlaine's own followers. Marlowe, however, specifically gives the number as five hundred.[97]

Now, the thousand horsemen are mentioned by a number of authors besides Mexia and Perondinus; but it is much more important to note that the number of Tamburlaine's men — not given at all by Mexia and Perondinus — is given as five hundred by at least two authorities, one of whom must certainly have been available to Marlowe.

At the end of his life of Tamburlaine, Mexia gives a list of authors consulted, in the most approved modern fashion:

This then that I here geue you, that al haue I borrowed of *Baptista Fulgotius*, Pope *Pius*, *Platina* vppon the life of *Boniface* the ninth, of *Mathew Palmier*, and of *Cambinus* a Florentine, writyng the historie, and exploytes of the Turkes.[98]

If Marlowe did read Mexia, he must have seen this bibliography; and — once acquainted with the names of these authors, treating of a subject that interested him — what more natural than to hunt up their books, most of which were ready to hand in the university library or in the library of Corpus Christi. The works of Pope Pius were given to the university in 1574, by Bishop James Pilkington. Those of Paulus Jovius were acquired in 1581, just as Marlowe entered, and Jovius' *Turcicarum Rerum Commentarii* had been in the library of Corpus Christi for several years, being part of Archbishop Parker's bequest of books.[99] Baptista Ignatius' *De Origine Turcarum Libellus*, Baptista Fulgotius' *Exemplorum Libri IX*, and Pope Pius' *Asiae Europaeque elegantiss. descriptio*, all filled with accounts of Tamburlaine, were part of the same bequest.[100]

If Marlowe became sufficiently interested in these authors, he may have found in Fulgotius [101] a full account of the way in

---

[97] I *Tamb.* 317.
[98] *The Foreste* (1576), chap. XIV, fol. 87v, HCL copy.
[99] See the Cambridge University Library's old *Catalogus Librorum MS* (Donors' Book); C. Sayle: *Annals of the Cambridge University Library*, pp. 49, 52; *Rough List of the Parker Books* (MS.), no. 298, in the Corpus Christi Library.
[100] *Rough List of the Parker Books*, nos. 47, 251, 298.
[101] Book III, chap. IV, p. 379, of the Corpus Christi copy (no. 47 of the Parker printed books). The book is also called *De Dictis Factisque memorabilibus*. The 1509 ed. has no page numbers. The passage quoted is on p. 104 of the 1578 ed. It is copied almost word for word by Philip Lonicer in his *Turcicae Historiae* (1578), p. 15r, tom. I, bk. I.

which Tamburlaine won over the Persian general, Theridamas. This is like Mexia's account, but with one important detail — the exact number of Tamburlaine's forces — that Mexia omits:

> Arma equosque comparare [Tamburlaine] iussit. *Hoc numero ad quingentos enim pervenerant*; quasdam mercatorum societates quae per eas regiones magno numero praesidii gratia commeare solent: & vulgo caravane dicuntur: armis devicit. . . . Ad companscendam praedonum audaciam *cum mille* equitibus dux in eius regionis finues ubi haec a diversis mercatoribus gesta erant: a persarum rege missus: cum a latronum duce in colloquium vocatus esset: latronis arte verbisque delinitus ex hoste comes ei factus.

This passage, then, is presumably the origin of the five hundred soldiers whom Marlowe gives to Tamburlaine; but it is not quite certain that Marlowe took them from Baptista Fulgotius, for the same number is given by Ruy Gonzales de Clavijo, who about 1403 journeyed as ambassador from the King of Spain to the court of Timur at Samarkand. Among other things, Clavijo writes:

> One day, when he had plundered a caravan of merchants, he obtained great wealth, and went to a land called Seistan, where he stole sheep and horses, for that land is very rich in flocks: *and he had as many as five hundred followers.*[102]

Reference to Bajazeth as Tamburlaine's footstool is equally significant. Though Mexia does not give the story at all and Perondinus does not use the word "footstool," the story was famous, and various other works frequently refer to Bajazeth as a "footstool" or "scabellum." It is not, therefore, pure chance that Marlowe hit upon this particular word.

"Bring out my —" he must have written one night in Corpus Christi, and memory, whether of tradition or of the printed page, supplied the final word. Here again we may refer to Mexia's useful bibliography. If we follow up once more the references he gives, we shall find in Baptist Fulgotius' *Factorum dictorumque memorabilium libri ix* a chapter "De Superbia," and, as an example, the story of Tamburlaine's treatment of Bajazeth, which concludes:

---

[102] *Narrative of the Embassy of Ruy Gonzales de Clavijo to the Court of Timur at Samarkand, A.D. 1403–06,* translated by Clements R. Markham. There is a later translation by Guy de Strange, London: Routledge, 1928. [CUL]

Cauea Baiazites inclusit, atque ita currui impositū, quocunque ipse proficisceretur, secū trahebat, *eo pro scabello utens,* ut faciliorem in equum pararet ascensum.[103]

Does this definitely prove that Marlowe used Fulgotius? Not conclusively; but it is certainly significant that in one of the books named by Mexia *two* details should appear which are in Marlowe's play but neither in Mexia nor in Perondinus.

Wagner and Herford make much of the close analogy between the descriptions of Timur's person given by Marlowe and by Perondinus. "The description of his person given by Perondinus, *but by no other of the Italian or Latin sources known to me,*" says the article, "is somewhat closely followed by Marlowe. Compare the phrases with which both begin — 'of stature tall,' 'statura fuit procera,' 'his joints so strongly knit,' 'valida erat usque adeo nervorum compage.'"

This sounds very plausible, but Wagner and Herford did not follow up Mexia's list of sources carefully enough. Had they done so, they would have found in Paulus Jovius' *Elogia virorum bellica virtute illustrium* [104] Timur's personal appearance thus described:

Erat Tamerlanes ore truculento redendentibusque oculis semper minaci; corpore autem ingenti, validisque nervis, adeo formo lacertosoque.

Surely this is quite as close to Marlowe as Perondinus; and we know that, if Marlowe read Mexia at all, he saw mention of Paulus Jovius in his bibliography. Thus, for the third time, matter in Mexia's sources appears in the play, though not in Mexia. In the two previous cases the material was not available in Perondinus either. In this case, however, Marlowe might have found it there.

There is thus good reason for questioning whether Marlowe ever read or even saw Perondinus' book. If we grant him access to Mexia and a few of the books that Mexia lists, we can supply every detail of the play except the Zenocrate episodes, which

---

[103] Ed. 1578, fol. 329, of the copy in HCL, which also has a 1509 ed. under the title *De dictis factisque memorabilibus collectanea.* The italics in the passage above are not in the original.

[104] Ed. 1561 (Florence), p. 93 [CUL]. HCL has the 1575 (Basel) ed., in which this passage appears at p. 102.

Perondinus practically ignores, and the history of Tamburlaine's wars with Bajazeth and Sigismund of Hungary, which neither Mexia nor Perondinus mentions.

From Paulus Jovius, Mexia, and three authors named in Mexia's bibliography — Baptista Fulgotius, Andrew Cambine, and Pope Pius II — Marlowe might have taken most of the rest of his play, including the Bajazeth episodes but not including the love story of Tamburlaine and Zenocrate or the wars with Sigismund. These books could have given him practically everything in Perondinus; Tamburlaine's shepherd origin, his accession to the crown, his revolt after aiding Cosroe, the exact number of his followers and opponents, the details of the Bajazeth story — cage, footstool, death, and everything except the kings as chariot horses (these appear in no source, and bear all the earmarks of a stage manager's inspiration)[105] — the attack on Damascus, the deputation of virgins, the white-red-black flags or tents.[106] Even the notion of Tamburlaine as "the scourge of God," on which Marlowe dwells and which was widely familiar, might easily have been drawn from this group of sources, in which it occurs repeatedly. Actually on the shelves at Corpus was Pope Pius' *Asiae Europaeque elegantiss. descriptio*, in which Tamburlaine is made to say: "Ira dei ego sum & orbis vastitas."[107] The account of Tamburlaine in this book concentrates innumerable details which Marlowe expanded in his play:

Thamerlanes genere Parthus . . . inter suos vimentis & corporis agilitate excelluit, vt breui multarum gentium dux fieret: . . . Pazaitem Turcarum dominum . . . viuum cepit, caueaque in modum ferae inclusum, per omnem Asiam circuntulit. . . . Soldanum Aegypti bello superatum, vltra Perlusum repulit. . . . In obsidionibus vrbium, prima die albo tentorio utebatur, secunda rubeo, tertia negro: qui sese dabant in albo sedenti, salutem consequabantur. Rubeus color

---

[105] See I. 239.

[106] Mexia says flags; Perondinus, Paulus Jovius, Cambine, and Pope Pius say tents. Marlowe wavers between "my milkwhite flags" and "my coleblack tents" (I *Tamb.* 1849, 1853). Douglas Bush in MLN, 24: 255–256 (1909), points out that the knight whose colors vary daily is a commonplace of medieval romance and appears in *Ipomedon*, 3039 ff., *Richard Coeur de Lion*, 267 ff. See also J. L. Weston: *Three Days Tournament* and Gaston Paris in *Journal des Savants*, p. 449, Ag 1902. This must be coincidence, as Marlowe is plainly following his sources.

[107] *Asiae Europaeque elegantiss. descriptio*, pp. 85–87; *Rough List of the Parker Books*, no. 251.

moriendum patribus familiarum indicabat: niger ciuitatis excidium
& omnia in cinerem conuertenda. Fama est populosæ cuiusdam
ciuitatis, quae prima die deditionem neglexisset, pueros, puellasque
omnes in candida veste ramos oliuæ præferentes exiuisse, vt principis
iram placerent: illum omnes ab equitatu conculcari atque conteri
iussisse, vrbem captam incendi. . . . duos filios reliquit regni successores.

Let us add two more minute details to the list of correspondences between the play and the various possible sources: the
spelling of the name of Bajazath's son, whom Marlowe calls
"Callapine," and of Orcanes, King of Natolia. So far as Callapine is concerned, Mexia omits all reference to him and, indeed,
all reference to Tamburlaine's wife and family. Perondinus
gives no name to Bajazeth's wife, but he does mention a son
named "Celebinus." The obvious change of two vowels and a
consonant restore this name to the same form used by Marlowe,
who was simply following another authority in this case.

Two of the authors in Mexia's list use essentially the same
spelling as Marlowe. Baptista Ignatius — "a diligent searcher
of auncient antiquities," says Mexia, approvingly [108] — after
describing the fate of Bajazeth, adds:

Huic duo fuere liberi mares, Orchanes, quem alij Calepinum & Maometes quem nostri Moysen magno, ut video, errore dicunt.[109]

Not only was Ignatius (or Egnatius) mentioned in Mexia and
available at Corpus,[110] but his *De Origine Turcarum* was actually bound up with the second edition of Perondinus in Clauser's
1556 collection of books on the Turks. Hence, if Marlowe read
either Mexia or Perondinus, he very probably read Ignatius
also.

The Turkish prince's name is given as Calapino by Andrew
Cambine [111] and by Paulus Jovius, the 1546 translation of whose
Shorte Treatise upon the Turkes' Chronicles declares that he

was cleped Cyryscelebes, and not Calepyne after the opinion of
Nicholaus Secundinus, whiche dedicated to Pius bysshop of Rome,
the genealogie of the Turkes, written in Latyne: whiche thyng was the

---

[108] Mexia, *op. cit.*, fol. 87r.
[109] *De Origine Turcorum* (1556), p. 185.
[110] *Rough List of the Parker Books*, no. 298. See I. 220.
[111] Andrew Cambine, *op. cit.*

occasion that al other, in a maner (the true pronuntiation of his proper name, beynge corrupte) for Cyriscelebes, named him Calepyne.[112]

Marlowe may have seen this passage, but the opening lines of the first scene of Act III, in the Second Part of *Tamburlaine*, where Orcanes crowns the heir to the Turkish throne, is evidently from Philip Lonicer's *Chronicorum Turcicorum*. In the play this runs: "*Calepinus Cyricelibes*, otherwise *Cybelius*." [113] In Lonicer's book the chapter heading is "Calepinus Cyrice-. libes, qui et Cibelinus," and the text of the same page adds, "Calepinus Cyricelebes, quem & Cibelium nominant." [114]

Baptista Ignatius gives the name Orchanes as that of one of Bajazeth's sons, whereas in the play Marlowe applies it to one of Bajazeth's vassals, Orcanes, King of Natolia. Evidently Marlowe, assured by Mexia that Bajazeth "left too Sonnes," found this confirmed by Ignatius, who, however, gave three names for two princes, only one of whom he decided to use in his play. Whereupon, with an attentive ear to the strange foreign sound of Orcanes and Callapine, he gets rid of the commonplace Mahomet ("Maometes"), which is likely at best to be confused with the "god" of the Turks; gives the Sultan's son the name of Callapine; and retains the name Orcanes for the Sultan's vassal, thus getting both names into his play. Marlowe may also have found in Lonicer's book [115] the name of Orchanes, second Turkish emperor and grandfather of Bajazeth.

A third similarity in name may indicate that Marlowe was depending on something more than the two books of Mexia and Perondinus. He gives the name of Bajazeth's queen — Zabina — which appears in none of the old chronicles of western Europe. The historical Bajazeth, the last of the Turkish emperors to marry, had a consort named Dastina, or Despina, a daughter of the Serbian prince, Lazar Gresljanovitch, to whom he actually showed all the devotion that he shows in the play, and who shared his disgrace at the hands of Tamburlaine. It is striking, to say the least, that Marlowe should have selected a name so closely resembling a real one; but there is no evidence to show why he did so.

[112] Fol. xiii, chap. 5, sig. B.v, r and v.   [113] II *Tamb.* 3111.
[114] Ed. 1578, fol. 16r, bk. I, tom. I.
[115] *Chronicorum Turcicorum Tomus Primus* (1578), fol. 10r.

The origin of the other feminine character in Marlowe's play — whose name is obviously adapted from a Greek philosopher's — offers the most mysterious problem of all. The true role of Zenocrate in the drama — at first the prisoner of Tamburlaine, then his greatly loved wife — has only recently been understood.[116] Marlowe tries very hard to get variety amid the excessive sameness of his story, for it is hard to go through ten acts merely defeating enemies and proclaiming victories. In the reconciliation of Zenocrate and her father, the Soldan of Egypt, he gets a climax for his first play, the full value of which appears only on the stage. Through half the play, ever since she gave her heart to her captor, Zenocrate has been looking forward to some such reconciliation; and this scene therefore gives us a union of forces which justifies putting a period to the dramatic action at this point.

Furthermore, Tamburlaine must be made something more than a far-off, outlandish conqueror in the eyes of the Elizabethan audience; and Marlowe accomplishes this by making him, the hero, the world-conqueror, also a man like other men — loving and losing, conquering the world but sickening and dying in the end, overmastered by a fate too powerful even for the "scourge of God." Zenocrate establishes a relationship of sympathy between Tamburlaine and the audience on the ground of their common humanity.

Hitherto only two references to the wife of Tamburlaine have been known. Mexia says nothing of her, merely remarking of Tamburlaine that "in the ende, he paieth, the debte due vnto nature, leauyng behinde hym twoo soonnes, not such as was the father," [117] a hint which Marlowe develops into the one effeminate son of the conqueror and his two warlike sons. Perondinus devotes an exceedingly short chapter to "the wife of Tamerlane and his children," in which he says:

Accepit in matrimonium cuiusdam Bactriani reguli filiam, ex qua duos suscepisse liberos scriptores omnes asseverant, nulla ex parte & virtute bellica & fortuna Tamerlani comparandos. quod postea rei exitu comprobatum vidimus.[118]

---

[116] See George Pierce Baker: "Dramatic Technique in Marlowe," *Essays and Studies*, 4: 172–182 (1913).

[117] *The Foreste* (1576), chap. XIV, fol. 87r, HCL copy.

[118] Ed. 1556, p. 245.

The other reference is found in *The Bondage and Travels of Johann Schiltberger* (1396–1427), a Bavarian who was actually in personal contact with the historical Tamburlaine, and who writes:

It is to be noted, that three causes made Tämerlin fret, so that he became ill, and died of that same illness. The first cause was grief that his vassal had escaped with the tribute; the other it is to be noted was, that Thämerlin had three wives, and that the youngest, whom he loved very much, had been intimate with one of his vassals whilst he was away.... He ... ordered that she should be immediately beheaded.... It fretted him so much that he had killed his wife, and that the vassal had escaped, that he died.[119]

Here, if we lay aside the infidelity, are the elements of the story of Tamburlaine's love, his sickness, and his death, very much as Marlowe presents them. Observe that Schiltberger says that he fretted "so that he became ill." This is very like Marlowe's hero, grieving for Zenocrate and ultimately dying of a lingering illness.

Schiltberger's account of his travels lay in manuscript until 1859, so that it is practically impossible to imagine Marlowe ever saw it. Someone must have read the manuscript, however, and from this source or from others, garbled versions of the story of Tamburlaine's wife must have been in oral circulation in Europe.

The taunt of concubinage which Zabina throws at Zenocrate [120] is suggested by an insulting message actually sent to the historical Tamburlaine by the historical Bajazeth. This is recorded by the Byzantine historian, Laonicus Chalcocondylas, whose *De Origine et Rebus Gestis Turcorum* is bound up with Perondinus in Clauser's edition of 1556. The passage runs:

Nisi cum exercitu aduersum nos procedat, precor ut uxorem suam ter repudiatam tandem iterum assumat. Hoc quidem uergit in contumeliam Turcorum, uidelicet ter uxorem suam recipere, nisi persuadeatur.[121]

[119] Translation into German from the Heidelberg MS., edited in 1859 by Professor Karl Friedrich Neumann, and translated into English by Commander J. Buchan Telfer, R.N., pp. 29–30. [HCL, CUL]   [120] I *Tamb.* 1264.

[121] Also in *Corpus Scriptorum Historiae Byzantinae* (ed. B. G. Niebuhr, 1843), XLIII. 105–106. The Greek text runs:

"εἰ τοίνυν μὴ ἐπίῃ μαχούμενος ἡμῖν, ἐς τρὶς τὴν ἑαυτοῦ γυναῖκα ἐχέτω ἀπολαβών." τοῦτο δὴ οὖν ἐς ὕβριν φέρει τῷ γένει τούτῳ, Μεχμέτῃ ἐξορκῶσαι ἐς τρὶς ἤδη ἀπολαβεῖν τὴν ἑαυτοῦ γυναῖκα, ἂν μὴ πείθηται.

One other casual and passing reference to the strong influence of a wife over the conqueror seems never to have been previously noted. Heinrich von Efferhen, in a sixteenth-century book of sermons,[122] writes that Tamburlaine

temeraria petitione ducum Asiae & *uxoris suae commotus*, arma cepit bellum gesturus cum Baiazete.

Such a passage certainly makes it possible that other stories of the sort were afloat at the time. The books of the period bear further witness to a lively and general interest in this mysterious Asiatic conqueror, who had in such a welcome manner relieved the pressure of the Turks.

The Mulfuzat Timury

The *Mulfuzat Timury*, or *Memoirs of Timur*, attributed to Tamburlaine himself, still exist. If we turn to this work, we shall see at once that the whole Zenocrate episode, the binding link that gives the play whatever unity it possesses, is not, as Wagner and Herford suppose, "supplied in germ by the tradition" and then developed by Marlowe. Instead, it is a fairly accurate transcript from history, in which the Elizabethan dramatist took liberties with fact not much greater than those taken by Mr. John Drinkwater in *Abraham Lincoln* and *Oliver Cromwell*, or by M. Sascha Guitry in *Pasteur* and *Deburau*.

The *Mulfuzat Timury* as we have it today is a Persian manuscript of 457 pages, which was first brought to England from India about 1784, among the papers of Major William Davy, of the Honourable East India Company's Service, who had for twelve years been interpreter to Sir Robert Baker, commander-in-chief in Bengal. After his death, en route to England, Major Davy's papers were sent home, and his manuscript of the *Mulfuzat Timury* lay unexamined until 1829, when Major Charles Stewart translated it into English.[123]

Abu Taulib ul Husseyny, the Persian translator, says that he found the Turki original in the library of Jafir, Pasha of

---

[122] Henricus von Efferhen: *XIII Homiliae in Caput XXXVIII. et XXXIX. Prophetae Ezechielis de Gog & Magog, seu de Turcis* (1571), fol. i 8*v*. Cf. chap. I of bk. II of the section "Historia de Oguziorum seu Ottomanidum Origine," fol. h4.

[123] Printed for the Oriental Translation Committee, London: J. Murray and others, 1830. Copies in LC, HCL.

Yemen; and as *Astley's Collection of Voyages* mentions such a
man as Pasha of Yemen in 1610, and as the translation is dedicated to the Emperor (Shah) Jehan,[124] we have a fair idea of
the time when the Persian translation was made. Major Davy
himself expressed his entire belief in the authenticity of the
work. Numerous copies exist, some of them in royal hands,
and it is everywhere accepted in the East as genuine. Major
Stewart, the English translator, was able to collate two other
Persian manuscripts with the one brought back by Major Davy.

What do we find in the *Mulfuzat Timury?* A close approximation of the Zenocrate story. It is idle to pretend that we
have here much more than approximation of the story as Marlowe tells it, but the resemblances are so close that we are
forced to conclude either that this document gave Marlowe the
love story of Timur which is hinted at by Schiltberger and von
Efferhen, or else that the facts on which it is based reached Marlowe in some other way through some unknown intermediary.

The historical Tamburlaine was not, of course, the model
(if somewhat stormy) husband whom Marlowe depicts, but in
all essentials the two accounts are the same. The historical
Timur, like Marlowe's hero, did capture a lady whom he afterward married. Among his numerous wives (Marlowe, of course,
makes his hero more romantically appealing by giving him only
one), there was a favorite whom he especially loved; who, like
Zenocrate, shared many of her husband's perils and adventures
in the field; and who died when he was in the midst of his career
of conquest.

All this we have from the *Mulfuzat Timury.* Two other Persian sources confirm the stories. In the *Rauzat-us-Safa,* of Mir
Khwand,[125] the elder, it is related that after a victory over the
King of the Jattas, a Mongol tribe, the Timur of history really
did capture the king's daughter. Exposed to the conqueror,
she caught his fancy, and he married her. Both the *Rauzat-us-
Safa* and the *Zafar-nāmeh,* of Ali-i-Yazdi,[126] tell how the death

[124] Roughly a contemporary of Charles I.
[125] The story of the capture and marriage is in Mir Khwand's *Rauzat-us-Safa* (Tehe-
ran, 1854), vol. VI, fol. 15v.
[126] This story is in Mir Khwand, *op. cit.,* vol. VI, fol. 15r, and also in Ali-i-Yazdi's
Zafar-nāmeh (Calcutta: Bibliotheca Indica), vol. I, pp. 356–357. Cf. vol. II, pp. 1–5.
The Persian texts were searched for me by M. Minovi, Esq., of London.

of this lady and another wife caused Tamburlaine such distress that he withdrew from the world and sought consolation among the devout.

Most of this is close to Marlowe's play and much of it is paralleled in Schiltberger's narrative. Such similarities are too marked to be mere coincidence; but, before speculating, let us have the apposite passages from the *Mulfuzat Timury*. Marlowe's version of the capture of Zenocrate, daughter of a king (the Soldan of Egypt), by Tamburlaine is closely akin to this passage:

> During this time, the officers and chiefs of the enemy being quite discomfited, were retreating towards Khezar, and it so happened that Arzū Melk Aghā, the daughter of Amyr Jelayr, and the wife of Amyr Musā, who in the confusion of the defeat, had been left behind, having joined the runaways, was overtaken; when I saw her, I instantly sent to her my canopy to conceal her from public view, and gave her in charge of Dūlet Shāh, the pay-master, who was a eunuch, or pilgrim; and what was very extraordinary, the lady being big with child, was safely delivered of a daughter in that desert.[127]

This daughter afterward became Timur's wife. She is not, it is true, identical with the favorite wife who was the prototype of Zenocrate; but the telescoping of two individuals is a liberty at which no dramatist would hesitate.

Timur himself describes the death of his favorite wife in these terms:

> At this place, I received intelligence that (my wife) the illustrious Aljay Tūrkān Aghā, whom I had left very ill, had departed this life; on hearing this, I said, "verily we belong to God, and to him shall we return." [128]

In the following passage the *Mulfuzat* comes very close to a passage addressed by Tamburlaine in the play to his recreant son, Calyphas:

> It also came into my mind that no legitimately born person would have acted in the infamous manner these two scoundrels had done; I therefore addressed Bughā, and said to him, "may your face be black, if your mother had been a virtuous woman, you never would have been guilty of such ingratitude. ... it has been truly said that 'a

[127] Bk. V, chap. xxi, p. 104.
[128] Bk. V, chap. xix, p. 94.

bastard never quits this world till he has injured his patron,' you are the son of a whore, as you have clearly proved."

Compare that with:

> Bastardly boy, sprong from some cowards loins:
> And not the issue of great *Tamburlaine*.[129]

Two incidents from the *Mulfuzat Timury* recall the expedition of Theridamas, with his thousand horse, against Tamburlaine. One Tukel Behader attacks Timur with a thousand cavalry — a coincidence in numbers that one might dismiss as nothing more, were it not that so many later chroniclers and Marlowe himself are insistent upon this number (always of horsemen) as being the strength of the hostile force.

In the *Mulfuzat Timury*, also, a hostile chief deserts to Timur under circumstances somewhat similar to the desertion of Theridamas:

> Melk Hussyn also mounted his horse, and pretending to his people that he meant to fight with me, came out of the fortress and advanced against me in battle array; . . . while we were in this state of suspense, Melk Hussyn, accompanied by his own attendants, came over to me; . . . we met, and embraced each other on horseback; many of his officers also came over, and laid aside all animosity.[130]

These close correspondences suggest a definite relationship between Marlowe's play and the *Mulfuzat Timury*, even though in Marlowe's lifetime that document had not yet been translated from Turki into Persian, much less into English. Several hypotheses may be suggested: We may, first of all, fall back on oral tradition. All Europe was full of the story of Tamburlaine, and throughout England, France, and Germany there were chronicles in Latin, Greek, German, French, Italian, and English recounting his adventures. The sailors from Queen Bess's England were everywhere. Is it too much to believe that when interest in the exploits of Tamburlaine was so general in the Orient that his memoirs were treasured by kings, when the whole Occident was eagerly reading and talking about him, when ships were plying between the two, some Elizabethan mariner may have carried back the eastern version of his story?

[129] II *Tamb.* 2638–2639; *Mulfuzat Timury*, bk. V. xxv, p. 118.
[130] *Ibid.*, bk. V. v, pp. 36–37.

After all, Mexia and Perondinus would never have been able to write the life of Timur at all had there not been communication of some sort with the Orient to give them facts, however distorted.[131]

This is all the more credible since at least two Europeans penetrated to Timur's very court. Clavijo came back to Spain only a few years before Mexia must have begun to write. If Mexia's story reached England, is it too much to suppose that Clavijo's story may have reached England, too? Schiltberger's manuscript was never printed during Marlowe's lifetime. But did Schiltberger never show his manuscript to any friends, or did he never *tell* so interesting a story, when he had been at pains to write it?

The study of Oriental languages had begun in Europe, and perhaps in England as well, long before Marlowe. By 1636 Jacob Golius was actually printing from Arabic type in the Low Countries; and if type had already been cast to print these languages, we may assume a period of at least half a century during which the language was cultivated and a body of readers and book buyers built up. Back and forth between England and the Low Countries a constant stream was pouring — soldiers, sailors, traders, players, and ambassadors, most of whom went through Canterbury on the main line of travel, where young Kit Marlowe, the shoemaker's boy, was growing up. Is it too much to assume an eager English lad with a keen ear for travelers' tales of Tartar kings and conquests?

Perhaps in this way, perhaps in some lost book, perhaps through his own travels on the Continent in government secret service, the link between Marlowe and the far-off countries of his dreams was established. At least we may be sure that there was some link of this sort, and it is permitted to hope that it will some day be discovered.

THE SIGISMUND EPISODES

One more group of sources remains. No one has ever yet pretended that either Mexia or Perondinus afforded material for

---

[131] Timur had diplomatic correspondence with Charles VI, of France. Cf. Silvestre de Sacy: "Memoire sur une correspondance inédite de Tamerlane avec Charles VI," *Mem. de l'Acad. des Inscriptions*, 6: 470–522 (1822).

the scenes in which the Hungarians, led by King Sigismund, appear; but here again, when Marlowe followed up Mexia's bibliography, he found material lying ready to his hand. Paulus Jovius describes the defeat of Sigismund by Callapine near the Danube, though he does not afford authority for the poetic justice of Sigismund's death, as in the play.

But Marlowe was not content with Paulus Jovius, for he has here compressed, for the sake of dramatic effectiveness, two sets of historical facts, much as Mr. John Drinkwater allows his Abraham Lincoln to deliver parts of the Springfield speech in the theatre in Washington. The historical facts that Marlowe describes are those of the battle of Varna in 1444, long after Tamburlaine was dead. King Ladislaus of Hungary (not Sigismund) had made a ten-year truce with the Turkish emperor, Amurath II, in the treaty of Szedin (1443); but he was later persuaded by the papal legate, Cardinal Julian, to break the truce and attack the unsuspecting Turks. Amurath, however, rallied his troops, crossed the Bosphorus, met the Christians at Varna, and conquered them, killing both Ladislaus and the Cardinal.

Marlowe has replaced Ladislaus with Tamburlaine's contemporary, Sigismund, and has provided two tempters instead of one — Frederick and Baldwin, lords of Buda and Bohemia. He has also put Orcanes, King of Natolia, in place of the Sultan Amurath.

As a matter of historical fact, the Turks were eager to make peace with the Hungarians because the King of Carmania was threatening them. For him, Marlowe substitutes Tamburlaine. Gazellus, Viceroy of Byron, says:

> Since *Tamburlaine* hath mustred all his men,
> Marching from *Cairon* northward with his camp,
> To *Alexandria*, and the frontier townes,
> Meaning to make a conquest of our land:
> Tis requisit to parle for a peace
> With *Sigismond* the king of *Hungary*:
> And saue our forces for the hot assaults
> Proud *Tamburlaine* intends *Natolia*.[132]

[132] II *Tamb.* 2371–2378. I am indebted for these facts to Miss Ethel Seaton's article, "Marlowe and His Authorities," TLS, 20: 388, 16 Je 1921. They confirm the view that Marlowe went beyond Mexia and Perondinus.

In three important respects Marlowe closely approximates history: the manner of ratifying peace; the arguments used to induce the king to break the truce; and the prayer of the indignant Turkish leader to the Christian God. Marlowe represents Orcanes as demanding that the Christians shall swear by Christ Himself, while he, as leader of the Turks, swears by Mahomet:

> [*Orcanes.*] But (*Sigismond*) confirme it with an oath,
>   And sweare in sight of heauen and by thy Christ.
> [*Sigismund.*] By him that made the world and sau'd my soule
>   The sonne of God and issue of a Mayd,
>   Sweet Iesus Christ, I sollemnly protest,
>   And vow to keepe this peace inuiolable.
> [*Orcanes.*] By sacred *Mahomet*, the friend of God,
>   Whose holy Alcaron remaines with vs . . .
>   I sweare to keepe this truce inuiolable.
>   [II *Tamb.* 2456–2467]

This is almost exactly the account of the event given by Antonius Bonfinius in his *Rervm Vngaricarvm Decades Qvatvor*:

Turci iuramentum in Eucharistiam à Rege postulant. . . . Conuentum tandem est vtrinque, vt in Euangelio nostri, illi in Alcorano iurarent. Scriptis igitur eodem argumento, lingua tamen duplici, cõditionibus pacis, eas inter se perpetuas inuiolatasq*ue* fore, sanctissimo vtrique iuramento asseuerarunt.[133]

Set this side by side with Marlowe's lines and the resemblance is clear:

>   . . . this truce inuiolable:
>   Of whose conditions, and our solemne othes
>   Sign'd with our handes, each shal retaine a scrowle:
>   As memorable witnesse of our league.   [2467–2470]

Practically the same story is told by Philippus Callimachus, who writes:

Et cum Turci peterent q*uid* in confirmandis pacis conditionibus, prolata in mediũ Eucaristia rex iuraret. . . . Constitutũ est in confirmanda pace proferri utrinq*ue* in mediũ sacram historiã suam, quod euangelium nostri, alcoranũ illi vocant, quibus ubi su*æ* quisq*ue*

---

[133] Ed. 1581, p. 457. There are copies of this book in HCL and NYPL, the latter also having the 1568 ed.

dexterā admouit religiose iuratū est, conuenta executum iri, atque inviolata permansura.[134]

When it is proposed that the Christians shall break the truce, Marlowe allows his "lords of Buda and Bohemia" to use the same arguments as Cardinal Julian:

> ... With such Infidels,
> In whom no faith nor true religion rests,
> We are not bound to those accomplishments,
> The holy lawes of Christendome inioine.[135]

Thus Bonfinius:

Iulianus tempestiuius adoritur: Si quis vestrum (inquit) Proceres, fortasse miretur, quòd de rescindenda pace, ac violanda fide, sim verba facturus: is primùm intelligat, me nil aliud hodie, quàm de seruando fœdere vobiscū acturum. . . . In quas miserias præceps consilium nos planè coniecerit, considerate: pacem cum Turca fecimus infideli, vt sanctam fidelium fidem violaremus, & sacrosanctum cum summo Pōtifice sociisque Principibus initum antè fœdus rescinde-remus.[136]

Finally, we have the outburst of Orcanes as Marlowe imagined him (the Amurath of history), when he learns of the Hungarians' perfidy:

> Thou Christ that art esteem'd omnipotent,
> If thou wilt prooue thy selfe a perfect God,
> Worthy the worship of all faithfull hearts,
> Be now reueng'd vpon this Traitors soule,
> And make the power I haue left behind
> (Too litle to defend our guiltlesse liues)
> Sufficient to discomfort and confound
> The trustlesse force of those false Christians.
> To armes my Lords, on Christ still let vs crie,
> If there be Christ, we shall haue victorie.
>   [II *Tamb*. 2912–2921]

This is little more than a poet's transcript from history. The actual words of Amurath, as reported by Bonfinius, were:

Nunc Christe, si Deus es (vt aiunt, & nos hallucinamur) tuas measque

---

[134] *De Clade Varnensi* (1519), lib. II. An edition of this book is also bound with Lonicer's 1578 ed. See tom. II, lib. II, p. 67. Both in HCL.
[135] II *Tamb*. 2827–2830. Bonfinius reverses the argument of *The Jew of Malta*.
[136] *Op. cit.*, pp. 457–458.

hîc iniurias, te quaeso, vlciscere: & his qui sanctum tuum nomen nondum agnouere, violatæ fidei pœnas ostende.[137]

How Marlowe happened to read Bonfinius, it is impossible to determine, but a volume printed at Frankfort was surely no more inaccessible than Perondinus, printed in Basel and Florence.

The oath of Amurath is a good illustration of the way in which the study of sources sometimes throws light upon an author's mind. This passage has long been supposed to illustrate Marlowe's "atheistic" leanings and has been pointed out as an example of the sort of blasphemy about which Richard Baines bore tales to the authorities. But when the "blasphemy" turns out to be merely a vivid bit of history, we see that it is merely one more instance of the selective skill with which Marlowe has sifted the material in his sources. As Miss Seaton very happily puts it: "Upon Marlowe no longer rests the responsibility of their invention, but merely the responsibility of choice."

Ortelius and His Map

As much might be said for the bewildering geography of *Tamburlaine*, with which Marlowe has often been reproached. The Black Forest — "*Nigra Silua*, where the Devils dance" — appears near Odessa; Zanzibar is "the Westerne part of *Affrike*" [138] instead of an island on its east coast; Rome appears to be somewhere in the Balkans; and many of the place names are quite untraceable on ordinary maps. Since Marlowe, like Milton and Keats after him, has a great love for high-sounding geographic names, this series of blunders has usually been set down as mere indifference to scientific nicety.

This is an error. Marlowe actually made careful use of the maps in the *Theatrum Orbis Terrarum* compiled by the German geographer, Abraham Ortels, or Wortels (1527–1598), usually known as Ortelius. First printed in 1570, this atlas was constantly reprinted throughout Marlowe's lifetime, and was probably used by his friend Raleigh. Marlowe might easily have

---

[137] *Op. cit.*, p. 464. Miss Seaton quotes the version given by Knolles, whose *Historie of the Turkes* was not printed until 1603, long after Marlowe was dead.
[138] II *Tamb.* 2764.

seen it at Cambridge.[139] A copy had been given to the university library in 1581 by Bishop Richard Barnes; and another copy, the bequest of Archbishop Parker, had been in the library of Corpus Christi for several years when Marlowe arrived.[140]

If we examine these maps, the source of most of Marlowe's geography is at once apparent. Ortelius shows a Nigra Silva near Odessa; and Mercator (1619) supplies a note about the "Forest noir," which is part of "La Forest Hercynie," in which exist "les monstreuses terreurs des Faunes espouventables." [141] Ortelius places the island of "Zenzibar" on the east coast of Africa; he also has a province of "Zanzibar" in the west. Rome is probably located in the Balkans in *Tamburlaine* because Ortelius inadvertently separated "Roma" from "nia" by too much space when he labeled Roumania.

When Techelles marches

Along the riuer *Nile*,
To *Machda*, where the mighty Christian Priest,
Cal'd *Iohn* the great, sits in a milk-white robe,
[II *Tamb.* 2755–2757]

he is thinking of the town of Machda on a tributary of the Nile, as shown in the map by Ortelius with the note: "Hic longe lateque imperitatt magnus princeps Presbiter Ioannes titus Africae potentiss: Rex." When Techelles says

From thence vnto *Cazates* did I martch,
Wher Amazonians met me in the field,
[II *Tamb.* 2760–2761]

he is alluding to the town of Cazates shown by Ortelius with the note "Amazonum Regio," and so on throughout the play.

"Without a single exception," says Miss Seaton, "every non-classical name appears in the *Theatrum*. Marlowe must have turned the atlas to and fro, and picked out a name here and there, attracted partly, but not entirely, by its sonority." [142]

[139] Cf. Ethel Seaton: "Marlowe's Map," *Essays and Studies*, 10: 13–35 (1924).

[140] Cf. the university library's *Catalogus Librorum MS.* (Donors' Book), p. 21; C. Sayles: *Cambridge University Library Annals*, p. 52; *Rough List of Parker Books* (MS.) in the Corpus Christi Library.

[141] French text of 1619, p. 227. Cf. A. H. Gilbert: *Geographical Dictionary of Milton*, s.v. "Hercynian Wilderness."

[142] *Op. cit.*, pp. 27–28.

These, then, were the sources of *Tamburlaine*: an Asiatic chief, a young English poet, and between them league upon league of tossing sea, of burning desert, of snow-capped mountains; priestly chroniclers upon the vellum covers of whose pious labors the dust of four centuries lies thick; the strange screed of a barbarian chief — and between these two, also, maps of strange regions, the hurrying ships of England, and the living word upon the lips of men.

INFLUENCE

The play, however, is the thing. What did Marlowe make of his widely varied sources, and how did *Tamburlaine* affect the audience and readers — and also the writers — of its day?

There is no doubt that *Tamburlaine* was a successful play. The evidence of that is clearly to be seen in the hasty composition of a second part, obviously to follow up an assured success, and in the wealth of contemporary references, of which the best-known is Pistol's

> These be good humours, indeed! Shall pack-horses
> And hollow pamper'd jades of Asia,
> Which cannot go but thirty mile a-day,
> Compare with Caesars and with Cannibals
> And Troian Greeks? [143]

which is, of course, a ludicrous garbling of Tamburlaine's cry to his team of kings:

> Holla, ye pampered Iades of *Asia*:
> What, can ye draw but twenty miles a day?
> [II *Tamb.* 3980–3981]

Now the humor of that passage is quite lost and its introduction wholly pointless unless the listening pit and crowded galleries instantly recall the fiery ranting of the Scythian chief, in absurd comparison with the doughty mouthing of mine Ancient Pistol. The shrewdest man of the theatre in London was perfectly sure that every soul in his audience was perfectly familiar with the original source of the "hollow pamper'd jades of Asia." Such a passage is in itself proof positive that *Tamburlaine* had

[143] II *Henry IV*, II. iv. 176–180. See also II. 209 of the present work.

been a successful play; for of course a play with which everyone is familiar has been a commercial success.

Other dramatists likewise seized on this well-known line. Indeed, it became so well known that it is worth seeing exactly what Marlowe had written and how he came to write it. The stage directions in the Second Part of *Tamburlaine* run:

> Tamburlaine drawen in his chariot by [the kings of] Trebizon and Soria with bittes in their mouthes, reines in his left hand, in his right hand a whip, with which he scourgeth them. . . . [Kings of] Natolia, and Ierusalem led by with fiue or six common souldiers.[144]

Tamburlaine opens the scene with the famous line,

> Holla, ye pampered Iades of *Asia*.

Neither the stage directions nor the line appears to have been entirely original with Marlowe, although both probably enjoyed more contemporary fame than anything else he wrote. Quite probably he was familiar with the similar scene in *Jocasta* (1566), which is thus described by George Gascoigne:

> There came in uppon the Stage a king . . . sitting in a Chariote very richely furnished, drawne in by foure Kinges in their Dublettes and Hosen, with Crownes also upon their heades.[145]

Jocasta thus introduces four as the conventional number of kings drawing chariots in these triumphal scenes. Marlowe follows this convention, and thereafter four captives, usually Moors, draw triumphal cars through one Elizabethan play after another. Very likely it was always the same property car.

The "pampered jades" speech — probably borrowed [146] from "pampred Jades of *Thrace*" in Golding's translation of Ovid — is parodied and ridiculed by Beaumont and Fletcher in *The Coxcomb*:

> Weehee,
> My pamper'd jade of Asia; [147]

in *Women Pleased* ("Away, thou pamper'd jade of vanity"); [148]

---

[144] IV. iii, p. 120 of Brooke's ed. (1910).

[145] G. Gascoigne: *Complete Works*, ed. J. Cunliffe (1907), I. 246.

[146] *Shakespeare's Ovid* (ed. W. H. D. Rouse), p. 186, l. 238. See also Douglas Bush: *Mythology and the Renaissance Tradition*, p. 136n.

[147] *Coxcomb*, II. ii; Dyce's (1843) ed., III. 152.

[148] *Women Pleased*, IV. i; Dyce's (1843) ed., VII. 63.

and by Ford and Dekker in *The Sun's Darling* ("I sweat like a pamper'd jade of *Asia*").[149] John Taylor, the water poet, uses it twice:

> And fulsome Madams, and new scuruy Squires,
> Should iolt the streets in pomp, at their desires,
> Like great triumphant *Tamberlaines*, each day,
> Drawne with the pamper'd Iades of Belgia.[150]

As a Thames waterman, Taylor naturally detested the coaches which were becoming popular, and the Belgian horses that drew them. Hence his contemptuous description of a ride in a coach. "I was but little inferiour to *Tamberlaine*, being iolted thus in state by those pampred Iades of Belgia." In *The Blind Beggar of Bednall Green*, by Day and Chettle, the character Swash is offered the privilege of seeing "a stately combate be-twixt *Tamberlayn* the Great, and the Duke of *Guyso* the less." A few lines further on, Swash exclaims, "I'll murther your *Tamberlayn* and his Coatch-horses." [151] The famous lines are again quoted in the *Quintessence of Witt* (ca. 1607), a manu-script provincial satire, which appeared in evidence at Taunton Assize.

> What holloe hoo, ye pampred Asyian Iades,
> must men of not[e] and worth be yor Comrades? [152]

There are accurate quotations in the second act of *Eastward Hoe* (1605); in *The Fleire* (1607), by Edward Sharpham; [153] and in *A Strappado for the Diuell* (1615), by R. Braithwaite.[154] Thomas Lodge provides an imitation, with every appearance of seriousness, in *The Wounds of Ciuill War*.[155] The much-quoted passage makes its final appearance in English literature when George Eliot permits a character in *Middlemarch* to read into Marlowe's scene some strangely Victorian metaphysics: "I take Tamburlaine in his chariot for the tremendous course of the world's physical history lashing on the harnessed dynasties"![156]

---

[149] *Sun's Darling*, III. ii (1657 ed. in LC).
[150] John Taylor: *Works* (ed. 1630), pp. 121 (wrongly numbered 111), 239.
[151] Bang's ed. (Materialien), ll. 1640, 1660–1661; sig. G2r of the 1659 ed.
[152] Original texts in the minutes of Lord Ellesmere on the Assize at Taunton, in Bridgewater MSS., Huntington Library. See also Charles J. Sisson: *Lost Plays of Shakespeare's Age*, pp. 175, 177, 184.
[153] Nibbe's ed. (Materialien), p. 22.
[154] Ed. 1872, p. 159.
[155] See I. 265.
[156] *Middlemarch*, chap. XXII.

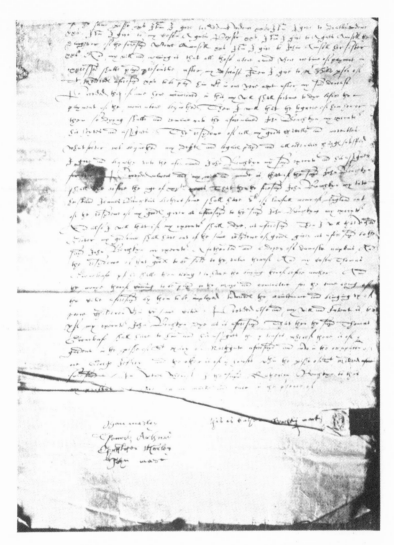

LAST PAGE OF THE WILL OF KATHERINE BENCHKYN, WITH
SIGNATURES OF JOHN AND CHRISTOPHER MARLOWE

The mildly derisive note that gradually creeps into the later Elizabethan and Jacobean allusions to *Tamburlaine* is at least partly due to the gradual advance in standards of dramatic criticism. Marlowe's faults as a playwright, which are apparent enough to modern readers, had not at first been very obvious to the earlier Elizabethan audiences; but the later Elizabethans demanded better structure, more plausibility, and more finished characterization.

Ben Jonson is quite justified in complaining that plays like *Tamburlaine* "fly from all humanity." [157] His criticism is essentially the same as that of Joseph Hall (1574–1656), who in his *Virgidemiarum* pokes fun at "the Turkish Tamberlain,"

> Graced with huff-cap terms and thund'ring threats,
> That his poor hearers' hair quite upright sets.

Similarly derisive is the allusion in Marston's *Antonio and Mellida*: "Rampum scrampum, mount tufty Tamburlaine! What rattling thunderclap breaks from his lips," or the question in *Satiro-Mastix*:

> Dost stampe mad Tamberlaine, dost stampe? [158]

The humiliation of Bajazeth seems to have made almost as deep an impression, and later playwrights frequently alluded to it. Dekker in *Old Fortunatus* writes:

> Poor Bajazet, old Turkish Emperor,
> And once the greatest monarch in the East;
> Fortune herself is sad to view thy fall,
> And grieves to see thee glad to lick up crumbs
> At the proud feet of that great Scythian swain,
> Fortune's best minion, warlike Tamburlaine:
> Yet must thou in a cage of iron be drawn
> In triumph at his heels, and there in grief,
> Dash out thy brains.[159]

In *The Travels of the Three English Brothers* (1607) there is

---

[157] *Discoveries* (ed. G. B. Harrison, Bodley Head Quartos), p. 33.
[158] *Hall's Satires*, bk. I, Satire III, p. 10 of the ed. by Thomas Wharton, expanded by Samuel Weller Singer; Bullen's Marston, I. 11; Scherer's ed. of *Satiro-Mastix* (Materialien), ll. 1975–1976; William John Olive: *Burlesque in Elizabethan Drama*, p. 135.
[159] I. i, pp. 299–300 of the Mermaid ed.

another allusion to Bajazeth's cage. Sir Thomas Shirley, defying the Turkish emperor, exclaims:

> Thy selfe (as sometimes were thy Ancestors)
> Fed in a cage and dragd at conquerors heeles.[160]

Heywood's *Golden Age* (1611) alludes indirectly to Tamburlaine's use of Bajazeth as his footstool:

> Down, treacherous lord, and be our foot-pace now,
> To ascend our high tribunal.[161]

Massinger, in *Believe as You List*, alludes to both episodes simultaneously:

> Then by the senators, whom I'll use as horses,
> I will be drawn in a chariot . . .
> Our enemy, led like a dog in a chain,
> As I descend or reascend in state,
> Shall serve for my foot-stool.[162]

Massinger makes a second allusion to the footstool in *The Maid of Honour*:

> *Page.* . . . I'll make
> Thy back my footstool.
> *Sylli.* Tamburlaine in little!
> Am I turned Turk! [163]

As late as 1640 the episode is still remembered in William Habington's *Queen of Arragon*:

> . . . An emperor did serve
> As footstool to the conqueror, and are we
> Better assur'd of destiny? [164]

Even the revisers who produced the 1616 text of *Doctor Faustus* borrowed it. Bruno is brought before the Pope, "led in chaines." Then:

> *Pope.* Cast downe our Foot-stoole.
> *Ray[mond, King of Hungary].* Saxon *Bruno* stoope,
> Whilst on thy backe his hollinesse ascends
> Saint *Peters* Chaire and State Pontificall.[165]

---

[160] Bullen's reprint (1881), p. 80.
[161] Shakspere Soc. ed., III. i, p. 48.
[162] Mermaid ed., III. iii, vol. II, pp. 424–425.
[163] Mermaid ed., II. ii, vol. I, p. 325.
[164] Hazlitt's Dodsley, XIII. 396.
[165] Brooke's ed. (1910), 889–892, p. 203.

A host of other references in various unimportant authors[166] show clearly enough just how successful the play had been, for these are not elaborate or detailed references, but hasty allusions made in passing, as if the writers were quite sure of being understood by an audience already thoroughly familiar with the original. Dekker alludes to the play at least eight times, and the unknown author of *The Taming of a Shrew* also makes very free with it.[167]

It needs but little imagination to fancy the enthusiasm with which the Elizabethan audiences must have greeted the new stage technique of Marlowe. They had been regaled hitherto with such exercises in the encyclopedic drama as *The Troublesome Raigne of John, King of England*, the pointless imitation of Seneca in *Gorboduc*, or the refined inanities of Lyly. Suddenly there burst upon them the dazzling genius of this youth from Cambridge. In place of the old sprawling formless plays, we have the close-knit structure of *Tamburlaine* — which, to be sure, seems sprawling and formless enough to us today, but which, seen in its own time and place, is a miracle of structure and serves the only purpose that dramatic structure ever does serve: to lift the men and women who see the play quite out of their own lives and into the represented action of the mimic world. It appeals, likewise, to the Elizabethan lust for conquest and the new interest in strange lands and peoples then stirring in men's minds. And this new and fascinating kind of play makes use of a new and beautiful kind of language. Ears that had been bored by wooden verses suddenly heard the passionate music of the mighty line, into which poured all the fire and vigor, the longing grasp for things impossible, which were the very echo of the spirit of that time. What wonder if the subjects of Queen Bess thronged to the playhouse when Alleyn was playing *Tamburlaine*![168]

Successes in the theatre are notoriously of short life. Within a hundred years all the noise and stir, the mimic war and con-

---

[166] Collected by Tucker Brooke: "Reputation of Christopher Marlowe," *Trans. Connecticut Acad.*, 25: 366–373 (1922).

[167] See II. 248–253.

[168] My debt at this point to Professor George Pierce Baker's illuminating essay on "Dramatic Technique in Marlowe" is evident enough here to need no acknowledgment. See *Essays and Studies*, 4: 172–182 (1913).

quests, had been forgotten. When Charles Saunders produced his halting tragedy, *Tamerlane the Great*, in 1681, it wakened only vague recollections of the last revivals of Marlowe's play, and these only in the minds of the oldest theatre-goers. Had not some such play on some such subject been famous on the older stage when Elizabeth was Queen? There must have been a great thumbing of dusty diaries and an industrious searching of *Momus Triumphans* and similar handbooks of the stage, and perhaps even a little jealous innuendo among fellow-craftsmen as to the originality of Master Saunders; for when he publishes his play, his sarcastic preface bears all the earmarks of the dudgeon of a much-nettled man. Some people, he complains, "will yet in spight of Stupidity have their share too in Damning the Reputation of an Author; and the means they took, was to give out, that this was only an old Play Transcrib'd." Then Saunders launches forth in the full tide of his indignation:

But I hope I may easily unload my self of that Calumny, when I shall testifie that I never heard of any Play on the same Subject, untill my own was Acted, neither have I since seen it, though it hath been told me, there is a Cock-Pit play, going under the name of the *Scythian Shepherd*, or *Tamberlain the Great*, which how good it is, any one may Judge by its obscurity, being a thing, not a Bookseller in *London*, or scarce the Players themselves, who Acted it formerly, cou'd call to Remembrance, so far, that I believe that whoever was the Author, he might e'en keep it to himself secure from invasion, or Plagiary; But let these who have Read it Convince themselves of their Errors, that this is no second Edition, but an entirely new Play.[169]

To clinch the matter, Saunders revealed his actual source. "I drew the design of this Play, from a late *Novell*, call'd *Tamerlane* and *Asteria*, which I'm sure bears not half the Age of the Tragedy before mention'd."

Posterity, to be sure, has once again played at ducks and drakes with literary reputations. Marlowe's *Tamburlaine* is by no means so obscure as it was in 1681, and Saunders' stupid concoction has sunk deep into the oblivion it deserves. But the indignation of Master Saunders at being confused with so in-

---

[169] *Tamerlane the Great* (1681), preface, p. 2. [LC,JB]

significant a person as "whoever was the author" of *Tambur-laine* and his contemptuous asseveration that Marlowe's old play was "a thing not a bookseller in London, or scarce the players themselves who acted it formerly, cou'd call to remem-brance," shows how the Scythian shepherd was fallen from his high place in popular esteem. In 1598, eleven years after *Tamburlaine* was first produced, a Shakespeare was certain that every groundling would recognize his passing reference to a single scene. In 1681 a Saunders assures us, with a sincerity as evident as his heat, that the very booksellers had forgotten it! In this low estate *Tamburlaine* was to remain for hard upon two hundred years. Many a nineteenth-century editor was loth to admit that this play could have come from Marlowe's pen at all." [170]

Yet probably no play has exerted so great an influence on the history of English drama as *Tamburlaine*. It helped to free English tragedy from foreign leading strings, especially Italian dominance. It gave English drama a new force and passion. It established blank verse — hitherto only tentatively used — as the chief medium of tragedy. It provided the first example of the subtlety and feeling that blank verse could attain; and, even though Marlowe himself was not always capable of the heights of poetry, it was this quality which Shakespeare carried on and upward a few years later. It set up a conquering hero of quenchless ambition as a dramatic type upon whom other dramatists immediately seized. It first gave dramatic unity to English tragedy, by using a single hero, surrounded by other characters who seem his mere shadows.

The resulting bloodlessness of subordinate characters is, in-deed, one of Marlowe's faults. His other faults, bombast, rant, and bloodshed, were re-enforced by the influence of Seneca; and together they encouraged the welter of bloodshed in which Elizabethan playwrights delighted. This evil influence is felt almost to the closing of the theatres in 1642.

The Elizabethans themselves were not all blind to these shortcomings in Marlowe. Jonson's remark that the mighty lines were "fitter for admiration than for parallel" [171] has a very

[170] See I. 194–195.
[171] "Address to the Reader," preceding William Bosworth's *Chast and Lost Lovers*

double meaning. *The Returne from Pernassus* seems to be ridiculing *Tamburlaine* in the lines put into the mouth of "Furor Poeticus," a character who is further identified as a former Cambridge student:

> Ile cause the Pleiades to giue thee thanks,
> Ile write thy name within the sixteenth spheare:
> Ile make the Antarticke pole to kisse thy toa,
> And *Cinthia* to do homage to thy tayle.[172]

Marlowe had made frequent allusions to the Antarctic pole and to Cynthus. Another similar outburst by Furor Poeticus resembles Greene's strictures on *Tamburlaine*:

> Hang him whose verse cannot out-belch the wind:
> That cannot beard and braue *Don Eolus*,
> That when the cloud of his inuention breakes,
> Cannot out-cracke the scarr-crow thunderbolt.[173]

Still another line in the *Returne* probably reminded the audience at St. John's College of "Awake ye men of *Memphis*" and the "pampered jades" speech, neatly dovetailed. This was:

> Awake you paltry trulles of *Helicon*.[174]

Furor Poeticus is described as "a nimble swaggerer with a goosequill." He alludes to his own verse as "my high tiptoe strouting poesye," and swears

> By that cælestiall fier within my brayne,
> That giues a liuing genius to my lines.[175]

Once or twice there seem to be jeering allusions to *Faustus*. There is reference to the "very terrible roaring muse" of Furor Poeticus — "nothing but squibs and fireworks." Again, one character says to another, "How like thy snowt is to great Lucifers!"

In passages like these, the dialogue suggests that academic

(1651). See George Saintsbury: *Minor Poets of the Caroline Period*, II. 527. See also II. 133–134 of the present work.
[172] The MS. of the *Returne* is Rawlinson D.398, at the Bodleian. Reference here is to the ed. by W. D. Macray (Oxford, 1886). This passage is from ll. 1667–1670, p. 134.
[173] Ll. 495–499, p. 94.
[174] I *Tamb.* 1372, 3980: *Returne*, 1349, p. 123.
[175] Ll. 1342–1343, p. 123. Cf. l. 509, p. 95.

Cambridge remembered Marlowe very well indeed, without in the least remembering him kindly.

Tamburlaine remained so familiar to readers that, for years, allusions to the play itself or even to specific scenes and lines abound. Even its title was plagiarized for the lost *Timur Khan*, of which only a "plotte" remains.[176] It cannot be identical with Marlowe's play, for the incidents described in the "plotte" are entirely different; Ben Jonson in *Discoveries* sneers at it in words which imply the existence of two plays, not one: "the *Tamerlanes*, and *Tamer-Chams*, of the late Age, which had nothing in them but the *scenicall* strutting, and furious vocifer-ation, to warrant them then to the ignorant gapers." [177] The title was again borrowed in 1590, when a ballad appeared on *The True Comical Discourse of Tamberlein the Scythian Shepparde*.[178]

The tremendous success of *Tamburlaine* worked an instant revolution in the tastes of the theatre-going public. There had been nothing like it before. The old-fashioned plays seemed stodgy; their rhymed and stanzaic verse ridiculous. Naturally, other dramatists made haste to write plays of the same sort. Among the early Elizabethan dramatists who thus show the influence of *Tamburlaine* are Greene, Peele, Lodge, Dekker, Kyd, Shakespeare himself, Anthony Munday, Henry Chettle, Marlowe's friend George Chapman, and the unknown authors of *The Wars of Cyrus* and *Scanderbeg*.

Among the later dramatists who are clearly influenced, in greater or less degree, are John Webster, Philip Massinger, and John Ford, the two latter also suggesting the school of Jonson. *Tamburlaine's* influence on Munday, Middleton, Chettle, Chapman, and Dekker is relatively slight. In Munday's *Down-fall of Robert Earl of Huntington*, in Munday's and Chettle's joint *Death of Robert Earl of Huntington*, and in Chettle's *Hoff-man*, the rant, blood, and violence suggest Marlowe, though we must not forget that in this respect most Elizabethans were pretty much alike. Dekker, in *Old Fortunatus*, echoes *Tam-burlaine* in the language of Fortune and the kings. He borrows

176 Reproduced in James Boswell's revised ed. of Malone's Shakespeare (1821), III. 356–357, from originals in Malone's collection. Also in Greg's *Elizabethan Playhouse Documents*.
177 Ed. G. B. Harrison (Bodley Head Quartos), p. 33.
178 SR 14 August 1590.

a situation from Marlowe when Fortune "treads" upon kings as she mounts her "chair." He borrows a character in Bajazet. He also borrows heavily from *Faustus*.[179] Middleton alludes to Marlowe's play — "the ordnance playing like so many Tamburlaines" — in *Father Hubburd's Tales*.[180] Chapman's *Bussy d'Ambois*, *Conspiracy of the Duke of Biron*, and *Tragedie of the Duke of Biron* show plain traces of Marlowe's love of the extraordinary hero and situation.[181]

The blood and violence of Webster and Tourneur probably owe something, if not directly to Marlowe, at least to the tradition he did so much with the aid of Kyd to establish. Like Ancient Pistol in *Henry IV*, Quicksilver, the apprentice in *Eastward Hoe*, quotes the rant of *Tamburlaine*, which the more sophisticated playgoers of a later generation may not have taken very seriously. It is satirized in the induction of *A Warning for Fair Women*:

> How some damnd tyrant, to obtaine a crowne,
> Stabs, hangs, impoysons, smothers, cutteth throats.[182]

ROBERT GREENE

Although he seized every opportunity to ridicule Marlowe's work in general and *Tamburlaine* in particular, Robert Greene shows Marlowe's influence more clearly than any other contemporary. He borrows Marlowe's plot, structure, and verbiage, and so far as in him lies he also imitates the mighty line. Only in the grim horror of Marlowe's climaxes did he decline to follow him. He preferred happy endings. Tamburlaine, Faustus, Barabas, Edward, Dido, Chatillon, and the Guise all meet with violent and unhappy ends; but Greene's Alphonsus retains his hard-won power; James IV's story ends before Flodden Field; Friar Bacon repents in time.[183]

Powerfully influenced by *Tamburlaine*, Greene is less influenced by *Doctor Faustus* and seems to have been very little influenced, if at all, by later plays. The influence of *Tamburlaine* is most obvious in his *Alphonsus, King of Aragon*; it is so

---

[179] See I. 308–309.
[180] Dyce's Middleton, V. 588.
[181] Hermann Ulrici: *Shakespeares dramatische Kunst*, I. 318.
[182] Fol. A2v, of the 1599 ed., Tudor Facsimile Texts.
[183] Cf. C. H. Herford: *Studies in the Literary Relations of England and Germany*, p. 191.

clear in *Selimus* and *Locrine* that some critics would attribute both plays to Marlowe; and there are evident traces in *Orlando Furioso*, *Friar Bacon and Friar Bungay* (which is closely related to *Doctor Faustus*), *George à Greene*, and *A Looking-Glass for London*. It was presumably the ill-success of his efforts to imitate Marlowe that so embittered Greene.

His *Alphonsus, King of Aragon*, is an attempt to outdo Marlowe in an episodic conquest play, marked by perpetual slaughter, laid in the Orient with mainly Oriental characters, in language, versification, and style as close to Marlowe's as Greene was able to make them. The first two acts are constructed in exact imitation of the First Part of *Tamburlaine*. A comparative table [184] makes this clear enough.

Tamburlaine	*Alphonsus*
1. Tamburlaine plans conquest of Persia and Asia.	1. Alphonsus plans reconquest of Aragon.
2. Tamburlaine joins Theridamas and Cosroe to conquer Persia.	2. Alphonsus joins Albinus to conquer Aragon.
3. Tamburlaine encounters King Mycetes and seizes his crown.	3. Alphonsus kills King Flaminius and claims throne.
4. Theridamas, sent to attack Tamburlaine, is won over with all his forces.	4. Laelius, seeking to avenge his king, recognizes Alphonsus and is won over to his side.
5. Tamburlaine conquers Persia for Cosroe.	5. Belinus attributes his victory chiefly to Alphonsus.
6. The grateful Cosroe makes Tamburlaine regent and commander.	6. The grateful Belinus gives Alphonsus the domain of Aragon.
7. Tamburlaine seeks Cosroe's crown.	7. Alphonsus seeks Belinus' crown.
8. Tamburlaine conquers. His speeches resemble those of Alphonsus.	8. Alphonsus conquers. His speeches resemble those of Tamburlaine.

The play, as Storojenko observes, has "strong traces" of

---

[184] Adapted from E. Hübener: *Einfluss von Marlowe's Tamburlaine* (Halle Diss. 1901). See also Storojenko's life of Greene in Grosart's *Greene*, I. 175–176; C. M. Gayley: *Representative English Comedies*, I. 403; Thomas H. Dickinson's introduction to his edition of Greene (Mermaid), pp. xxxix–xl; G. E. Woodberry, in Gayley, *op. cit.*, I. 391; William John Olive: *Burlesque in Elizabethan Drama* (North Carolina Diss. [MS.], 1937), pp. 140–145.

being "an imitation of Marlowe's *Tamburlaine*." Alphonsus drops into a vein typical of Marlowe's heroes and plainly influenced by Marlowe's "Passionate Shepherd" [185] when he pleads with Iphigena, who is a fair equivalent of Zenocrate:

> Nay virgin stay. And if thou wilt vouchsafe
> To entertaine *Alphonsus* simple sute,
> Thou shalt ere long be Monarch of the world:
> All christned kings, with all your Pagan dogs,
> Shall bend their knees vnto *Iphigina*.
> The Indian soyle shalbe thine at command,
> Where euery step thou settest on the ground
> Shall be receiued on the golden mines;
> Rich *Pactolus*, that riuer of account,
> Which doth descend from top of *Tmolu's* mount,
> Shall be thine owne, and all the world beside,
> If you will graunt to be *Alphonsus* bride.[186]

This parallels the passage beginning, "Disdaines *Zenocrate* to liue with me," in which Tamburlaine makes similar promises.

These comparisons bring us to the end of Greene's second act, and a clearer case of borrowing it would be hard to find. Thereafter Greene follows his great model a little less slavishly, but he still continues to make free with Marlowe's work. He alludes to Tamburlaine specifically in one passage.

> . . . remember with your selues
> What foes we haue; not mightie Tamberlaine,
> Nor souldiers trained vp amongst the warres,
> But feareful boors, pickt from their rurall flocke,[187]

which is important as providing pretty definite proof that Marlowe's play was already on the stage. In both *Tamburlaine* and *Alphonsus* the leaders of the opposing forces exchange billingsgate before the battle; both the victorious heroes reward their faithful followers with crowns; both the victors feast; both conquer Turkish emperors whose demeanor as captives is strangely similar; both heroes win the love of unwilling princesses, daughters of foreign potentates; and both ungallantly give the ladies reason to fear concubinage instead of legitimate marriage; both have armies which are said to exceed

---

[185] In Grosart's Greene, I. 170. See II. 157–160 of the present work.
[186] I *Tamb*. 278–301; *Alphonsus*, 1762–1773, Grosart's Greene, XIII. 400–401.
[187] *Alphonsus*, 1577–1580, Grosart's Greene, XIII. 393.

those of Xerxes, and both battle like the Titans against Jupiter.
Both defy Mahomet,[188] and both assert their control over
Fortune. Alphonsus says:

> I clap vp Fortune in a cage of gold,
> To make her turne her wheele as I thinke best.

Tamburlaine boasts:

> I hold the Fates bound fast in yron chaines,
> And with my hand turne Fortunes wheel about.

Later, Anippe repeats his vaunt to Zenocrate:

> Your Loue hath fortune so at his command,
> That she shall stay and turne her wheele no more.[189]

Greene's Alphonsus and Amurack defy the gods like Tamburlaine. Alphonsus says that Mars

> . . . dares not stir, nor once to moue a whit,
> For feare *Alphonsus* then should stomack it.[190]

Amurack describes himself as one

> Whose mighty force doth terrify the gods,

all of which is exactly in the vein of Tamburlaine, particularly
the defiance of Mahomet just quoted. Similarly, Marlowe's
hero refuses to crown Zenocrate "Vntil with greater honors I
be grac'd"; Alphonsus gives crowns away, while hoping for a
mightier realm.

There are also occasional verbal echoes, some of which
may be accidental. Thus Greene refers to "*Phœbus* borrowed
beames," to "*Phœbus* with his golden beames," and — in almost the same words — to "*Phœbus*' golden beams"; while
Tamburlaine alludes to "*Phœbes* siluer eie." [191] All of this might
be either accident or imitation.

It is noticeable that almost every parallel, whether of phrasing or construction, is with the First Part of *Tamburlaine*,
though Marlowe's habitual repetition occasionally leads to cer-

<hr/>

[188] *Alphonsus*, III. ii; II *Tamb.* 4290.
[189] *Alphonsus*, 1619–1620, Grosart's Greene, XIII. 395; I *Tamb.* 369–370, 2155–2156.
See I. 264–265, II. 280 of the present work.
[190] I *Tamb.* 2155–2156; *Alphonsus*, 1625–1626, Grosart's Greene, XIII. 395.
[191] I *Tamb.* 1004; *Alphonsus*, 1407, 1268, 559, Grosart's Greene, XIII. 386, 380, 353.

tain verbal parallels with the Second Part as well. This seems to indicate that Greene wrote *Alphonsus* immediately after the production of the First Part of *Tamburlaine*, while Marlowe was at work on his sequel.[192] Grosart is doubtless being over-subtle when he suggests that *Alphonsus* satirizes *Tamburlaine*, although it is true, as J. M. Brown observes, that "a little more exaggeration would produce the impression of burlesque."[193] Storojenko supposes that Marlowe ridiculed *Alphonsus* and thus irritated Greene.[194] More probably Greene was irritated by his own failure to comprehend the magic of the mighty line and to reproduce Marlowe's devices for varying the monotony of blank verse.

ORLANDO FURIOSO

Greene's other plays show less imitation, though Marlowe's influence is still more or less apparent. *Orlando Furioso* repeats the conquering-hero type of play initiated by *Tamburlaine*; employs Marlowe's characteristic use of geographic names for their color and sound; and indulges in a degree of bombast which may be due either to imitation of Marlowe merely or to the fact that Greene was also an Elizabethan.

Storojenko professes to see in the Circassian count, Sacripant, "a very transparent parody of Tamburlaine," especially as regards "his stupid self-satisfaction and childish longing for a crown."[195] But this is reading modern attitudes into the Elizabethan mind. Greene more probably meant Sacripant as a serious rival to Tamburlaine's popularity with the playgoing public, and therefore made his own character as much like Marlowe's as he could. Sacripant says:

A Scepter then comes tumbling in my thoughts.

A crown is

. . . the golden marke
Which makes my thoughts dreame on a Diademe.[196]

---

[192] Grosart: Introduction to *Life and Works of Robert Greene*, I. xxvii–xxviii.
[193] *New Zealand Magazine*, 2: 107 Ap 1877. File in NYPL.
[194] "Life of Greene" in Grosart's Greene, I. 89, 169–170.
[195] Translated in Grosart's Greene, I. 180, 181.
[196] Grosart's Greene, XIII. 128, 130. See E. H. Wright: *Influence of Christopher Marlowe on His Immediate Contemporaries*, p. 4; E. Hübener: *Einfluss von Marlowe's*

His "chaire presents a throne of maiestie"; his "dreames are Princely, all of Diadems." His "glorious genius" makes him "coequall with the gods" — a passage which suggests such Marlowe phrases as "coequall with the cloudes" and "co-equal with the crown," the latter in I *Henry VI*.[197]

There is a further parallel in

> Heauen, earth, men, beasts, and euery liuing thing,
> Consume and end with Countie Sacrepant.
> > [*Orlando* (Grosart, XIII. 187)]
>
> For *Tamburlaine*, the Scourge of God must die.
> *Amy.* Meet heauen & earth, & here let al things end.
> > [II *Tamb.* 4641–4642]

OTHER PLAYS BY GREENE

George à Greene contains a specific reference to Marlowe's play:

> Least I, like martiall Tamburlaine, lay waste
> Their bordering countries,[198]

and there are certain minor similarities, such as ambitions for the crown and bestowal of awards upon faithful followers. These, however, arise naturally out of the subject matter of Greene's play and may well be independent.

A Looking-Glass for London and England, in which Greene collaborated with Thomas Lodge, belongs to the general type inspired by *Tamburlaine* and thus shows certain resemblances. The dialogue is in the high-flown vein, filled with hyperboles, which *Tamburlaine* had made popular. Rasni, King of "Niniuie," is, like Tamburlaine, surrounded by three chieftains who are mere puppets, and he boasts in the vein of Tamburlaine: "Rasni is God on earth, and none but he." [199] And again:

> Is not great Rasni aboue natures reach,
> God vpon earth, and all his will is law.

The heroine Remilia corresponds to Zenocrate. There is the

Tamburlaine, pp. 26–31; Adolf Geissler, *op. cit.*, chap. VII. Hübener professes to detect still further analogies, but they seem rather strained.

[197] I *Tamb.* 261; Grosart's Greene, XIII. 128; I *Henry VI*, V. i. 33.

[198] Grosart's Greene, XIV. 123.

[199] Grosart's Greene, XIV. 9, 12.

suggestion by the author that the gods themselves envy the hero his love, exactly as in Marlowe. Remilia boasts:

> For were a Goddesse fairer then am I,
> Ile scale the heauens to pull her from the place,

which is clearly borrowed from *Tamburlaine*. Rasni's lines in the opening speech:

> Six hundreth Towers that toplesse touch the cloudes:
> This Citie is the footestoole of your King,

seem to show the joint influence of the "topless towers" passage in *Faustus* and the footstool passage in *Tamburlaine*. Another line from the *Looking-Glass*:

> A hundreth Lords do honour at my feete,[200]

is very like Tamburlaine's

> Then shalt thou see a hundred kings and more
> Vpon their knees, all bid me welcome home,
> [II *Tamb.* 2519–2520]

or the earlier passages:

> Me thinks I see kings kneeling at his feet
> [I *Tamb.* 251]

and

> A hundreth Tartars shall attend on thee.
> [I *Tamb.* 289]

Remilia's praise of her own beauty:

> Tell me, is not my state as glorious
> As Iunoes pomp, when tyred with heauens despoile,
> Clad in her vestments spotted all with starres,
> She crost the siluer path vnto her Ioue?
> Is not Remilia far more beautious,
> Richt with the pride of natures excellence,
> Then Venus in the brightest of her shine?
> My haires, surpasse they not Apollos locks?
> Are not my Tresses curled with such art
> As Loue delights to hide him in their faire?
> . . . Haue I not stolne the beautie of the heauens,
> And plac't it on the feature of my face? [201]

[200] Grosart's Greene, XIV. 8, 9, 12, 29.
[201] Grosart's Greene, XIV. 26–27.

curiously echoes Marlowe's verse and mood, and seems also to
owe something to Faustus'

> Clad in the beauty of a thousand starres,
> [DF, 1342]

as well as to Tamburlaine's praise of Zenocrate:

> *Zenocrate,* louelier than the Loue of *Ioue.*
> [I *Tamb.* 283]

Rasni's lament over Remilia's death is clearly modeled on
Tamburlaine's lament over Zenocrate's.[202]

There is, however, a strong temptation to exaggerate the significance of these parallels. Men in love and women in love
with themselves talk very much alike, both in life and on the
stage, and Greene's actual borrowing from Marlowe in some of
these plays is rather slight.

The opening line of the fourth act of the First Part of *Tamburlaine* seems to have made an equally deep impression on
Greene and on John Fletcher. Marlowe wrote:

> Awake ye men of *Memphis,* heare the clange
> Of Scythian trumpets.
> [I *Tamb.* 1372–1373]

Greene gives to his character Jonas the line

> Repent, ye men of Niniuie, repent! [203]

Fletcher puts Marlowe's line into the mouth of Judas in
Bonduca and uses "Thou man of Memphis" in *Wit Without
Money.*

George Peele

George Peele, whom Greene couples with Marlowe in the
malicious address in his *Groats-worth of Witte,*[204] seems to have
been influenced by *Tamburlaine* in three extant plays, *The
Battle of Alcazar, Edward I,* and *David and Bethsabe.* He was
certainly familiar with *Tamburlaine* in 1589, when Norris and

---

[202] II *Tamb.* 3046–3110; Grosart's Greene, XIV. 31–32.
[203] Grosart's Greene, XIV. 85. Cf. *Bonduca,* II; *Wit Without Money,* V. ii.
[204] Grosart's Greene, XIV. 85. See also I. 123 of the present work.

Drake left England on their expedition to Spain and Portugal. His *Farewell to Norris and Drake* contains the lines:

> Bid Mahomet's Poo [head], and mighty Tamburlaine, . . .
> Adieu.[205]

Peele's lost *Turkish Mahomet and Hiren the Fair Greek*, to which Pistol alludes in II *Henry IV*, was probably an imitation of the love story of Tamburlaine and Zenocrate.[206]

THE BATTLE OF ALCAZAR

Though *The Battle of Alcazar* shows the influence of *Tamburlaine* clearly enough, it is not, like *Alphonsus*, a mere imitation. It does, however, repeat the conquest motif, which soon grows wearisome in the plays of this period:

> Sit you, and see this true and tragic war,
> A modern matter full of blood and ruth,
> Where three bold kings confounded in their height,
> Fell to the earth, contending for a crown.[207]

The scenes of conquest in Africa, the strange potentates and their courts, the pomp of war, the elaborate costuming are all drawn from Marlowe's play. Stukely, like Theridamas, goes over to the enemy and yearns to be a king. Tamburlaine threatens to wound his sons to give them lessons in courage; Peele makes his Moorish ambassadors thrust their hands into the flame of torches to attest their veracity. The body of Zenocrate is carried about with Tamburlaine's army; the body of Peele's Abdemelec is placed upon the throne to see a victory.

Peele, like Greene, refers specifically to Tamburlaine and even quotes his dying words, slightly altered. In Marlowe's play this line is

> For *Tamburlaine*, the Scourge of God must die.

Peele writes:

> Convey Tamburlaine into our Affric here,
> To chastise and to menace lawful kings:

---

[205] Dyce's Peele, II. 170.

[206] II *Henry IV*, IV. iv. 174. Cf. *Jests of George Peele* (ed. 1809), p. 22, and *The Returne from Pernassus*.

[207] Reference is to Dyce's Peele (1829). This passage is on p. 89. Attribution of this play to Peele has been questioned. See W. W. Greg: *Two Elizabethan Stage Abridgements*, and Edith A. White: *Two Hands in the Battle of Alcazar*.

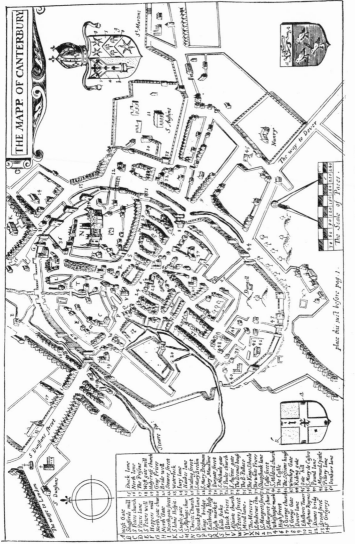

MAP OF CANTERBURY AS MARLOWE KNEW IT

Tamburlaine, triumph not, for thou must die,
As Philip did, Cæsar, and Cæsar's peers.[208]

Marlowe's emphasis on "the sweet fruition of an earthly crown"
recurs in a later passage:

There shall no action pass my hand or sword,
That cannot make a step to gain a crown;
No word shall pass the office of my tongue,
That sounds not of affection to a crown;
No thought have being in my lordly breast,
That works not every way to win a crown;
. . . Huff it, brave mind, and never cease t'aspire,
Before thou reign sole king of thy desire.[209]

The Moor's furious speech at the opening of the third scene
of Act II has much of the exaggeration, though none of the
music, of Tamburlaine's lament over Zenocrate:

Fight, earthquakes, in the entrails of the earth,
And, eastern whirlwinds, in the hellish shades.
Some foul contagion of the infected heaven
Blast all the trees, and in their cursed tops
The dismal night-raven and tragic owl
Breed and become fore-tellers of my fall.[210]

The same familiar sound is heard in the concluding passage of
the fourth act:

Ride, Nemesis, ride in thy fiery cart,
And sprinkle gore amongst these men of war,
That either party eager of revenge
May honour thee with sacrifice of death;
And having bath'd thy chariot wheels in blood,
Descend and take to thy tormenting hell
The mangled body of that traitor king.[211]

The opening of Peele's fifth act seems to be based on three lines
of Tamburlaine:

And when the princely Persean Diadem,
Shall ouerway his wearie witlesse head,
And fall like mellowed fruit, with shakes of death. . . .
[I Tamb. 499–501]

---

[208] II Tamb. 4641; Dyce's Peele, p. 96. See also I. 253 of the present work.
[209] Dyce's Peele, p. 106.
[210] Dyce's Peele, pp. 106–107.
[211] Dyce's Peele, p. 133.

Peele takes over this imagery, causes Fame to hang "crowns upon a tree," and calls the crowns a "fruit new ripe to fall." [212]

Certain other scattered passages at least seem like echoes of Marlowe. Peele's line:

> When he that should give essence to thy soul [213]

is certainly related to Marlowe's

> Your soul giues essence to our wretched subiects.
> [II *Tamb.* 4557]

Other similar passages are:

> That almost brent the Axeltree of heauen.
> [I *Tamb.* 1494]
> Fire, fire about the axletree of heaven.
> Whirls round.   [*Alcazar*, p. 135]

> Compast with *Lethe*, *Styx* and *Phlegeton*.
> [II *Tamb.* 3203]
> Of Lethe, Styx, and fiery Phlegethon.
> [*Alcazar*, p. 140]

> Reuenge it *Radamanth* and *Eacus*.
> [II *Tamb.* 3846]
>   . . . yet when we meet in hell:
> Before grim Minos, Rhadamanth, and Æacus,
> The combat will I crave upon thy ghost.
> [*Alcazar*, p. 140]

The significance of individual similarities of this sort is easily exaggerated, since both writers were university men familiar with the metaphysical view of essences and also with classical mythology; but their abundance is striking. They are re-enforced by other parallels too close to leave any doubt:

>   . . . and euery fixed starre
> To sucke vp poison from the moorish Fens.
> [I *Tamb.* 1449–1450]
> Thou fatal star, what planet e'er thou be,
> Spit out thy poison bad.
> [*Alcazar*, p. 139]

---

[212] Dyce's Peele, pp. 134–135. See also P. H. Cheffaud: *George Peele*, pp. 75–76; Erna Landsberg: *Der Stil in George Peeles sicheren und zweifelhaften dramatischen Werken*, p. 100; E. Hübener: *Einfluss von Marlowe's Tamburlaine*, pp. 37–41.

[213] Dyce's Peele, p. 108.

For if his chaire were in a sea of blood,
I would prepare a ship and saile to it.
[II *Tamb.* 2658–2659]
Such slaughter with my weapon shall I make,
As through the stream and bloody channels deep,
Our Moors shall sail in ships and pinnaces.
[*Alcazar*, p. 97]

And fall as thick as haile vpon our heads.
[II *Tamb.* 2872]
And they, my lord, as thick as winter's hail
Will fall upon our heads at unawares.
[*Alcazar*, p. 131]
. . . with smaller shot, as thick as hail.
[*Alcazar*, p. 136]

Making a passage for my troubled soule,
Which beates against this prison to get out.
[II *Tamb.* 3915–3916]
Whose weapons have made passage for my soul,
That breaks from out the prison of my breast.
[*Alcazar*, p. 141]

Make a bridge of murthered Carcases.
[II *Tamb.* 2662]
Hoisted vp their slaughtered carcases.
[I *Tamb.* 1912]
March on their slaughtered carkasses.
[I *Tamb.* 592]
And lay huge heaps of slaughter'd carcases,
As bulwarks in her way.
[*Alcazar*, p. 110]
And of those slaughter'd bodies shall thy son
A huge tower erect.
[*Alcazar*, p. 97]

Wil take occasion by the slenderest haire.
[II *Tamb.* 4632]
. . . will watch occasion,
And take her fore-top by the slenderest hair.
[*Alcazar*, p. 108]

Puissant, renowmed and mighty *Tamburlain.*
[I *Tamb.* 1194]
Thrice puissant and renowned Abdilmelec.
[*Alcazar*, p. 93]

Fortune her selfe dooth sit vpon our Crests.
[I *Tamb.* 596]
Send victory to light upon my crest.
[*Alcazar*, p. 124]
And Victory adorn'd with Fortune's plumes
Alights on Abdilmelec's glorious crest.
[*Alcazar*, p. 101]

Batter the shining pallace of the Sun
[II *Tamb.* 3073]
Vp to the pallace of th'imperiall heauen.
[II *Tamb.* 3003]
And glister like the palace of the sun.
[*Alcazar*, p. 103]
All like the palace of the morning sun.
[*Wounds of Civil War*, p. 18] [214]

Earth cast vp fountaines from thy entralles.
[I *Tamb.* 2129]
Within the massie entrailes of the earth.
[*Faustus*, 176]
Fight, earthquakes, in the entrails of the earth.
[*Alcazar*, p. 106]

And all the trees are blasted with our breathes.
[I *Tamb.* 973]
Some blasted grove. . . .   [*Alcazar*, p. 98]
Blast all the trees. . . .   [*Alcazar*, p. 107]

Edward I

Like Greene, Peele seems to have yielded less to Marlowe's influence after being strongly influenced in a single play. Though much has been made of the specific resemblances of *Edward I* to *Tamburlaine*, they are really very slight. There are, however, several echoes of Marlowe's *Edward the Second.*[215] In

[214] Reference is to Hazlitt's Dodsley (1874), VII. 113.
[215] See II. 401–402.

Marlowe's play Bajazeth's cage is drawn by Moors; in Peele's play Edward's triumphal chariot is drawn by Moors. Tamburlaine's own team of captive kings were probably made up as Moors, and the Second Part contains the line:

> With naked Negros shall thy coach be drawen.
> [II *Tamb.* 2531]

This is an echo of Marlowe's "Passionate Shepherd," which *Edward I* echoes together with *Tamburlaine* in the lines:

> Whose footpace, when she progress'd in the street[s]
> Of Acon and the fair Jerusalem,
> Was [upon] nought but costly Arras points,
> Fair island tapestry, and azur'd silk.

This compares to Marlowe's:

> The pauement vnderneath thy chariot wheels
> With Turky Carpets shall be couered:
> And cloath of Arras hung about the walles.[216]

Otherwise such similarities as have been noted are certainly trivial and probably accidental.[217]

David and Bethsabe

Tamburlaine affects Peele's *David and Bethsabe* chiefly in the military scenes of the "tragedy of Absalon." The boasts of the leaders and the abuse exchanged by the two armies before battle are probably borrowed from Marlowe. Absalon's yearning for a crown is drawn from the Bible, but is expressed very much as in *Tamburlaine*. Peele probably borrowed this material from the Bible because he had seen how effective Marlowe had made similar material. David's emotional raptures over Bethsabe are like Tamburlaine's over Zenocrate.

There is one other echo:

> And make our strokes to wound the sencelesse aire.
> [I *Tamb.* 1256]
> And makes their weapons wound the senseless winds.
> [D&B, p. 13]

---

[216] II *Tamb.* 2533-2535; Dyce's Peele, p. 122.

[217] Hübener, *op. cit.*, pp. 41-43; Erich Kroneberg: *George Peele's Edward the First,* pp. 71-74. For other echoes of *The Passionate Shepherd,* see II. 157-160, 208 of the present work.

THOMAS KYD: THE SPANISH TRAGEDY

Caution is necessary in discussing the relationship between Kyd's *Spanish Tragedy* and *Tamburlaine*, since both plays appeared about the same time. Marlowe's play was probably the earlier, but this is by no means certain. T. W. Baldwin [218] argues for the priority of *The Spanish Tragedy*. Both plays are in the same wild, bombastic vein; both exerted a distinct influence over later work; and both are frequently referred to. One cannot always be sure which influence is uppermost, nor be sure whether Kyd is imitating Marlowe or vice versa.

Since Marlowe does not seem to have been imitative, however, and since *Tamburlaine* at least seems to be the earlier play,[219] we shall assume here that Marlowe influences Kyd.

Not only are the plays similar in tone, but there are specific resemblances. Hieronimo, in agony at his son's death, digs into the earth with his dagger, exclaiming:[220]

> Away! I'll rip the bowels of the earth,
> And ferry over to th' Elysian plains.
> [ST, III. xii. 70–71]

Tamburlaine, in agony over the death of Zenocrate, cries:

> What, is she dead? *Techelles*, draw thy sword,
> And wound the earth, that it may cleaue in twaine,
> And we discend into th'infernall vaults,
> To haile the fatall Sisters by the haire.
> [II *Tamb.* 3064–3067]

Hieronimo's words:

> A comedy?
> Fie! comedies are fit for common wits:
> But to present a kingly troop withal,
> Give me a stately-written tragedy,
> [ST, IV. i. 152–154]

sound faintly like the prologue to *Tamburlaine*.

---

[218] "On the Chronology of Thomas Kyd's Plays," MLN, 40: 349 (1925). See II. 176, 179 of the present work.

[219] Marlowe speaks as an innovator in the prologue to *Tamburlaine*. He would hardly have done this if he were imitating *The Spanish Tragedy*, nor would Greene have been so angry at anyone but an innovator.

[220] References are to the ed. by J. Schick (Temple Dramatists).

The scenes of lamentation and real or feigned insanity in both plays are very much alike; but this is to be expected, since both dramatists were holding the mirror up to the same nature.[221] Bajazeth's lines:

O life more loathsome to my vexed thoughts,
Than noisome parbreak of the Stygian Snakes, . . .
O dreary Engines of my loathed sight,
[I *Tamb.* 2036–2040]

seem almost parodied in Hieronimo's

O eyes! no eyes, but fountains fraught with tears;
O life! no life, but lively form of death.
[ST, III. ii. 1–2]

JERONIMO

The First Part of *Jeronimo*, probably first produced in 1588 and certainly acted in 1591, falls within the period when the influence of *Tamburlaine* was at its height.[222] The play is probably, though not certainly, by Kyd. It exhibits typical imitation of Marlowe in everything except the versification, which tends toward rhyme; but his influence is on the whole rather weak, and there is none of the wholesale borrowing which appears in other plays. The imitation consists mainly in the bombastic diction, the flamboyant speeches of Balthazar, and one striking parallel:[223]

Wade vp to the chin in blood.
[II *Tamb.* 2653]
Make a bridge of murther'ed Carcases.
[II *Tamb.* 2662]
I'd wade up to the knees in blood, I'd make
A bridge of Spanish carcases,
[*Jeronimo*, p. 364]

which recalls passages in *The Battle of Alcazar*. Mr. Ernest Hunter Wright certainly goes too far in saying that in these two plays "Kyd is practically free from Marlowesque influence."[224]

221 Cf. E. Hübener, *op. cit.*, pp. 51–52.
222 The induction to *Cynthia's Revels* (1600) refers to it as "departed a dozen years since," i.e., 1588. Henslowe refers to a production of April 10, 1591.
223 Cf. I. 259. References are to Hazlitt's Dodsley, vol. IV. *Jeronimo* begins on p. 345.
224 *Influence of Christopher Marlowe on His Immediate Contemporaries*, p. 5.

Soliman and Perseda

Soliman and Perseda, which has also been attributed rather doubtfully to Kyd, continues the *Tamburlaine* tradition of successive slaughters in an Oriental setting, a romantic love story, a single hero who is the terror of all other characters, and his tragic death at the height of his success. Marlowe's lines, already imitated by Greene,[225]

> Your Loue hath fortune so at his command,
> That she shall stay and turne her wheele no more
> [I *Tamb.* 2155–2156]

are again copied when Fortune says:

> . . . though Fortune have delight in change,
> I'll stay my flight, and cease to turn my wheel.
> [S&P, p. 259]

Other parallels are fairly close:

> . . . thrice renowmed man at armes.
> [I *Tamb.* 711]
> . . . thrice renowned Englishman.
> [S&P, p. 264]

> Come back again (sweet death) & strike vs both:
> [II *Tamb.* 3423]
> Come therefore, gentle death, and ease my grief.
> [S&P, p. 284]

> If all the christall gates of *Ioues* high court
> Were opened wide, and I might enter in . . .
> It could not more delight me than your sight.
> [II *Tamb.* 2722–2725]

> But say, my dear, when shall the gates of heaven
> Stand all wide open for celestial gods, . . .
> And Cupid bring me to thy nuptial bed.
> [S&P, pp. 291–292]

> And bring him captiue to your highnesse feet.
> [II *Tamb.* 3173]
> And bring him bound for thee to tread upon.
> [S&P, p. 295]

---

[225] See I. 251, 265, II. 280. References are to Hazlitt's (1874) Dodsley, vol. V.

. . . cowards and fainthearted runawaies.
                              [I *Tamb.* 326]
. . . that Coward, faintheart, runaway.
                              [II *Tamb.* 3339]
. . . that faint-hearted runaway.
                                  [S&P, p. 325]

THOMAS LODGE: WOUNDS OF CIVIL WAR

Thomas Lodge's *Wounds of Civil War, or Marius and Sylla*, produced about 1587,[226] is presumably one of the earliest imitations of *Tamburlaine*. It follows the general model of *Tamburlaine* in character, plot, incidents, and tone, but is not closely built around a single central figure in Marlowe's manner. Sylla triumphs in Act III, drawn by four Moors. The humiliation of the conquered Carbo suggests that of Bajazeth. Sylla is called "the scourge of Asia." There is the usual emphasis on the felicity of royalty:

> Yet kings are gods, and make the proudest stoop,
>   [*Wounds*, p. 187]

which [227] is very like the dialogue of Theridamas with Usumcasane in *Tamburlaine*:

> *Vsum.* To be a King, is halfe to be a God.
> *Ther.* A God is not so glorious as a King:
>   [I *Tamb.* 761–762]

There is an obvious echo of the passage about fortune, which both Peele and Greene had echoed: [228]

> Pompey, the man that made the world to stoop,
> And fetter'd fortune in the chains of power,
> Must droop and draw the chariot of fate.
>   [*Wounds*, p. 194]

Other echoes are:

> And make whole cyties caper in the aire.
>   [II *Tamb.* 3251]
> . . . with the Cannon shooke *Vienna* walles,
> And made it dance vpon the Continent.
>   [II *Tamb.* 2412–2413]

---

[226] For various opinions on date, see N. Burton Paradise: *Thomas Lodge and His Friends*, p. 129.
[227] References are to Hazlitt's Dodsley (1874), vol. VII.
[228] See I. 251, 264, II. 280.

> ... will make the towers of Rome to shake,
> And force the stately capitol to dance.
>
> [*Wounds*, p. 109]

> Brighter than is the siluer Rhodope.
> [I *Tamb.* 284]
> In brightness like the silver Rhodope.
> [*Wounds*, p. 113]

Passages of boasting or description often show a marked similarity to other passages in *Tamburlaine* without specific parallelism. Mr. Paradise [229] believes that the *Wounds of Civil War* was the earlier play and that Marlowe was the borrower. There are various parallels with *Edward the Second* and with Peele's *Battle of Alcazar*.[230]

MASSINGER AND FORD

Philip Massinger and John Ford are not greatly influenced by Marlowe, though Massinger's tragic and passionate speeches sometimes have the ring of *Tamburlaine*. Like Shakespeare in *Henry IV*, both borrow bombastic lines or allusions to put into the mouths of comic characters.[231] Thus, in Massinger's *Believe as You List*, a humorous priest wishes to use Roman senators to draw his triumphal chariot — surely a reminiscence of Tamburlaine and his team of kings.[232] The same character uses the Roman Flaminius as a footstool, precisely as Tamburlaine uses Bajazeth. Ford, like Beaumont and Fletcher, merely quotes from Tamburlaine occasionally.[233] His most interesting quotation is of the famous passage:

> Is it not passing braue to be a King,
> And ride in triumph through *Persepolis*?

which reappears in *Love's Sacrifice* as:

> Thus do we march to honour's haven of bliss,
> To ride in triumph through Persepolis.

[229] *Op. cit.*, pp. 130–137.
[230] See II. 28, 31 and Edith A. White: *op. cit.*, p. 9.
[231] Cf. E. Koeppel: *Quellenstudien, Münchener Beiträge* (1895), and *Strassburger Quellen und Forschungen*, Heft 82 (1897).
[232] III. ii. 52 and II *Tamb.* IV. iv.
[233] See I. 240.

There is a similar echo in *Soliman and Perseda*:

And ride in triumph through the wicked world.[234]

THE WARS OF CYRUS

The anonymous author of *The Wars of Cyrus* seems to have been a rather pedantic individual, given to moralizing, who tried to tone down the conquering hero of Marlowe's invention and make a Christian gentleman of him. Cyrus never blasphemes or rants like Tamburlaine. Marlowe's influence is clear, however, in the general treatment of the theme — conflicting Asiatic empires, each supported by tributary kings and chieftains — and in the highly romantic treatment of love and war. The love story of Panthea, Araspas, and Abradates shows strong resemblance to the story of Olympia and Theridamas [235] in the Second Part of *Tamburlaine*. The play is, as its German editor observes, "a work of Marlowe's school but not one of its masterpieces." [236]

Though *The Wars of Cyrus* was not published until 1594, it was probably written several years earlier, thus coming directly under the influence of its model. Like other imitators of Marlowe's early style, the author catches some of his mannerisms but fails to reproduce the beauty and subtle variety apparent in his verse from the beginning.

Mr. W. J. Lawrence has endeavored to show that *The Wars of Cyrus* dates from 1578 and was written by Richard Farrant (d. 1580), founder of the first Blackfriars Theatre.[237] If this were true, the play could not possibly be influenced by *Tamburlaine*, but Mr. Lawrence's conclusions are very doubtful. He bases them on a lyric dealing with the love of Abradates and Panthea, which might be fitted into this play in the fifth act. This lyric exists in a manuscript dated 1581 in the Part Books transcribed by Robert Doe, one copy of which is in Christ Church, Oxford, while the other is in the British Museum.[238] At the very least, he holds, "a date subsequent to 1580 cannot now be assigned to *The Warres of Cyrus.*"

[234] I *Tamb.* 753–754, 755, 759; *Love's Sacrifice*, II. i, p. 310 of the Mermaid ed.; *Soliman and Perseda*, Hazlitt's Dodsley (1874), V. 373.
[235] See I. 209.   [237] TLS 20: 514, 11 Ag 1921.
[236] Wolfgang Keller, *Jahrb.* 37: 1 (1901).   [238] Addit. MSS. 17786–91.

Mr. Lawrence has, however, no ground for believing the lyric to be part of the play except the rather thin argument that no other treatment of the story of Abradates, taken from Xenophon's *Cyropaedia*, is known. Sir Edmund K. Chambers, after reviewing the evidence, concludes "that *Wars of Cyrus*, as it stands, is clearly post-*Tamburlaine*, and although there are indications of lost songs at ll. 985, 1628, there is none pointing to a lament of Panthea. But conceivably the play was based on one by [Richard] Farrant." [239]

DEKKER: OLD FORTUNATUS

While Dekker's *Old Fortunatus* is more clearly under the influence of *Faustus*,[240] it shows at least one trace of *Tamburlaine*. The four captive kings, who grow almost monotonous on the Elizabethan stage of this period, make their entry, and are used as footstools by Fortune, precisely as Tamburlaine uses Bajazeth, who is named as one of Fortune's captives in a passage already quoted, which begins:

> Here stands the very soul of misery,
> Poor Bajazet, old Turkish Emperor,
> And once the greatest monarch in the East;
> Fortune herself is sad to view thy fall.[241]

Dekker also has an allusion in his pamphlet, *A Knight's Conjuring*: "The very bowels of these infernal Antipodes shal be ript vp and pull'd out before that great Dego of Diuells his own face: Nay, since my flag of defiance is hung forth, I will yeelde to no truce, but with such Tamburlaine-like furie march against this great Turke and his legions, that Don Beelzebub shall be ready to damme himselfe and be horne-mad: for with the coniuring of my pen, all Hell shall breake loose." [242] This certainly suggests Marlowe at his worst.

GEORGE CHAPMAN

George Chapman plainly borrows from Marlowe: [243]

> The horse that guide the golden eie of heauen,
> And blow the morning from their nosterils.
> [II *Tamb.* 3986-3987]

---

[239] *Eliz. Stage*, III. 312. [241] *Old Fortunatus*, I. i. Mermaid ed., pp. 299–300.
[240] See I. 241, 308–309. [242] Percy Society *Publications*, V. 24.
[243] Collier erroneously imagines these lines of Chapman's to come from *Cæsar and*

As when the fiery coursers of the sun,
Up to the palace of the morning run,
And from their nostrils blow the spiteful day.
[*Hymnus in Cynthiam*, 205–207]

He also borrows another line which still another poet, Richard Barnfield, borrows twice!

RICHARD BARNFIELD

Barnfield (1574–1627) probably knew Marlowe personally. He was certainly a friend of Marlowe's friend, Thomas Watson,[244] and his abundant quotations from Marlowe's poems show his admiration. He borrows much less freely from the plays, but does take over one line of *Tamburlaine* which Marlowe himself had developed from an earlier experiment of his own in *Dido*. The sequence is interesting:[245]

And teares of pearle, crye stay, Æneas, stay.
[*Dido*, 1202]
Rain'st on the earth resolued pearle in showers.
[I *Tamb.* 1923]
And rayning downe resolued Pearls in showers.
[Barnfield's *Cynthia*, st. IX, p. 71]
Rayning downe pearle from his immortall eies.
[Barnfield's *Cassandra*, p. 106]
Rains on the earth dissolved pearl in showers.
[Chapman's *Poems* (1875), p. 431]

MILTON

By far the clearest of all traces of Marlowe in Milton comes from *Tamburlaine*:

In number more than are the quyuering leaues
Of *Idas* forrest, where your highnesse hounds,
With open crie pursues the wounded Stag.
[II *Tamb.* 3507–3509]

This is certainly akin to the Vallombrosa passage in *Paradise Lost*:

Thick as autumnal leaves that strow the brooks
In Vallombrosa.

Pompey. See HEDP, III. 124. The passage is most easily found in the 1875 *Poems*, p. 14.
[244] See DNB, III. 262–263, and II. 37, 131, 159–160 of the present work.
[245] References are to A. B. Grosart's (Roxburghe Club) ed. of Barnfield (1876). On the probable date of *Dido*, see II. 54–58.

There are various odds and ends of quotation. Ben Jonson's friend, William Drummond of Hawthornden, shows faint traces of *Tamburlaine* in his collected *Poems*. The line:

> And fills the World with Wonder and Delight

certainly suggests Marlowe's

> Wounding the world with woonder and with loue.

Henry Petowe, who emulated Chapman in continuing Marlowe's unfinished *Hero and Leander*, seems to glance at the same passage in

> . . . the world's faire wonder.[246]

Drummond also seems to have read *Hero and Leander* and *Edward the Second*.

The Times' Whistle (ca. 1614) has the lines:

> . . . Charles the Fift of Spaine
> Was nothing to him, nor great Tamburlaine.[247]

END OF TAMBURLAINE'S INFLUENCE

The last traces of *Tamburlaine* are found in three plays of the late seventeenth and early eighteenth centuries: *Tamerlane the Great* (1681), by Charles Saunders; *The Sacrifice* (1686), by Sir Francis Fane; and *Tamerlane the Great* (1702), by Nicholas Rowe.

Saunders' play seems to have been the author's only work. It was written while he was still at Westminster School, was corrected by Dryden, and through his influence was presented at the Theatre Royal. As nothing further is heard of Saunders, he presumably died young.

The relationship of his work to Marlowe's is not clear. Saunders denied that he had ever heard of the Elizabethan play; but it is hard to believe that his mentor, Dryden, was equally ignorant. The play opens with Bajazet conquered by Tamerlane and in chains. The victory has really been achieved

---

[246] II *Tamb.* 3050; Drummond's *Poems* (2nd ed., 1616), sigs. B1*v*, B2*v*; Petowe's *Philocassander and Elanira* (1599), sig. B3*r*. See also II. 109–111, 128 of the present work.

[247] Ed. J. M. Cowper, ll. 685–686, p. 25. (Early English Text Society, no. 48 [1871].) See I. 313 for a further discussion of this satire.

by Tamerlane's banished son, Arsanes, who is disguised. The rest of the play is concerned with his love for a mysterious princess, who turns out to be the daughter of Bajazet. The resemblance to Marlowe's play is slight.

Sir Francis Fane's play, *The Sacrifice*, published in 1686 but never produced, has no very close relation either to Marlowe, Saunders, or Rowe; but in Sir Sidney Lee's opinion is a late and faint echo of Marlowe.[248] It is a dull and stilted piece of work, which introduces Tamerlane, Bajazet, and Bajazet's empress — the latter under the historically correct name of Despina, not Zabina as in Marlowe.[249] The episode of Bajazet in the cage appears, but Tamburlaine, become strangely devout, declares, "there is no jesting with divinity." Bajazeth beats out his brains because he believes that Despina is faithless to him with Tamburlaine, whereupon that redoubtable warrior exclaims:

> Bless me, 'tis sad!

This is anything but Marlowe!

Since the play is partly in heroic couplets, the chance for imitation in dramatic diction is limited. Verbal parallels are lacking. Fane may never have read Marlowe at all, but may have been indirectly influenced through Saunders. Tucker Brooke says that "the relation seems dubious," [250] and believes that both Rowe and Saunders are wholly uninfluenced by their Elizabethan predecessor.

Rowe's play leans heavily on Richard Steele's *Christian Hero*, which had appeared in 1701 — a curious source for a play on the scourge of God. The violent barbarian chief of Marlowe's play has become a model of amiable moderation, who piously prays:

> Grant that my sword, assisted by thy Pow'r,
> This day may Peace and Happiness restore,
> That War and lawless Rage may vex thy world no more,[251]

and who virtuously insists upon religious toleration. This is because Tamburlaine is meant as a portrait of William III and

---

[248] Article "Marlowe," DNB, XII. 1067.
[249] See I. 225.
[250] *Trans. Connecticut Acad.*, 25: 384 (1922).
[251] Ed. 1703, I. i. p. 9.

the villainous Bajazet as a portrait of Louis XIV. The political undertone made the play popular, and it was given at Drury Lane every year on November 5, the anniversary of William's landing in England as well as the anniversary of the Gunpowder Plot. This practice persisted until 1815.[252] There is a close resemblance between the Saunders and the Rowe play, either because Rowe borrowed from his predecessor or because they were using the same sources.[253] A manuscript of *Tamerlane, Tragedy, Part II*, turned up in the possession of Stephen Jones, coauthor of the *Biographia Dramatica*, early in the nineteenth century, but has since disappeared. It is supposed to have been a continuation of Rowe's play.

If he really did influence Rowe, we may regard Marlowe as, in a distant sense, the founder of the American as well as the Elizabethan drama; for Thomas Godfrey's *Prince of Parthia*, the first American play produced (1754) on the professional stage, was written under Rowe's influence — a curious link between Elizabeth's London and the wild new continent.[254]

The Tamburlaine theme turns up repeatedly elsewhere, but without any very precise relation to its originator. "Monk" Lewis wrote a melodrama, *Timour the Tartar*, which is dated 1802 but was not produced at Covent Garden until 1811. The same theme was treated in an opera, *Tamerlane*, produced at the King's Theatre, 1724. There is also a Portuguese play, *Comedia Nova Intitulada; Os Tragicos Effeitos da Impaciencia de Tamerlao da Persia.*[255] The British Museum's copy is dated Lisbon, 1783.

The influence of Marlowe on all these late reproductions of the story is questionable, since by this time his reputation had fallen into its eighteenth-century night, whence it was restored toward the end of the period by the interest of scholars like Heber, Reed, Steevens, and Malone. For a century, *Tamburlaine* had been an influence on the English theatre. Tastes

[252] This was pointed out and ridiculed by Gibbon: *Decline and Fall*, cap. lxv, ii; and by Prescott: *Mexico* (ed. 1855), II. 152n.

[253] DNB, article "Rowe," by C. H. Furth, XLIX. 342. Cf. Eduard Bunning: *Nicholas Rowe Tamerlane (1702)*, pp. 26–44.

[254] Thomas Clark Pollock: "Rowe's Tamerlane and The Prince of Parthia," *American Literature*, 6: 150–162 My 1934.

[255] There is a copy in the Ibero-American Collection, Catholic University, Washington, D. C.

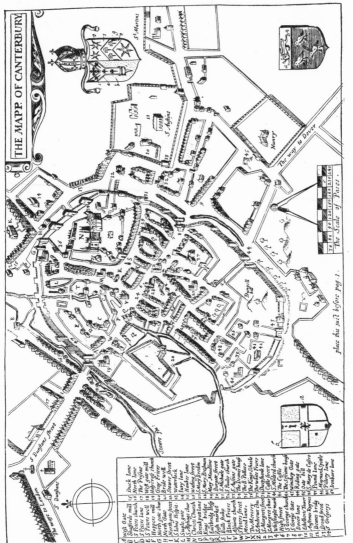

THE MAPP OF CANTERBURY

St Martins

The way to Dover

place this just before pag. 1.

| 70 | 60 | 120 | 150 | 180 | 210 | 240 |

The Scale of Paces.

St Dunstans street

The waye to London

St Dunstans

Stoure fiu:

Duugeill hill

Numry

St Augustins

MAP OF CANTERBURY AS MARLOWE KNEW IT

changed, the stage itself and the language and structure of the plays upon it changed, but Marlowe had given the Elizabethan drama the direction out of which its new plays grew, and his mighty line was a force forever in the poetry of England and America.

CHAPTER VIII

DOCTOR FAUSTUS

Learning, in despight of Fate,
Will mount aloft, and enter heauen gate.
Hero and Leander, I. 465⌐466

IN *DOCTOR FAUSTUS* we have the finest of all Marlowe's plays. The poet will live forever as the author of one long poem, *Hero and Leander*; one lyric, "*The Passionate Shepherd*"; and four plays, *Tamburlaine, Doctor Faustus, The Jew of Malta,* and *Edward the Second*. With these, such lesser works as *The Massacre at Paris,* and *Dido, Queene of Carthage,* are obviously not to be compared; nor do the translations and various attributed minor poems add greatly to his literary stature.

We may lay *Hero and Leander* aside as incomplete, and regard "The Passionate Shepherd" as at best a charming trifle, showing no ability on the poet's part to sustain an effort. Even Marlowe's greater plays can hardly be compared to *Faustus*. No one is likely to pretend that *Tamburlaine* and *The Jew of Malta* remotely approach it. *Tamburlaine*, no doubt, is a great play. Certainly, it is an important play, because it represents the first strivings of a genius and because it contains a few passages of the finest poetry in English. It is important, too, because it is one of the first great formative influences in English drama. But *Tamburlaine* is, after all, an experiment by a young poet, unused to the theatre and without models suited to his time or to the stage for which he wrote. It also exhibits at its very worst Marlowe's typical rant, from which he later largely freed himself. *The Jew of Malta* is only half Marlowe's. For good or ill, it is impossible to judge him on it.

The only rival of *Doctor Faustus* is *Edward the Second*, which some critics have preferred for its greater maturity and more perfect structure. Yet, granting all the merits of *Edward the Second*, it is hard to see why anyone should choose as Mar-

lowe's finest play a work which contains few of Marlowe's
finest lines and no dramatic situations so agonizingly intense as
the great scenes in *Faustus*.

That relatively few critics have shared this view of the matter
is doubtless due to the corrupt state of the text in all editions;
to the fact that the two versions of *Doctor Faustus* are so different as to leave doubt as to what Marlowe really wrote; and
to the efforts of well-meaning playhouse hacks to introduce a
grotesquely inappropriate comic element, which in earlier and
less critical days was attributed to Marlowe himself.

All this has somewhat served to cloak the brilliance of the
play from undiscerning eyes. Yet no lines in English verse are
finer or more widely known than the "thousand ships" passage
of Faustus' apostrophe to Helen. The philosophic dialogue between Faustus and Mephistophilis is almost as great. Nothing
in dramatic literature produces a more vivid effect than the
concluding scene. And no conception more truly tragic than
the struggle of the powers of Darkness for a human soul has
ever graced the English stage.

In this play we come closer than in anything else he ever
wrote to the proud, fiery, agonized spirit of the poet himself,
grasping forever at what he never would attain, the scholar
"still climbing after knowledge infinite," and the man hope-
lessly caught in a web that was not of his own weaving.

DATE

It has long been held that Marlowe probably wrote *Doctor
Faustus* about 1588 or 1589, just after the young dramatist's
first great success with *Tamburlaine*; [1] though Mr. Boas and
Mr. Brooke, as we shall presently see, prefer a later date.
Internal evidence — the increasing maturity, the powerful
effect due to improved dramatic structure, and the meter —
plainly put the date of composition after *Tamburlaine*, the
Second Part of which was probably written in the latter part of
1588. It was natural that a penniless young writer, just down
from Cambridge, should hasten to take advantage of his first
dazzling success by rushing out another play.

---

[1] Mr. J. M. Robertson says it was "admittedly played in 1588" (*Marlowe: A Con-
spectus*, p. 34). As a matter of fact, very few scholars admit anything of the sort.

External evidence points in much the same direction. There is a reference to the "fiery keele at *Antwarpes* bridge,"[2] clearly identical with the fire-ship which the Dutch used to destroy a bridge built by the Duke of Parma, besieging Antwerp in 1584–85. There is a reference[3] to the Duke himself when Faustus proposes to "chase the Prince of *Parma* from our land." This allusion to Parma's discomfiture would be good theatre immediately after the Armada's defeat. After 1590 Parma was fighting in France, and the boast would have no point. It has been argued that these passages are later interpolations, but that is hardly reasonable, since they would have been dull and ancient history in 1604 when the revisers commenced work.

There is further external evidence for a date in 1588 or 1589 in the fact that Robert Greene in his *Friar Bacon and Friar Bungay* — written about 1589 and listed by Henslowe, apparently as an old play, February 19, 1591/2—is plainly imitating *Doctor Faustus*. We know, moreover, that the Admiral's Company produced *Faustus*; and we also know that their productions were temporarily stopped November 6, 1589, by the Lord Mayor, acting on complaints by the Master of the Revels,[4] though they were again showing "feats of activities" at court on December 28, 1589, and that they were again playing publicly March 3, 1590. Presumably, then, Greene had seen a production of *Doctor Faustus* by November, 1589.

It is true that there is no extant record of a production prior to 1594;[5] but as the play had been revised in 1592, it must even then have been old. The entry in the *Stationers' Register* February 28, 1588/9, of a "ballad of the life and deathe of Doctor FFAUSTUS the great Cunngerer"[6] suggests that a popular publisher was already taking advantage of the vogue of Marlowe's play.

Mr. F. S. Boas and Mr. C. F. Tucker Brooke are inclined to push the play forward to the year 1592. Mr. Boas admits that external evidence indicates a date in 1588/9, and Mr. Brooke in 1910 wrote that external evidence "points with tolerable

---

[2] Line 124.   [3] Line 121.

[4] J. P. Collier, HEDP (1879), I. 264–265; E. K. Chambers: *Eliz. Stage*, II. 136.

[5] *Henslowe's Diary*, September 30, 1594.

[6] Arber's reprint, II. 516. Perhaps the ballad now in the Roxburghe Collection, III. 280 (British Museum).

certainty to the winter of 1588/9 as the date of the play's completion." [7] Both, however, are troubled by the fact that the English Faust Book, which was certainly the source of *Doctor Faustus*, did not appear in print until 1592. In 1922 Mr. Brooke wrote that "there is no good reason for assuming that *Doctor Faustus* was in existence prior to the publication of P. F.'s translation of the Faustbuch." [8]

There are, however, several ways of accounting for the appearance of the only known edition of the source book after the play had been written.[9] After all, the same thing happened in the case of Paul Ive's *Practise of Fortification*, which appeared after *Tamburlaine*, though there is no possible question of their relationship.[10] In the case of *Doctor Faustus* most authorities prefer to be governed by the weight of external evidence and date its composition about 1588/9, immediately after the production of *Tamburlaine*.[11]

[7] Boas' ed., p. 11; Brooke: *Works*, p. 139.
[8] "Marlowe Canon," PMLA, 37: 384 S 1922.
[9] See I. 288–289.
[10] See I. 210–211.
[11] Dates have been assigned as follows:

1831. Collier: "Very soon after his *Tamburlaine*." [HEDP, III. 126]
1850. Dyce: "*Tamburlaine* had not been long before the public, when Marlowe produced his *Faustus*." [ed. 1850, I. xv]
1874. A. Reidl: "About 1590." [p. vii]
1878. A. W. Ward: "Some time before February, 1589, and very possibly in 1588." [*Faustus* ed., p. lxxxiii]
1880. A. C. Bradley: "Probably in 1589 or 1590." [Ward's *English Poets*, I. 411]
1881. Theodor Delius: "Marlowe's Faustus spätestens 1589 entstanden sein muss." [*Marlowe's Faustus und seine Quelle*, p. 7]
1885. A. H. Bullen: "Soon after *Tamburlaine*." [I. xxvi]
1887. Ellis: "Not long after *Tamburlaine*.... The exact date is very doubtful." [p. xxxvi and note]
1887. Fleay: "The entry of the ballad [in SR] Feb. 28, 1588–9, is almost positive proof that the play had then been quite recently put on the stage." [Appendix A, Ward's ed., p. clxviii]
1887. Ernest Faligan: "Secundum est Marlovii drama." [*De Marlovianis Fabulis*, p. 148]
189?. J. LeGay Brereton: "Written about 1591." [*Passages*, p. xix]
1899. Ward: "The internal evidence which points to 1588, or to the very beginning of the following year, as the date of the earliest performance of this tragedy, is remarkably strong." [HEDL, I. 329]
1904. Ingram: "Appears to have been originally put upon the stage ... in 1588." [p. 133]
1909. Venzlaff: "Marlowe's Doctor Faustus ist in der ersten Hälfte des Jahres 1588, vielleicht schon im Winter 1587/8 geschrieben worden." [p. 72]
1910. Brooke: "External evidence verifies the conclusions of literary criticism and

SOURCES

The source material of *Doctor Faustus* raises four unusually difficult problems. First comes the question of the historical (or rather, biographical) basis of the play. Second, the addition to this rather slender substratum of a vast mass of tradition and folklore relating to magicians and magic power attained by selling the conjurer's soul to the Devil. Third, the mystery of the precise manner in which this material reached Marlowe. Fourth, the question how much material from this and perhaps other sources was added to the play by a series of revisers working on Marlowe's original, long after his death.

THE HISTORICAL FAUST

To the first question a partial answer is possible, while to the others a complete answer is probably forever impossible. Dr. Johannes Faustus was an historical personage, who flourished at the beginning of the sixteenth century and who probably died within thirty years of Marlowe's birth. His existence is attested by the register of Heidelberg University, which records that Johannes Faust, of Simmern, took the degree of Bachelor of Divinity in 1509.[12] Not only did the great conjurer thus begin his career in the odor of sanctity — the register even re-

---

points with tolerable certainty to the winter of 1588–9 as the date of the play's completion." [*Works*, p. 139]

1912. William Modlen: "1588 or 1589." [p. xviii]

1912. W. L. Phelps: "It is assumed that Marlowe's play was acted in 1588 or 1589; but, as a matter of fact, nobody knows." [pp. 12–13]

1922. Brooke: "There is no good reason for assuming that *Doctor Faustus* was in existence prior to the publication of P. F.'s translation of the Faustbuch in 1592." [PMLA, 37: 384 1922]

1923. Chambers: "A probable date is 1588–9." [*Eliz. Stage*, III. 423]

1926. Gollancz: "It may with some degree of certainty be assigned to the year 1588–9 (before November 1589)." [Temple ed., p. viii]

1927. Ellis-Fermor: "We must conjecture the date, and the latter part of 1588, or the earlier part of 1589 is that generally accepted." [*Christopher Marlowe*, p. 4]

1929. Oliphant: "The chances are that it was produced in 1588." [*Shakespeare and His Fellow Dramatists*, I. 152]

1931. Robertson: "*Faustus* was admittedly played in 1588." [*Marlowe*, p. 34]

1932. Boas: "Though it has been usual to push the composition of the play back to 1588–9, there is no compelling evidence for so early a date." [*Faustus*, p. 8]

1936. Rupert Taylor: "Traditional date of 1588." [PMLA, 51: 660 S 1936]

[12] *Acts of the Philosophical Faculty*, University Archives, I. 3, no. 50, fol. 36*r*. [MS. at Heidelberg]

minds us by an affixed "d" [*dedit*] that this devil's disciple began by honestly paying his fee.

Even before he took his theological degree, however, suspicion had begun as to his actual studies and pursuits. On August 20, 1497, the learned abbot Johannes Trithemius (1462–1516) warns a friend against a certain "Georgius Sabellicus, Faustus iunior. fons necromanticorum, astrologus, magus secundus, chiromanticus, agromanticus, pyromanticus, in hydra arte secundus," whom he describes as a knave "dignus qui uerberibus castigetur, ne temere deinceps tam nefanda et ecclesiæ sanctæ contraria publice audeat profiteri." [13]

German literature of the period is full of references to one, or several, men of this name — references which, as collected by Alexander Tille, fill a fat volume. In 1520 we find the Prince-Bishop of Bamberg paying a "Doctor Faustus pho" [philosopher] ten florins for casting his nativity. [14] In 1528 the Ingolstadt town archives note that "one who calls himself Dr. Jörg Faustus of Heidelberg has been told to spend his penny elsewhere." [15]

Amid innumerable similar references, a few are especially important. It is interesting to note that Martin Luther's friend, Melanchthon, was personally acquainted with "Joh. Faust von Knütlingen," whom he regarded as an impostor, and that he for the first time connects Faustus with the story of the grapevine conjured into existence in midwinter, which appears both in the *Faustbuch* and in Marlowe's play. [16] He also mentions the conversion of Faustus, attempted by a pious old man, an incident which is taken over by the *Faustbuch* and by Marlowe. This story originally comes from the *Confessions* of St. Augustine, who as a young man was warned by the wise physi-

---

[13] *Joannis Trithemii Abbatis Spanhemensis Epistolarum familiarium libri duo* (Haganoae, 1536), p. 312. There are copies of this work in HCL, NYPL, LC. The reference is reprinted in Alexander Tille: *Faustsplitter*, no. 1, pp. 1–2. Tille's is the best collection of Faust references in brief. For more extended reprints, see the series in J. Scheible: *Das Kloster*. Much of this material is also in Ward's ed. and in the ed. of the English Faust Book by William Rose (Broadway Translations).

[14] See Tille, *op. cit.*, p. 6, for much fuller references.

[15] Tille, *op. cit.*, p. 6.

[16] Hermann Witekind (1522–1603), professor at Heidelberg, writing under the pseudonym of Augustin Lercheimer von Steinfeld, tells the story in his *Christlich Bedencken vnnd Erinnerung vor Zauberey* (1586). See J. Scheible: *Das Kloster*, II. 205–218; Tille, *op. cit.*, no. 48, p. 92.

cian Vindicianus against *libri genethliacorum*, [17] unless it relates to a Franciscan effort to convert the German Faust.

Other episodes in Marlowe's play appear very early in the development of the Faust legend. Johann Gast, in his *Tomus Secundus Convivalivm Sermonum* (Basel, 1548),[18] tells both of the miracles and the death of Faustus:

Basileæ cum illo cœnatus sum in collegio magno, qui uarij generis aues, nescio ubi emerat, aut quis dederat, cum hoc temporis nullæ uenderentur, coquo ad assandum præbuerat. quales etiam ego nunquam in nostris regionibus uiderim. . . . Atqui miser deplorandum finem sortitus est, nam a satana suffocatus, cuius cadauer in feretro facie ad terram perpetuo spectans, etsi quinquies in tergum uerteretur.

This is the first suggestion that Faustus was in league with the Devil, the earlier accounts suggesting at worst that he was a magician, charlatan, and wandering scholar of dissolute habits. Thereafter there is much comment on his terrible death, and the corpse with the twisted head turns up again and again, even making a modern appearance in a contemporary short story.[19]

Such is the evidence for the life and works of the John Faust of history down to the appearance of the German *Faustbuch* which became the source of the English Faust Book, which in turn became the source of Marlowe's play.

With this shadowy but fairly consistent personage, legend and history have probably confused several other historical individuals. Twardowski, the magician of Cracow and lecturer on magic in the university there, also styled himself Faust, Junior. He distinguished himself by raising from the dead the second wife of King Sigismund August, who fainted at sight of her — a feat reminiscent of the legendary Faust's raising of Helen. He openly boasted of his connection with the Devil, from which he extricated himself in time by insisting that the Devil either take Madame Twardowski to wife or break the compact. The prudent fiend wisely chose the latter alternative. This may have been the man with whom Melanchthon

---

[17] *Doctor Faustus*, 1270 ff.; *Confessions*, IV. 5 and VII. 6; Tille, *op. cit.*, p. 235; Hermann Grimm in *Preussische Jahrbücher*, 47: 454–457 My 1881; Ward's ed., p. lxvii.

[18] There is a copy of this work in the Congressional Library. See p. 281 and Tille, *op. cit.*, no. 8, p. 12. The first (1543) ed. lacks the story.

[19] "The A-flat Major Polonaise" in Albert Hickman: *Canadian Nights*.

talked, especially as he is said to have been at Heidelberg at the same time as Johann Faust of Simmern.

There is also probably some confusion with the printer, Johann Fust, or Faust, an associate of Gutenberg who was accused of magical practices. Daniel Defoe falls into this error.[20]

Many other reputed wizards may have contributed something to the form which the Faust legend ultimately assumed, among them Vergil, Pope Sylvester II, Michael Scott, Klingsor, the Bohemian Zito, and Friar Roger Bacon, who like Faustus gave his name to an Elizabethan play.

The Legendary Faust

The attitude of the Middle Ages and the Renaissance toward magic and magicians wholly differs from that of pagan antiquity. To the pagan world, supernatural powers were divine and desirable gifts. Plato had looked upon poets as possessed;[21] and Pythagoras — to whom both Marlowe's Faustus and Greene's Vandermast, in *Friar Bacon and Friar Bungay*, make allusion [22] — was both prototype and model of the Greco-Roman magicians.

With the coming of Christianity, the pagan deities who bestowed magic power underwent a change for the worse. They were no longer divine, nor even admirable. They were evil spirits, commerce with whom was forbidden to the believer, although — as the life of the historical Faust shows — believers, even of episcopal rank, could sometimes wink at the prohibition. That is why, when St. Paul preached at Ephesus, "many of them also which used curious arts brought their books together, and burned them before all *men*." [23]

Strange to say, it seems rarely to have occurred to the early Christians that pagan deities simply did not exist. They did exist, and their late worshipers, after conversion to Christianity, still never doubted it for an instant. Only they were no longer gods but demons, no longer friends but foes.

---

[20] See I. 315.
[21] *Phaedrus*, 22 E. See also Aristotle: *Poetics*, XVII. 2. 4; Longinus: *On the Sublime*, VIII. 4.
[22] *Doctor Faustus*, 1461; *Friar Bacon*, sc. IX. 30.
[23] Acts xix. 19.

Miracles were, of course, divine in origin, signs of the per-
former's Christian power and the extent of God's favor to him;
but signs and wonders could also be performed by diabolical aid.
There was a sharp distinction between white (legitimate) magic
and black magic, which required diabolical aid and therefore
involved damnation of the magician's soul. But in spite of the
horror with which it was regarded, and the appalling risk which
it involved, black magic would not down, for it was supposed
to provide wealth, women, and unbounded though temporary
power.

A central figure in these conflicts between pagan sorcery and
the legitimate miracles of divine grace is the Samaritan sorcerer, Simon Magus, founder of the Simonian heresy. Popular
tradition and the rather scanty facts of history are very imper-
fectly recorded in the account of his overthrow by St. Peter,[24]
which is, for obvious reasons, the only mention of him in the
canonical Scriptures. To the orthodox believer, Simon is merely
one among many converts, who has given his name to the ecclesiastical offense of simony.

Behind that scant account of him lies an obscure but fascinating story of religious hatred and rivalry, magic and feats of
wizardry, vaguely cloaked in the diatribes of the good fathers
who struggled with the evil works of the wicked Simon. There
is even the fantastic possibility that Simon never existed as an
historical figure at all; but that he was originally a satirical
parody of St. Paul, set up by the saint's enemies, who eventually slipped into the New Testament by mistake — living in
history as Paul's enemy, when he was actually Paul's double.

Our knowledge of the Simon Magus of noncanonical history
is based mainly upon the New Testament Apocrypha and the
patristic writings, especially those of St. Clement of Alexandria,
whose father and brother were both named Faustus.[25] Simon
is repeatedly referred to in the New Testament Apocrypha,
notably in the apocryphal Acts of Paul; the Acts of Peter
(where he is specifically described as "the angel of Satan");
the Epistle of the Apostles, where he is denounced as a false
prophet; and the Passion of Peter and Paul, in which Simon

[24] Acts viii. 9–24.
[25] *Légende dorée*, clvii, pp. 644 ff.

performs various magic feats later attributed to Faustus.[26] The condemnatory attitude toward magicians which came with the new Christian orthodoxy is very clearly shown in these books and is even clearer in the Apocalypse of Peter and the Second Book of the Sibylline Oracles, both of which specifically doom sorcerers and sorceresses to damnation.

Specific resemblances between the story of Simon and the story of Faustus are: First, the feat of flying through the air; second, the education, professional wizardry, and boastful personalities of the two men; third, their direct relation to Helen of Troy; fourth, the magic transformation of a horse into a "bottle" [bale] of hay; fifth, the story of the homunculus, whom both Simon and Faustus fashion; and sixth, the appearance of the name Faustus [fortunate] in both stories.

1. It is easy to attribute undue importance to Simon's ability to fly through the air by magic. This was an ordinary achievement of any self-respecting magician. The idea was probably old when it appeared in the *Clouds* of Aristophanes and in the *Medea* of Euripides, plays with which Marlowe, the Cambridge scholar, was certainly familiar. Taken, however, in relation to the other coincidences, even this commonplace of magic seems significant.

2. The description of Simon in the *Recognitions of Clement*, a highly pious romance of the second or third century,[27] anticipates the exact personality of the historical Faustus: "by profession a magician, yet exceedingly well trained in the Greek literature; desirous of glory, and boasting above all the human race." Most of the early accounts of Faustus lay stress on his habit of boasting.

3. The presence of Helen of Troy in both stories is equally curious. Simon the Gnostic, who seems to have been identical with Simon Magus or at least to have been confused with him, takes Helen for his paramour, exactly like Faustus.

"Simon is going about in company with Helena," writes St.

---

[26] Montague R. James: *Apocryphal New Testament* (Oxford, 1924), pp. 288–289, 306–309, 331, 332, 470, 485, 487. Cf. *Acta Apostolorum Apocrypha* (ed. R. A. Lipsius and M. Bonnet, Leipzig, 1891–1903).

[27] Bk. II. chap. VII. St. Clement is probably identical with the Clement mentioned in Philippians iv. 3. See the *Recognitions*, X. 58, for the story of how Faustus, father of the saint, became the double of Simon Magus.

Clement in his *Recognitions*.[28] ". . . And he says that he has brought down this Helena from the highest heavens to the world; being queen, as the all-bearing being, and wisdom, for whose sake, says he, the Greeks and barbarians fought, having before their eyes but an image of truth; for she, who really is the truth, was then with the chiefest god." This is strangly like Faustus' "none but thou shalt be my paramour," and the likeness is heightened by the fact that the Helen whom Faustus raised from the dead was herself but a shadow, "but an image of truth."

4. The curious story of the horse that vanished under his rider, leaving only the hay that he had eaten, is in both traditions and reappears in Marlowe's play.[29]

5. Marlowe, however, neglects the story of the homunculus, whom Simon fashions out of air and Faustus from chemicals.[30] Goethe retains this story.

6. Finally, it is certainly significant to find the name of Faustus already [31] associated with these particular magic practices. The name was, of course, common enough under the Roman Empire, and even down to the Renaissance; but its association with magic practices more than a thousand years before the historical Johann Faust is remarkable.

Simon's evil repute was kept alive in treatises on magic, and it is especially interesting to find him referred to in Milich's *Zauberteufel* (1563) as the very model of a modern magician.[32] The *Zauberteufel*, as we shall see, may have contributed to the original German *Faustbuch*, though very little of its material seems to have reached Marlowe's play.[33]

It is easy to exaggerate the importance of these odd similarities; but there seems no reason to doubt that the legends which grew up around the names of Simon Magus and Simon the

[28] *Recognitions*, II. 25, in the *Ante-Nicene Christian Library*, XVII. 43–44. See also the *Recognitions*, II. 5–15 and especially 12; *Clementine Homilies*, II. 22–26; G. N. L. Hall: article "Simon Magus," in *Encyclopedia of Religion and Ethics*, XII. 517; English Faust Book, chap. LV.

[29] Ll. 1148–1162.

[30] *Clementine Homilies*, II. 26; *Recognitions*, II. 15.

[31] *Clementine Homilies*, XV. 4.

[32] Milchsack; *Historia D. Johannis Fausti*, p. cxxxvi, p. cxlvii, n. See p. 407.

[33] *Zauberteufel* (Milchsack's ed.). Also Wolfenbüttel MS. l. 5, 2 Aug. 2°. bl. 166v; G. Zart: *Goethejahrbuch*, 3: 339 ff. (1889).

Gnostic (presumably one individual) were through the centuries in some degree incorporated into the general group of legends which later centered about the unhappy Johann Faust of Germany.

The process was helped by at least two faintly similar stories in the canonical Scriptures. The first of these is the story of the Fall, which involves a lust for knowledge much like that of the Faust presented by Marlowe and Goethe. The second is the story of the temptation of Christ by Satan. In the story of the Fall, Eve yields to the tempter and wilfully violates a divine command for the sake of that knowledge which is power. In the story of Christ's temptation, the Tempter uses essentially the same bait he employs against Faust — power, wealth, and glory. Numerous legendary temptations of saints and Martin Luther's contest with a visible Devil must have helped to keep the tradition alive.

The sixth-century story of Theophilus of Syracuse must also have contributed to the Faust legend. Theophilus was an ecclesiastic who, having declined a bishopric out of modesty, found himself removed even from the post of archdeacon, and disgraced. Through the agency of a Hebrew magician, he sells himself to the Devil, forswears God and the saints, but not the Virgin, and is at length saved through her intercession. The original version is in Greek, and is written by one Eutychianus, who asserts that as a pupil of Theophilus he beheld his master conferring with the Devil and the signing of the compact in the victim's blood — a Faustian touch.

The most important literary version of the Theophilus story is a Latin play by Hrotsvitha, the learned nun, who wrote at Gandersheim in the late tenth century. In this version, a soldier indignant at losing his promotion is substituted for Theophilus. Another is the *Miracle de Théophile* (1245–65) of Rutebeuf. The story was retold in an English poem by William Forrest in 1572.[34] This is the first story known in which a man sells his soul to the Devil, and it is worth noting that the contract in blood has already appeared.

The whole idea of a compact with the Devil to obtain superhuman power of knowledge is, however, very ancient. It orig-

[34] A. W. Ward, HEDL, I. 330; H. Sutherland Edwards: *Faust Legend*, p. 20.

inates in Jewish traditions of before and just after the time of Christ. Jewish rites to invoke evil spirits form the basis for later magic of this sort and partly explain why, in medieval stories of this type, the Devil's agent is usually a Jew.

The brilliant, cynical, and at times pathetic character of Mephistophilis nowhere appears before the German *Faustbuch*. Efforts to explain the name Faust as equivalent to the Greek φάω [to shine] and Mephistophilis as either μὴ Fausto φίλος or else as μὴ φωτὸς φίλος are merely absurd, though Herman Grimm mentions demons *qui lucem oderint*.[35] It is also suggested that the name is a distortion of "Hephaistophilos," Hephaistos being a medieval name taken over from the Greek and used for the Devil. It is regarded as a kind of opposite to the name of Theophilus, Faust's prototype.[36] An effort to derive the name from other Hebrew names for angels like Ariel, Raniel, Gabriel, Raphael, Uriel, has also been made. This would give the form "Mephistophiel." The Bible mentions Mephibosheth, son of Saul, and another Mephibosheth, Saul's grandson, but as Mr. H. Sutherland Edwards observes, "there is nothing Mephistophelian in either of them." [37] The derivation of one of his most moving and searching characterizations thus remains, like so much of Marlowe's life, a mystery.

The Faust Books

There is, however, no doubt about the immediate source of Marlowe's *Doctor Faustus*. The play is obviously based on the version of the Faust legend which Johann Spies entitled the *Faustbuch* and published at Frankfurt-am-Main in 1587. This was later translated and adapted as *The Historie of the Damnable Life and Deserved Death of Dr. John Faustus*, the earliest extant edition of which was published in 1592.[38]

Spies, the German printer, says that the story was "recently communicated and sent" to him "through a good friend from Speyer," in the Rhenish Palatinate. The book was reprinted

---

[35] Ward's ed., p. 119, and Milchsack, *op. cit.*, p. ccxlviii (numbered cciil); Grimm, *Preussische Jahrbücher*, 47: 447 My 1881.

[36] *Praxis Cabulae Nigrae Doctoris Johannis Fausti*, p. 612.

[37] *Faust Legend*, p. 69. Cf. Scheible's *Kloster*, 11: 349 ff., and 5: 135–136.

[38] Copies are distributed as follows: Ed. 1592, BM, Bodleian; 1608, BM; 1618, Bodleian; 1636, Huntington.

in Hamburg in the year of publication. Another edition, also in 1587, enlarged the original story, apparently by borrowings from the *Christlich Bedencken vnnd Erinerungen vor Zauberey* of "Augustin Lercheimer" (Hermann Witekind).[39]

Three more editions, at least one of them a reprint of the original, appeared in 1588; another in 1589; and another in 1590 — the last containing six additional chapters which correspond to the Erfurt Chronicle. Very late versions, appearing in 1597 and 1598, obviously have no relation to Marlowe. The earlier editions are rare.[40]

The sources of the German *Faustbuch* are only partly clear. The unknown author obviously drew mainly on the popular legend. He must, however, have borrowed his geography from Schedel's *Chronik* (1493). The main outline of Faust's travels with diabolical aid are taken over from this work, pass into the English Faust Book, and to some extent reappear in Marlowe's play. There are certain textual correspondences and the order in which the cities are named is essentially the same. The unknown author has merely eliminated from Schedel's list very distant cities like Jerusalem and Nineveh, which he seems to have felt were beyond even the Devil's reach, and has slightly adapted the order of the others. He takes his local color from Schedel.

Marlowe follows this list as far as Rome, where he has an opportunity for anti-Catholic propaganda sure to be acceptable to a Protestant audience. He therefore dwells no further on Faustus' travels. A scene in Constantinople may possibly have dropped out of Marlowe's text. Schedel mentions the city and there is one allusion to it in the play, the complaint of Mephistophilis: "From *Constantinople* am I hither come." [41]

Another source on which the original German *Faustbuch* drew is the *Processus Belial* by Jacobus de Theramo, which deals with Christ's descent into Hell and probably is related to the Apocryphal Gospels. The description of Hell itself is full of

---

[39] Milchsack, *op. cit.*, p. cclxx, thinks that the *Faustbuch* had been completed before Lercheimer wrote.

[40] Ward's ed., pp. lxxii-lxxiii. See also the introduction to Braune's reprint (1878) and Zarncke: "Zur Bibliographie des Faustbuches," *Berichte der Königl. Sächsischen Gesellschaft der Wissenschaften*, 40: 181–200 (1888).

[41] Line 995.

crude horrors and seems to have been culled from various works of piety. Nothing is more characteristic of Marlowe's genius than the refined and intellectualized conception which he substitutes:

> Why this is hel, nor am I out of it:
> Thinkst thou that I who saw the face of God,
> And tasted the eternal ioyes of heauen,
> Am not tormented with ten thousand hels,
> In being depriv'd of euerlasting blisse? [42]

At a stroke, he discards all mere physical terrors in favor of a subtle and poetic ethical idea. One sees why this man was held unorthodox.

Some of the *Faustbuch's* descriptions of magic practices are taken from a work by Ludovicus Milichius (Frankfurt a.M., 1563) called *Der Zauber Teuffel*, but little of this appears in Marlowe except Faust's feat of producing fresh fruit in midwinter:

Also kan auch der Teufel im Winter Obs vnnd andere zeitige frucht den Zauberern zubringen, welches er auss Indien oder Aphrica holet, denn in denselbigen Landen trifft sich der Sommer vnd Winter nicht mit vnsern Landen.[43]

This is a common story about magicians, however, which appears in various works on magic.[44] It might therefore have reached the *Faustbuch* from various sources, but in view of other borrowings it probably did come through the *Zauber Teuffel*, which thus becomes, in a sense, a Marlowe source, though the poet probably never heard of it.

The correspondences between the play and the English Faust Book are so detailed as to make it perfectly clear in what mine the dramatist has been digging.[45] For once Marlowe seems to have been content with a single main source. Though he has drawn slightly on the native English legends of Friar Bacon and occasionally on the classics, he has not pushed his study further. There was, indeed, no reason to do so. The

---

[42] Ll. 312–316.

[43] *Zauber Teuffel*, chap. XX.

[44] Cf. Jodocus Hoecker: *Der Teufel selbs* (Frankfurt a.M., 1568?), p. 50; Milchsack, *op. cit.*, pp. cxviii-cxx, and notes; *Theatrum de Veneficis* (Frankfurt a.M., 1586), p. 310.

[45] For table of correspondences between Marlowe's play, Goethe's play, and the Faust books, see author's MS. dissertation, HCL.

Faust Book contained ample material, dramatic, vivid, picturesque, ideally suited to the stage. There was so much material that he had to discard nine-tenths of it in order to compress his play within the time limits of the Elizabethan theatre. He might very easily have picked up by word-of-mouth any of the Faust legends which were afloat on the Continent, but he really had no need of them.

Though Marlowe's play follows the English *Historie of the damnable life, and deserued death of Doctor Iohn Faustus* so closely — repeatedly echoing its exact wording and agreeing with it wherever it differs from the German — that the most skeptical critic cannot deny the relationship, it is difficult to see just how Marlowe got hold of it if *Doctor Faustus* was composed by 1589 or earlier, since the earliest known edition was published in 1592.

Some critics would evade this difficulty by dating the play 1592 or later. Others have sought refuge in the idea that Marlowe used the German *Faustbuch*. The first idea, as we have seen,[46] is in conflict with internal evidence as to date. The second is quite impossible. Few Elizabethans knew German, and there is no evidence that Marlowe was one of them. Moreover, the correspondence in phraseology between the play and the English Faust Book is too close to be accidental; and it is impossible, of course, for Marlowe to have translated into precisely the same phrasing that the English Faust Book later used. No two translators ever use the same language.

The English Faust Book is a very free translation of the German text. It is the work of one "P. F., *Gent.*," who had traveled on the Continent and who took the liberty of correcting and expanding his original from his own observations. He had a fair knowledge of German but evaded difficulties by leaving out the hard parts, notably Chapter LXV of the original, which is especially obscure. His identity is a complete mystery. The suggestion that "Gent" is a surname, which has at times been put forward,[47] is plainly impossible. This is the common Elizabethan abbreviation for "gentleman." It is set in italics

---

[46] See I. 275-277.

[47] H. Logeman: *Faustus Notes*, p. 144; John Ashton: *The Devil in Britain and America*, p. 38.

on the title page, while the initials are in Roman type. More-over, the Elizabethans very rarely used two initials with a surname.

Logeman has discovered in the *Dictionary of National Biography* three contemporaries with the requisite initials — Bishop Patrick Forbes, of Aberdeen (1564–1635); Patrick Fitzmaurice, Lord Kerry (1551?–1600), who was in prison from 1587 to 1591, when the translation was probably made; and Philip Ferdinand (1555?–1598), a Polish Jew who had been converted. Nothing, however, seems to identify any one of these men as the translator, and the initials may have been a com-plete blind. Logeman conjectures that they may have been a misprint as well.

Marlowe's play — or at least the text as it has come down to us — not only follows the structure and general arrangement of the English *Historie* but in scores of passages borrows its lan-guage word for word and line for line.[48] To make the argument still more convincing, the play often borrows passages which exist only in the English, not in the German. One of the most interesting of these is the allusion to "ayrie mountaine tops" encircling the city of Trier. Neither the German nor the Eng-lish Faust book has any reference to mountains, but the English book has an allusion to "monuments." Marlowe, glancing carelessly at the text, evidently mistook this for "mountains." The German has only "Palast" and "Werck." [49]

The English contains an impressive description of "the Castle of S. Angelo, wherein are so many great cast peeces as there are dayes in a yeare, *and* such Pieces that will shoote seuen bullets off with one fire." This passage plainly reappears in Marlowe's lines:

> Vpon the bridge call'd *Ponto Angelo*,
> Erected is a Castle passing strong,
> Within whose walles such store of ordonance are,
> And double Canons, fram'd of carued brasse,
> As match the dayes within one compleate yeare.[50]

The German *Faustbuch* has not a line of this.[51] A little further

---

[48] Only a few examples are given here. See author's MS. dissertation, HCL.
[49] Chap. XXII; *Doctor Faustus*, 805.   [50] Chap. XXII; *Doctor Faustus*, 839–843.
[51] Cf. Wilhelm Scherer's (1884) reprint, pp. 102–103.

in the English *Historie* is mention of "the PYRAMIDE that IULIUS CÆSAR brought out of AFRICA." This puts in an appearance in Marlowe's play as

> . . . high piramides,
> Which *Iulius Caesar* brought from *Affrica*.[52]

This African marvel is likewise missing in the German.

The "thousand ships" passage, the most famous Marlowe ever wrote, has a direct relation to the English *Historie*. Marlowe had already experimented with the phrases that were to make him famous. In *Dido* there is an allusion to waves as Neptune's "toples hilles," and the line

> And heele make me immortall with a kisse.[53]

He had already alluded twice to Helen and the thousand ships, once in *Tamburlaine*:

> *Hellen*, whose beauty sommond Greece to armes,
> And drew a thousand ships to *Tenedos*,

and again in *Dido*:

> Tell him, I neuer vow'd at *Aulis* gulfe
> The desolation of his natiue *Troy*,
> Nor sent a thousand ships vnto the walles.[54]

He may possibly have been thinking also of the passage in the *Iliad* [55] where the elders praise Helen's beauty, and the number of his ships corresponds exactly with classical tradition — specifically, with the *Aeneid*, with the Eighteenth Dialogue in Lucian's *Dialogues of the Dead*, and with the *Iphigenia in Tauris* of Euripides, works with which a Cambridge Master of Arts was likely to be familiar.[56] The passage in Lucian is a conversation between Menippus and Hermes, in which Menippus asks

---

[52] Ll. 844–845; chap. XXII.
[53] Ll. 1162, 1329.
[54] II *Tamb*. 3055–3056; *Dido*, 1610–1612. See II. 251.
[55] Gamma, 156.
[56] The parallel with Lucian was first pointed out by F. Biehringer, in *Globus*, 89: 94, 8 F 1906, and was repeated a month later by Frederick Tupper, Jr., writing independently in MLN, 21: 76–77 (1906). It has since been pointed out by Burton Rascoe in *A Bookman's Daybook*, pp. 196–197, and in *Titans of Literature*, p. 268 — apparently under the impression that it is his own discovery.

to see the famous beauties of antiquity, much t.ie same request that Faustus makes of Mephistophilis:

MEN. "Ὅμως τὴν Ἑλένην μοι δεῖξον· οὐ γὰρ ἄν διαγνόιην ἔγωγε.
EPM. Τουτὶ τὸ κρανίον ἤ Ἑλένη ἐστίν.
MEN. Εἶτα διὰ τοῦτο αἱ χίλιαι νῆες ἐπληρώθησαν ἐξ ἀπάσης τῆς Ἑλλά-
δος καὶ τοσοῦτοι ἔπεσον Ἕλληνές τε καὶ βάρβαροι καὶ τοσαῦται
πόλεις ἀνάστατοι γεγόνασιν.

The *Aeneid* refers merely to the "mille carinae." [57]
The passage from *Iphigenia* is in the opening speech:

ἐνταῦθα γὰρ δὴ χιλίων ναῶν στόλον
Ἑλληνικὸν συνήγαγ' Ἀγαμέμνων ἄναξ,
τὸν καλλίνικον στέφανον Ἰλίου θέλων
λαβεῖν Ἀχαιούς, τούς θ' ὑβρισθέντας γάμους
Ἑλένης μετελθεῖν, Μενέλεῳ χάριν φέρων.

But Marlowe's own lines notoriously hovered in his restless head. He may merely have been thinking of his own earlier work when, in Chapter LXV of the English Faust Book, he came upon a passage which itself provided one half of his most famous lines, and by suggestion called forth from his brain the thousand ships again: "fayre HELENA of GREECE, for whom the worthy town of TROIE was destroyed and razed downe 'to the ground." This he transformed into

Was this the face that lancht a thousand shippes?
And burnt the toplesse Towres of *Ilium*? [58]

If this is not evidence as to Marlowe's source, what is? Other similar examples of direct parallelism with the English Faust Book are too numerous to detail.

The famous concluding passage of *Doctor Faustus* seems likewise to have been borrowed. The lines

Cut is the branch that might haue growne ful straight,
And burned is *Apolloes* Laurel bough

are among the most moving that Marlowe ever wrote, not least because they foreshadow his own melancholy end. But they are amazingly like a couplet in *Shore's Wife*, a poem by the obscure Thomas Churchyard, which was published in the 1563 edition of the *Mirror for Magistrates*, which also contains an account of the "Young Mortimer" who appears in *Edward*

---

[57] *Aeneid*, II. 198.
[58] EFB, chap. XLV; *Doctor Faustus*, 1328–1329.

the Second. Marlowe may, in browsing through this book, which was well known in his time, have found the lines:

> They brake the bowes and shakte the tree by sleight,
> And bent the wand that mought haue growne full streight.[59]

These lingered in his mind, sank below the level of conscious thought, and returned again when the fate of Faustus made them appropriate.[60]

It is tempting to suppose that Marlowe borrowed the final line of Faustus:

> Terminat hora diem, Terminat Author opus

from a manuscript in Archbishop Parker's collection at Corpus Christi, where the same line occurs.[61]

TEXT

The text of *Faustus* is one of the most corrupt known. Indeed, J. P. Postgate in his article on "Textual Criticism" in the *Encyclopædia Britannica* remarks that "where there is great or complicated divergence between the editions, as in the case of Marlowe's *Faustus*, the production of a resultant text which may be relied upon to represent the ultimate intention of the author is well-nigh impossible." [62]

There are, in all, ten early editions, published in 1604, 1609, 1611, 1616, 1619, 1620, 1624, 1628, 1631, and 1663. There is some ground for suspecting that an edition, now lost, may have been published in 1601, as Hermann Breymann long ago suggested and as Mr. Percy Simpson has recently reiterated.[63] It is entered by Thomas Bushell in the *Stationers' Register* for January 7, 1601/2, but no copies survive. It is easy to understand how this edition may have completely vanished, for of the ten extant editions, six are represented by unique copies.

Marlowe's original manuscript probably underwent more or less adaptation while the play was in the actors' hands when it

---

[59] CHEL, III. 198. The lines are in st. 24 of the Haslewood (1815) ed. of the *Mirror*, II. 467.

[60] Cf. Alwin Thaler: "Churchyard and Marlowe," MLN, 38: 90–91 F 1923.

[61] Parker MS. 281, fol. 78v.

[62] Fourteenth (1929) ed., XXII. 7.

[63] Breymann's Heilbronn ed., pp. xxiv–xxv; Percy Simpson: "The 1604 Text of Marlowe's 'Doctor Faustus,'" *Essays and Studies by Members of the English Association*, 7: 143 (1921).

was first being produced; it was certainly much modified after the author's death. The early editors were confused on this point by the fraudulent entry in *Henslowe's Diary* indicating payments to "Thomas dickers [Dekker]" for "adycyons to ffostus" in 1597.[64] There is, however, pretty general agreement that the play had been revised even before this, probably in 1594, when it had a series of new productions. Fleay asserts that "the forger of the 1597 entry . . . was right in his conjecture, and that the author was Thomas Dekker." [65] Breymann regards this as unproved, but agrees that there was revision of some kind. Fleay is convinced that parts of even the earlier texts are not Marlowe's and that he can recognize Dekker's thought, style, and meter.

From the manuscript which resulted from this first revision, the lost edition of 1601/2 and the extant editions of 1604, 1609, and 1611 seem to have been printed. Before any of these extant editions had appeared, however, the already revised playhouse manuscript was again revised by William Birde and Samuel Rowley. This was in 1602. *Henslowe's Diary* has a genuine entry, recording payment to them of four pounds "for ther adicyones in doctor fostes." [66] Since this was a generous sum by Henslowe's standards, the "adicyones" must have been fairly considerable.

Not until 1616, however, do the results of their collaboration, or perhaps even an earlier one,[67] appear in a printed edition. In that year the publisher, John Wright, who had followed Bushell's 1604 text in his own editions of 1609 and 1611, suddenly brought out a new edition using a new text. He did this without explanation or comment; but his next (1619) edition carries on its title page the line, "with new additions."

The 1616 quarto had added about 550 lines and minor variations, with which all later editions agree, except for a few lines and individual variant readings. The 1663 edition makes more and worse additions to the play.

The text of *Faustus* thus falls into two main divisions, known

---

[64] Fol. 19v, ll. 13–16; Collier's ed., p. 71; Greg's ed., I. 38. See I. 196–197 for a discussion of these frauds.

[65] Appendix A to Ward's (1901) ed., p. clxvii; Breymann's ed., p. xxxi.

[66] *Henslowe's Diary*, fol. 108v; Greg's ed., I. 172.

[67] See also II. 250–251.

respectively as the A and B texts. Mr. E. H. C. Oliphant suggests [68] that there are really three versions. Presumably he
would erect the 1663 quarto into a C text.

In general the additions and alterations after the A text is
abandoned consist of a toning-down of religiously doubtful
passages; alteration of words and phrases, usually for the worse
from a literary standpoint; and the interpolation of a few new
scenes from the English Faust Book. Breymann printed the
1604 and 1616 texts on opposite pages; Brooke printed the
1616–1663 alterations as an appendix; while Boas, basing his
edition on the B text as given in the 1616 quarto, prints only
the 1663 variants as an appendix.

It is impossible to state whether Birde and Rowley, the revisers, ever had Marlowe's authentic original manuscript before them. Assuming that they worked from an already revised
manuscript only, Breymann has diagramed the relationship
between the texts as follows:

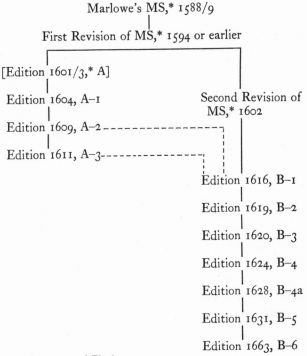

Marlowe's MS,* 1588/9

First Revision of MS,* 1594 or earlier

[Edition 1601/3,* A]

Edition 1604, A–1

Second Revision of
MS,* 1602

Edition 1609, A–2

Edition 1611, A–3

Edition 1616, B–1

Edition 1619, B–2

Edition 1620, B–3

Edition 1624, B–4

Edition 1628, B–4a

Edition 1631, B–5

Edition 1663, B–6

In the light of our knowledge today we need no longer star the edition of 1611, of whose existence Breymann had his doubts but which is now known to exist in a single copy in the Huntington Library. It is also necessary to interpolate the 1628 edition, which was entirely unknown to Breymann. If we assume that Marlowe's original manuscript still lay about the playhouse when the second revision was undertaken, Breymann would rearrange this table as follows:

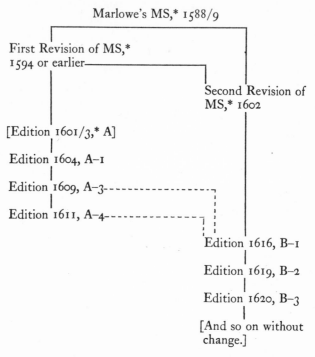

Marlowe's MS,* 1588/9

First Revision of MS,*
1594 or earlier——————

Second Revision of
MS,* 1602

[Edition 1601/3,* A]

Edition 1604, A–1

Edition 1609, A–3- - - - - - - - - - - - - - -

Edition 1611, A–4- - - - - - - - - - - -

Edition 1616, B–1

Edition 1619, B–2

Edition 1620, B–3

[And so on without
change.]

The most famous passages in *Doctor Faustus* — the opening soliloquy, the metaphysical conception of hell expressed by Mephistophilis, the apostrophe to Helen, and the final scene — appear in all texts. They bear his stamp so clearly that, were external evidence lacking, they might be attributed to Marlowe solely on the basis of style; but as a matter of fact the texts fully support this view.

STAGE HISTORY

The chief puzzle in the stage history of *Doctor Faustus* is the fact that we have no written record of performance prior to September 30, 1594, when Henslowe enters the receipts from "docter ffostose" as "iij^{ll} xij^s." [69] This performance must have been given at the Rose Theatre, whither the Lord Admiral's men had gone after separating from the Lord Chamberlain's in June, 1594. The date is more than a year after Marlowe's death, and the play is not marked as a new one. The unusually large takings may have been due to special scenic effects, to which the play lends itself so well — one of which must certainly have been the "j dragon in fostes," which appears in Henslowe's inventory of stage properties for 1598.[70] The complete record of Henslowe's takings is as follows:

October 9, 1594	44*s*.
October 21	33*s*.
November 5	38*s*.
November 20	18*s*.
December 8	15*s*.
December 20	18*s*.
December 27	52*s*.
January 9, 1594/5	22*s*.
January 24	24*s*.
February 8	18*s*.
April 31, 1595	22*s*.
June 5	17*s*.
September 11	30*s*. 2*d*.
September 26	13*s*.
February 13, 1595/6	25*s*.
May 5, 1596	20*s*.
June 12, 1596	17*s*.
July 3, 1596	14*s*.
October 28, 1596	27*s*.
November 4	17*s*.
December 17	9*s*.
January 5, 1596/7	5*s*.

These figures leave no doubt that *Doctor Faustus* was one of the great successes of its day; but when at the last performance

[69] Fol. 10*r*; Greg's ed., I. 19.
[70] *Diary* (Collier's ed.), p. 273.

receipts had sunk to five shillings and the public enthusiasm seemed to have been exhausted, Henslowe took it off the boards. In the fall of 1597 the Lord Admiral's and Lord Pembroke's men began to act together at the Rose, and the old play was revived. There was a production October 11, 1597, but, as Henslowe makes no record of his takings, they may not have been worth entering.[71]

The Lord Admiral became Earl of Nottingham October 22, 1597, and Henslowe begins to refer to these players as the Earl of Nottingham's men on May 26, 1599. The title page of the 1604 quarto, describing the play as "acted by the Right Honorable the Earle of Nottingham his seruants," implies that there were other later performances. This is confirmed by the payments to Birde and Rowley for their additions in 1602, since Henslowe was far too thrifty to lay out money on rewriting which led to no performances.

The vivid contemporary descriptions of productions of the play give hints as to costuming and production and also as to the play's terrifying effect upon its audience. The first of these is in *The Blacke Booke* (1604) by "T. M.," who was presumably Thomas Middleton. This is a collection of tales of low life which owes its title to the fact that "it doubly damns the devil." In it, a certain "villanous lieutenant" is described as possessing "a head of hayre like one of my Divells in Dr. Faustus when the old Theatre crackt and frighted the audience."[72] "The old Theatre" may have been the original Theatre in Shoreditch, where the Admiral's men were acting in 1590/1. If so, this is the earliest allusion to a stage production of *Doctor Faustus*.

Later, we have a clear picture of the stage during a performance at the Fortune Theatre. This appears in John Melton's *The Astrologaster, or, The Figure-caster* (1620):

Another will fore-tell of Lightning and Thunder that shall happen such a day, when there are no such Inflamations seene, except men goe to the *Fortune* in *Golding-Lane* to see the Tragedie of Doctor *Faustus*. There indeede a man may behold shagge-hayr'd Deuills runne roaring ouer the Stage with Squibs in their mouthes, while

[71] Fol. 27v; Greg's ed., I. 54.
[72] Works of Middleton (ed. A. H. Bullen), V. 515, where text is modernized.

Drummers make Thunder in the Tyring-house, and the twelue-penny Hirelings make artificiall Lightning in their Heauens.[73]

William Prynne in his *Histriomastix* (1633) tells a startling tale of how the Devil in person appeared among the actors impersonating stage devils during a performance of *Doctor Faustus*. This is one of his series of edifying accounts of disasters which have shown the "just, though terrible judgement of God upon these Play-haunters and prophaners of his holy day," [74] and the *"fearefull precedents of others, who by communicating with the Devill at Stage-playes, have fallen quite away from God."* Among these was an unfortunate lady who had been so corrupted by the drama that on her deathbed, instead of crying for mercy, she cried out: "Hieronimo, Hieronimo; *O let mee see* Hieronimo *acted*; *(calling out for a Play, in stead of crying unto God for mercy,) and so closed her dying eyes."* [75]

There is also an allusion to the tragical ends of men either slain in playhouses or in quarrels there commenced — which may be a distorted reference to Marlowe's assassination. On the same page is a reference to the *"visible apparition of the Devill on the Stage at the Belsavage Play-house, in Queene* Elizabeths *dayes, (to the great amazement both of the Actors and Spectators) whiles they were there prophanely playing the History of* Faustus (the truth of which I have heard from many now alive, who well remember it,) *there being some distracted with that fearefull sight."* [76]

This apparition must have seemed natural enough to Prynne, who believed that the devils had theatrical performances in hell every Sunday evening: *"euery Lords day at night, (a time which some men consecrate and set apart for Stage-Playes, . . . the Deuils did vse to meete in Hell, and there did recreate, and exhilarate themselues with Stage-Playes: . . ."* [77]

Others must have been equally credulous, for the story of the extra and genuine devil in *Faustus* reappears. There is the

[73] Page 31. There is a copy in HCL. Cf. Brooke, *Trans. Connecticut Acad.*, 25: 375 (1921–22).
[74] There are two editions of *Histriomastix* in 1633, which do not agree in pagination. References here are to the Columbia University copy. See pt. I, fol. 557*r*.
[75] *Ibid.*, fol. 556*r*.
[76] *Ibid.*, fol. 556*r*.
[77] *Ibid.*, p. 13. The Columbia copy is paged, not foliated, at this point.

story of a performance at Exeter which ended in terror when
the players in the conjuring scene found that they had unin-
tentionally summoned Satan in person and that "there was
one devell too many amongst them." The story is recorded by
one J. G. R., who bases it on a manuscript note "on the last
page of a book in my possession printed by Vautrollier in
1585." [78]

This passage runs:

Certaine Players at Exeter acting *upon* the stage the tragicall storie
of Dr. Faustus the Conjurer; as a certain nomber of Devels kept
everie one his circle there, and as Faustus was busie in his magicall
invocations, on a *sudden* they wer all *dasht*, every one harkning other
in the eare, for they were all perswaded there was one devell too many
amongst them; and so after a little pause desired the people to pardon
them, they could go no further *with this* matter: the people also understanding the thing as it was, every man hastened to be first out of
dores. The players (as I heard it) contrarye to their custome spending the night in reading and in prayer got them out of the towne the
next morning.

By 1673 the story was being retold to include the celebrated
actor, Edward Alleyn:

The Tradition concerning the Occasion of the Foundation [of Dulwich College], runs thus; That Mr. *Alleyne*, being a Tragedian, and
one of the Original Actors in many of the celebrated *Shakespear*'s
Plays [*sic*], in one of which he play'd a *Dæmon*, with six others, and
was in the midst of the Play surpriz'd by an *Apparition* of the *Devil*,
which so work'd on his Fancy, that he made a Vow, which he perform'd at this Place. [79]

It is interesting to have Alleyn thus connected with the play,
but Aubrey is wrong in supposing that he played a demon.
Early references make it clear that he played the part of
Faustus himself. The most interesting of these appears in *The
Knave of Clubbes* (1609), by S. Rowlands:

The Gull gets on a surplis,
With a crosse vpon his breast,

[78] *Gentleman's Magazine*, 2nd ser., 34: 234 S 1850. See also Chambers: *Eliz. Stage*,
III. 424. Thomas Vautrollier was a sixteenth-century Huguenot printer, a refugee who
had presses in both London and Edinburgh. See J. Q. Adams: *Life of Shakespeare*,
p. 126.
[79] John Aubrey: *Natural History and Antiquities of Surrey* (ed. 1718–1719), I. 190.

Like *Allen* playing *Faustus*,
In that manner he was drest.[80]

This corresponds fairly well with the various woodcuts on the title pages of the early editions, which may, therefore, be taken as portraits of Alleyn. They are not unlike the known portrait at Dulwich College.

The play continued to be popular after the Restoration, though the corrupt form of the 1663 quarto and the words on the title page, "as it is now acted," hint at the mutilation it had suffered. Samuel Pepys went May 26, 1662, "to the Redd Bull, where we saw Dr. Faustus, but so wretchedly & poorly done that we were sick of it." The play was produced again on September 28, 1675, by the Duke of York's Company, in the presence of Charles II.[81] In the same year Edward Phillips in his account of Marlowe in the *Theatrum Poetarum* (1675) observed: "Of all that he hath written to the Stage his Dr. *Faustus* hath made the greatest noise with its Devils and such like Tragical sport." [82] In 1687 William Winstanley echoes and improves on this: "None made such a great Noise as his Comedy of *Doctor Faustus* with his Devils, and such like tragical Sport, which pleased much the humors of the Vulgar." [83]

The seventeenth-century actor Betterton seems to have taken over Alleyn's part of Faustus, and Mountfort (Munferd) the part of Mephistophilis. At least in the 1663 copy at the British Museum (644.b.69) "Mr. Baterton" is scribbled in an early hand opposite the name of Faustus, and "Mr. Munferd" opposite Mephistophilis. This period began the degeneration of the great tragedy into mere spectacle. The intellectual pathos of Marlowe's hero was not for the groundlings. But the Devil was as popular with them as he had been in the days of the miracle and morality plays, when the mere threat to withhold his "abominable presence" was a sufficient device to elicit coins from the spectators.[84] We have already seen that the Devil was the

---

[80] *Complete Works of Samuel Rowlands* (Hunterian Club, 1880), II. 29. See also A. Tille: *Faustsplitter*, pp. 65 ff.

[81] Allardyce Nicoll: *Restoration Stage*, p. 310. The King's presence is probable but not proved.

[82] II. 25 (Modern Poets).

[83] *Lives of the most Famous English Poets*, p. 134.

[84] J. Q. Adams: *Shakespearean Playhouses*, p. 4.

one great attraction that most impressed Middleton, Melton, and Prynne. The temptation was to develop this aspect of the play and emphasize spectacular staging, and to this temptation the later producers readily succumbed.

The process had already been helped forward by the Continental tours of English actors early in the seventeenth century. The German folk story in its new English dramatic dress had been carried back to Austria by wandering companies of London players as early as 1608.[85] Both *Doctor Faustus* and *The Jew of Malta* were acted at Graetz in the carnival of that year; and presumably the English actors, who, we know, visited other parts of Germany, carried *Faustus* far and wide as an especially popular part of their repertoire. Certainly "eine Tragoedia von Dr. Faust" was performed by English comedians at Dresden on July 7, 1626, to be followed by *The Jew of Malta*. Playing before audiences of alien speech, the English actors were naturally compelled to rely for effect on gesture, stage business, and spectacle, and doubtless exaggerated the grotesque side of the play. In Vienna the Faustus story remained popular during the seventeenth and eighteenth centuries; but, as the Jesuits objected to Faustus' skepticism, the later versions tended to make a libertine of him.

Thus both at home and abroad the play of *Doctor Faustus* degenerated with its leading character. Mountfort presently reworked it into a farce — *The Life and Death of Doctor Faustus*, with which he combined *The Humours of Harlequin and Scaramouche*. In this he emphasized precisely those elements of Marlowe's play which owed least to his genius — if, indeed, he had anything to do with them — the Seven Deadly Sins, the horse-courser, the carter, and the buffoonery in the palace of the Pope. The scenes in the study of Faustus and the terrible finale remained, but in a sadly mutilated form, when this travesty was acted at the Queen's Theatre in Dorset Garden at intervals from 1684 to 1688. It was later revived at the theatre in Lincoln's Inn Fields, and was finally published in 1697.

---

[85] Johannes Meissner: *Die englischen Comoedianten zur Zeit Shakespeares in Oesterreich*, p. 90; Albert Cohn: *Shakespeare in Germany*, pp. lxxxiii, xciii, cxv-cxvii; Karl Weiss: *Die Wiener Haupt- und Staatsaktionen* (1854), p. 36.

In the early part of the eighteenth century the Faust story was being employed, as Pope observes in his notes to the *Dunciad*, in "a set of farces, which lasted in vogue two or three seasons, in which both playhouses strove to outdo each other in the year 1726, 27." [86] Sad to say, they were "frequented by persons of the first quality in England to the twentieth and thirtieth time." Pope satirized these and kindred productions in the lines in which, he says, Colley Cibber

> . . . look'd, and saw a sable Sorcerer rise,
> Swift to whose hand a winged volume flies:
> All sudden, Gorgons hiss, and Dragons glare,
> And ten-horn'd fiends and Giants rush to war.
> Hell rises, Heav'n descends, and dance on Earth,
> Gods, imps, and monsters, music, rage, and mirth,
> A fire, a jig, a bottle, and a ball,
> Till one wide conflagration swallows all.[87]

The chief offender seems to have been John Thurmond, whose *Harlequin Dr. Faustus* was published in 1724. It was performed at Drury Lane. Pope can even cry, addressing personified Dullness,

> Hell thou shalt move; for Faustus is thy friend.[88]

He complains especially that the two theatres "rival'd each other in showing the Burnings of Hell-fire in Dr. Faustus." [89] Martin Powell's puppet-theatre under the Covent Garden piazzas, to which the *Spectator* alludes,[90] had already taken over the unfortunate Faustus.

A good many of the more recent performances have been academic. *Doctor Faustus* was produced at Cambridge University in 1907, with Rupert Brooke and George Mallory (later famous as a mountaineer) in the cast. The play was so successful that it led to the organization of the Marlowe Dramatic Society in 1908. There were other Cambridge productions in 1924 and again in 1934, though not under the Society's auspices.

In America *Doctor Faustus* was produced at Princeton University in 1907; at Williams College May 1, 2, and 30, and June

[86] Bk. III, ll. 229–236, and notes to l. 229.
[87] *Dunciad*, III, ll. 227–234.
[88] *Ibid.*, III, l. 307.
[89] Note to III, l. 310.
[90] No. 14, March 16, 1710/11.

2, 1908, and again May 28 and June 22, 1912; by Carnegie
Institute, Pittsburgh, at Schenley Park, February 25 to March
14, 1921, with Russell Collins as Faustus and costumes from the
collection of William Poel, under the direction of Frederick
McConnell; at Yale in 1932, under the direction of Miss Jane
Ogburn; and at Stanford University in 1934.[91] The play has
also been produced at Dartmouth College and at Brown
University.

There have been numerous professional productions. In
December, 1885, W. G. Wills produced a spectacular adaptation at the Lyceum Theatre, London, with Henry Irving as
Mephistophilis. Beerbohm Tree appeared in a spectacular
adaptation about 1908, and Ben Greet staged a production at
the Garden Theatre, New York, in 1910.[92] Sam Hume produced the play with his own settings at the Detroit Arts and
Crafts Theatre in 1918, using a modified text. There was a
Cleveland production in 1922 with Russell Collins, who had
played in the Carnegie Institute production the year before,
again as Faustus. This was revived at the opening of the new
playhouse, the Francis E. Drury Theatre, and ran at intervals
throughout the 1927–28 season. The production of Orson
Welles, with himself as Faustus, was one of the great successes
of the New York season of 1937. Another production, by
Walter Armitage, ran in New Orleans, June 8–13, and in At-
lanta, July 17–August 3. Curiously enough, there was a small
production in London the same year. The Mary Ward Set-
tlement gave the play at the Tavistock Little Theatre in
November.

Almost all productions on the Continent have been German.
The Heidelberger Hebbelverein produced the play December
16 and 17, 1903, using an undecorated stage. The general
direction was by Ernst Leopold Stahl.[93] There were productions in Göttingen, Essen, and Frankfurt in 1910, and at

[91] Data largely from college and university authorities. See also Palo Alto *Times*,
May 7; San Francisco *Chronicle*, May 7; Oakland *Tribune*, May 5; Stanford *Daily*,
May 7, 1934.

[92] Boston *Evening Transcript*, March 19, 1910.

[93] Ernst Leopold Stahl: *Der Hebbelverein in Heidelberg*, p. 10; *Jahrb.* 44: 23 8-n.
(1908); Ernst Thaumann in *Frankfurter Zeitung*, December 17, 1903 (Abendblatt).
There is a copy of Dr. Stahl's book in the University of Illinois library.

SIGNATURES OF JOHN MARLOWE

Reading down: Deposition regarding Benchkyn will, 1586; Parish records of St. Mary Bredman, 1591/2; Deposition of witnesses, Parfect *vs.* Doggerell, 1593; Deposition of witnesses, Byssell *vs.* Johnson, 1602

Hamburg October 23, 1911.[94] At the meeting of the German Shakespeare Society April 24, 1928, there was another German production under the general direction of Max Brock, with Dr. Franz Ulbrich as Generalintendant. Hans Illiger appeared as Faustus, and Bernhard Vollmer as Mephistophilis. The German text was a new translation — as yet unpublished — by A. Morsbach and A. Rapp, based on the 1604 text but with some borrowing from that of 1616.[95]

The Danish Shakespeare Society sponsored a production in Copenhagen, at a date which no one now seems to remember. The actors were drawn from the younger members of the Royal Theatre Company and the title role was entrusted to Steffen Tvede. A lecture on Shakespeare and Marlowe preceded the production.[96]

Since the introduction of radio drama *Doctor Faustus* has even had a certain vogue on the air, to which its length — it can be fitted neatly into an hour — and the relative unimportance of scenery especially suit it. There were New York productions under the auspices of the National Broadcasting Company, October 16, 1931; October 17, 1932; September 30, 1933; January 28, 1935; January 15, 1937; September 12, 1937; November 6, 1938; and November 3, 1940.[97]

Of greater interest, however, are Marlowe's modern successes on the scenes of his ancient struggles and triumphs. On July 2 and 4, 1896, the Elizabethan Stage Society put on a revival in St. George's Hall, London, using a reproduction of the Fortune stage.[98] Swinburne wrote a special prologue for the occasion. The Society again produced the play at the Court Theatre, in October, 1904, under the direction of William Poel. Terry's Theatre toured England and Scotland with it for six weeks. There was another London revival under the auspices of the Phoenix Society in October, 1925.

On July 24 of the same year scenes from *Doctor Faustus* were among the episodes from Marlowe's plays produced under Mr. Poel's direction for the benefit of the Marlowe Memorial at

[94] *Jahrb.* 49: 160 (1913).
[95] Otto Francke in *Jahrb.* (OS) 64 (NS) 5: 240–242 (1928).
[96] Data from Professor Josias Bille, Egede, Gjentofte, Denmark.
[97] Data from National Broadcasting Company, New York.
[98] W. Davenport Adams: *Dictionary of the Drama*, I. 582.

Canterbury. On August 20, 22, and 24, 1929, the doors of the Chapter House, Canterbury, opened for three performances by the Norwich Maddermarket Theatre players, under the direction of Nugent Monck. The "atheist" poet, the shoemaker's boy of Canterbury, had come into his own at last.[99]

No Elizabethan play, except the greatest of Shakespeare's, has had so long a life on the stage, or has moved the minds of men so deeply.

Contemporary Influence

Not only did *Doctor Faustus* hold the stage in a purely literary way long after it had ceased to be commercial drama. It also influenced the drama of its own day and the poetry of all succeeding generations.

It is interesting to note one line which Marlowe seems to have borrowed from the *Spanish Tragedy* and which Shakespeare then seems to have borrowed in turn:

> Had I as many lives as there be stars.
> [*Spanish Tragedy*, IV. iv. 178]
> Had I as many soules as there be starres.
> [DF, 338]
> Had I as many eyes as thou hast wounds.
> [*Julius Caesar*, III. i. 200]

The clearest imitation of *Doctor Faustus* is Robert Greene's *Friar Bacon and Friar Bungay*, in which, however, Greene deals far more cautiously with the material of Marlowe's second success than he had with his first. Thomas Dekker, in *Old Fortunatus* and in *If It Be Not Good, The Diuel is in it*; Barnabe Barnes in *The Divils Charter*; and the anonymous authors of *The Merry Devil of Edmonton*, *Two Merry Milkmaids*, *A Knacke to Knowe a Knaue*, the *Contention* plays, and *The Taming of a Shrew*,[100] all borrowed in some degree from *Doctor Faustus*. It is just possible that Sacrapant, in Peele's *Old Wives' Tale*, is meant as a burlesque Faustus.

Doctor Faustus helped to restore to favor as a dramatic char-

---

[99] See Boas' ed., pp. 50–52; Harold Child in RES (1917); Flasdieck in ES, 64: 320–351 (1929); and contemporary files of the London newspapers.

[100] Not discussed in this chapter. See II. 248–253. On Sacrapant, see William John Olive: *Burlesque in Elizabethan Drama*, p. 139.

acter a devil whose popularity on the stage had waned since the days of the mystery, miracle, and morality plays. Such plays as Jonson's *The Divil is an Asse* (1616), in which Pug the devil is carried back to hell somewhat as Faustus is snatched away; *Grim, the Collier of Croydon*; *The Devil and His Dame*, attributed to William Haughton; and John Wilson's late seventeenth-century play, *Belphegor, or the Marriage of the Devil*, presumably owe their origin, if not to Marlowe, at least to the fashion he established. It can even be argued that Dekker's prose *Seauen Deadly Sinnes of London* originates in the pageant of the seven deadly sins in Marlowe's play, which Dekker may have studied carefully while revising it.[101] This is all the more plausible since he introduces a partial list of the deadly sins into *If It Be Not Good, The Diuel is in it.*[102] There had been no allusion to them on the Elizabethan stage before Marlowe. None of this last group, however, can be regarded as directly and consciously imitative of *Doctor Faustus*. They were following a tradition of whose origin they were, at most, dimly conscious.

One gets, however, some idea of the effect produced on the Elizabethan mind — to which the Devil was a real and not a metaphysical entity — when one finds the play being published as late as 1663, sixty years after the great queen's death and three years after the Restoration, and the fantastic stories about the Devil's personal appearance on the stage continuing still later.

Friar Bacon and Friar Bungay

Robert Greene's *Friar Bacon and Friar Bungay* is an effort to set up a home-grown English magician as a rival to the German Faustus, which leads to a natural effort on the author's part to outdo the supernatural feats of Marlowe's conjuror. In detail the play borrows little from *Doctor Faustus*, and its episodes are taken with little change from the prose pamphlet on *The Famous History of Friar Bacon.*[103] Such verbal echoes as exist are all from *Tamburlaine*.

[101] See I. 294.
[102] Pearson's ed. (1873), III. 287.
[103] Reprinted in *Miscellanea Antiqua Anglicana*.

The theme was probably suggested to Greene by the success of Faustus. Marlowe himself, struck by the similarity between Roger Bacon and John Faust, had made a fellow-magician suggest to Faustus "wise *Bacons*" works, and had even appropriated one of Bacon's miracles when he makes Faustus boast:

> Ile haue them wall all *Iermany* with brasse,

and alludes in *The Jew of Malta* to "walls of brasse." [104]
These passages have three parallels in Greene's play:

> Thou meanst ere many yeares or daies be past,
> To compasse England with a wall of brasse.

> The brazen walles framde by Semiramis, . . .
> Shall not be such as rings the English strond.

> But I will circle England round with brasse.[105]

Greene also alludes to Helen of Troy, as if with an eye on Marlowe.

Greene's treatment of his theme, however, is very different. *Friar Bacon and Friar Bungay* is a gay and jovial play, confines itself to English scenes, carefully avoids Marlowe's passionate utterances, and ends happily. Similarities of vocabulary are mainly due to the fact that both men were "university wits."

THOMAS DEKKER: OLD FORTUNATUS

Dekker's *Old Fortunatus* owes something not only to *Tamburlaine* but also to *Faustus*.[106] Dekker found himself confronted with material presenting certain resemblances to Marlowe's play, that is, a German tale of a mortal who sought supernatural aid of a questionable sort and was deluded by it.

Technically, the play owes little to *Doctor Faustus*. Dekker's talent for delineating homely, everyday Elizabethan life had little in common with Marlowe's gift for high astounding terms, and there is no borrowing of lines or phrases.

---

[104] Ll. 183, 116; *Jew of Malta*, 631.
[105] *Friar Bacon and Friar Bungay*, sc. II. 30; sc. XIII. 17, 22.
[106] Tucker Brooke in *Trans. Connecticut Acad.*, 25: 373 (1922); Ward, HEDL, II. 457–459; Mary Leland Hunt: *Thomas Dekker*, p. 31; C. H. Herford: *Literary Relations of England and Germany*, pp. 213–215, 175n.

The general treatment, however, and the employment of the chorus to bridge the gap between the hero's magic flights show a degree of similarity, while the adventures of Fortunatus' son as a wonder-worker at court are not unlike those of Faustus. The allegorical figures of Virtue and Vice faintly suggest the good and evil angels who strive for Faustus' soul. Faust tricks the Pope; Fortunatus the Sultan. Faust's Helen is won by magic; so is Agripyne. Faust rejects religion for magic power; Fortunatus wisdom for wealth. Both prosper, but their prosperity ends in catastrophe. Both repent in vain. Dekker's Fortune is nearly as inexorable as Mephistophilis, and Fortunatus' body is carried off by satyrs much like the fiend who bears Faustus to hell.[107]

There are several traces of *Doctor Faustus* in *If It Be Not Good, The Diuel is in it*, though it looks forward to Goethe rather than backward to Marlowe. This is, like Goethe's *Faust*, a bringing up to date of the old story of the Devil and his temptations, placed in the realistic setting that Dekker knew so well how to depict.[108] Scenes of incantation, allusions to most of the deadly sins, Lucifer, infernal spirits, and the stage manager's fireworks all come from Marlowe's play.

BARNABE BARNES: THE DIVILS CHARTER

Though slight, the influence of *Doctor Faustus* upon *The Divils Charter*, by Barnabe Barnes, first produced in February, 1606/7, is apparent enough. The play is concerned with the crimes of the Borgias. Pope Alexander has already signed a compact with Astaroth when the play opens, so that the signing does not take place on the stage, as in *Faustus*. Alexander's death occurs because Astaroth changes wine glasses, so that the Pope gets poisoned wine intended for others. This very faintly resembles the horseplay of Faust and Mephistophilis in the papal palace. There are scenes of incantation and the raising of spirits which resemble *Macbeth* quite as much as *Faustus*, but the final scene in which the Devil comes for Alexander VI and carries him off in agony is obviously borrowed from Marlowe.

[107] Cf. C. H. Herford: *Literary Relations of England and Germany*, pp. 213–214.
[108] Mary Leland Hunt: *Thomas Dekker*, p. 153.

The Merry Devil of Edmonton

The anonymous *Merry Devil of Edmonton* shows obvious traces of Marlowe's play in theme, structure, and occasional echoing lines. As the play is referred to in *The Black Book* (1604) and was probably being written about 1600, it clearly belongs to a period when *Doctor Faustus* was still being acted. Occasional alexandrines suggest Marlowe's influence.[109]

The hero, Fabell, is discovered in his study, like Faustus. He has long since made a compact with the Devil which has reached its end; but, more ingenious than Faustus, he tricks the fiend into extending the period for seven years. The prologues have a certain resemblance, the closest of which appears in the lines:

> Now is he borne, his parents base of stocke,
> In *Germany*, within a towne calld *Rhodes*.
> [DF, 11–12]
> In Middle-sex his birth and his abode.
> [*Merry Devil*, 12–13] [110]

The scenes in which the diabolical compacts expire are very similar, though in *Faustus* this occurs in the last scene, and in *The Merry Devil* in the first. Faustus, horrified at the thought of an eternity of punishment, exclaims:

> Let Faustus liue in hel a thousand yeeres,
> A hundred thousand, and at last be sau'd.
> O no end is limited to damned soules.
> [DF, 1456–1458]

Fabell, in the same dismay, cries:

> Yet ouerwhelme me with this globe of earth,
> And let a little sparrow with her bill,
> Take but so much as shee can beare away,
> That euery day thus losing of my load,
> I may againe in time yet hope to rise.
> [*Merry Devil*, I. i. 22–26]

---

[109] Cf. Warnke and Proescholdt's ed., p. xvi, and II. ii. 66; III. i. 68; IV. i. 129 and 145.

[110] Sig. A4r of the Tudor Facsimile Text (1911), reproducing the 1608 ed. (Capell R.23) of the *Merry Devil*, at Trinity College, Cambridge.

Marlowe's Mephistophilis orders Faustus to

> Write a deede of gift with thine owne blood.
>   [DF, 467]

Fabell's familiar spirit, Coreb, says:

> Didst thou not write thy name in thine owne blood?
> And drewst the formall deed twixt thee and mee . . .? [111]
>   [*Merry Devil*, I. i. 27–28]

Since *The Merry Devil* is primarily a love story, however, the similarities to Marlowe's work are very limited. Hazlitt remarks that it "sets out with a sort of story of Doctor Faustus, but this is dropt as jarring on the tender chords of the rest of the piece." [112]

THE TWO MERRY MILKMAIDS

Another anonymous play, *The Two Merry Milkmaids*, opens, like so many of the plays imitating *Doctor Faustus*, with a magician in his study. It is a kind of parody of the magic element in *Faustus*. The would-be magician, Bernard, raises not a real devil but only his own tutor, disguised as "Asmody" [Asmodeus, the evil spirit in the apocryphal book of Tobit]. His miracles consist merely in bringing fresh flowers for a lover, as Faustus brought fresh fruits. There is one specific allusion to Marlowe's character:

> Why, haue we it not recorded, *Faustus* did
> Fetch *Bruno's* Wife, Duchesse of *Saxonie*,
> In the dead time of Winter, Grapes she long'd for? [113]

Later, however, the tutor himself turns conjuror and raises a real spirit, who produces a miracle of invisibility which is used for such pranks of stealing food and drink as appear in *Doctor Faustus*. There is a faint echo of Marlowe's most famous line in

> This is the Face that wud not let me rest. [114]

---

[111] Both passages on sig. A4r. See William John Olive: *Burlesque in Elizabethan Drama*, pp. 136–139.
[112] *Lectures on the Dramatic Literature of the Age of Elizabeth* (ed. 1840), p. 206.
[113] Sig. G.
[114] Sig. E3; *Nero*, I. iy (Mermaid ed., p. 18).

There is a similar echo in the anonymous *Nero* —

> But thou, than wrangling Juno far more fair
> Staining the evening beauty of the sky,

which certainly owes something to Marlowe's apostrophe to Helen.

Knacke to Knowe a Knave

The anonymous *Knacke to Knowe a Knave*, acted by Lord Strange's men in 1592 with Alleyn in the cast,[115] contains an obvious borrowing from the last scene of *Doctor Faustus*, in which these very actors had played. The wicked bailiff dies — penitent too late — with these lines:

> But hark, my sons: methinks I hear a noise,
> And ghastly visions make me timorous. . . .
> My heart is hardened, I cannot repent,
> And I am damned to ever-burning fire.
> Soul, be thou safe, and body fly to hell.
>   *[He dieth.*
> *Enter Devil, and carry him away.*[116]

The contract in blood appears in Richard Johnson's *Famous History of the Seven Champions of Christendom* (1596), which was made into a play about 1634 and published 1638. The sorceress Kalyb makes a bargain much like Faustus' and in the end the spirits come to tear her in pieces.[117]

Pseudo-Shakespearean and Other Plays

A few scenes in the *Contention* plays show the influence of *Faustus*, notably the death of Beaufort, which is very like that of Marlowe's hero, and the parting of Margaret and Suffolk, which has some likeness to the scenes between Faustus and Helen of Troy.[118] The *Taming of a Shrew* borrows a number of lines from *Faustus* and is also influenced by *Tamburlaine* and *The Jew of Malta*.[119]

---

[115] *Henslowe's Diary*, fol. 8r; Greg's ed., I. 15.
[116] Cf. Hazlitt's Dodsley, VI. 520; J. P. Collier: *Five Old Plays* (Roxburghe Club, 1850), p. 365.
[117] Frederick Brie: "Romane und Drama im Zeitalter Shakespeares," *Jahrb.* 48: 142 (1912). The play has been edited by Dr. Giles E. Dawson.
[118] Shakespeare Society (1843) ed., p. 46.
[119] See II. 248–253.

Mere allusions are fairly abundant. Shakespeare, Jonson, Shirley, Fletcher, and Thomas Randolph all quote from the play or allude to characters or situations in it. Randolph even borrows the words of Faustus in his *Amyntas*:

> . . . My blood congeales
> Within my quill, and I can write no more.[120]

This is almost word for word Marlowe's

> My bloud conieales and I can write no more.
>   [DF, 494]

The Times' Whistle

The Times' Whistle (ca. 1614), by "R. C., Gent.," an anonymous satire preserved in manuscript in the Cathedral Library, Canterbury, shows numerous traces of Marlowe. One passage may refer directly to his religious views:

> Thou w*hi*ch wilt never graunt a Diety,
> Vnlesse it be in poynt of pollicie,
> W*hi*ch by religion dost not set a strawe,
> Devisde, thou thinkst, but to keep fooles in awe.[121]

The last line echoes the Baines libel almost verbatim, and the whole passage expresses the attitude of Barabas in *The Jew of Malta*. The ideas are, of course, commonplaces, but it is significant that "R. C." alludes specifically to Marlowe on p. xxi, and to Jonson and other writers throughout his satire. Whoever he was, he was obviously interested in the literature of his day.

A lengthy passage in the fourth "Satira" practically duplicates the final scene of *Doctor Faustus*:

> Another Faustus, haplesse, hopelesse man,
> What wilt thou doe, when as that litle sand
> Of thy soone emptied houreglasse, is spent?
> When horrour of thy conscience keeps repent
> From thy black spotted soule? O (but in vaine)
> Thou wilt then wish . . .
> Thoug*h* I liv'de ne're soe miserablie poore, . . .
> Millions of yeares, I could be well content

---

[120] Ed. 1638, IV. vi.

[121] The original is MS. Y.8.3. It has been reprinted by the veteran Canterbury antiquarian, J. M. Cowper, in the series of publications by the Early English Text Society (no. 48, vol. 1871). Quotation here is ll. 19–22, p. 5.

To 'scape the everlasting punnishment. . . .
Then wilt thou curse thy selfe, thy wretched fate,
The wombe that bare thee, him that thee begat;
Wish thou hadst been a beast, a sencelesse stone.[122]

MILTON

Doctor Faustus provides one of the clearest Marlowe-Milton
parallels — the idea, common to both poets, that the individual
soul can be its own hell. Even this is not an undoubted parallel,
for the conception is one which Milton was quite capable of
evolving himself; and it had actually already been used by
Omar Khayyam, who was unknown to both Marlowe and
Milton.[123] However, Milton knew his Shakespeare and could
hardly have been entirely incurious with regard to Marlowe,
like himself a Cambridge student who had declined the priesthood. The parallels between *Faustus* and *Paradise Lost* are
very close: [124]

> *Fau.* How comes it then that thou art out of hel?
> *Me.* Why this is hel, nor am I out of it.
>   [DF, 312–313]
> Hell hath no limits, nor is circumscrib'd
> In one selfe place, for where we are is hell,
> And where hell is, must we euer be.
>   [DF, 553–555]
> The mind is its own place, and in it self
> Can make a Heav'n of Hell, a Hell of Heav'n.
>   [PL, I. 254–255]
> The Hell within him, for within him Hell
> He brings, and round about him, nor from Hell
> One step no more than from himself can fly.
>   [PL, IV. 20–22]
> Which way I flie is Hell; my self am Hell.
>   [PL, IV. 75]

That the play was still being read during this period is shown
by a reference in the *Britanicus Vapulans*, one of the controversial pamphlets that pullulated during the Civil War: "Your

---

[122] Ll. 1625–1641, pp. 53–54 of Cowper's text.
[123] See FitzGerald's version, LXVI. Milton recurs to the idea in *Comus*, 381–384.
[124] Stephen Phillips: "Diabolic in Poetry," *Poetry Review*, 5: 145 O 1914; S. C.
Sarcar's ed., pp. iii, xxii; Henry Morley: *English Plays*, p. 119; A. C. Edmunds' MS.
dissertation, pp. 54 ff.; Leigh Hunt: *Imagination and Fancy* (ed. 1845), pp. 139–140.

Oxford Scholars conjuring up Popery in the likeness of Prelacie is as ridiculous in the matter, as your other quibs were in the words. It would become the Tragedy of Doctor *FAUSTUS*, or rather a Puppet play farre." [125]

DEFOE

The most interesting of the eighteenth-century allusions is in Daniel Defoe's *History of the Devil*.[126] Marlowe's play had given rise to a proverb, "the Devil and Dr. Faustus," which eventually became "the Devil and Dr. foster." Even Henslowe at least once alludes to the play as "doctore foster,"[127] and *Knavery in All Trades* (1664) has an allusion to "the devil in *Doctor Faustus*."[128]

Defoe had no idea that the proverb had anything to do with a once-successful play, and his queer idea that the proverb alluded to the printer Fust, or Faust, shows how far Marlowe's reputation had declined. Defoe, in his *History*, mentions "the famous Dr. Faustus, or Foster, of whom we have believed such strange things, as that it is become a proverb, 'as great as the Devil and Dr. Foster:' whereas poor Faustus was no doctor, and knew no more of the Devil than another body." There is a passing reference in *The Review*.[129]

The proverb has a long life. It appears in *Tom Jones* as a mild oath: "What the Devil and Doctor Faustus";[130] and is still familiar enough in the nineteenth century to appear in William Carleton's once-popular novel, *Fardorougha the Miser* (1839), in Irish dialect form as "the divil an' Docthor Fosther."[131]

[125] *Britanicvs Vapvlans*, "Numb. 1," p. 5. Copy at Worcester College, Oxford.
[126] I owe the exact reference to Mr. Merrill V. Eaton, working under the direction of Dr. John Robert Moore. The passage appears in the Second Part of the *History of the Devil*, chap. XI, Bohn ed., *Novels and Miscellaneous Works of Daniel De Foe* [sic], III. 560; Hazlitt ed. (1843), III. 102; Tegg-Talboys ed. (1840), X. 347. See also Alexander Tille: *Faustsplitter*, no. 214, p. 515.
[127] *Henslowe's Diary*, fol. 25r. Greg's ed., I. 49.
[128] Fol. E r of the copy at Worcester College, Oxford.
[129] *Review*, vol. III, no. 81, p. 323, bk. VIII of the Facsimile Text Society Reprint, no. 44. I owe the reference to the courtesy of Dr. John Robert Moore.
[130] *Tom Jones*, bk. XVIII, chap. VIII. The passage is in vol. II, p. 391, of the 1924 ed. (New York: Knopf). See also G. L. Apperson: *English Proverbs and Proverbial Phrases*, p. 145, entry no. 39, under "Devil."
[131] Ed. 1848, p. 233. On this novel, see G. Barnett Smith: article "Carleton, William," DNB, IX. 98.

A critic in *Blackwood's* probably had the proverb as much in mind as the play when he wrote in 1817 that the catastrophe of Lord Byron's *Manfred* was "somewhat too much in the style of the Devil and Dr Faustus." [132]

GOETHE

The most important influence exerted by Marlowe's *Doctor Faustus* was probably upon the mind of Goethe, to whom it seems to have suggested parts at least of his own most famous work — a rare instance of one master-work influencing another. The exact nature of this relationship is in some dispute, but there is no question that a direct relationship of some kind exists, and the preponderance of evidence indicates that it is fairly close.

Faust occupied Goethe during a large part of his working life, and has been called a record of his spiritual development. He first became interested in the story in 1770 and worked on it while he was also working on *Götz von Berlichingen*. The latter, published in 1773, was followed the next year by *Werther*. In 1775 *Faust* had reached the stage represented by the so-called Göchhausen Transcript, or *Urfaust*, discovered in 1887 by Erich Schmidt, editor of *Faust* in the Weimar edition. It was in the possession of Major von Göchhausen, among papers that had descended in his family, containing odds and ends from various writers, including Ossian and Shakespeare. The complete version represented by the *Urfaust* was unlike any other surviving.[133] As it is known that Goethe did no work on *Faust* between 1776 and 1786, this manuscript is supposed to represent the state of his work on his removal from Frankfurt to Weimar. It must date from 1775. This version is closer to Marlowe's than any other — so close structurally that it is hard to imagine the two plays to be without a relation of some kind.

Later, in 1790, Goethe published *Faust: A Fragment*, in some two thousand lines of verse. This was followed in 1808 by *Faust: A Tragedy*, in 4,700 lines. In 1832, immediately after his death, a second five-act drama, almost twice as long as the first part, was published as the *Second Part of Faust*.

---

[132] *Blackwood's*, 1: 295 Je 1817. But see I. 323–325 of the present work.
[133] Cf. R. McLintock: *Goethe's Faust*, pp. xii ff. and n.

Before Goethe touched it, Faust as a dramatic subject had suffered the same degeneration in Germany as in England. It was a popular puppet play and little more. Goethe was certainly familiar with these marionette shows. No German, indeed, could very well fail to be so acquainted. Moreover, they were actually being performed at Strassburg and Leipzig, as he himself specifically mentions.[134] Some critics have therefore tried to show that these plays were the sole sources of his *Faust*.

Even if this were true, however, there would still remain a single frail link connecting the two great Faust dramas; for the German puppet plays themselves are by some scholars attributed to the indirect influence of Marlowe's *Faustus*, carried back to its German homeland by wandering English players, and then imitated by the puppet-masters. Probability favors this theory, so attractive to English-speaking scholars, especially since at least two German princes, the Duke of Brunswick and the Landgraf of Hesse, are known to have been patrons of English companies before 1600, when *Doctor Faustus* was still a new play at the height of its popularity.[135]

These German puppet plays fall into four main groups: the Ulmer Spiel; the Augsburger Spiel (including versions associated with Augsburg, Strassburg, Leipzig, Weimar, and Oldenburg); the Berliner and Niederoestreichischer Spiel; and the Kölner Spiel. A fifth Bohemian version is even closer to the Faust story as Marlowe tells it.[136]

A direct connection between Marlowe's work and Goethe can, however, be made very probable, though entirely satisfactory proof is lacking. Different in tone and feeling though the two plays may be, they nevertheless exhibit a distinct similarity in structure and sometimes in phrasing. Their structural likeness becomes especially clear when plot summaries are placed side by side. Goethe's plot is very close indeed to Marlowe's in

---

[134] *Dichtung und Wahrheit* (Weimar ed.), Bk. X. I. xxvii, 321; *Kunst und Altertum* (Weimar ed.), II. XLI; pp. 290–292 in the article, "Helena, Zwischenspiel zu Faust"; Letters to W. von Humboldt and Sulpia Boisserée, October 22, 1826, IV. XLI, p. 202.

[135] R. McLintock, *op. cit.*, p. xx; Erich Schmidt: "Deutsche Litteratur im Elsass," [Schnorr's] *Archiv f. Litteraturgeschichte*, 8: 359–360 (1879); W. Creizenach: *Versuch einer Geschichte des Volksschauspiels vom Doctor Faust*, pp. 45–46, 182.

[136] Otto Heller: *Faust and Faustus*, pp. 131–132.

the beginning, and becomes more and more independent only as he introduces new material and his own conceptions develop.

The chief difference is that Goethe develops the Marguerite story, already hinted at in the *Faustbuch* and earlier accounts; while Marlowe has, as usual, relatively little interest in romantic love.

Not only is there thus marked structural resemblance between the two plays, but there are also in Goethe's version a number of those telltale echoes which so frequently betray a poet's use of sources. Most of these appear in the *Urfaust* and run through the later versions. Highly significant is the opening monologue on the vanity of learning (known in Germany as the *Fakultätenschau*), which appears neither in the Faust books nor in the puppet plays, but which does appear in both Marlowe and Goethe. In this opening passage, both poets ridicule jurisprudence and both extol medical skill.[137] There are various parallels. Marlowe's Faustus exclaims:

> This night Ile coniure though I die therefore. [195]

Goethe's Faust soliloquizes:

> Du musst! du musst! und kostet' es mein Leben!
> [F 481, Fgt 128, Urf 128]

Marlowe's Faustus greets Lucifer, master of Mephistophilis:

> O who art thou that lookst so terrible? [699]

Goethe's Faust greets the Erdgeist, also master of Mephistophilis:

> Schreckliches Gesicht! [F 482, Fgt 129, Urf 130]

It is, to be sure, a natural way to greet the Devil, but the parallel becomes more striking when we find that the magical formulae are also much the same in both. Mephistophilis reports for duty with the same airy insolence in both plays. Marlowe's devil begins:

> Now *Faustus*, what wouldst thou haue me do? [270]

Goethe makes his devil say:

> Wozu der Lärm? was steht dem Herrn zu Diensten? [F 1322]

[137] Otto Heller, *op. cit.*, pp. 51 ff.; James Taft Hatfield in JEGP, 24: 450 (1925).

Marlowe's Faustus is careful to bid Mephistophilis three times to come — three being a magic number.

> ... come *Mephastophilus,*
> *Veni, veni Mephastophile.* [460–461]

When Faust cries, "Herein!" Goethe's Devil explains:

> Du musst es dreimal sagen. [F 1533]

Sometimes Goethe seems to be practically translating Marlowe, as in the following passages:

> That I shal waite on Faustus whilst he liues. [DF 463]
> Ich will mich *hier* zu deinem Dienst verbinden. [F 1656]

> And write a deede of gift with thine owne blood. [467]
> Du unterzeichnest dich mit einem Tröpfchen Blut. [F 1737]

> And *binde* thy soule, that at some certaine *day.* [482]
> *Verbinde* dich; du sollst, in diesen *Tagen.* [F 1672]

> This word damnation terrifies not him. [294]
> Das Drüben kann mich wenig kümmern. [F 1660]

> Yet art thou still but *Faustus*, and a man. [51]
> Du bist am Ende — was du bist. [F 1806]

Deliberate and admitted verse translation is often no closer to its original than this.

Even more convincing, however, is the spiritual similarity of the main characters. To both poets, Faust and his tempter are tragic figures charged with a profound symbolism. In the Faust books and the puppet plays, on the other hand, one is a cheapjack mountebank, and the other the seriocomic Devil of the miracle and morality plays.

It is, furthermore, perfectly established that Goethe was acquainted with Marlowe's play in the latter part of his life, though it is true that none of Marlowe's works appeared in his library after his death. Goethe's best-known allusion to *Doctor Faustus* is his remark to Henry Crabb Robinson (1775-1867), which is quoted in Robinson's *Diary* in 1829:

I mentioned Marlowe's "Faust" [*sic*]. He burst out into an exclamation of praise. "How greatly is it all planned!" He had thought of translating it. He was fully aware that Shakespeare did not stand alone.[138]

Unfortunately, this is twenty-one years after the publication of the First Part of *Faust* and does not prove that Goethe was acquainted with Marlowe's version of the story while working on his own.

There is, however, abundant reason for believing that this is actually the case. It is, in the first place, very probable in itself. Like most German writers of the *Sturm und Drang* period, Goethe had a lively interest in English literature, and *Werther* abounds in allusions to English authors. The youthful Ludwig Tieck had begun translation from the English as early as 1791 and was occupied with the Elizabethans from 1791 onward.[139]

As early as 1799 Goethe had interested himself in the Elizabethan drama. In 1800 A. W. Schlegel writes him casually, as if dealing with a familiar theme: "Die Stücke von Sh.'s berühmtesten Vorgängern, Marlowe, Heywood, Lilly, seyn so schlecht und unkünstlich," and refers to Dodsley's collection of plays.[140] How, under the circumstances, Goethe could have missed *Doctor Faustus* it is hard to imagine.

There is an additional bit of evidence to show that Goethe at least knew about Marlowe's play, though here again the date is later than the publication of the First Part of *Faust*. There is a casual allusion in Goethe's diary, dated June 11, 1818:

> 11. Früh spazieren gegangen. Anfang der Translocation der Bibliotheken. Hofmedicus Rehbein. *Vimariensia*. War der Kleine inoculiert worden. Dr. Faust von Marlowe. Rehbein zu Tische. . . .[141]

This must have been the translation "des altenglischen Faust"[142] which L. Achim von Arnim says, in a letter of

---

[138] Cf. *Diary* (Macmillan, 1869), August 2, 1829, II. 434, and Eckermann's *Goethe Gespräche*, VII. 108, August 2, 1829.

[139] Edwin Hermann Zeydel: "Ludwig Tieck as a Translator," PMLA, 51: 221–242 (1936).

[140] A. W. Schlegel to Goethe, January 7, 1800, in Carl Schüddekopf and Oskar Walzel: *Goethe und die Romantik. Briefe mit Erläuterungen*, no. 37, I. 60. (Schriften der Goethe-Gesellschaft, 1899.)

[141] *Tagebücher. Goethes Werke* (Weimar ed., 1894), III. Abth. 6. Band, p. 215.

[142] L. Achim von Arnim to Goethe, May 20, 1818. Carl Schüddekopf and Oskar Walzel, *op. cit.*, no. 14, II. 155.

May 20, 1818, he is sending to Goethe — presumably Wilhelm Müller's recent version.

Goethe evidently sent the book on to Charlotte von Schiller, widow of the poet, who wrote him on "Freytag Abend," sometime in the "Anfang Juni 1818," about a book — obviously *Doctor Faustus* — which she had received from him and which had much delighted her:

Sie haben mir ein recht seltsames Werck gesendet, es hat mich äuserst beschäftigt, und das Alter des Stücks, wie der wunderbare Gang der Begebenheiten, sind sehr merckwürdig. Da ich so nahe am Paradiese [i.e., the "Paradise" on the River Saale] wohne, so habe ich durch dieses Werck auf eine wunderbare Art die Sieben Todt Sünden kennen lernen sollen, durch ihr Erscheinen in dieser Poesie, und hoffe sie sind deswegen nicht in mein Gemüth eingedrungen.[143]

As June 5, 1818, was Friday, it is evident that the letter was written then. When Goethe made his entry in the diary, he was still thinking, six days later, of the book he had presented to Frau von Schiller, which from her description can only have been *Doctor Faustus*. Presumably this is why no copy of Marlowe's play was found in his library.[144] Goethe had given his copy away. Was he willing to part with it because the First Part of *Faust* had been published? If so, may he not have known it for a long time?

Copies of Marlowe's works were at this time hard books to get. Oxberry's reprint, the first since 1663, appeared in this very year. If Goethe had read *Doctor Faustus* in English, he must have read one of the quartos, since no other editions existed.

This is not so impossible as it sounds. If the 1628 quarto of *Faustus* could reach Sweden and if the only known copies of the 1594 *Edward the Second* are in Cassel and Zürich, it ought not to have been impossible for the director of the Court Theatre at Weimar to get one of these books, which were not then of any great value.

Eckermann mentions a conversation with Goethe on January 2, 1824, in which the German Boswell referred to Jonson,

---

[143] "Mittheilungen aus dem Goethearchiv. ... VI. Briefe von Charlotte von Schiller," *Goethe-Jahrb.*, 8: 47 (1887), Letter no. 36. See note by L. Geiger, p. 112.

[144] Heller, *op. cit.*, p. 19. See also p. 15, and Erich Schmidt, *loc. cit.*

Massinger, Marlowe, Beaumont and Fletcher as having provided a background for Shakespeare's genius. Goethe replied: "Sie haben vollkommen recht." Again, Goethe's letter to Schiller on December 6, 1799, shows that he had been reading Edmund Malone's "Attempt to Ascertain the Order in which the Plays of Shakespeare were Written," which abounds in references to Marlowe.[145]

There is a third bit of evidence, hitherto overlooked, which also suggests Goethe's special interest in Marlowe. His friend Gottfried Körner, sending news of Goethe to Schiller from Leipzig, May 29, 1796, wrote: "Auf Hero und Leander sind wir äusserst gespannt." [146] This was in reply to a letter from Schiller, dated May 23, 1796, and written after a visit to Goethe. In this Schiller remarked: "Hero und Leander hat er noch nicht angefangen." [147]

This clearly refers to some literary project which Goethe had in mind but abandoned. The subject, in view of Goethe's classical interests, is not surprising; yet for present purposes it is highly significant. Considering the limited number of Marlowe's titles, it is certainly interesting to find Goethe hitting upon two of them, especially as these letters were written while *Faust*, still unfinished, was very much in his mind. Comments on *Doctor Faustus* by Sir Walter Scott, whose work Goethe knew, were published about this time and may have helped draw his attention to the play.[148] It seems scarcely probable that Goethe was influenced by Calderón's *El mágico prodigioso*, or that Calderón owed anything to Marlowe.

To sum up, then, we may say that Goethe probably, but not certainly, was influenced by Marlowe's *Doctor Faustus*. This is plausible because Goethe's play shows similarities; because Goethe had a general familiarity with Elizabethan literature; because Schlegel was writing casually to him about Marlowe long before the 1808 *Faust*; because Goethe later specifically mentions *Doctor Faustus*; and because he seems also to have

---

[145] *Goethes Briefe. Goethes Werke* (Weimar ed., 1893), IV. Abth. 4. Band, p. 232. See also Heller, *op. cit.*, p. 17.

[146] *Goethe-Jahrb.*, 8: 54 (1887), Letter no. 43.

[147] *Schillers Briefe* (ed. Fritz Jonas), IV. 451, Letter no. 1038; Gaedeke's ed., II. 42.

[148] "Essay on the Drama," *Misc. Prose Works*, VI. 251; Lockhart: *Memoir*, I. 244 (chap. VIII).

been interested in the story of Hero and Leander, again indicating familiarity with one of Marlowe's subjects.

BYRON'S MANFRED

The close resemblances between Lord Byron's *Manfred* and
Doctor Faustus were noted as soon as Byron's poem reached
the reviewers. Like Faustus, Manfred is a necromancer, raises
spirits in his study, discusses the exact form in which the spirits
shall appear to him, seeks forbidden knowledge, laments the
vanity of learning, raises Astarte (instead of Helen) from the
dead, is obdurate to the entreaties of the Abbot who seeks to
reclaim him (and who replaces the Old Man and the Good
Angel who plead with Marlowe's Faustus), and — in a final
scene — dies as the evil spirits come for him.

In *Blackwood's* for July, 1817, Henry Maitland wrote an
article on *Doctor Faustus*, in which he commented on "the general resemblance of its subject to that of Lord Byron's last
poem," and after describing some of Marlowe's more striking
scenes raised the question "whether Lord Byron had them, or
had them not, in his mind during the composition of some passages of Manfred." [149] Finally, he suggested that "excessive
admiration is bestowed on *one* great living Poet"; and that
"there are so many glorious works of the mighty dead, unknown
or disregarded — works from which that illustrious person has
doubtless imbibed inspiration, and which, without detracting
from his well-earned fame, we must think are far superior, in
variety, depth, and energy of passion, to the best poems which
his powerful genius has yet produced."

In its August number the *Edinburgh Review* leaped to Byron's
defense:

It is suggested, in an ingenious paper, in a late Number of the Edinburgh Magazine [i.e., *Blackwood's*], that the general conception of
this piece, and much of what is excellent in the manner of its execution, have been borrowed from 'the Tragical History of Dr Faustus' of
Marlow; and a variety of passages are quoted, which the author considers as similar, and, in many respects, superior to others in the poem
before us. We cannot agree in the general terms of this conclusion; —
but there is, no doubt, a certain resemblance, both in some of the

[149] *Blackwood's*, 1: 388–389, 394 Jy 1817.

topics that are suggested, and in the cast of the diction in which they are expressed.[150]

The anonymous critic, whom Byron [151] believed to be Jeffrey himself, then quoted three passages [152] from *Doctor Faustus*, the

> Shadowing more beautie in their ayrie browes

passage, the lines to Helen, and the concluding lines, after which he went on:

But these, and many other smooth and fanciful verses in this curious old drama, prove nothing, we think, against the originality of Manfred; for there is nothing to be found there of the pride, the abstraction, and the heart-rooted misery in which that originality consists. Faustus is a vulgar sorcerer, tempted to sell his soul to the Devil for the ordinary price of sensual pleasure, and earthly power and glory — and who shrinks and shudders in agony when the forfeit comes to be exacted. The style, too, of Marlow, though elegant and scholarlike, is weak and childish compared with the depth and force of much of what we have quoted from Lord Byron.

All of this John Murray duly forwarded to Byron in Italy. His Lordship was extremely emphatic:

I *never read*, and do not know that I ever saw, the *Faustus* of Marlow. . . . As to the *Faustus* of Marlow, I never read, never saw, nor heard of it — at least, thought of it, except that I think Mr. Gifford mentioned, in a note of his which you sent me, something about the catastrophe; but not as having any thing to do with mine, which may or may not resemble it, for anything I know. . . . I deny Marlow and his progeny, and beg that you will do the same.[153]

In another letter Byron wrote: "the devil may take both the Faustuses, German and English, — I have taken neither." He did admit having listened upon one occasion when George Henry Lewes translated orally some scenes from Goethe's *Faust*, but insisted he could point out the exact geographical locale which had inspired his own poem, without recourse to any source book.

[150] *Edinburgh Review*, 28: 430–431 Ag 1817.
[151] Letter to John Murray, October 12, 1817. *Letters and Journal* (ed. R. W. Prothero, later Baron Ernle), IV. 174–175.
[152] *Doctor Faustus*, 156–158; 1328 ff.; 1478 ff.
[153] Letters to John Murray, October 12, 17, 1817. See *Letters and Journal*, IV. 175, 177, 178; Samuel C. Chew: *Dramas of Lord Byron*, p. 174.

Poor Maitland qualified his views in the October *Black-wood's*, explaining that he had never "accused Byron of plagiarism from Marlow," but had merely pointed out "a general resemblance in the subjects." Finally, "that 'Faustus' is, as a composition, very inferior to Manfred, we perfectly agree with the [Edinburgh] Reviewer; for the wavering character of the German magician will not bear comparison for a moment with that of the Princely Wanderer of the Alps: and the mixed, rambling, headlong, and reckless manner of Marlow, in that play, must not be put into competition with the sustained dignity of Byron." [154]

It was a perfect example of abject snobbery.

Oxberry's edition of Marlowe, which appeared about this time, was, for obviously commercial reasons, careful to declare "MARLOW'S FAUSTUS decidedly superior to the 'Manfred' of Lord Byron."

In our own day, a rather dubious trace of *Doctor Faustus* may perhaps be found in Henry Arthur Jones's play, *The Tempter*. There is a conceivable echo of the clock's stroke that heralds the doom of Faustus in the clock scene in W. B. Yeats's *Hour Glass*. In a similar scene in Middleton's *Changeling*, Beatrice had counted the strokes aloud. Yeats keeps this part of his scene in silence. [155]

In *Elizabeth the Queen*, Maxwell Anderson makes Her Majesty exclaim to the doomed Essex:

> I tell you if Christ his blood
> Ran streaming from the heavens for a sign
> That I should hold my hand you'd die for this.

This, the author says, is "a deliberate echo" of Marlowe's

> See see where Christs blood streames in the firmament.

"I supposed Elizabeth to be familiar with Marlowe," Mr. Anderson adds, "and quite likely to use a figure of his to reinforce her meaning." There is a similar oblique quotation of this line in *The Merry Devil of Edmonton*. [156]

---

[154] *Blackwood's*, 2: 30–n O 1817.
[155] W. J. Lawrence: *Those Nut-Cracking Elizabethans*, pp. 89–90.
[156] *Elizabeth the Queen*, p. 166; *Doctor Faustus*, 1432; sig. A4r of the Tudor Facsimile Text (1911) of the *Merry Devil*. Mr. Anderson's comments are from a letter to the author.

The "thousand ships" passage has always been a favorite with modern poets. Edward Robert Bulwer-Lytton ("Owen Meredith"), in his juvenile *Clytemnestra* (1855), uses it twice.[157] In the first passage, Clytemnestra herself remembers a speech by the ghosts of those killed at Troy:

> . . . For such a crime
> A thousand ships were launch'd, and tumbled down
> The topless towers of Ilion, tho' they rose
> To magic music in the time of Gods!

In the second, he misquotes:

> Make me immortal with one costly kiss!

a line chiefly remarkable as an example of the harm a single adjective can do. Stephen Phillips, in his *Marpessa*, has the lines:

> Nor for the face that might indeed provoke
> Invasion of old cities.[158]

In Brian Hooker's translation of Edmond Rostand's *Cyrano de Bergerac*, which was produced by Walter Hampden, the "thousand ships" passage is adroitly slipped into Cyrano's speech on his nose, replacing an allusion to Théophile de Viau's *Amours tragiques de Pyrame et Thisbé*, which would have meant nothing to an English-speaking audience:

> Or — parodying Faustus in the play —
> "Was this the nose that launched a thousand ships
> And burned the topless towers of Ilium?" [159]

— a grotesque conclusion to two hundred and fifty years of literary influence!

Thus the Faust epic, beginning dimly amid the legends and realities of the Greco-Roman world, scarcely distinguishable now from one another, is passed down the centuries. The legends connect themselves dimly with the name of some charlatan or impostor of the early German Renaissance. They pass thus into popular tales. Thence they find their way to the mind

[157] *Clytemnestra, The Earl's Return, The Artist, and Other Poems* (London: Chapman and Hall, 1855), pp. 4–5, 47. Copy in HCL.
[158] Ed. of 1901, p. 24.
[159] Page 41.

of Christopher Marlowe, and from his mind in some mysterious way provide an impulse to the mind of Goethe, and perhaps — in spite of his denials — to the mind of Byron. A tale gradually built up over a period of some fifteen hundred years has finally produced one of the great dramas of English literature and a national monument of German letters.

CHAPTER IX

THE JEW OF MALTA

> . . . *All the golden Mines,*
> *Inestimable drugs and precious stones,*
> *More worth than* ASIA.
>
> II *Tamburlaine,* 4544–4546

THE *JEW OF MALTA* is not a great play, for it lacks almost, though not quite, all the ingredients of greatness. It is not even a good play; for, breaking squarely in two in the middle, it lacks even the saving virtue of unity. It is, indeed, not so much a play at all as the great beginning of a play, or the remnant of a play that once was great.

Yet, with all its ill qualities thick upon it, the *Jew* has a fascination peculiarly its own. None of Marlowe's other works is so closely bound up with the life and works of the great businessman of Stratford. Elsewhere the relation of Marlowe to Shakespeare is largely a matter of reasonable inference and plausible conjecture; but there is no shadow of doubt that *The Merchant of Venice* emerges directly from *The Jew of Malta*, and that, if there had been no Barabas, there would hardly have been a Shylock.

Then, too, the *Jew* has all the lure of mystery. There is no room for doubt that the first two acts are mainly Marlowe's. But who has been tampering with the rest? Who is the author of the extraordinary farrago that hustles the play to its ridiculous, though highly Elizabethan, conclusion? No man knows.

Finally, *The Jew of Malta* is not an obscure play or a stage failure, but one of the most brilliant successes of its time; a play much clapper-claw'd by the vulgar, it is true, but a play that royalty also applauded; a play that refused to be driven from the boards even when Shakespeare had reworked most of its essentials in *The Merchant of Venice*; a play based upon historical events — though heaven alone knows exactly what those historical events may have been — and called back to popular attention by nothing less than a court scandal.

Such, then, is *The Jew of Malta*: a wretched work shot through with genius, the standing puzzle of the English stage, and the inspiration of the greatest poet that ever set pen to paper, Shakespeare himself.

DATE

Marlowe probably wrote *The Jew of Malta* some time in the year 1589 or 1590. As usual, we cannot be sure of the date, but this guess seems rather better than most for a variety of reasons. There are two bits of concrete evidence. One is an entry in that quaint and invaluable document, *Henslowe's Diary*:[1]

ß at the Jewe of malltuse the 26 of febrearye 1591 [i.e., 1592] ... l[s]

As Henslowe fails to put his customary "ne" opposite this entry, we may conclude that this is an old play which had already been produced before the *Diary* was opened in 1591. The second, and less certain, clue appears in the third line of the prologue —

And now the *Guize* is dead ...

— a reference to the assassination of the Duke of Guise on December 23, 1588, not long after Marlowe had returned from his secret mission, whatever it was, as an agent of the English government.

Though plays and their prologues are not invariably written at the same time, there is good reason for believing that this play and its prologue must have been written fairly close together. There had been, at most, but four years between Marlowe's leaving the university and Henslowe's note. Marlowe had written two other plays — really three, since *Tamburlaine* is in two parts — and his leisure for turning out still another before 1590 would have been very scanty. We may assume, then, that the *Jew* was finished some time toward the end of 1589 or early in 1590;[2] and that the rising young drama-

---

[1] Henslowe is using a small *l* for the Roman *L*. In other words, he took in fifty shillings. Greg's ed., I. 13.

[2] There is unusual agreement as to the date of this play. The most important suggestions are:

1831. Collier: "Probably written about 1589 or 1590." [HEDP, III. 135]

tist, with two successes already to his credit, found the canny Henslowe ready to accept it and Lord Strange's men glad enough to produce it — probably at the Cross Keyes Inn in Grace Church Street, in which they were playing about this time.[3]

Shakespeare may have joined this very company a few months before this time; though, to believe that, we must accept the theory that he had joined the Earl of Leicester's players when they visited Stratford in 1586/7, and that he was among the men from Leicester's Company who in 1588 joined Lord Strange's men, the company with which, under its various changes of name, we find him connected until his retirement from the stage.[4]

AUTHORSHIP

While there is no doubt that Marlowe wrote the original form of *The Jew of Malta*, the play has been badly mangled, and

1850. Dyce: "Composed after 23rd Dec. 1588." [I. xx]

1870. Cunningham: "Mr. Collier considers that *The Jew of Malta* was written in 1589 or 1590, and on such a point the opinion of no other man is of equal weight." [p. xv]

1880. A. C. Bradley: "Probably in 1589 or 1590." [Ward's *English Poets*, I. 411]

1885. Bullen: "Not earlier than December 1588." [I. xxxix]

1887. Faligan: "Scriptum et actum fuisse . . . (1589) vel anno sequente videtur." [*De Marlovianis Fabulis*, p. 164]

1888. Wagner: "Wir können . . . nur behaupten, dass dieser Prolog nach dem 23. Dezember 1588 geschrieben ist: das Stück selbst kann früher verfasst sein." [p. iv]

1899. Ward: "The third of Marlowe's tragedies." [HEDL, I. 338]

1908. W. W. Greg: "Soon after 23 Dec. 1588." [Greg's Henslowe, II. 151]

1909. Lewis Perry: "Edward Alleyn played the part of Barabas in London, in the year of our Lord 1590." [Williams College ed., p. xviii]

1910. Brooke: "The year 1590 cannot be far wrong." [*Works*, p. 230]

1912. Phelps: "No one knows when it was written." [p. 15]

1922. Brooke: "Composition in 1589 would best suit this allusion [to the death of Guise], and would best explain the violence of the plot which *The Jew of Malta* shares with *Tamburlaine*." [PMLA, 37: 384–385 (1922)]

1923. Chambers: "Date of performance later than 23 Dec. 1588." [*Eliz. Stage*, III. 424]

1927. Ellis-Fermor: "Probably written in 1589 or 1590, but we have few means of judging." [*Christopher Marlowe*, p. 5]

1931. H. S. Bennett: "*Tamburlaine* was written by 1588, and there seems nothing to gainsay our placing *The Jew* in the next year, or very shortly after." [p. 5]

1936. Rupert Taylor: "Some time in 1590." [PMLA, 51: 659]

[3] E. K. Chambers: *Eliz. Stage*, III. 424–425; Fleay: *Chron. Hist. . . . London Stage*, II. 61.

[4] John Tucker Murray: *English Dramatic Companies*, I. 36, 75; J. Q. Adams: *Life of Shakespeare*, pp. 130–131.

there is some doubt how much of its latter half is really his. Thomas Heywood's revival under Charles I is presumably responsible for this; and there is good reason to suppose that Heywood himself was the adapter. As the play exists only in the edition of 1633, there is no opportunity to improve the text by comparing editions.

On May 14, 1594, while *The Jew of Malta* was at the height of its popularity, the enterprising publisher, John Danter, entered in the *Stationers' Register* "a ballad intituled *the murtherous life and terrible death of the riche Jew of Malta.*" The next day Nicholas Linge and Thomas Millington entered for publication a copy of the play itself; but of the edition thus proposed not a single copy has ever come down to us, a melancholy fact over which many a bibliophile's tears have fallen. They may have fallen in vain, however, for it is quite possible that the edition never appeared at all, a protest from Henslowe or the actors sufficing, perhaps, to prevent publication of a play which was still a valuable stage property.

Heywood refers to the 1633 edition, in the dedication, as "newly brought to the Presse." This would normally indicate a reprint, but not necessarily so, for the first edition of *Tamburlaine* is also described as "Now first, and newlie published."

If *The Jew* was never printed until 1633, the playhouse parts must have lain about unnoticed for nearly forty years; and Heywood, as he set about preparing the old play for his up-to-date seventeenth-century audience at the court of Charles I, may well have felt justified in taking liberties with the quaint text of an earlier day. Scruples over altering the handiwork of a great genius meant no more to him than to some modern editors.

Whether Heywood or some earlier and now forgotten predecessor is to blame, liberties someone has certainly been taking. *The Jew of Malta*, as we now have it, splits fairly in two at the beginning of the third act. The play opens greatly, with the unforgettable soliloquy of Barabas, alone in his counting-house, and moves swiftly and evenly through acts one and two, with many passages that are authentically great verse, written with the ease and consistent skill of a young dramatist who had by this time won his spurs. The plot itself may be the typical blood-and-thunder of the Elizabethan stage; but the plot is merely the raw material which Marlowe has fused to poetry and drama at the point of a brilliant pen.

Then suddenly the poetry is gone. The greatly conceived character of a human and credibly wicked miser has vanished, none knows whither; and in its place we have a conventional villain, a miserable farrago of scarecrow corpses, the bungling comic relief afforded by a whore and a blackamoor, and the banal stage convention of promiscuous slaughter. This is obviously not Marlowe's, or so we are tempted to declare. But to say that every passage which falls below one's private conception of a genius's best must be denied his authorship is a little too easy a method of literary criticism, numerous and famous though the critics be who have practised it.

The argument for the initial authorship of *The Jew of Malta* by Marlowe is fairly simple. Contemporary sources repeatedly assign it to him, and there is not much doubt that his handiwork runs through it from end to end. It is not likely that he wrote half a play — nor is it likely, on the other hand, that the players who bought his manuscript were charily respectful of an author's rights, or hesitated to alter at their own good pleasure.

Many passages scattered here and there through the latter, inferior portions of the play have the right Marlowe ring about them — the vivid, passionate touch that none may imitate or counterfeit. Barabas' outburst against his unfilial daughter, for example,

> Oh vnhappy day,
> False, credulous, inconstant *Abigall*!
> But let 'em goe: And *Ithimore*, from hence
> Ne're shall she grieue me more with her disgrace;
> Ne're shall she liue to inherit ought of mine,
> Be blest of me, nor come within my gates,
> But perish vnderneath my bitter curse
> Like *Cain* by *Adam*, for his brother's death,[5]

was written by Christopher Marlowe — and by no other man who ever trod the stage or the planet.

Other passages of equal brilliance occur here and there to the end of the play, very like gold nuggets in the sands of well-used

[5] Ll. 1328–1335.

metaphor. One such passage is of especial interest because in it Marlowe, not for the first time, parodies, or at least echoes, his own most famous lyric:

> Content, but we will leaue this paltry land,
> And saile from hence to *Greece*, to louely *Greece*,
> I'le be thy *Iason*, thou my golden Fleece;
> Where painted Carpets o're the meads are hurl'd,
> And *Bacchus* vineyards ore-spread the world:
> Where Woods and Forrests goe in goodly greene,
> I'le be *Adonis*, thou shalt be Loues Queene.
> The Meads, the Orchards, and the Primrose lanes,
> Instead of Sedge and Reed, beare Sugar Canes:
> Thou in those Groues, by *Dis* aboue,
> Shalt liue with me and be my loue.[6]

The famous passage had been running in Marlowe's head for some time before he gave it final form in "The Passionate Shepherd." It is obvious and authentic Marlowe, yet it appears in the fourth act in a setting which is very doubtfully his.

Marlowe's lack of all save a very grim sense of humor, a quality which is as clearly marked as his characteristic intensity and violence, suggests that he may even have had rather more to do with the grotesque efforts at humor in the latter half of the play than critics generally give him credit for. These humorous scenes are not very funny, at best; but they mark a slight advance on the vague clowning that appears here and there in *Tamburlaine* and *Doctor Faustus* — presumably an effort on Marlowe's part to provide the comic relief that the actors wanted, even though he was temperamentally unsuited to provide it. On the other hand, this element in *The Jew of Malta* may be interpolation by Heywood or some other hack, as many critics think. A genius forcing himself into a vein not naturally his own and a pure stage hack trying solely to please the Elizabethan mob might easily write very much alike.

Even the falling off in pure poetry in the latter part of *The Jew of Malta* is not by any means proof that Marlowe did not himself write the play from end to end, essentially as it has come down to us. Brave beginnings and botched endings are no novelty in dramatic literature; nor was Christopher Marlowe a sober, workaday youth whose methods of creation showed any-

[6] Ll. 1806–1816. For other parallels, see II. 153–160.

thing resembling exemplary regularity. If we assume careful
and painstaking writing at the beginning of the play, and hasty
writing under pressure to finish it in time to meet the theatre's
demands, toward the end — with a good deal of strong drink
between times — we shall assume nothing inherently improbable; and we shall account beautifully for every line, good or
bad, of *The Jew of Malta* as it now exists.

Later, of course, Heywood may have helped matters along
with a few touches of his own, meant to improve and modernize,
but in actual fact nicely calculated to mar the play. No one can
work such infinite havoc in a little room as your thoroughgoing
modernizer.

SOURCES

The doubt about the authorship of *The Jew of Malta* adds a
complexity to its source material, since it is quite possible that
the reviser added material to that already employed by Marlowe. No one satisfactory source for the entire play has ever
been made out. Probably none exists.

The historical event on which the play is ostensibly based is
the siege of Malta in 1565, one year after the dramatist who
was to immortalize it had been born. Other details seem to come
in a general way from various incidents of the long wars waged
against the infidel by the Knights of Malta, also known as the
Knights of St. John and the Knights Hospitalers. Marlowe
seems to have borrowed suggestions from the lives of two quite
real Mediterranean adventurers, the Portuguese Jew João
Miques, also known as Joseph Nassi, and a certain David
Passi, and perhaps from one or two others. He borrowed also
from various books of travels; and his subplot bears a suspicious resemblance to episodes in Thomas Heywood's *The
Captives*. This is the material most likely to have been introduced by Heywood during his revision of 1633.

History, however, furnishes the groundwork for the play.
Europe, with very good reason, had taken an anxious interest
in the exploits of the Turkish armies, which, under the great
Sultan Solyman the Magnificent, had been victorious from
Aden and Baghdad to the gates of Vienna. In 1522 the Knights
of St. John had been driven out of Rhodes. The Turkish attack

on Malta in 1565, if successful, would have given the infidel a
naval base from which to conduct operations in the two halves
of the Mediterranean — precisely the use to which the modern
British navy put the island until the airplane made it difficult.

The breathless interest with which all Europe watched the
siege is reflected in the little newsbooks that took the place now
filled by newspapers and gave the general public its only tidings. The earliest of these pamphlets were naturally published
in Italy, where the news was first received; but the speed with
which they reappeared in French, German, Dutch, and English
editions is mute evidence of the agonized anxiety all Europe
felt.[7]

Distribution of important news by these means had begun
soon after the introduction of printing and was by this time
a well-established practice. Thus in August, 1565, while the
siege was still in progress, we find a tiny booklet of four and a
half pages, less than the length of a modern newspaper column:
Vltimi Avisi Venuti da Messina circa la Impresa di Malta. A
similar brochure at Naples bears the title *Discorso sopra le cose
de lisola di Malta.* In the Low Countries appeared a strange
little blackletter newsbook, *Een sekere ende warachtighe goede
nyeuse tijdinghe van het Eylant van Malta.* In Nurnberg there
was a *Kurtzer ausszug der geschichten so sich zugetragen haben
mit kriegsübung vnnd belegerung der Insul Malta.* This was
written at Malta itself, on September 24, 1565, just after the
Turkish defeat, by one Martin Croua, who surely deserves an
humble niche in the history of war correspondence. English
interest was lively enough to induce a London printer, Thomas
Marshe, to expend fourpence for "his lycense for pryntinge of a
boke intituled *the tru Copye of the laste advertismente that cam
from Malta,*" written within a few months of the siege.[8]

After the war was over, in very modern fashion, came a flood
of war books. A catalogue of the library of the Knights of St.

---

[7] Cf. Matthias A. Shaaber: *Some Forerunners of the Newspaper in England*; Lucy
Maynard Salmon: *Newspaper and Authority*; Margaret Bingham Stillwell: *Incunabula
and Americana: 1450–1800.* News of the discovery of America was reported in this way
within five years in seventeen editions and in four languages.

[8] Arber's reprint, I. 301. The London printer, Thomas Marshe, must not be confused with the Yorkshire printer of the same name. See E. Gordon Duff: *Century of the
English Book Trade*, p. 100; R. B. McKerrow: *Dictionary of Printers and Booksellers*,
p. 187.

John, published in 1781,[9] lists a dozen or more such volumes, written in Italian, English, Latin, French, and German, all of which were published in Marlowe's lifetime. Marlowe, however, seems to have chosen for the most part to ignore these works, though as he probably used the newsbooks for *The Massacre at Paris* [10] he may also have glanced through a few of them, if any survived in libraries accessible to him.

Though Marlowe bases his play upon history, he departs from its facts with a truly Elizabethan freedom. The Turks of sober history were not victorious and did not capture Malta, as in the play. The "historical" figures whom Marlowe introduces are mostly wrong. The gallant La Valette of history never appears, but is replaced by a governor named [11] Ferneze, who cannot be identified with any known historical figure. The Turkish general Selim — later Sultan Selim II — did not direct the siege in person, and his name was not Selim Calymath, as the dramatist asks us to believe. Nassi and Passi, the supposed originals of Barabas, had little or nothing to do with Malta.

In short, Marlowe was not writing a play on the siege of Malta as it actually occurred, but was basing his work on a combination of several picturesque bits of Mediterranean history.

The "Originals" of Barabas

There is nothing to guide us as to the origin of Barabas — one of Marlowe's most successful characterizations and the source of Shakespeare's Shylock — beyond a certain vague similarity between his stage adventures and the careers of two Jewish adventurers who played disreputable but exciting parts in Near Eastern politics during the sixteenth century.

The first candidate for the ungrateful role of Marlowe's hero-villain was proposed in 1886 by the Austrian scholar, Leon Kellner, who felt so sure of his ground as to venture the assertion: "Der 'Jew of Malta' ist fast ein historisches drama." [12]

---

[9] *Catalogo della biblioteca del sagro militar ordine di S. Giovanni Gerosolimitano oggi detto di Malta*. Compilato da Fra Francesco Paolo de Smitmer.

[10] See II. 73–77.

[11] See I. 345–346.

[12] "Die Quelle von Marlowe's 'Jew of Malta,'" ES, 10: 85 (1886).

MARLOWE'S ROOM, CORPUS CHRISTI COLLEGE, CAMBRIDGE

The historical original suggested by Kellner was the Portuguese Jew, João Miques — a name Latinized as Johannes Michesius or Miches — who headed the emigration of a band of some five hundred Jews from Italy to Constantinople in 1555. This talented rogue became a confidential adviser to the Sultan; and when Selim II ascended the throne of Turkey — to win for himself the title of "Selim the Sot" — João Miques was made Duke of Naxos and the Cyclades, exchanging his former Christian name for the Jewish name of Joseph Nassi.[13] His career, according to Kellner, presents three striking similarities to that of Barabas; and I shall presently suggest not only a fourth point of resemblance but also an avenue whereby knowledge of his career might have reached Marlowe.

The resemblances between the Barabas of Marlowe's play and the Joseph Nassi of history, as pointed out by Kellner, are rather striking. In the first place, Marlowe's Barabas boasts how he

> . . . in the warres 'twixt *France* and *Germanie*,
> Vnder pretence of helping *Charles* the fifth,
> Slew friend and enemy with my stratagems.[14]

The historical Nassi was actually in political and financial relations with the courts of France and Germany, though later unmasked as the enemy of both.

In the second place, Marlowe's Barabas, in the famous "infinite riches in a little roome" soliloquy which opens the play, boasts of the range of his commercial dealings — with Persia, Uzz, Spain, Greece, Egypt, Arabia, and half the world besides.[15] The historical Nassi had similarly wide commercial relations and on such a scale that the French government at one time owed him 150,000 ducats.[16]

In the third place, Marlowe's Barabas, in league with the Turks, becomes the Jewish governor of a Christian island — a sufficiently remarkable event in the sixteenth century. Nassi not only governed Naxos, but even kept a crown and royal banner conveniently at hand, firmly believing that he would

---

[13] For a more favorable estimate of Nassi, see H. Graetz: *History of the Jews*, vol. IV, chaps. 16 and 17.

[14] Ll. 952–954.

[15] Ll. 36–83.   [16] Graetz, *op. cit.*, p. 595.

eventually be made king of Cyprus.[17] He died a natural death in 1579, not a violent death like that of Barabas; but the discrepancy need not prevent his being regarded as the prototype of Marlowe's villainous hero. Almost any Elizabethan dramatist would, in any case, have felt it necessary to kill off so base a villain — no matter what the source book said — in order to send the groundlings home in a good humor.

The difficulties with what may be conveniently called the Nassi theory are first that, as Kellner presents it, it accounts at best for no more than the skeleton of the play; and second that there is no book from which Marlowe can be shown to have taken his raw material. Kellner does, indeed, show that one Uberto Foglietta gives a cursory description of Nassi in a book called *De Sacro Foedere in Selimum Libri Quattuor* [18] and that there is further allusion to him in *De Bello Belgico*, by the Jesuit Famiano Strada.[19] The first description, however, is incomplete, and the latter was written after Marlowe's death.

There were, however, innumerable other references to this international busybody, which Kellner fails to note.[20] These ultimately made him widely, if not favorably, known. There is a reference to him in the *De Bello Cyprio Libri Tres*, by Joannis Antonius Guarnerius,[21] which almost falls within Marlowe's lifetime and which brings us a step nearer to Marlowe's wealthy Barabas by referring to Nassi as "vir prædiues." We hear the same account of Nassi in 1624 — much too late, alas, to be a source — in Antonio Maria Graziani's *De Bello Cyprio Libri Quinque*,[22] which dwells on the wealth and the influence at court which Nassi gained by "prædiuitis fœminæ nuptijs."

Here, then, is a fourth point of resemblance between the historical Nassi and the histrionic Barabas, whose immense wealth Marlowe emphasizes throughout the play — an example which Shakespeare followed in characterizing Shylock. Marlowe never could have read either the book by Guarnerius or that by Graziani; but their writings are at least evidence that writers of the period were well aware of Nassi's wealth, and that infor-

---

[17] *Ibid.*, p. 600. [18] Pp. 2–3.
[19] I. 240–242, 321.
[20] Kellner is quite mistaken in saying (*loc. cit.*, p. 99) that contemporary authorities passed Nassi over in silence.
[21] Pp. 6a–7. [22] Page 19.

mation of the sort most likely to catch Marlowe's errant fancy
was available to him.

Books on the Near East were almost as abundant then as
now. Any number of volumes in Latin, German, and Italian
dealing with the Turkish wars appeared during the sixteenth
century; and several which were printed within Marlowe's
brief lifetime tell something of Nassi's story. We find him described as a Turkish intelligence agent in Giovanni Pietro
Contarini's history of the war, which was published in Italian
at Venice in 1572, in Latin at Basel in 1573, and in German in
1574.[23] The frequency of editions shows how lively and wide-
spread interest in the wars must have been and how easily
Marlowe could have learned about them. The Latin history of
the war by Pietro Bizari, which was translated into French
by F. de Belleforest and published in Paris in 1573, devotes
several pages to "Ieã Michs grãd ennemy des Venetians,"
who is represented by Belleforest as urging the Sultan to begin hostilities,[24] and as delivering a lengthy harangue on the
desirability of war.

It is abundantly evident, then, that Nassi's career was well-
known in Western Europe. He had dealt directly with the
Venetian, French, Austrian, and Polish governments, as well
as with the Flemish nobility and William of Orange.[25] There
were even poems on "Giosuf Hebreo," and Marlowe might
conceivably have heard all about the rogue from his friends
the Walsinghams, who were intimately in touch with foreign
affairs.

In any case, he could scarcely have missed Contarini's book,
for it was bound up with the second (1584) edition of Philip
Lonicer's two books of *Chronicorum Turcicorum [sic]*, which he
had certainly read while writing *Tamburlaine*.[26] This contains
the following account of Nassi:

Accidit deinde, non longo post tempore, vt Iudæi quidam ex Occidente
Constantinopolin scripserint ad Ioannem Michetem Marranum (quo

[23] *Historia delle cose svccesse dal principio della gverra mossa da Selim Ottomano a' Venetiani.* Copy in HCL.

[24] *Histoire de la gverre qui c'est passee entre les Venitiens et la saincte ligue, contre les Turcs pour l'Isle de Cypre, és années 1570. 1571. & 1572. Faicte en latin par Pierre Bizare, & mise en Françoys par F. de Belleforest.* Copy in HCL.

[25] Graetz, *op. cit.*, IV. 601-602.   [26] See I. 211-212.

nomine vocantur Iudæi, qui vi timoreque aliquo baptizantur) eique
significarunt, Venetorum armamentarium, accenso in pulvere bom-
bardico igni, vna cum multis aliis eorum munitionibus, Idibus
Septembris exustum esse, anno seruatoris nostri M. D. LXIX. &
vrbem ipsam cum tota ditione magna annonae caritate laborare,
vescique eos solo pane ex milio facto. Quibus rebus imperatori nun-
ciatis, Ioannes Miches, qui illi familiaris erat, iamque ipsius cogita-
tiones de Cypri regno intellexerat: hâc commodam occasionem esse,
magnæ huius expeditionis suscipiendæ & rei feliciter gerendæ monuit:
cumque illæ res fama magis magisque confirmaretur, Selymo facile
persuasit, vt quod de Cyprico regno dudum animo conceperat, exequi
conaretur.[27]

There are references to Nassi in two other books, which Marlowe might also have seen, easily enough. One of these is the
Verdadera Relacion[28] of Francisco Balbi de Corregio, which
alludes in passing to "Iuan Miques judio estanto en Con-
stantinopla." The other is François de Belleforest's (1530–
1583) *Cosmographie Universelle,* which twice alludes to Nassi
under the name Miqué, and from which Marlowe had already
taken the incident of Olympia's slaughter of her children, in
Tamburlaine.[29] The first passage runs:

Micqué Iuif homme turbulent. — Cette tempeste apaisee, Selim
homme adonné à ses plaisirs, . . . & vn vray image de Sardanapale,
se tenoit en repos, si vn paillard Iuif nommé Micqué, homme subtil,
rusé & malicieux, ne luy eut proposé, quel gaing il le feroit s'il se ruoit
sur les Chrestiês, veu que touts les plus grands Monarques Latins
estoyent empeschez à accorder & vuider leurs differents aduenuz pour
le fait de la religion: & luy conseilla d'attacher les Venitiens, & leur
oster l'Isle de Chipre, comme des dependances du Royaume &
Soltanie d'Egypte. A quoy Selim presta l'oreille.[30]

Belleforest's second passage gives much the same picture:

Iean Micqué Iuif quel homme. — A cecy fut il poussé par vn meschant
Marran appelé Iean Micqué, Iuif & Espaignol, ou sorty des Iuifs que
iadis Ferdinand chassa d'Espaigne, hôme fin & cauteleux, & lequel
n'auoit laissé Prouince Chrestienne où il ne se fut arresté, car il auoit
demeuré vn long temps à Lyon negotiant en France, puis à Marseille,
de là passa à Rome, visita la Sicile, & puis prit son addresse à Venise,
où il fut fort solicité de se faire Chrestien: mais comme il est cauteleux
& meschant, piqué de haine contre cette Seigneurie, s'en partit lors

---

[27] Tom. II, p. 3; see Ethel Seaton, RES, 5: 390–393 (1929).
[28] Barcelona, 1568, fol. 6.   [29] See I. 209.
[30] II. 580. This work is frequently catalogued under Muenster, Sebastian.

que moins on y pensoit, & garda cette charité en son coeur, iusqu'à tant que se retirant auec les Turcs en Constantinople, il gaigna l'amitié de Selim, & son pere estant mort, il le rendit mal vueillant de la Seigneurie Venitienne. Ce paillard retaillé mit en auant au Turc circoncis de quelle consequence luy estoit l'Isle de Chipre, & combien ce luy estoit de deshonneur, qu'au milieu de son Empire les Venitiens tinssent vne si belle piece: ce qui incita le tyran à la redemander, & en defaut de la luy quitter de denoncer la guerre aux citoyens de saint Marc.[31]

A manuscript [32] in the Hofbibliothek (now the National-bibliothek) in Vienna seems to link *The Jew of Malta* still more closely to Joseph Nassi. The play lives up to the German repu-tation for lengthy titles. It is styled *Comoedia Genandt Dass Wohl Gesprochene Urtheil Eynes Weiblichen Studenten oder Der Jud von Venedig*. It is a queer combination of Marlowe and Shakespeare, including the pound of flesh story, and is clearly a relic of the numerous visits to the Continent of the English companies who often went on tour there when times were hard in London. In this version of the story, the villainous Jew, Barrabas of Cyprus, smuggles himself aboard ship in disguise and under the alias "Joseph." The juxtaposition of the proper name Joseph and the very island over which the historical Joseph Nassi ruled is striking. The name reappears in what must have been a similar play, *Comödia von Josepho Juden von Venedigk*, which was produced at Dresden in 1626.[33]

Kellner's suggestion that Joseph Nassi was the original of Marlowe's Barabas held the field for nearly forty years. If it was not a wholly satisfactory suggestion, it was at least the only one; and Nassi was tentatively accepted as an "interesting parallel" to Barabas by Mr. C. F. Tucker Brooke in his 1910 edition of Marlowe's *Works*.[34] In 1922, however, Mr. Brooke called attention to the existence of another Jew whose notoriety reached its height at the very time when Marlowe was pre-sumably beginning work on *The Jew of Malta*.

[31] II. 785.
[32] Codex 13791. Reprinted by Meissner in *Die englische Comoedianten*.
[33] Karl Elze, *Jahrb.*, 6: 137–138n (1871); Rudolf Genée: *Geschichte des Shake-speare'schen Drama*, pp. 164 ff., 409 ff. Schelling, I. 232; Meissner, *Jahrb.*, 19: 130, 137 (1884); Cohn: *Shakespeare in Germany*, pp. cxv and cxvii. See I. 366–367.
[34] Page 233. See also his article in TLS: 21: 380, 8 Je 1922.

This was David Passi, whose career can be fairly accurately traced through the confidential reports made by the diplomatic agents of the city-state of Venice. It is true that Marlowe can have had no access to the secret papers of a foreign state, but he was certainly in close association with men steeped in Elizabethan diplomacy, who were watching the course of Near Eastern affairs.

The historical Passi is in some respects more closely akin to Marlowe's Barabas than Nassi. According to the Venetian diplomatic reports, he enjoyed high favor with the Sultan, whom he kept informed of events in Christendom. The reports describe him as a man of "natural ability and sufficient knowledge," who is "able to do great harm and great good." He was known to the English ambassador, and there is a strong suggestion that he may have been in touch with the English secret service about 1585, perhaps coming into direct contact with Marlowe himself.[35]

On February 16, 1591/2, the Venetian ambassador writes in obvious exasperation: "This David, for one truth tells a hundred lies" [36] — which would certainly qualify David to be the original of Barabas, were such habits at all unique either in diplomacy or in the Near East. Passi aided the Turks in constructing models of Crete and Malta in preparation for their attacks; and according to Richard Knolles's *Generall Historie of the Turkes* (1603), he was eventually handed over to the Janizaries and tortured to death.

All this suggests Marlowe's Barabas in a general sort of way, but the comparison breaks down when pushed into detail, and there is no satisfactory way of showing exactly how Marlowe learned about Passi. The most striking difference between the rascal of history and the rascal of the stage is that David Passi never became a ruler. But here the historical Joseph Nassi, sometime Duke of Naxos and the Cyclades, comes conveniently to the rescue. The names are very similar (the reader must certainly have been at some pains to avoid confusion), and if Marlowe got their stories by word of mouth, he too may have become confused. Or, even if he had known he was dealing

---

[35] *Cal. State Papers, Venetian, 1581–1591*, nos. 296, 301, 994.
[36] *Ibid.*, no. 1015. See also no. 1023 for Passi's service to Don Antonio.

with separate individuals, he would hardly have hesitated to make any convenient combination. The compression of two workaday adventurers into one glorious villain was a trifle at which no Elizabethan playwright was likely to stick — Marlowe least of all.

Marlowe, indeed, seems to have enjoyed working topical allusions into his plays; and nothing would have pleased him better than to transport either or both of these Mediterranean adventurers from the Near East to the London stage. As printed sources for Nassi were plentiful rather than complete, it is reasonable to suppose that Marlowe eked them out by word-of-mouth reports, on which he must have depended entirely for anything he knew about Passi.

Perhaps, however, Marlowe did not go so far afield as the Mediterranean to find a prototype for his Barabas. There was in England Edward Brandon, the converted Jew to whom the impostor Perkin Warbeck had once been servant. This man, like Barabas, was wealthy, for he had twice married wealthy Christian women. He was involved in political intrigue, and he became governor of the Channel Islands. With Malta or the Turks he had nothing whatever to do, but even so he may have afforded Marlowe some useful hints.[37]

GEOGRAPHICAL WORKS

Marlowe's knowledge of Malta and conditions there was probably derived from *The Nauigations, peregrinations and voyages, made into Turkie by Nicholas Nicholay, Daulphinois. . . . Translated out of the French by T. Washington the younger*, which was published in London in 1585. The much-traveled M. Nicholay devotes an entire chapter, full of local color, to Malta; and he is quick to note, in true Gallic vein, that "aboue all there is great aboundaunce of Curtisans, both Greeke, Italian, Spaniards, Moores, and Maltez" [38] — a passage which neatly accounts for the courtesan Bellamira in Marlowe's cast of characters.

[37] Cf. J. L. Cardozo: *Contemporary Jew in Elizabethan Drama*, p. 44.
[38] Bk. I, chap. XVI, p. 17r of the 1585 ed. There is a copy in LC, from which this and the following quotations are taken. Unfortunately, this copy has a great many blanks. See also the reprints in J. and A. Churchill: *Collection of Voyages and Travels*, vol. VII, and in Thomas Osborne's unsigned *Collection of Voyages and Travels*.

Marlowe's debt to Nicholay's book is probably heavier than has hitherto been realized, however. His description of Malta is immediately followed by a description of the siege of Tripoli, of which he was an eyewitness. This is important, for one of Nicholay's episodes is strikingly similar to an episode in the siege of Malta, as Marlowe describes it on the stage. As has been said, the Malta of history was never captured, and the baffled Turks were compelled to withdraw. But, according to our playwright, they did capture the island fortress — through treachery from within, committed by the villainous Barabas. Now, Nicholay describes in detail a similar episode at Tripoli, where the enemy was enabled to breach the wall in just this way:

... An vnhappie souldier from Prouence, born in Cauaillon, being the Popes countrie, which by the long frequentation he hadde in those countries, had learned the language and serued as a spie vnto the enemie, seeyng the occasion to be come to that passe which his knauery and dissimuled treason hadde wished for, and being corrupted with money, found the menes to flee vnto the campe, where he declared vnto the Turkes the weakest places of the castle, by the which it might be battered and soone taken, & it was against the gouernours lodging, which standing towards the ditch, and hauing vnderneath it the cellars to retyre the munition, could not be repayred nor fortified: which the Bascha hauing vnderstanded, caused the battery there to be planted, laying the peeces so lowe that easily they dyd beat the vautes and cellars in suche sorte as in small time they did pearse the walles.[39]

This is not unlike the scene in which Barabas escapes to the Turks:

> *Caly.* Whom haue we there, a spy?
> *Bar.* Yes, my good Lord, one that can spy a place
>   Where you may enter, and surprize the Towne.

The method by which Barabas betrays Malta is not identical with the betrayal of Tripoli, but it is not unlike:

>   ... here against the Sluice,
> The rocke is hollow, and of purpose digg'd,
> To make a passage for the running streames
> And common channels of the City.
> Now whilst you giue assault vnto the wals,

[39] Bk. I, chap. XIX, p. 22*v*, of the 1585 ed.

> I'le lead 500 souldiers through the Vault,
> And rise with them i'th middle of the Towne,
> Open the gates for you to enter in,
> And by this meanes the City is your owne.[40]

The breaching of the wall by the conquerors is alluded to later in the play:

> Thus haue we view'd the City, seene the sacke,
> And caus'd the ruines to be new repair'd,
> Which with our Bombards shot and Basiliske,
> We rent in sunder at our entry.[41]

This same chapter contains the description of a slave market, on which Marlowe is plainly drawing in the scene where Barabas purchases Ithamore.[42]

Marlowe, following up a hint given by Nicholay, may have read the *Discours de la Guerre de Malte*, by Nicolas de Ville-gagnon,[43] just as he followed up the bibliography given by Mexia when he was writing *Tamburlaine*.[44] Nicholay had met Villegagnon at Malta and specifically mentions his book. The author of the *Discours* was writing in 1553, twelve years before the siege of Malta, but he describes the taking of Tripoli and the treacherous Provençal. From him Nicholay certainly — and Marlowe possibly — learned the story:

Entre ceux, qui estoient dedans, y auoit le Prouincial Cauaglion, qui pour auoir demouré long temps en ce païs la, estoit deuenu heretique, & seruoit d'espie à noz ennemis, leur communiquoit & rapportoit toutes noz entreprinses, ayant pour ce fait, salaire d'iceux. Il se retira deuers leur costé, craignãt ou d'estre pris, ou bien pour auoir ainsi accordé auec eux, ausquelz il enseigna l'endroit du chateau, qui estoit le plus foible & plus aisé à batre: car au-parauãt il auoit congneu toutes les incommoditez & dangiers qui y pouoient estre.[45]

If Marlowe really saw Villegagnon's book, he may quite likely have mistaken the account of the historical capture of Tripoli — which is particularly vivid — for an account of the

---

[40] Ll. 2071–2073, 2089–2097.
[41] Ll. 2226–2229.
[42] Ll. 762–902. See also Bk. I, chap. VIII, p. 8r; chap. XIX, p. 21v; chap. XXI, p. 27v; Samuel C. Chew: *Crescent and the Rose*, p. 386n.
[43] Also called Nicolas Durand de Villegagnon.
[44] See I. 220–223.
[45] *Discours*, pp. 61–62. Cf. pp. 63, 109.

siege of Malta. The descriptions of the two cities come so close together in the book that it is not easy, even for the modern reader, to disentangle them.

As Villegagnon mentions one "Octauio Ferneso" and "le seigneur Fernese," [46] we can hazard a shrewd guess where Marlowe hit upon the name "Ferneze" for the heroic defender of Malta, instead of doing proper honor to La Vallette, the real commander.

A further significant paragraph in Nicholay's book likewise escaped Kellner. This is his comment on the rich costumes and easy morals of Greek and Peratine women in the sixteenth century: "They forget not also to attyre themselues after such a sort, that if a man did see them as they do march, he woulde take them to be Nymphes or Spouses."

"I know she is a Curtezane by her attire," [47] says Marlowe's Ithamore. It is not a very imposing piece of evidence, but convincing enough when taken together with all that has gone before.

The proper names of the characters in *The Jew of Malta* give a few vague hints as to its author's literary browsings. We have already seen [48] that the name Ferneze may have come from Villegagnon's work. Two other proper names are worth noting. It is certainly odd that the Corpus Christi library during Marlowe's student days contained a rare manuscript *Miracula Sancti Ithamari*; [49] and Marlowe, a recreant candidate for holy orders, may have found a malicious amusement in bestowing the name of a sainted bishop upon the ruffian Ithamore created by his fancy. We know that a manuscript, said to be the only one in existence, [50] was in the Corpus library while Marlowe was still at Cambridge, since it was part of Archbishop Parker's bequest of 1575; but there is obviously no means of showing that Marlowe ever read it. When, however, the Turkish leader addresses one of his pashas as "Callapine," we may feel pretty

[46] Page 98. The name Farnese was again connected with Malta after Marlowe's death, when Giovanni Fratta dedicated his *Malteide* to Ranuccio Farnese.

[47] Line 1177. Nicholay, *op. cit.*, bk. II, chap. XXV, p. 66r. There is a somewhat similar passage in chap. XVI, p. 17.

[48] See also I. 336.

[49] Jacobus Nasmyth (ed.): *Catalogus Librorum Manuscriptorum*, etc., p. 230, no. CLXI. 10; M. R. James: *Descriptive Catalogue*.

[50] M. R. James: *Descriptive Catalogue*.

sure that the name has lingered in the playwright's mind from the days when he was writing *Tamburlaine*.[51]

MACHIAVELLI'S INFLUENCE

Amid the general doubt that envelops the sources of *The Jew of Malta*, there is one point of certainty. That is the influence of Machiavelli's *Il Principe* on *The Jew*, *The Massacre at Paris*, and to some degree on *Tamburlaine*, though in this last the Machiavellian trace is not nearly so clear. Barabas is an example of Machiavellian craft; the Guise and Tamburlaine are examples of Machiavellian thirst for power at all costs. Doubt may remain as to precisely how this influence was exerted; that it was exerted there can be no doubt at all.

In *The Jew of Malta* Machiavelli makes his first appearance on the Elizabethan stage — though references to him had been common in nondramatic literature for twenty years[52] — to speak a prologue which sets the keynote for the whole play. His spirit — or rather, his spirit as conceived by Elizabeth's England — pervades the entire piece, and thereafter becomes a commonplace of dramatic allusion in later plays.

Machiavelli had not been translated into English in Marlowe's lifetime, and there is no evidence for the poet's first-hand acquaintance with *Il Principe*. It is even doubtful whether he read Italian.

It is possible, however, to exaggerate the importance of these facts. A number of the newsbooks which dealt with the siege of Malta were also in Italian; yet the dramatist seems to have had a working knowledge of their contents. In the intellectual circles which he frequented — which had at one time included Giordano Bruno[53] — there must have been several men who interested themselves in Italian studies; and in any case Elizabethan England was rapidly becoming so Italianate that it was hard for any mind to escape the contagion. Furthermore, *Il Principe* had already been extensively translated into French and Latin. There were two French versions, one in 1553 and

---

[51] See I. 224–225.
[52] Mario Praz: *Machiavelli and the Elizabethans*, pp. 6–7.
[53] See I. 129. There is no evidence, however, that Marlowe ever met Bruno.

one in 1586, and four Latin versions between 1560 and 1589.[54] It is worth noting that Machiavelli, like Marlowe, indulges in ridicule of Moses; [55] and that Robert Greene, who like Marlowe had studied at Cambridge, where Machiavelli was much admired, includes in his diatribe against Marlowe the question: "Is it pestilent Machiuilian pollicie that thou hast studied?" [56]

Marlowe's knowledge of Machiavelli may have come through chance conversations with his friends — perhaps through Sir Philip Sidney, Sir Francis Walsingham's son-in-law, who alludes to Machiavelli in his correspondence; [57] through Spenser, who elsewhere [58] exercises a clear influence over Marlowe and who had taken over Machiavellian doctrine bodily in his *View of the Present State of Ireland*; [59] or through Raleigh, whose *Cabinet Council Containing the Chief Arts of Empire* and *The Prince, or Maxims of State*, borrow heavily from *Il Principe* and from the *Discorsi*. Italian texts of both these last had been published in London dated — though perhaps falsely — 1584.[60]

More probably, Marlowe derived most of his knowledge of Machiavelli's ideas from an attack on the cynical Italian penned by Innocent Gentillet,[61] a Huguenot jurist of the sixteenth century. Gentillet's *Commentariorum de regno aut quovis principatu recte et tranquille administrando, libri tres*, or *Discours sur les moyens de bien gouverner et maintenir en bonne paix un royaume . . . Contre N. Machiavel*, ran through many editions. The first French version is dated 1576, and the first Latin version probably appeared in 1577. This was translated into English by Simon Patericke, or Patrick, presumably in 1577, since

---

[54] Edward Meyer: *Machiavelli in Elizabethan Drama*, p. 3; Elmer Edgar Stoll: *John Webster*, pp. 204–205; Mario Praz, *loc. cit.*

[55] Cf. *Il Principe*, VI, and the Baines libel.

[56] Grosart's Greene, XII. 142. See I. 123 of the present work.

[57] Steuart A. Pears (ed.): *Correspondence of Sir Philip Sidney and Hubert Languet* (1845), p. 215; Meyer, *op. cit.*, pp. 18–19.   [58] See I. 205–209.

[59] E. A. Greenlaw: "Influence of Machiavelli on Spenser," MP, 7: 187 (1909).

[60] C. E. Sayle: *Cambridge University Library. Early Printed Books*, I. 399. See also his Appendix, p. 793, no. 8023, and Joseph Ames (ed. William Herbert): *Typographical Antiquities*, pp. 1180, 1181, 1284.

[61] On Gentillet, see Hans Josef Schäfer: *Innozenz Gentillet, sein Leben und besonders sein "Anti-Machiavel"* (Bonn Diss., 1929); *Biographie universelle [Michaud]* (1856), XVI. 196–197; *Nouvelle Biographie universelle* (Didot, 1857), XIX. 949–950, where a bibliography is given. Authorities do not agree as to dates of editions, and reference is occasionally made to a 1571 ed. This does not appear in the printed catalogues of the British Museum and Bibliothèque Nationale.

the dedication is dated "Kalends Augufti. Anno 1577." The English title was *A discovrse vpon the meanes of wel governing and maintaining in good peace, a kingdome, or other principalitie. . . . Against Nicholas Machiavel the Florentine.* Commonly known as the "Anti-Machiavel," or "Contre-Machiavelli," it was not published in England until 1602, with a second edition in 1608, but it probably circulated in manuscript long before that.

Gentillet expresses the anti-Italian feeling in France caused by the influx of Italians with Catherine de' Medici, of which Marlowe's *Massacre at Paris* is a belated echo. Gentillet himself is very specific on this point, complaining repeatedly "that *Machiavell* by his doctrine and documents, hath changed the good and antient government of France, into a kind of Florentine government, whereupon wee see with our eyes, the totall ruine of all France." [62]

He condemns the whole Machiavellian doctrine as "beastly vanitie and madnesse, yea, full of extreame wickednesse," [63] and sets forth "the end and scope which I haue proposed unto my selfe, that is, to confute the doctrine of Machiavell." [64] Marlowe's exposition of Machiavelli's views reproduces Gentillet's misstatements and may be contrasted with the original about as follows: [65]

Machiavellianism of "The Prince"	*Machiavellianism of Marlowe*
1. Applies only to political affairs.	1. Applies also to personal affairs.
2. Does not necessarily distinguish between *virtù* and virtue.	2. Opposes *virtù* to virtue.
3. Advocates *virtù* for good of the state as a whole.	3. Advocates *virtù* for personal ends.
4. Admits that *fortuna* (element of luck) must be considered.	4. Neglects *fortuna*.
5. Employs *virtù* for a single purpose.	5. Seeks power for its own sake.
6. Requires psychological insight.	6. Conspicuously lacks psychological insight.

[62] English (1608) ed., sig. Aiiijr. Columbia University has a copy of this book.
[63] *Ibid.*, sig. Aijv.   [64] *Ibid.*, sig. ijr.
[65] Cf. Chester Louis Reiss: *Christopher Marlowe and Atheism*, New York University, Master's thesis (MS.), 1932.

In his prologue to *The Jew of Malta*, Marlowe seems also to have been influenced by a poem, "Epigramma in Effigiem Machiavelli," written by his arch-enemy, Gabriel Harvey. This begins with the Latin heading, "Machiavelli ipse loquitur." Harvey practically sums up Gentillet's view of Machiavellianism, and accuses Machiavelli of the four crimes usually attributed to him by Marlowe and later dramatists: murder, poisoning, fraud, and general violence. One rather obscure line,

Aut nihil, aut Cæsar: noster [i.e., Machiavelli's] alumnus erat,

may have suggested

What right had *Cæsar* to the Empire?

in Marlowe's prologue.

Harvey seems to have been one of the earliest students of *Il Principe* at Cambridge. He was trying to borrow a book by Machiavelli as early as 1573, when he was himself still a student of twenty-three, as we know from an extant letter to a certain "Mr. Remington":

Mr. Remington, you remember I was in hand with you not long agoe for your Machiavell, ye greate founder and master of pollicies. I praie you send me him now bi this schollar, and I wil dispatch him home againe, God willing, ere it be long, as politique I hope as I shal find him.[66]

Harvey kept up his interest in Machiavelli, and just before Marlowe entered the university was writing to a friend:

I warrant you sum good fellowes amongst us begin nowe to be prettely wel acquayntid with a certayne parlous booke callid, as I remember me, Il Principe di Niccolo Macchiavelli.[67]

In his marginal notes on his own books, Harvey is constantly quoting Machiavelli.[68] If we had the whole truth about Marlowe's relations with Harvey and his brothers, we might find that they had been on friendlier terms in the university than in after life. At any rate, Marlowe probably became interested in Machiavelli while a student, for in April, 1580, only a few

[66] E. J. L. Scott (ed.): *Letterbook of Gabriel Harvey* (Cambridge Society, 1884), p. 174. See also pp. 135, 175.
[67] *Ibid.*, p. 79; Grosart's Harvey, I. 69.
[68] G. C. Moore Smith (ed.): *Gabriel Harvey's Marginalia*. See index.

months before Marlowe entered, Harvey remarks in a letter to Edmund Spenser [69] that the sinister Italian is the favorite reading of all the young men.

While no single Machiavellian line in *The Jew of Malta* can be shown to come directly from *Il Principe* or the *Discorsi*, or even directly from Gentillet, the play is saturated with Machiavellianism as expounded, for purposes of refutation, by the indignant Huguenot. The following borrowings from this source are most important:

1. *The idea of revenge at all costs and refusal to forget an injury.* This theme is reiterated in the first two acts of the play. Gentillet, in the sixth maxim of his third book, sets forth the Machiavellian view "that an offence ought to take so deepe root in the heart of the offended, that by no pleasures, services, or other meanes it can be rased out." [79] It is possible to exaggerate this coincidence, however, since revenge is a common human motive, and is also prominent in Seneca's plays, which influence the entire Elizabethan drama.

2. *The idea that religion is mere "policy."* The word "policy," in its common Elizabethan meaning of hypocritical self-seeking, is drawn directly from Machiavelli. Word and idea pass together into Marlowe's verse in such passages as:

> I count Religion but a childish Toy

in the prologue and such other passages as:

> For I can see no fruits in all their faith
> But malice, falshood, and excessiue pride,
> Which me thinkes fits not their profession.
> [154–156]
>
> I, policie? that's their profession,
> And not simplicity, as they suggest.
> [393–394]
>
> Thus hast thou gotten, by thy policie,
> No simple place, no small authority. . . .
> And since by wrong thou got'st Authority,
> Maintaine it brauely by firme policy.
> [2128–2137]

[69] Grosart's Harvey, I. 69.
[70] English ed. (1608), p. 177.

All this might easily come from Gentillet's assertion in the first maxim of his second book that "this Atheist *Machiavell* teacheth the prince to be a true contemner of God and of Religion, and onely to make a shew and a faire countenance outwardly before the world, to be esteemed religious & devout, although he be not." [71]

Barabas acts on much this principle, and his assertion that

It's no sinne to deceiue a Christian [72]

— a view plainly contrary to the Talmud — is related to it. The Christians themselves apply the same principle to the infidel in the Second Part of *Tamburlaine*, when Baldwine exclaims

> . . . for with such Infidels,
> In whom no faith nor true religion rests,
> We are not bound to those accomplishments,
> The holy lawes of Christendome inioine.[73]

3. *The related idea that religion is a cloak for crime.* This is not very far from the opinion, attributed to Marlowe in the Baines libel, that "the first beginning of religion was onely to keepe men in Awe." It reappears in Barabas' observation that

> Religion
> Hides many mischiefes from suspition.[74]

Gentillet discusses the effect of this maxim on the moral conduct of Machiavelli's disciples, and concludes that "being fraughted with all impietie and Atheisme, and having well studied their *Machiavel*, which they know vpon their fingers, they make no scruple nor conscience at any thing." [75] It is a fair description of Barabas himself.

4. *The idea that one is bound to keep faith only when profitable.* Gentillet sums this up by saying that "a Prince ought not to hold any faith or promise, but so farre, as concernes his profit: and that he ought to know how to counterfeit the foxe, to catch and entrap other beasts, and as soone as hee hath them in his nets, to play the lyon in slaying & devouring them." [76] This is a

---

[71] English ed. (1608), p. 92. The same principle is set forth in *Il Principe* (18) and in *Discorsi* (II. 2).

[72] Line 1074.

[73] Ll. 2827–2830.

[74] Ll. 519–520.

[75] English ed. (1608), p. 93.

[76] English ed. (1608), p. 94. See also pp. 224, 255, Maxim 21.

perversion of *Il Principe* and of similar views expressed in the
Discorsi and the *Florentine History*.[77] It reappears clearly in the
words of Barabas when he is made governor of Malta:

> . . . why, is not this
> A kingly kinde of trade to purchase Townes
> By treachery, and sell 'em by deceit? [78]

5. *The idea of complete egoism.* This is implicit in all Gentillet's interpretation of Machiavelli, nor is it wholly unfair to
the original. The idea is equally implicit in all that Barabas
does and in much that other Marlowe heroes do. It is clearly
expressed in such lines as

> Ego mihimet sum semper proximus,

though the Latin is not Marlowe's, but a slightly garbled quotation from the *Andria* of Terence. It is even clearer in

> For so I liue, perish may all the world,

and

> Thus louing neither, will I liue with both,
> Making a profit of my policie;
> And he from whom my most aduantage comes,
> Shall be my friend.[79]

The Jew of Malta thus introduces a new phase of Marlowe's
work. Hitherto his plays had dealt with the lust of power, the
power of political dominion and armed might in *Tamburlaine*,
the power of the intellect, lawful or unlawful, in *Doctor Faustus*.
Both had been "one-man plays." In *The Jew of Malta* Marlowe
continues the theme of human lust for power — this time, the
power of wealth; and he continues to center his play upon a
single character.

But when the actor personating Machiavelli steps upon the
stage to speak the prologue, there enters with him a theme new
in Marlowe's work — statecraft and the devious intrigues of
Machiavellian "policie" — which reappears in *The Massacre
at Paris* and in *Edward the Second* and which Marlowe would

---

[77] *Il Principe*, 18; *Discorsi*, I. 9 (42); *Florentine History*, VII. 193.
[78] Ll. 2329–2331.
[79] *Andria*, IV. i. 12. Terence wrote: "Proxumus sum egomet mihi." *Jew of Malta*,
2292, 2213–2216.

have carried further had he lived. This development helps to confirm the order of composition of his plays, already determined on other grounds.

Marlowe never abandons his older theme. Barabas is as eager for power as Tamburlaine or Faustus. As governor of Malta he even adds political power to the power that his wealth has already given him. The evil favorites in *Edward the Second* are also, in their own way, selfishly eager for power, which they exercise through their control of the weak king. The Duke of Guise in *The Massacre at Paris* seeks power likewise. But in the plays of "policie" there is a new motive. ·In Barabas, in the Guise, in the evil favorites, in Young Mortimer and the barons, we find the ruthless, deliberate, and unscrupulous execution of devious schemes which the Elizabethans knew indifferently as "policie" or Machiavellianism. If we go further, and attribute to Marlowe *The True Tragedie* and *The Contention*, we shall find this theme again in Richard of York, and we also find it carried over from Marlowe into Shakespeare's earlier work.[80]

Into these plays of policy there enter characters of a new sort and a new complexity, the Marlowe villains, best exemplified in Barabas, the Guise, and Richard of York, but also plainly visible in Young Mortimer. Vigilant, scheming, cunning, sinister, and cold-blooded, these characters are unlike the hotheaded Tamburlaine or the hesitant Faustus. They are not quite human, and yet all too humanly credible. Shakespeare takes them up. Ford, Webster, and the others follow him, and the type never quite drops out of English literature. Old Scrooge is just a little like Barabas. It is the logical development of Marlowe's favorite power motive after his mind has begun to work on Machiavellian doctrines.

THE BIBLE

Ironically enough, *The Jew of Malta*, which shows clearer traces of Machiavellian doctrine than any other play of Marlowe's, is also the play which shows the clearest evidence that he read the Bible. Apparently he used either the Geneva Bible of 1560, like Shakespeare, or the Bishops' Bible, translated under the direction of Archbishop Parker, who had provided

[80] See Chapter XVI.

funds for the scholarship on which the future dramatist went to
Cambridge. Apparently Marlowe had studied the Book of Job
and had gained from it an understanding of the Jewish character in prosperity and adversity.

The clearest trace of this is the comment of Barabas on the
wealth of Job:

> What tell you me of *Iob*? I wot his wealth
> Was written thus: he had seuen thousand sheepe,
> Three thousand Camels, and two hundred yoake
> Of labouring Oxen, and fiue hundred
> Shee Asses.[81]

This is almost a direct transcription of Job i. 3, which in the
Geneva Bible reads:

His substance also was seuen thousand shepe, and thre thousand
camels, and fyue hundreth yoke of oxen, and fyue hundreth she
asses.

Marlowe changes the five hundred yoke of oxen to two hundred.
This is a slip either by the author or by the printer, but it
should be noted that in the black letter of the Bishops' Bible
"five" and "two" look very much alike.

In this same speech, there is another echo of Job:

> But I may curse the day,
> Thy fatall birth-day, forlorne *Barabas*;
> And henceforth wish for an eternall night,
> That clouds of darkenesse may inclose my flesh,

which is obviously related to

Afterward Iob opened his mouthe, and cursed his day. And Iob cryed
out, and said, Let the daye perish, wherein I was borne, and the
night when it was said, There is a manchilde conceiued. Let yt day
be darkenes.[82]

Another line,

> 'Tis in the trouble of my spirit I speake,

is almost word for word from the Geneva Bible:

> Therefore I . . . wil speake in the trouble of my spirit.[83]

[81] Ll. 414–418.
[82] Ll. 424–427; Job iii. 1–4.   [83] Line 440; Job vii. 11.

Other details of the play are also Biblical. Abigail, the name of Barabas' daughter, is the name of one of David's wives.[84] When Barabas exclaims

> The man that dealeth righteously shall liue

he is echoing an Hebraic idea that appears in Job, Proverbs, and Ezekiel.[85] The name "*Kirriah Iairim, the great Iew of Greece*," [86] appears to come from Chronicles,[87] where the Geneva Bible gives the name as "Kiriath-iearim," and the Bishops' Bible as "Kiriath Jarim." This is a place name — "city of woods" — which occurs repeatedly in the Old Testament, usually in contexts which make clear its geographical meaning. Only in the second chapter of First Chronicles is the allusion so obscure that it might be either a geographical name or the personal name for which Marlowe mistook it. The blunder indicates that he knew no Hebrew, which was not a required part of the Cambridge curriculum.

Sources of the Subplot

Even when we have disposed of the main plot of *The Jew of Malta*, a secondary source, or set of sources, must be found. There is still the vexed question of the subplot, especially the slaying of Friar Bernardine, the setting up of his dead body, and the second "slaying," when Friar Iacomo, in exasperation, strikes the corpse, which he supposes to be alive, for refusing to answer him; and then, in an ecstasy of remorseful terror, admits that he is a murderer.

The identity of the adapter of the last three acts, who is probably responsible for this element in the play, is controversial. One of the few definite facts we can be sure of with regard to *The Jew of Malta* is that Thomas Heywood was the impresario of the court and Cockpit productions in 1633. He himself says specifically, "I vsher'd it unto the Court, and presented it to the Cock-pit." [88] Heywood, therefore, lies — not very unjustly, in all probability — under the heaviest suspicion.

---

[84] I Samuel xxv. 42.
[85] Line 349; Job iv. 7; Proverbs x. 2 and xii. 28; Ezekiel xviii. 8, 9, 22.
[86] Line 162.
[87] I Chronicles ii. 50, 52, 53.
[88] "Epistle Dedicatory" to the 1633 ed. Brooke's (1910) ed., p. 237.

Not only was he an impresario; he was also a constant and copious hack writer, likely to undertake just such rewriting as the play has suffered. Its subplot, moreover, is one that he twice uses, elsewhere, in his admitted work. There is, therefore, abundant ground for suspecting Heywood; and there is no particular ground for suspecting anyone else.

Efforts to prove his authorship of the scenes of the subplot by vocabulary tests have been rather fruitless. Heywood had an especial fondness for the words "monomachy," "mediate," "aspersed," "courtesy," "modesty," "noble," "strange," "confine," "obdure" (for the adjective "obdurate"), "comrague" (for "comrade"), "infallid," "strage" (destruction), "apology" (as a verb), "ecstasied," "gratulate," and the odd phrase, "unite consent." These have been used as guides in detecting his supposed share in his collaboration with John Webster.[89] Of these, "mediate" actually appears in line 2402 of *The Jew of Malta*. "Ecstasy" appears as a noun in line 443. "Courtesy" appears in lines 252, 991, 2344, and 2394. "Modesty" appears in line 1764, but it also appears in line 868 of *Dido*. "Noble" appears only in line 617, which is certainly Marlowe's, and reappears throughout Marlowe's other works and in most of the dramatists of the period. The other typical Heywood words do not appear at all, and the effort to assign the latter part of *The Jew of Malta* through vocabulary tests thus breaks down at once. The versification does not differ markedly from Marlowe's, nor does it greatly resemble Heywood's; but as it is obviously hasty the matter is of no great importance. The failure of these tests does nothing to advance Heywood's claims, though it in no wise invalidates them.

The story of the subplot — the setting up of a dead body and the accusation of murder against a man who strikes it down — appears in Heywood's play, *The Captives*, and again in his Γυναικεῖον: or, *nine Bookes of various History, concerninge Women*. *The Captives* has been dated 1624, and the story of the murdered corpse might easily still have been in his mind

---

[89] Henry David Gray: " 'A Cure for a Cuckold,' by Heywood, Rowley, and Webster," MLR, 22: 389 (1927); Rupert Brooke: *John Webster and the Elizabethan Drama*, pp. 176–194; H. Dugdale Sykes, N&Q, 11th ser., 7: 423–424, 31 My 1913; 9: 383–384, 16 My 1914.

when he revised Marlowe's work for the court seven years later.[90]

In spite of the extreme probability that Heywood revised the play, we can never be entirely sure that there was actually any revision at all. Marlowe and Heywood may, quite accidentally, have stumbled on the same story, and all our critical cogitations may be wasted over nothing more puzzling than the hurried and consequently botched work of a somewhat dissipated young man of genius, who happened to want some money.

Whoever discovered it first, as dramatic material, the essential elements in the story of the dead man and his second "killing" appear and reappear in folk tales all over Europe and Asia. At least five Old French *fabliaux* tell the story, and there are Scotch versions, a version in the *Arabian Nights*, and another in the English *Gesta Romanorum*.[91] The story may have reached England through Masuccio di Salerno (1420–c.1476), who tells it in the first *novella* of a series of fifty printed at Naples in 1476. As another of his *novelle* furnishes some of the material that Shakespeare uses in *Romeo and Juliet*, it is reasonable to regard him as an Elizabethan source. The tale might also have reached Marlowe through a collection of tales, mainly Italian, which appeared in Paris in 1555, under the title *Comptes du monde adventureux*. There is also a native English tale in verse, *A mery Jest Of Dane Hew Munk Of Leicestre*, which Marlowe may have known from childhood.[92]

Heywood, in *The Captives* and in the Γυναικεῖον, is certainly following Masuccio, for the correspondences are too close to be accidental. This version of the story, like Marlowe's, deals with two friars, whereas the story of Dane Hew deals with a friar and an abbot. The latter version was, however, published in Marlowe's lifetime.[93] The unique copy preserved at the Bodleian bears no date, but the printer's name is given as John Allde, who does not appear in the *Stationers' Register* after 1584. It was therefore readily available to Marlowe in 1589 or 1590.[94]

[90] Arthur Melville Clark: *Thomas Heywood: Playwright and Miscellanist*, p. 119.

[91] Emil Koeppel in *Archiv*, 97: 323–329 (1896).

[92] Most readily accessible in W. Carew Hazlitt's *Remains of the Early Popular Poetry of England*, III. 130–148.

[93] See A. G. Judson (ed.): *The Captives*, p. 20.

[94] R. B. McKerrow: *Dictionary of Printers and Booksellers*, p. 6; E. Gordon Duff: *Century of the English Book Trade*, p. 2.

The rather gruesome trick of setting up a dead body to be knocked down again by chance passersby, which appealed to the taste of Elizabethan book-buyers as a "mery Jest," is given in much greater detail by Masuccio and the unknown author of *Dane Hew* than by Marlowe. Dane Hew is "foure times slain and once hanged." Heywood, who follows Masuccio, has the body carted back and forth repeatedly and indulges in other macabre details, both in *The Captives* and in his Γυναικεῖον.

Marlowe — assuming that he wrote these scenes — contents himself with only one re-killing. This restraint, taken together with his reluctance to include the more shocking incidents of Edward II's murder, suggests that the young University Wit, though eager for violence of the splendid sort, had no liking for the unsavory horrors with which his successors regaled the groundlings. What Ford or Webster or Tourneur would have done with such a scene is only too easy to imagine.

For the first time, if this part of the play is really his, we can credit Marlowe with the literary virtue of restraint. This may be more significant than it at first appears. Except for a few passages in *Faustus*, it is the earliest sign of restraint in Marlowe's writing, but it is not the last. In *Edward the Second* there also appears a toning down of that early exuberance by which *Tamburlaine* had been marred.

Perhaps, amid all the bombast that still mars *The Jew of Malta*, we are watching here the beginning of a new Marlowe, ready at last to lay aside the exaggeration that was his besetting literary sin. But we shall never know. Before the new promise of a young poet who was already great could come to its fruition, Ingram Friser's dagger had ended the chance of future achievement.

The little that can be positively stated as to Marlowe's sources is painfully slight; but, in general, the main origins of the play are clear enough: Marlowe became familiar in some way with the story of the Turkish wars and with the lives of the Jewish adventurers who were involved with the Turkish government. He was steeped in Machiavellian ideas of "policie," derived mainly from Gentillet. He gathered a detail or two of the siege of Tripoli and some general information from Nicholay's book, drew some Jewish lore from the Bible, and — if he

wrote the scenes of the subplot at all — drew them from either
Masuccio or the tale of Dane Hew.

STAGE HISTORY

The Jew of Malta must have caught the public fancy almost
at once. Though it was already an old play when Henslowe
first noted it in his *Diary*, it was one of the most popular in the
repertoire of that exceedingly astute manager, who enters in all
thirty-six performances, the last of which is in 1596. As we find
him in May, 1601, lending the large sum of five pounds "to bye
divers thing*es* for the Jewe of malta," the old play must have
retained a trace of its old popularity until it was revived at the
Cockpit and at a court performance in 1633, nearly half a century after Marlowe wrote it. This is an extraordinary record
for any play but a masterpiece — an exalted title to which the
poor *Jew* has no claim at all.

So frequent are the performances that it has been suggested
that Henslowe lent it to any company that happened to be using
his theatre, a theory which would account for the fact that *The
Jew of Malta* is successively presented by Strange's men, by the
Queen's and Sussex's men in conjunction, then by the Admiral's or Lord Chamberlain's men; and at last passes into the
permanent possession of the Admiral's men in 1594. When the
properties of the Admiral's men were listed in 1598, they included "j cauderm for the Jewe," [95] which must have been used
for the death of Barabas in the fifth act.

Part of the play's immense popularity in its day is due to the
fact that *The Jew of Malta* is, by Elizabethan standards, a delightful play. The good are very good, and the bad are satis-
fyingly wicked, while even Elizabethan records for mimic
slaughter are surpassed by the casual extermination of a whole
nunnery. When at the end the romantic villain of the piece was
boiled to death, the Cross Keys Tavern and the Rose Theatre
must have rocked with lusty, innocent Elizabethan laughter
and general enthusiasm.

The purely literary faults of *The Jew of Malta*, which are clear
enough in the study, disappear in the theatre; for the mutila-
tions were originally made for the sake of a theatrical effect,

[95] *Henslowe Papers*, p. 118.

which they still produce. "Critics of this particular play have united in saying that the interest falls off after the second act and that the play deteriorates into such a succession of horrors that all dramatic interest is lost," says Mr. Lewis Perry in his introduction to the Williams College acting version.[96] "We did not find this to be the case when the play was acted. There was, on the other hand, a steadily rising interest from first to last." Even the humorous scenes, tedious enough to read, proved "surprisingly effective" on the stage.

But not all the success of the play need be laid to its dramatic merit — if we can call it dramatic rather than merely theatrical, and if merit is not too strong a word. A fair share of the stage success may also be credited to the lucky chance that in 1594 a Jewish physician, prominent at the Virgin Eliza's court, got himself hanged and thus roused popular interest in the Jews and the Jewish question at the very moment when public interest in Marlowe's botched play was beginning to lag.

Henslowe was not the man to lose such a chance, and *The Jew of Malta* promptly began a series of performances that crowded thick upon one another, as we can see from the dates in the *Diary*; and that filled the house day after day, as we may infer from the daily takings, which Henslowe notes down with characteristic care.

The unfortunate Jew whose untimely elevation thus provided Henslowe and the players with such an agreeable and timely bit of publicity was the physician Roderigo Lopez, who had for thirty-odd years successfully evaded the laws that banned all Jews from English soil; and who at length contrived to make himself so welcome and so useful at court that he became a personal favorite of the Queen's — who liked him so much that in the end she hesitated four months after sentence of death had been passed upon him, before she could bring herself to sign the warrant for his execution.

The Lopez case provides a somewhat melodramatic answer to a question that once puzzled the earlier devotees of the old English drama. A law passed in 1290 had ordered the expulsion of all Jews from England, whither none could legally return until in 1650 Oliver Cromwell called them back. But if there were no

[96] Page xviii.

Jews in Elizabethan England — as even so careful an historian as Green specifically asserts [97] — why the lively interest in them that was unmistakably evinced by the common run of London playgoers? A play called simply *The Jew* had been popular as early as 1579.[98] Then came Marlowe's tremendous success with *The Jew of Malta*, and finally *The Merchant of Venice*, an equal Shakespearean success.

It will not do to say that Marlowe and Shakespeare made stage monsters of an unknown race on the principle *omne ignotum pro magnifico* — or *horrifico*. Both writers, however horrible they may make their villains to divert the groundlings, have caught several real characteristics that have been Jewish for many centuries: family affection, a habit of quoting the Old Testament, clannishness, religious strictness, and dietary observances. These have nothing to do with the vulgar libels of the Jew-baiters.

Such accurate portraiture may be unconscious on the dramatist's part, but it does not come by accident. Both Marlowe and Shakespeare have been observing Jews at some time or other. But where and how?

The answer is what one might naturally expect. It is hard enough to get any law enforced; and the rigors of the original enforcement of the anti-Jewish law — if it really was rigorous to begin with, which is by no means certain — had slowly relaxed during a period of three hundred years or more, when there were few Jews about, and the fires of Christian hatred burned somewhat languidly. It is not likely that all Jews were

---

[97] "From the time of Edward to that of Cromwell no Jew touched English ground."— J. R. Green: *Short History of the English People*, pt. II, p. 205 (ed. 1888). Green's view of the matter is supported in J. L. Cardozo's *Contemporary Jew in Elizabethan Drama*, in which the author argues that exclusion of the Jews was practically complete for centuries after the expulsion. This view is questioned by Sir Sidney Lee and M. J. Landa.

[98] There are two contemporary allusions to this play. One is in Stephen Gosson's *Schoole of Abuse* (1579), pp. 29–30 (Shakspere Society Publications, vol. XV): "And as some of the players are farre from abuse, so some of their playes are without rebuke. . . . The Jew and Ptolome, shown at the Bull, the one representing the greediness of worldly chusers, and bloody mindes of usurers; the other very lively describing how seditious estates . . . are overthrowne." There seems to be another allusion to this play in Gabriel Harvey's letter to Spenser, which ends: "He that is faste bownde vnto the in more obligations then any marchant in Italy to any Jewe there." Cf. Edward Scott: "Shakespeareana," *Athenaeum*, no. 2801, p. 14, 2 Jy 1881, and his *Letterbook of Gabriel Harvey*, p. xiii. This is dated too early to allude to either Marlowe or Shakespeare.

ever completely expelled. There must have been a good many half-hearted conversions and many downright evasions. There is even a scandalous theory that the Pilgrim Fathers were mainly the descendants of Jews who had been more or less forcibly converted under Edward I. It is a pleasantly infuriating theory, but we must get back to our hanging.

It is reasonably certain, then, that there were Jews in Marlowe's England. Henry VIII had brought a rabbi into the country. In 1591 a Portuguese Jewess was for a time lady-in-waiting to the Queen, and preferred her ancient faith to an English nobleman's offer of marriage. A casual allusion in an old play refers to the regular custom of hiring court suits from Jewish pawnbrokers. All through Elizabeth's reign, a house was maintained in Chancery Lane for the relief of converts from Judaism. Two or three Jews were sometimes in residence at once. Their signatures in Hebrew characters are preserved to this day. As the universities seem to have welcomed men learned in Hebrew and not to have been nicely curious about their faith, Marlowe may quite likely have known a Jewish scholar or two at Cambridge.

Of one notorious, though not very guilty, Jew's relations with Queen Elizabeth's court — and, quite by accident, with *The Jew of Malta* — there is no doubt, for the criminal records make it all clear. Dr. Roderigo Lopez settled in England just after Elizabeth came to the throne. He appears in the 1571 census of foreigners in London as "Doctor Lopus portingale howsholder Denizen," with the further information that he "came into this realme about xij yeares past to get his lyvinge by physycke." [99] Dr. Lopez, or Lopus, prospered and rose in the world. By 1569 he had already become a member of the College of Physicians. By 1571 he was attending the Queen's secretary, Sir Francis Walsingham. [100] (Again the name of Walsingham appears in relation to a man who touches Marlowe's life and work, and who is involved in state intrigue!)

A few years later Lopez is household physician to the most

[99] Returns of Strangers in London in 1571, SP 12/82, fol. 7, PRO. The text here is directly from the original and differs from other texts. See also N&Q, 2nd ser., 8: 448, 3 D 1859; Sidney Lee in *Trans. New Shakspere Society*, 1887-92, p. 158.

[100] *Walsingham's Diary* (*Camden Society Miscellany*, vol. VI), p. 12, November 21, 1571.

powerful nobleman of the time, the Earl of Leicester, whose enemies lampoon the doctor as "Lopez the Jew." In 1586 Lopez reaches the highest point of a British medical career: he becomes chief physician to the sovereign, who in 1589 grants him the monopoly of aniseed and sumac for all England. Monopolies of this sort were the economical Elizabeth's favorite method of rewarding her friends. They cost her nothing, yet were vastly profitable to the holders.

Lopez, the Portuguese Jew, had climbed so high and so fast during his thirty years in England that the sensation of his fall is comprehensible. He made a fatal mistake that other professional men have made since then and let himself become involved in politics. The Earl of Essex used him to get secret news from Spain. Then Essex brought to England one Don Antonio Perez, the half-Jewish pretender to the throne of Portugal — naturally a bitter foe of Philip of Spain, who actually was ruling Portugal; and, quite as naturally, a friend warmly received in England. Who could be so useful an interpreter as Dr. Lopez, the royal confidant and physician, with his mastery of five languages?

But there were quarrels, and in 1593, the year of Marlowe's death, Lopez committed the unpardonable offense of revealing medical secrets. Waxing merry in company with Don Antonio, "Lopez began bitterly to inveigh against the Earl of Essex, telling some secrecies, how he had cured him, and of what diseases, with some other things which did disparage his honour." [101] Dr. Lopez was more learned than discreet. What he had said was reported to Essex; and the Earl, then still high in royal favor, set himself to turn the Queen's mind against her Jewish physician, who presently found himself on trial for high treason. The specific charges were intelligence work for Spain and a design to poison the Queen.

That Lopez had ever been more than indiscreet is doubtful; but there is no doubt that he had accepted fifty thousand crowns from Spain and that he had threatened Don Antonio's life. His confessions of other treason, made under torture, he subsequently retracted. The Queen was a long time making up her mind, but she signed the death warrant at last, and Lopez

[101] Godfrey Goodman: *Court of King James the First* (ed. John S. Brewer), I. 152–153.

was hanged at Tyburn June 7, 1594, a year after Marlowe's death.

His dying assertion that he loved the Queen as he loved Jesus Christ was received with shouts of laughter from the highly Christian multitude that had come to enjoy the hanging, and the drop fell amid the cry: "He is a Jew!" The Queen allowed the widow to retain all her husband's property, which was legally forfeit to the Crown, except one jewel said to have been sent to Lopez by the King of Spain. This Elizabeth wore at her girdle for the rest of her life.[102]

It is not hard to imagine the stir all this created in the little Elizabethan capital, which for all its hundred thousand inhabitants retained the characteristics of a big village. The offender's race had been emphasized at his trial, and the unconscious irony of his last words caught the far from squeamish popular fancy. Forty years afterward poets and playwrights were still writing about Lopez the Jew. Middleton and Dekker tucked allusions to him into the *Game at Chesse* (1624) and the *Whore of Babylon* (1605/07); and even before the doctor's trial, he was already so familiar a London figure that Marlowe had casually referred to him in *Faustus* — "Doctor *Lopus* was neuer such a Doctor." [103]

Marlowe had been a whole year dead when Lopez was hanged and *The Jew of Malta* leaped into its sudden revival of popularity; but even during its author's brief lifetime his play had already become an extraordinary success. Henslow was producing it once or twice a month during the spring of 1591/2, and the receipts ran as high as fifty-four shillings a performance.[104] During 1593 this phenomenal popularity began to lag. The hero-villain Barabas was thrilling, the murders were delightful; but at last even the 'prentices had had enough, and the canny Henslowe moved his company on to more profitable ventures. For a year there was not a single performance.

Then came the Lopez trial and the hanging, which Henslowe

[102] For details of the Lopez affair, see Sir Sidney Lee: "The Original of Shylock," *Gentleman's Magazine*, (OS) 246, (NS) 24: 185–200 F 1880; "Elizabethan England and the Jews," *Trans. New Shakspere Society*, 1st ser., vols. 11–14: 143–166 (1887–1892); *Camden's Annales* (3rd ed. 1635), pp. 430–431; William Murdin: *Collection of State Papers Left by William Cecil, Lord Burghley*, p. 669.

[103] Ll. 1149–1150.

[104] *Henslowe's Diary*, fol. 7v, May 11, 1592; Greg's ed., I. 14.

must have regarded as a godsend. Public interest in Jews, especially bloody, plotting, wicked, murderous ones, went fever-high; and the players, who well understood how to gratify such tastes, dug up their parts of *The Jew of Malta*. Lopez was not arraigned until February; but a hint was enough for Henslowe, and on "the 18 of Jenewary" he produced *The Jew of Malta* before the biggest house it had ever enjoyed, with the largest takings so far on record for the play, three pounds. There were two productions in February, two in April, one in May; and in June, the month when Lopez was hanged, there were four. The public was thoroughly aroused and so interested in Jewish villains that the play could run on without missing a month, and sometimes with several productions a month, until February of the following year. After that, interest fell off rapidly, and the takings sank to a single pound. In June, 1596, when the receipts were a bare thirteen shillings, Henslowe abandoned the old play.

In 1601 he and his aides tried to revive it, not very successfully, for there is no record of actual performances. All we know about the attempt is contained in Henslowe's businesslike record of loans for the purchase of properties and costumes: [105]

Lent vnto Robart shawe & mr Jube the 19 of maye 1601 to bye \ v^{ll}
divers thing*es* for the Jewe of malta the some of . . . . /
lent mor to the littell tayller the same daye for more thing*es* for \ x^{s}
the Jewe of malta some of   /

Thereafter *The Jew of Malta* languished in England until Thomas Heywood revived it at the Cockpit and at court in 1633. Heywood's production had the actor Perkins in place of "so vnimitable an Actor as Mr. *Allin*," who had created the role of Barabas. For some years before this, *The Jew* was one of the English plays which had a vogue in Germany. There is record of a performance at Graetz in 1608 and of several performances at Dresden in 1626.[106] Contemporary manuscript notes on the latter survived in an old almanac:

[105] *Henslowe's Diary*, fol. 87r. Greg's ed., I. 137.
[106] Karl Elze in *Jahrb.* 6: 137–138n (1871); Rudolf Genée: *Geschichte des Shakespeare'schen Drama* (Leipzig, 1870), pp. 164 ff., 409 ff.; Schelling: *Elizabethan Drama*, I. 232; Meissner in *Jahrb.*, 19: 130, 137 (1884); Albert Cohn: *Shakespeare in Germany*, cxv–cxviii.

1626

[Julius] 13. — Ist eine Comoedia von Josepho Juden von Venedigk
    gespielt worden. [Also November 5.]
[Julius] 31. — Ist eine Tragoedia von Barrabas, Juden von Malta
    gespielt worden.
[Augustus] 29. — Ist eine Tragoedia von Barrabas, Juden von Malta
    gespielt worden.

Thereafter, in spite of its Elizabethan successes, *The Jew of
Malta* was not often produced. Edmund Kean staged a version
adapted by the actor, S. Penley, on April 24, 1818. Kean was
encored in the scene in which Barabas disguises himself as a
musician — a scene for which a new song had been specially
written.[107] There was a revival at Williams College in 1907;
another by the Phoenix Society at Daly's Theatre, London,
November 5 and 6, 1922; and another by the Yale Dramatic
Association in June, 1940.

INFLUENCE

The influence that Marlowe exerted on other dramatists
through *The Jew of Malta* is not quite like the influence he
exerted through his other plays. In part it was exerted directly,
in part through Shakespeare and *The Merchant of Venice.* In
part it was a purely literary influence exerted on the structure
and characterization and language of later Elizabethan plays;
in part also it was an influence on the costume and make-up of
the stage Jews who followed Barabas and Shylock. The effects
are most obvious in the subsequent development of the conventional Elizabethan stage Jew; in the succession of Machiavellian villains who trod the boards; and in a new plot, or
subplot, dealing with the usurer and his daughter, on which
dramatists rang the changes constantly until the closing of the
theatres in 1642.

The large artificial nose of the stage Jew first appears with
Barabas and continues with Shylock and on down to the present
day. The red wig and beard of Shylock very likely had the same
origin, though this is less certain; and there were probably other
details of make-up and costume to which we have no allusions

107 M. J. Landa: *Jew in Drama,* p. 68.

today. Barabas, as originally played by Alleyn,[108] was made up with a large artificial nose. His slave Ithamore exclaims:

> Oh braue, master, I worship your nose for this,

and later refers to Barabas as a "bottle-nos'd knaue," or simply as "nose." [109] William Rowley, in his pamphlet, *The Search for Money* (1609), describes a character as having "his visage (or vizard) like the artificiall Jewe of Maltae's nose . . . upon which nose, two casements were built, through which his eyes had a little ken of us." [110] A similar make-up, together with a red wig and beard, was used when Shylock came on the boards. According to the old actor, Thomas Jordan, writing as "city poet" in 1664:

> His beard was red, his face was made
> Not much unlike a Witches;
> His habit was a Jewish Gown,
> That would defend all weather;
> His chin turn'd up, his nose hung down,
> And both ends met together.[111]

In Burbage's funeral elegy, there is a reference to his impersonation of "the red-hair'd Jew." [112]

The aquiline nose characteristic of Jews, Arabs, and other Semitic peoples seems to have impressed the English at an early date. There is a Middle English manuscript [113] which clearly contrasts Jewish and English faces in its illuminations. In the later Elizabethan drama the allusions are so frequent as to show that the convention was thoroughly established. Pisaro, in *Englishmen for My Money* (1616), is called "signor bottle-

---

[108] "Epistle Dedicatory" and "Prologue to the Stage," Brooke's (1910) ed., pp. 237, 239.
[109] Ll. 938, 1229, 1531.
[110] Percy Society Reprint (1890), p. 19.
[111] "The Forfeiture: a Romance," in Jordan's *Royall Arbor of loyal Poesie* [BM, C.38.a.24], pp. 36–37. See J. P. Collier: *New Particulars*, pp. 38–39; W. Creizenach: *Geschichte d. neueren Dramas* (1909), IV. 514; Edgar Elmer Stoll: "Shylock," JEGP, 10: 236 (1911), reprinted with typographical errors corrected in his *Shakespeare Studies* (1927); Furness Variorum *Merchant of Venice*, p. 461.
[112] J. P. Collier: *Memoirs of the Particular Actors in the Plays of Shakespeare*, pp. 52 ff.; Karl Elze in *Jahrb.* 6: 161 (1871).
[113] MS. Royal, 6.E.vi. Reproduced in H. D. Traill and J. S. Mann: *Social England*, II. 121. Gérard David's "Descent from the Cross," in the Basilique du St. Sang at Bruges is another early example of the typically Jewish physiognomy.

nose," and there are allusions to "Mammon the usurer with his great nose," [114] and two others of the same sort.

The Machiavellian influence is perhaps clearest in a play named for the hero, *Machiavellus*, produced at St. John's College, Cambridge, in 1597.[115] In this, Machiavelli struggles for the heroine's hand through a remarkable series of disguises, plots, and counterplots, his adversary being a Jew, Jacuppus, whose name recalls one of Marlowe's friars.

Machiavellian philosophy is implicit in the amazing series of Jews and usurers who follow in later plays. The first dramatic treatment of Jews, in the English mystery plays, shows no hostility. The characters are treated, not as aliens, but as part of the Biblical tradition. Even as late as *Three Ladies of London* (1584), by Robert Wilson (d. 1600), Gerontus is a sympathetic Jewish character; but immediately after Marlowe's play the tide turned the other way. It may perhaps have turned even before Marlow, for the anonymous *Timon*, which shows anti-Jewish feeling, may be dated between 1581 and 1590, and may therefore precede his work.

Jewish figures in the later drama are clearly modeled on the two familiar figures of Barabas and Shylock.[116] Among such characters are Abyssus in *Timon* (1581–1590); Abraham in *Selimus* (1588), a play which shows many traces of *Tamburlaine*; [117] Pisaro in William Haughton's *Englishmen for My Money* (1598); Mammon, the usurer, in *Iacke Drums Entertainment* (1600); and Zariph in *The Travels of Three English Brothers* (1607), apparently the joint work of John Day, William Rowley, and George Wilkins. There are verbal echoes or other traces of *The Jew of Malta* in four of Ben Jonson's plays, in *Arden of Feversham*,[118] and in Robert Greene's *James IV*. Many other plays borrow, directly or indirectly, from Marlowe's plot.[119]

[114] III. iii. 1, and sigs. B2r and D4r of the 1601 quarto.
[115] Ward: HEDL, I. 339n; Boas: *University Drama*, p. 313.
[116] For the relation between these two characters, see I. 367 and Chapter XVI.
[117] See II. 278–280.
[118] See II. 288
[119] Professor Rupert Taylor in PMLA, 51: 653, 658–659, cites various parallels with the pre-Shakespearean *King John*; but none of these are very close, and even the closest might be accidental.

Selimus

Abraham in the anonymous *Selimus* is probably the first stage Jew borrowed from Marlowe, and the play almost certainly antedates *The Merchant of Venice*. The borrowing is not, however, very important, as Abraham appears in but two scenes. Like Barabas, he is a poisoner.

Selimus himself owes almost as much to Barabas as to Tamburlaine. He is an intriguer, a Machiavelli who despises morals and religion like Barabas, as well as a conqueror like Tamburlaine. Though there are no verbal echoes of *The Jew of Malta*, there is marked similarity of content in some speeches; and Marlowe's prologue could readily be used for *Selimus*. Its main ideas are perfectly reproduced in the first speech by Selimus himself.

Englishmen for My Money

William Haughton's *Englishmen for My Money* opens exactly like *The Jew of Malta*, with the usurer meditating upon the ships at sea fraught with his wealth. Pisaro soliloquizes:

> How smugge this gray-eyde Morning seemes to bee,
> A pleasant sight; but yet more pleasure haue I
> To thinke vpon this moystning Southwest Winde,
> That driues my laden Shippes from fertile *Spaine*:
> But come what will, no Winde can come amisse,
> For two and thirty Windes that rules the Seas,
> And blowes about this ayerie Region;
> Thirtie two Shippes haue I to equall them:
> Whose wealthy fraughts doe make *Pisaro* rich.[120]

The pronunciation of the word "region" so as to make three syllables is characteristic of Marlowe,[121] though of course not exclusively his. Pisaro loses his two daughters, who fall in love with Christians and marry them by deceiving him. There are two allusions to his huge nose. Otherwise the play has no resemblances to Marlowe's.

Iacke Drums Entertainment

The character of Mammon, the Jewish usurer in *Iacke Drums Entertainment* (1601), shows plain traces of both *The Jew of*

[120] I. i. 1–9. Edited by Albert Croll Baugh (Pennsylvania Diss., 1915).
[121] See II. 194–195.

Malta and "The Passionate Shepherd." The play also contains one half-recollected line from *Edward the Second.*[122] Bloodthirsty like Barabas, Mammon is ready to "complot ten thousand deaths,"[123] and his exclamation on hearing that a ship is lost reminds one of both Shylock and Barabas:

> My shippe, my bonds, my bondes, my ship.[124]

He woos the heroine almost in the terms of "The Passionate Shepherd":

> My ship shall kemb the Oceans curled backe
> To furnish thee with braue Abiliaments,
> Rucks of rich Pearle, and sparkling Diamonds
> Shall fringe thy garments with Imbroadry:
> Thy head shall blaze as bright with Orient stone,
> As did the world being burnt by *Phaeton.*[125]

TRAVELS OF THREE ENGLISH BROTHERS

Bullen thought the Jew Zariph in John Day's (1569–1626) *Travels of Three English Brothers* (1607) was "a travesty of Shylock";[126] but Zariph is really far closer to Marlowe's Barabas — a mere bloodthirsty wretch, without Shylock's dignity, pathos, and other redeeming traits. It is significant of the strength of the tradition which Marlowe established that, just as Shakespeare remodeled the innocuous Jew of *Il Pecorone* into the malignant Shylock, so the author of *The Three English Brothers* transforms the kindhearted Jewish merchant who befriended Sir Thomas Sherley when imprisoned in Constantinople into the stage monster who had become conventional.[127] One passage contains echoes of both Marlowe and Shakespeare:

> A hundreth thousand Duckats! sweete remembrance.
> Ile read it againe; a hundreth thousand Duckats!
> Sweeter still: who owes it? a Christian. . . .
> Vnhallowed brats, seed of the bond-woman,
> Swine deuourers, vncircumcised slaues
> That scorne our Hebrew sanctimonious writte,

---

[122] See II. 38.
[123] Sig. F2r of the 1601 quarto.
[124] Sig. F3r.   [125] Sig. F2r. See II. 153–160 of the present work.
[126] See p. iii of Bullen's introduction to the play (1881). Rowley may have had a hand in this play. See Eduard Eckhardt: *Dialekt- und Ausländerstypen d. aelt. eng. Dramas* (Materialien, no. 32), II. 160–161, par. 479.
[127] Tract by Anthony Nixon, quoted by Bullen, *op. cit.,* p. iii.

Despise our lawes, prophane our sinagogues. . . .
Sweet gold, sweete Iewell! but the sweetest part
Of a *Iewes* feast is a Christians heart.[128]

After *The Jew of Malta* and *The Merchant of Venice*, the usurer — not always a Jew — became a stock figure on the Elizabethan stage. There are at least forty-five plays with usurers as characters, and in at least nine of them a gallant, cozened by the usurer, saves himself by marrying the usurer's daughter, niece, or ward.[129]

The plot becomes a mere formula. The gallant is a spend-thrift, modeled more or less accurately from the prodigal son. He is in debt to the usurer. Usually, like Shakespeare's Lorenzo, he elopes with the lady, taking with him the usurer's ill-gotten gains.

While this tradition owes much to Marlowe, it has other origins as well. It seems to owe nothing to Latin comedy, whose moneylenders have none of the cruelty typical of the Elizabethan stage figure; [130] but it owes a good deal to the Avarice of the morality plays. There are traces of this in the names which the later Elizabethan dramatists bestow on their usurers — Bartervile in Thomas Dekker's *If It Be Not Good*; Gripe, in *Wily Beguiled*; Lucre in Middleton's *Trick to Catch the Old One*; Hog in the anonymous *Hog Hath Lost His Pearl*; Hornet, in James Shirley's *Constant Maid*; and Sir Giles Overreach in Massinger's *New Way to Pay Old Debts*. Even Marlowe is careful to choose a name with evil connotations.

Marlowe establishes the stock plot of the later plays by introducing for the first time the rebellious daughter who steals from her usurious father. Shakespeare carries this one step further by making the rebellious daughter elope. Lorenzo, who calls himself "an unthrift love," anticipates the prodigal gallant who habitually falls in love with the usurer's daughter in the later plays.

In *A Knacke to Know an Honest Man*, which was acted in 1594, the rebellious daughter foils her usurious father by releas-

---

[128] Bullen's reprint (1881), pp. 59–60.

[129] Albert Croll Baugh's ed. of *Englishmen for My Money* (University of Pennsylvania Diss., 1915); Arthur Bivens Stonex: "Usurer in Elizabethan Drama," PMLA, 31: 190–210 (1916); Walter Reinecke: *Der Wucherer im aelteren englischen Drama* (Halle Diss., 1907).

[130] For a different view, see William Poel: *Shakespeare in the Theatre*, pp. 70, 75.

ing two prisoners, one of whom she marries. In *Wily Beguiled*, written about 1596, Gripe's daughter elopes with a poor scholar. In Thomas Heywood's *Fair Maid of the Exchange* (ca. 1602), Moll, the usurer's daughter, marries his victim, whereupon the usurer relents. In Robert Tailor's *Hog Hath Lost His Pearl* (1613), Haddit, the prodigal, elopes with the daughter of Hog, the usurer, carrying along some of the usurer's money.

In Richard Brome's *The Damoiselle* (1637/8), Brokeall is ruined by the usurer Vermine. Brokeall's son marries Vermine's runaway daughter and regains his father's property. Shackerley Marmion, in *A Fine Companion* (1633), varies the formula by giving the usurer two daughters, who wed two impoverished gallants. William Cartwright's *The Ordinary* (1634) adopts another variant — two usurers, one with a daughter who marries the impoverished hero, while the other is tricked into marrying her maid. In Middleton's *Trick to Catch the Old One* (1606) two usurers are tricked into marriage, one to the hero's cast mistress, while the hero marries a usurer's niece. In James Shirley's *Constant Maid* (1636–39), the hero elopes with Hornet's daughter and three thousand pounds. There are traces of the same theme in Davenant's *The Wits* (1634) and various other plays.

Most of these writers were probably following an established formula, of whose origin in Marlowe's *Jew of Malta* they were vaguely conscious, if conscious at all. Ben Jonson, however, who testified to his acquaintance with Marlowe's work by two specific allusions to it, knew exactly what he was doing. He introduced variations of the usurer-daughter-prodigal formula in *The Staple of Newes* (1625), *The Magnetick Lady* (1632), and *Volpone* (1606). The title role in the latter play owes something to classic comedy but a good deal more to Barabas.

Jonson practically quotes Marlowe's famous line,

Infinite riches in a little roome

when his miser in *The Sad Shepherd* refers to

The sacred treasure in this blessed room.

Chapman also quotes it in *Ovid's Banquet of Sense*:

And show their riches in a little room.[131]

[131] *Jew of Malta*, 72; *Sad Shepherd*, I. i. 13; *Ovid's Banquet of Sense*, 320 (II. 29 of the 1875 ed. of Chapman's *Works*). See also II. 208–211 of the present work.

All three have a perplexing relation to "great commoditie in a little roome" in William Harrison's (1534–1593) prose *Description of England*. This work first appeared in 1577, but there was a new and revised edition in 1586/7, almost at the beginning of Marlowe's career as a dramatist.[132] Marlowe may have taken his famous line from Harrison; the similarity may be mere coincidence; or it may be due to common echoing of Horace's "multum in parvo."

Other playwrights are casual snappers-up of Marlowe's unconsidered trifles, but their borrowings are too slight to be considered in detail. Traces of Barabas appear in Webster's *Devil's Law Case*;[133] in the character of Muley Mohammed in Peele's *Battle of Alcazar*; in Aaron in *Titus Andronicus*; and in Eleazar in *Lust's Dominion*.[134] There are traces of the mood of *The Jew of Malta* in Greene's *Alphonsus of Aragon* and *Orlando Furioso*. In the latter, Sacripant's malignancy suggests Barabas, but in both plays the influence of *Tamburlaine* is far more obvious.[135] Greene probably had Barabas in mind when he remodeled his villain Ateukin in *James IV* from Cinthio's *Hecatomithi*. Greene's villain has written "annotations upon Machiavel," and he hires Andrew and Slipper after listening to their own account of their abilities, in a scene much like that in which Barabas buys his slave Ithamore. This scene is not in the source.[136]

Arden of Feversham contains several parallels, and some lines on wealth in *A Shrew* faintly echo *The Jew*.[137] The lost *Jew of Venice* (1653), attributed to Dekker, probably showed similar traces.[138] Dekker's pamphlet, *News from Hell* (1606), alludes to a character as "my rich Iew of *Malta*."[139]

The anonymous *Skialetheia* of 1598 — which is almost certainly the work of Edward, or Everard, Guilpin — quotes two lines from *The Jew of Malta* with fair accuracy:

> Like to the fatall ominous Rauen which tolls,
> The sicke mans dirge within his hollow beake.

[132] CHEL, III. 366; F. J. Furnivall: article "William Harrison," DNB, IX. 46.
[133] E. V. Lucas' ed., II. 339; O. Schröder: *Marlowe und Webster*, pp. 8–11.
[134] See II. 271.   [136] Dyce's Greene, p. 204, col. 1, l. 8.
[135] See I. 248–253.   [137] See Chapter XVI and Rupert Taylor, *op. cit.*
[138] E. K. Chambers: *Eliz. Stage*, III. 301.
[139] Grosart's Dekker, II. 142.

This is in Epigram no. 8, addressed "To Deloney," that is, to Thomas Deloney, the balladist. The use of italics indicates that it is meant for a quotation of Marlowe's

> Thus like the sad presaging Rauen that tolls
> The sicke mans passeport in her hollow beake.[140]

The Jew of Malta's influence extends even to Elizabethan prose fiction, in *The Unfortunate Traveler* (1596), by Marlowe's quondam collaborator, Thomas Nashe. In this early novel we have an avaricious Jew, Zorach — a poisoner, bloody, cunning, Christian-hating, and revengeful — who prepares a mine to blow up the city of Rome, precisely as Barabas had prepared a mine to blow up the Turks in Malta, and who, like Barabas, meets death by torture.[141]

---

[140] See the Oxford ed. (1912) of Deloney's *Works* by Francis Oscar Mann, p. xiii, and the Shakespeare Association facsimile of *Skialetheia* (no. 2, 1931), which has also been reprinted by the Beldornie Press (1843); in Collier's *Miscellaneous Tracts* (1870); and by A. B. Grosart (1878). The Marlowe passage is JM, 640-641.

[141] McKerrow's Nashe, II. 304-316; Friedrich Brie: "Romane und Drama in Zeitalter Shakespeares," *Jahrb.*, 48: 141-142 (1912); Cazamian and Legouis: *Hist. Eng. Lit.*, I. 221-222.